Major Libraries

THE BRITISH LIBRARY
  <http://www.bl.uk/>
  The world's largest library.

LIBRARY OF CONGRESS HOME PAGE
  <http://lcweb.loc.gov/>
  The national library of the United States.

NEW YORK PUBLIC LIBRARY
  <http://www.nypl.org/index.html>
  Catalog of one of the great public research libraries.

OHIOLINK CENTRAL CATALOG
  <http://olcl.ohiolink.edu/search/>
  A pioneering statewide library catalog with more than 24 million items.

On-Line Texts

ELECTRIC LIBRARY
  <http://www.elibrary.com>
  Extensive, full-text database with hundreds of full-text newspapers and
  magazines (though not the most important ones), thousands of works of literature, and more.

ELECTRONIC TEXT CENTER—UNIVERSITY OF VIRGINIA
  <http://etext.lib.virginia.edu/>
  Extensive collection of on-line literary texts.

PROJECT BARTLEBY
  <http://www.bartleby.com>
  Extensive collection of on-line literary texts.

UNIVERSITY OF TORONTO LIBRARIES: Resources
  <http://library.utoronto.ca/www/utel/rp/utel.html>
  Extensive collection of on-line literary texts.

THE RESEARCH PROCESS

A Complete Guide and Reference for Writers

SECOND EDITION

Martin Maner

Wright State University

Boston   Burr Ridge, IL   Dubuque, IA   Madison, WI   New York   San Francisco   St. Louis
Bangkok   Bogotá   Caracas   Kuala Lumpur   Lisbon   London   Madrid   Mexico City
Milan   Montreal   New Delhi   Santiago   Seoul   Singapore   Sydney   Taipei   Toronto

McGraw-Hill Higher Education

*A Division of The **McGraw-Hill** Companies*

THE RESEARCH PROCESS: A COMPLETE GUIDE AND REFERENCE FOR WRITERS

Published by McGraw-Hill, a business unit of The McGraw-Hill Companies, Inc. 1221 Avenue of the Americas, New York, NY, 10020. Copyright © 2000, 1996 by The McGraw-Hill Companies, Inc. All rights reserved. No part of this publication may be reproduced or distributed in any form or by any means, or stored in a database or retrieval system, without the prior written consent of The McGraw-Hill Companies, Inc., including, but not limited to, in any network or other electronic storage or transmission, or broadcast for distance learning. Some ancillaries, including electronic and print components, may not be available to customers outside the United States.

This book is printed on acid-free paper.

4   5   6   7   8   9   0   BAH/BAH   9   8   7   6   5   4   3   2

ISBN: 0-7674-1139-0

Sponsoring editor, Renée Deljon; developmental editor, Rick Roehrich; production editor, Carla White Kirschenbaum; manuscript editor, Mark Gallaher; text and cover designer, Linda M. Robertson; art manager, Amy Folden; manufacturing manager, Randy Hurst. The text was set in 10/12 Janson by Thompson Type and printed on 45# Custom LG by Banta Book Group. *Cover:* © Rudi VonBriel/Photo Edit.

Library of Congress Cataloging-in-Publication Data
Maner, Martin.
  The research process : a complete guide and reference for writers /
  Martin Maner.—2nd ed.
    p. cm.
  Rev. ed. of: The spiral guide to research writing. c1996.
  Includes index.
  ISBN 0-7674-1139-0
  1. Report writing.   2. Research.   I. Maner, Martin. Spiral guide to research
writing. II. Title.
LB2369 .M344 2000   99-030605

www.mhhe.com

CONTENTS

3   GENERATING AN ARGUMENT   29

4   FINDING SOURCES   47

7   RESEARCH PAPER FORMATS: MLA AND APA   153

9 WRITING THE ROUGH DRAFT 268

PREFACE

A research paper is a creative opportunity to participate in generating new knowledge and challenging established opinions. This text does, of course, offer detailed advice on specific tasks, such as formatting, but it never loses sight of the larger purpose of research as an independent, creative process of rediscovery and reinterpretation. This philosophy underlies the features I've built into the text to help students learn how to write a research paper, a process that should be the capstone achievement of each college student's academic career.

AUDIENCE

The Research Process is a comprehensive guide intended to serve college students throughout their careers, from first-year composition to discipline-specific upper division courses and beyond. It makes a perfect companion to the *MLA Handbook,* the APA *Publication Manual,* or Kate Turabian's *Manual for Writers of Term Papers, Theses, and Dissertations.* My goal is to meet the needs of the student who has had little training in library research and has perhaps a blurry notion of what a research paper really is. To become a research writer means becoming a member of a discourse community that shares certain conventions in the communication of new arguments and new knowledge. These conventions are often unfamiliar to the beginning writer. Especially in the opening chapters, the guide confronts these basic questions: What is the difference between genuine research and repetition of what others have found? How can a mere beginner challenge the arguments of an expert in the field? What is the ultimate purpose of the research paper?

This text is aimed specifically at students writing *library* research papers. Though it discusses the use of questionnaires and non-print media, it does not address laboratory research. It emphasizes the MLA format for drafting, but because it is interdisciplinary and oriented toward writing across the curriculum, it should be useful to any student in any discipline who is doing library research.

FEATURES

I've included a number of features that I hope will make this guide a more useful learning tool for students tackling the research process.

▪ *Emphasis on process and the recursive nature of research.* Instead of suggesting that research writing is tidier and more systematic than it really is, the text presents research as a process that naturally involves backtracking and inevitably requires the writer to carry out several activities at once. Since the processes of asking questions, finding information, and reaching conclusions constantly modify each other, the title, *The Research Process*, is meant to suggest that research writing is a recursive, spiraling process that searches and researches, moving forward with each turn toward the goal of a well-crafted paper.

To show how each part of the research writing process relates to other parts, the text supplies extensive cross-references to related research activities—something in the nature of "hypertext" or decision trees. The reader can easily navigate through the book to find information. Important summary points are highlighted by text boxes.

"Quick View" sections at the beginnings of most chapters offer streamlined advice about the chapter topic. Often, these sections will suffice to answer students' questions; they also serve as useful previews or reviews of the research process.

▪ *Collaborative and flexible approach.* The tone of the text is collaborative, not prescriptive: It offers tips, points out dangers, suggests ways of saving time, and clarifies choices. Instead of imposing a single, inflexible method of research writing, the guide helps research writers find methods appropriate to their own learning styles. It takes into account the real working habits of students by assuming that writers may work from a variety of materials, including photocopies, note cards, printed material, computerized information resources, and word-processing files. A variety of organizing and drafting techniques helps the reader find comfortable, efficient, individualized approaches. Collaboration and peer evaluation are stressed throughout.

▪ *Emphasis on argumentation.* Instead of treating the research paper's argument only as an end result, the text explains how argument figures into every stage of the process. For example, the text presents looking for sources in the context of finding an original thesis, and it presents information gathering as a process of reading actively and analytically.

INTERNET ▪ *Thorough attention to computers and using the Internet.* The guide highlights the efficient use of word processing and computerized information services. In addition to offering a wide range of word-processing tips, the text encourages students to use the latest research technology, such as on-line and CD-ROM databases, for fast information retrieval. Guidelines for evaluating and properly documenting Web sources are also included. Up-to-date examples and guidelines for citing electronic sources are given for each of the four major research formats. An icon in the margin alerts readers to passages dealing with electronic sources and the Internet.

■ *Emphasis on problem solving.* The text includes a research journal that records the decisions I made as I worked through the exercises and realities of library research on a topic I knew little about. The completed paper—an analysis of part of the Romantic revolution in music—is included in Chapter 8. Short excerpts from my journal appear at the end of most chapters; showing students the problems I encountered and worked through can both encourage them and offer direction.

■ *Sample papers in most commonly used research formats.* Chapters 7 and 8 include complete papers in MLA format, APA format, CBE Citation Sequence format, and Chicago format. These papers exemplify the range and diversity of college research.

■ *Student examples of research activities.* Examples of prewriting, note taking, and drafting activities that contributed to the writing of the sample papers in Chapters 7 and 8 appear throughout the text, exemplifying the recursive nature of the research writing process.

■ *Exercises that directly support students' paper assignments.* Exercises throughout the text pose questions and tasks that students can apply to their own research papers. Each exercise helps students advance the progress of their papers rather than perform busy work without a context.

ACKNOWLEDGMENTS

I thank Wright State University and its College of Liberal Arts for granting me a one-year sabbatical to complete this book. I am grateful to my faculty colleagues, especially Richard Bullock, Peter Bracher, and Henry Limouze, for their support and for their many useful suggestions. Thanks also to Reneé Deljon, sponsoring editor; Rick Roehrich, developmental editor; Carla White Kirschenbaum, senior production editor; Amy Folder, art editor; and Glenda King, design manager at Mayfield Publishing Company, and the peer evaluators: Louise Ackley, Boise State University; Peggy Brent, Hinds Community College; Michael Delahoyde, Washington State University; Cathy Della Penta, Mesa Community College; William Peirce, Prince George's Community College; and James Stokes, University of Wisconsin at Steven's Point. Their invaluable suggestions have helped guide my revisions to make this book as practical and as constructive as possible.

To Jill Colak, Lisa Hewitt, Todd Rose, and Kristin Brucker, thanks for your interesting papers and your careful and curious attention to research. To the students in my research writing classes, thanks for your patience. Your comments and critiques were very helpful.

To Elizabeth, Jaimie, Karen, and Taylor, thank you for being the loving and beautiful family that makes hard work worthwhile.

Finally, to John Haefner and the faculty of University High School in Iowa City, Iowa, to whom this book is dedicated, thanks for nurturing in several generations of students a genuine love of knowledge and research.

INTRODUCTION:
Research—Who Needs It?

Library research is frustrating and time-consuming. It requires patience. It demands precision. It's not financially rewarding. Who needs it?

Everyone does. At its simplest, research writing entails merely knowing where to look something up—a universally useful type of knowledge. For example, suppose you are given the job of helping to put together a publicity campaign for an upcoming lecture series. Your media director asks you to write a short biographical sketch of Jonathan Miller. You know that Miller hosted a PBS series called *The Body in Question*, but that's all you know. How would you go about compiling an accurate, short biography of Miller? Test your library skills now by jotting down an answer. Just by trying to answer this question, you may understand the importance of such skills, no matter what your field of study or your occupation.

At its most complex, research writing is a highly creative endeavor that requires you to use all the skills that a good education fosters. It calls for originality, organization, critical thinking, and persuasive ability. If it is sometimes difficult and time-consuming, it is also eminently useful in school and beyond. And because research is inevitably an independent activity, it is the one area of schoolwork in which you may go wherever your curiosity leads.

To enjoy research, you have to go at it the way you'd ideally go at life itself: You need curiosity tempered with an awareness of your own limits; you need the detachment of a game player and the commitment of a person who knows that the game is serious. Much of our education has worked to prevent these healthy attitudes, however. Most of us have been educated in a system that requires the passive acquisition of information. We have gotten our knowledge prepackaged in textbooks and in lectures; we have seldom been encouraged to go out and search for it independently.

Passive learning, unfortunately, makes us dependent, naive, and cynical, even though our culture tells us we are independent and able to think for ourselves. Many students imagine that they must confine their research to libraries, and they forget to ask friends about experts they might know or to use the telephone. A student of mine who researched the history of the blues as a musical form discovered, after he made some phone calls to local musician friends, that a former disc jockey in the area owned one of the largest collections of blues recordings in the world, along with a plentiful supply of books and articles about the blues. The disc jockey himself was a willing interview subject and provided loads of information and anecdotes. The student also happened to hear a National Public Radio program dealing with the blues, and the program mentioned a center for blues studies located in a southern state. Letters to the center and to NPR turned up useful information for the student's paper. This student learned that the library and the world are open to each other.

The point is not just that library research can extend well beyond the library, but also that if you search creatively, it can sometimes seem to be raining information; all you have to do is hold out your hand. Everyone has had the experience of learning a new word and then immediately and repeatedly encountering the word in speech and print. It is as though the word was invisible until you learned it; then it appeared everywhere. Research works this way, too. Once your search for information picks up speed, sources may seem to just pop up, like those newly recognized words. The unexpected discovery of something useful is brought about by being in the right place, at the right time, with an openness to new experience.

The search for books, articles, bibliographies, interviews, recordings, films, and videotapes can become drudgery only if you forget the purpose of what you are doing, which is *to satisfy your own curiosity and ultimately to resolve your own reasonable doubts about a subject.* To the ordinary person, the library stacks may look like so many board feet of bound, printed pages; but to the research writer, the library is the knowledge hub of the universe. It is a network of living lines of communication, a spider's web of connections leading out to the world.

Given half a chance, most students will discover that research is not drudgery, busywork, or licensed theft. With a subject of genuine interest and a compelling question to resolve, most will get caught up in the pleasure of research. The crucial step is to make a commitment to a subject and a hypothesis early in the research process. Your hypothesis may be revised later, but you need to make a clear hypothetical statement as soon as possible and then stick to it. The prospectus should be an especially useful tool here (see Chapter 5, "Writing a Short Plan"). If you get discouraged by your research project, remember that although research entails some of the discomforts of detective work, such as boredom, frustration, and detailed record keeping, it also involves many of detective work's pleasures, such as suspense, challenge, and the thrill of serendipity.

If you must write on an assigned topic that you despise, I sympathize with you. Your challenge will be to find a way to make the topic more appealing to you and thus to make it more truly your own. The trick is to find your own angle, some aspect of the topic that interests you. Talk to the instructor about finding your angle, but only after you've come up with some ideas; simply complaining about the topic won't move you any closer to making it your own. For an example of a fresh approach to a seemingly unpromising topic, see Harold Herzog's discussion of mouse killing in the section "How to Make an Assigned Topic Interesting" in Chapter 2.

The first chapter of this book discusses some commonly misunderstood aspects of research writing, and it aims to reorient your thinking about research by emphasizing the circular nature of the process. But in addition to understanding the research process, you should give careful thought to something even more fundamental: your own feelings about the research writing you are about to begin. For virtually every research writer, the completion of a research paper entails movement through several emotional stages. Phyllis J. Perry has observed that when gifted children are allowed to do independent research, they go through several phases that she calls "finding motivation," "initial excitement," "anxiety," "procrastination and blaming," and "the fork in the road" ("Giftedness and Independent Research," *Full Flowering: A Parent and Teacher Guide to Programs for the Gifted* [Columbus: Ohio Psychology, 1985], 52–64). I like to use her labels to describe the same stages as they occur in the work of college research writers:

1. *Finding motivation.* I am not talking about working for a good grade. I am referring to your need to find a genuine research topic—a problem to be solved or a question to be answered. Your interest in the research problem or question must be genuine. By definition, a real question cannot have a predetermined answer, and the solution of a real problem cannot be measured against any predetermined criteria. Thus, you must believe at the outset that your success or failure is something that only you will be able to fully evaluate; that a high course grade is merely a side effect of satisfying yourself; and that satisfying yourself is more important than anything else. If you are working on an assigned topic that you detest, find an angle that you like (see "Arguing with Yourself" in Chapter 3).

2. *Initial excitement.* If passive forms of education have bored you, pursuing a research topic may feel truly liberating. If you have been turned loose from the constraints of assigned topics, you may feel at first that the research project is going to be pure fun. For once, you will be completely in charge, able to satisfy your own curiosity about your own questions.

3. *Anxiety.* After, or perhaps even during, the initial excitement of being free to work on your own, you may start to feel nervous about your adequacy for the task. Perhaps very early in the process, your research project will turn out to be harder than you expected. Soon unforeseen obstacles will pop up, and the project will begin to consume more time than you originally planned. Other classes and other commitments will begin to get in the way.

4. *Procrastination and blaming.* Usually around the time of midterm exams, you may begin to resent that the library staff seems rude, interlibrary loans are impossibly slow, other instructors have added assignments to your class load, and the sources you have found are badly written. Often your blaming is directly proportional to your fatigue and the amount of your procrastination. That is, the more you have delayed the crucial steps in getting projects under way, the more you may cast about to find others to blame. In any case, procrastination and blaming are both common reactions to fear and frustration.

5. *The fork in the road.* At this point, you may move in one of two directions: You may be tempted to fall back on familiar, perhaps inappropriate

solutions: padding, summary, omission of contradictory evidence, perhaps even academic dishonesty (such as plagiarism). Or you may face reality, address problems, master the material, find creative solutions to unexpected difficulties, make a few compromises, and finish the project with a sense of achievement.

Recognizing these normal emotional phases at the outset can save you some grief. Recognizing them can even help you minimize any disappointment you may later feel. Real achievement comes only with ambition, and ambition usually entails some disappointments along the way. If you expend some effort, however, you will achieve your goal. I cannot guarantee you an A for your effort, but I promise you that if you follow the processes explained in this book, the result will be a paper better than any you have ever written before.

CHAPTER 1

THE NATURE OF RESEARCH WRITING

Most research writing instruction presents the process of writing a research paper as a series of tidy steps: Find a subject, narrow the topic, gather information, organize the data, formulate the main idea, draft the paper, revise. But few people can write a paper following such rigid guidelines, because real library research always seems to involve doing several things at once. At any given moment you may be redefining the topic, gathering information, searching for sources, modifying the main hypothesis, drafting, and revising. To claim that these activities can be reduced to a series of steps makes you feel inadequate when you are unable to follow the tidy pathway from notes to outline to final draft. What is worse, the step-by-step approach may lead you to delay writing until you run out of time.

THE PURPOSE OF RESEARCH WRITING

Instead of trying to follow a step-by-step approach, be flexible about the research writing process, and keep asking yourself the basic question: "What is the purpose of my research writing?" The answer is that research writing aims to generate new knowledge or reinterpret old knowledge. Only this answer acknowledges that college research has a genuine goal beyond summarizing, quoting, and paraphrasing sources. If you believe that the task is simply to reorganize and reexpress the work of others, you may be demoralized by the thought of this busywork. But if you set out to say something new, you may be energized by the possibility of discovery. Furthermore, do not think of the purpose of writing only as producing an end product, a paper. The important point is to pursue the *goal* of generating new knowledge throughout the research writing process; pursuing it will make you think like a researcher. If, when the paper is done, you feel that you have not generated any new knowledge, don't be dismayed. You are bound to have done at least some reinterpretations of old knowledge.

Because research writing aims at generating and reinterpreting knowledge, many conventions of research writing derive from the way a research paper puts old information to new uses. For example, stating your main idea, your thesis, early in your paper is a courtesy to other researchers who are reading your work

1

quickly to see whether your research is relevant to theirs and who don't have time to search for the main point. Thus, you need to think of yourself as a researcher addressing other researchers, not as a student addressing a teacher. This does not mean that you and every other college writer should aim to turn into an expert who is writing for publication in some specialized field. But it does mean that every writer will be helped by understanding that each aspect of writing the paper—even such seemingly dry stuff as using the proper bibliographical format—is governed by the need to publish information effectively. More importantly, if you think of publication as a hypothetical objective, you will be helped by aspiring to the same goals that the best of the published research writers aspire to: originality, honesty, precision, and grace.

The principles just outlined have other far-reaching consequences. For instance, if your goal is to generate new knowledge, then an important first step is to survey the published literature to see that your main idea has not been adequately treated before. If a thoroughly adequate treatment—one that answers all your questions—already exists, then your paper will be only a rehash. It is important to find a fresh approach; for this difficult first step you may think you will have to survey the entire literature of the world! However, library catalogs and indexes, especially computerized ones, in conjunction with careful use of the Internet, make this apparently impossible task feasible (or nearly so). For now, just keep in mind that your early goals are to find the best possible sources on a limited topic and to survey the available sources thoroughly enough to avoid duplicating someone else's work.

RESEARCH AS NEW KNOWLEDGE

If you start with the radical (and subversive!) idea that you should aim to generate new knowledge, you quickly bump into some more questions: "What kind of knowledge can I create? And knowledge that's new to whom?" In answer to the first question, library research does not generate new conclusions the way a scientific experiment or a social scientist's questionnaire does. Since library research draws upon the writings of others, it can look like a mere borrowing—and in fact can degenerate into mere borrowing if it is badly done. But remember:

> Good library research generates new knowledge by reinterpreting old knowledge, by challenging flawed studies, by pointing out previously unnoticed patterns, by analyzing familiar data in new ways, and by synthesizing material that previously lay scattered.

In answer to the second question, it is probably best to assume that you are writing for a group of your peers in your academic major. But I suggest that you check with your instructor to see how he or she defines the audience for your research. Ask, too, whether your instructor agrees that a research paper should strive to present new conclusions or at least a new interpretation of published material. Remember that a professor who wants only an objective presentation of currently available information will still probably expect you to analyze, interpret, evaluate, and, perhaps, challenge your sources (see "Can I Really Challenge Experts?" in Chapter 3 and "Active Reading" in Chapter 6).

How can library research generate new knowledge through the reinterpretation of old knowledge? To answer this question, you must recognize that knowledge is far more than an accumulation of facts. One common way to define knowledge is to treat it as different from unsupported opinion. Consider these two statements:

I liked *Citizen Kane* better than any other movie I've seen.

Citizen Kane is the best movie ever made.

Which of these statements makes a claim that can be attacked or supported? In other words, which of these statements arouses doubt about the quality of *Citizen Kane*?

Clearly, the first statement does not. In fact, it is really not a statement about *Citizen Kane* at all; it is a statement about the speaker's feelings. If you doubt the statement, you will say to the speaker, "Did you really?" If you doubt the second statement, you will say to the speaker, "Is it really? How is it best? What do you mean by 'best'?" If the speaker has really thought hard about his statement, he might say, "Well, it is beautifully constructed, and it was the most innovative and influential film ever made." Now the two of you can argue about whether *Citizen Kane* really fits these three criteria (construction, innovation, influence) or even about whether these three criteria are appropriate to define a movie as "best." In either case, the two of you will have moved beyond the expression of unsupported opinion. You may end up arguing with each other by producing examples and counterexamples, and in the process you will be moving toward verifying or falsifying the speaker's original statement. You may never reach a final resolution of the question, but you will be arguing about something that can be "known" in the broadest sense.

I intentionally chose the most ambiguous sort of statement (an aesthetic judgment) to show that even questions of evaluation can be arguable as long as the arguers have a common ground, such as a set of criteria, on which to base their arguments. In many kinds of academic research, verification or falsification is carried out in much more objective, and sometimes more conclusive, ways. For instance, it may be possible to show that a drug either did produce therapeutic effects or didn't; a library research paper about the drug must survey the available evidence, marshal it effectively, and draw conclusions from the best available data. Even if the conclusions are drawn from published research, the researcher can analyze and evaluate that research in a fresh way.

A student in one of the social sciences once made this comment in my class: "Look, I understand how it's possible to generate a fresh hypothesis by doing library research in the humanities, where you're arguing subjectively about how to interpret things; but I'm studying sources in economics, where a fact is just a fact. How can I generate a fresh argument without going out and doing new research?" The answer is that it is false to assume that "a fact is just a fact" in any field. A fact is only as good as the instrument that produced it and the assumptions that surround it. For example, many people know this "fact": A 1992 Roper poll found that 22 percent of Americans doubt that the Holocaust really happened. However, it turns out that the survey question producing this "fact" was confusingly worded. When the question was rephrased, only 1 percent of the sample doubted that the Nazi regime exterminated millions of Jews.

Many readers have encountered the "fact" that the Eskimos have dozens of different words for snow. This "fact" nicely illustrates the point that a language reflects the environment and preoccupations of its speakers. Too bad the "fact" is a complete fabrication, based on a misunderstanding of a chance remark in Franz Boas's introduction to *The Handbook of American Indians* (1911). Boas mentioned four Eskimo root words for snow; another writer inflated the number to seven; an encyclopedia raised the number to nine; and some writers have claimed that the Eskimos use as many as two hundred words for snow (Geoffrey Pullum, "The Great Eskimo Vocabulary Hoax," *Natural Language and Linguistic Theory* 7.2 [1989]: 275–281). Skepticism, therefore, is the researcher's greatest asset.

You may not always be able to overturn errors as striking as these, but be sure to take a skeptical look at source material. Analyze your sources critically. A mediocre research paper presents only the conclusions drawn by its sources; an excellent research paper analyzes the sources' assumptions, arguments, and methods.

My central point, then, is this:

> Your main idea, your thesis, must be one worth doubting.

Understanding this principle helps you think clearly about what you are doing. If you cannot imagine a statement being doubted, why bother writing at length to support it? A biographical summary of an author's life, for example, is obviously a poor choice for a topic if the information summarized does not generate some argument. If there are arguable questions about the author—perhaps the facts of the author's life are in doubt, or perhaps the author embodied mysteries of personality or motivation—and if supporting evidence can be found on both sides of the doubtful questions, then the subject is probably workable. New knowledge, then, can be generated whenever doubtful statements are subjected to fresh examination.

DEFINING THE NECESSARY DEGREE OF DOUBT

Even though this philosophy of research writing seems reasonable, there is a problem concealed in it. How, precisely, do we define the degree of doubt necessary to make a thesis statement effective? There is no clear-cut answer to this question. But the most common mistake students make when confronted with this criterion of doubt is to feel that the doubtful question should be enormously controversial, mysterious, and full of uncertainty. We probably tend to overestimate the degree of necessary doubt because only dramatic, controversial research attracts wide public attention; we think of researchers as investigators of mysteries. A magazine or newspaper is not interested in the latest archaeological dig unless it reveals some provocative new truth or resolves some famous controversy. But only a tiny proportion of actual research is dramatic in this way.

Keep in mind the nature of the reader of research papers. The typical reader of a published research paper (remember that the conventions of publication affect the conventions of unpublished college papers, too) is not like a reader of tabloids, who needs to be lured with splashy, sensational headlines. The typical reader of a research paper is already interested in the subject. A research paper is usually a specialized argument written for specialists.

The type of doubtful thesis to be supported in a research paper will pack very little of the explosive punch of a tabloid headline. But after all, "Elvis Interviewed: He's Been Living with Aliens" arouses incredulity rather than doubt, anyway. The research reader does not need such sensational stimulants. "Hittite Burial Site Reveals Advanced Metallurgical Knowledge" will suffice. The key point to remember is that the reader must respond to the main statement with some degree of uncertainty. "Oh, really? I thought the Hittites knew very little about metal. Tell me more." That's all the writer really needs in the way of a curious response.

Not everyone cares about Hittite burial remains, but research is based upon a system of free inquiry in which a very narrow or specialized topic is regarded as worthwhile if it gives rise to doubtful questions. At the same time, a reader's interest and involvement should be fostered and encouraged by an introduction that establishes a context for the highly specific doubt or uncertainty the paper will discuss. What matters is that a genuine question, a real uncertainty, is under discussion; it need not be controversial, shocking, or mysterious. You should gently nurture your reader's interest by explaining why your topic matters.

DESCRIBING, NARRATING, EXPLAINING, AND ARGUING

If we define a research paper as a documented argument in support of a key statement, or thesis, that is doubtful enough to require support, do we mean that a research paper must be purely argumentative? The answer is no. Traditional rhetoric distinguishes four uses of writing, known as the four modes of discourse:

Description: to convey an impression in words

Narration: to tell a story or explain a process

Exposition: to explain or analyze a subject

Argumentation: to produce reasoning and evidence in support of a statement

(See also Chapter 3, "Generating an Argument.")

Usually, a writer will use all four modes in a research paper. In a paper dealing with the phenomenon known as mass hysteria, for example, the writer might describe its symptoms, narrate an example of its occurrence, and explain the psychological principles that govern it. However—and this is the point often overlooked—none of these modes is sufficient to make the writing a research

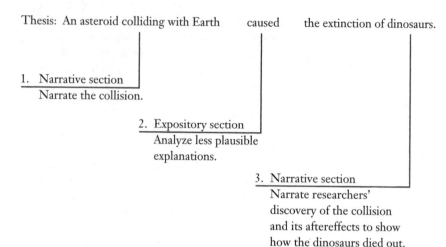

FIGURE 1.1   Subsections Supporting a Thesis

paper. There must be, in addition, an overall argumentative purpose that these descriptive, narrative, and expository portions of the paper all exist to support.

As another example, a research paper explaining the fossil evidence that shows when the dinosaurs became extinct might contain a narrative section telling about an asteroid's collision with the planet Earth, an expository section analyzing possible explanations for the extinction, and a narrative section explaining how researchers discovered that such a collision actually occurred. But like the harried, impatient reader of the research paper, the writer must keep asking: What is the point of all this? What argumentative point do these other sections support? Ultimately, these sections must serve some higher purpose. Thus, narrating the asteroid collision may be necessary to make the reader understand the collision's effects; analyzing other theories may be necessary to make the reader understand the advantages of the asteroid theory; and explaining the researchers' discoveries may be necessary to help the reader evaluate the evidence for and against the thesis. The result can be visualized as several subsections supporting one argumentative statement (Figure 1.1). Notice that the thesis sentence announces the subtopics in the order in which they will be discussed.

Argumentation primarily means persuading the reader to believe a statement by rationally evaluating evidence for and against it. To argue is not merely to express an opinion but to make a clear and persuasive statement that can be doubted, to give reasons for it, and to answer objections to it. To argue effectively, you may need to narrate, to describe, and to explain.

Argumentation is not just an end product, though; it plays a part in every stage of the research writing process. In the early stages, argumentation is an instrument of *inquiry:* You frame a tentative thesis, a hypothesis, which guides your research by focusing it on the gathering of evidence for and against your tentative statement. In the middle stages, argumentation is an instrument of *analysis:* By examining arguments for and against your hypothesis, you develop, modify, and support your thesis to make it as accurate and truthful as possible. In the later stages, argumentation becomes an instrument of *persuasion:* You present your case attractively and convincingly in order to win the agreement of your audience. (For a clear discussion of argumentation's functions, see Timothy W. Crusius and Carolyn E. Channell, *The Aims of Argument: A Rhetoric and Reader* [Mountain View, CA: Mayfield, 2000], especially pages 3–10.)

PREWRITING

In the early stages of developing a topic to write about, you can use a variety of idea-generating techniques. The least structured technique is brainstorming, which consists of writing down every idea that comes to mind. The key to effective brainstorming is to refrain completely from criticizing any ideas that come to you; write down everything, no matter how offbeat or silly it may seem. There are two reasons for being so uncritical. One is that self-criticism stifles creativity. Another is that today's oddball notion may, with a few creative twists, become tomorrow's brilliant idea.

If you get stuck and find yourself staring at a blank page, use the technique known as freewriting. Start writing and force yourself to keep writing. If you can't think of anything to say, write, "I can't think of anything to say." Keep this up until you've generated some ideas.

Mapping, or clustering, is another technique that many writers find useful. Take an idea or a subtopic generated during a brainstorming or freewriting session and write it in the middle of a page. Then come up with as many connected ideas as you can, laying them out on lines radiating from the central idea. Try to pursue each line of thought as far as you can, using the lines to show how the ideas relate to each other (Figure 1.2).

For some writers, clustering is so helpful that its effects are almost magical. The reason may be that some writers think visually and do their best work when they are imagining spatial relationships between ideas rather than struggling to put one word after another.

Although these techniques are usually treated as door openers for the early stages of writing, they can be useful at any point in the writing process. A writer who has completed most of a preliminary draft but is puzzling over one subtopic, for instance, should return to brainstorming or mapping to generate more ideas.

USING A RESEARCH JOURNAL TO DEVELOP THE ARGUMENT

Many writers envision the process of writing a research paper as finding a topic, gathering photocopies, and writing the paper. But by now it should be clear that the process is considerably more complex than that. The writing of a truly effective research paper involves searching, re-searching, writing, and re-writing, in a process that continuously turns back upon itself recursively. To

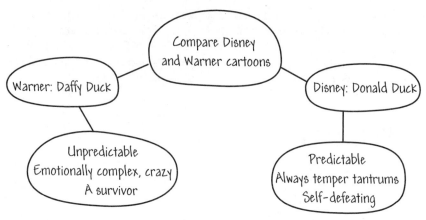

FIGURE 1.2 Clustering

support a thesis well, you have to mull over tentative ideas repeatedly while learning about the research topic. However, the research paper itself should sound confident and persuasive, even if you have felt tentative and confused while doing the research.

In other words, there is bound to be a huge gap between the tentative, mulling-it-over stage and the final, here-is-my-argument stage. This gap occurs because argumentation serves first as an instrument of inquiry and last as an instrument of persuasion. If you try to jump directly from gathering sources to writing a persuasive argument, your work will be shallow and unreflective because you will not have considered your material thoroughly enough. You will not have raised interesting questions in your rush to argue a case.

To bridge the gap between tentative first thoughts and persuasive final thoughts, start a research journal. It will serve as a special place where you can mull freely. You can say things in a journal that you would never say in a draft. Thus, the journal will free you to ask questions, to express doubts, and even to give vent to your frustrations about the paper. It will prevent a rush to judgment.

Because your journal will free you from a sense of audience, it will also help you to focus on inquiry before you get to persuasion. And because your journal will involve thinking aloud (on paper, at least), it will record a genuine development of thought rather than, say, a dry list of points. The journal, in other words, will go far to prevent the most common shortcomings of research writing.

There is an even more pressing reason to keep a journal: It will save time. "Sure," you're thinking. "I'll save a lot of time by writing a long journal that will never be handed in for credit! Not unless it's assigned, thank you." But if the journal does its job, much of it *will* be handed in, because your best ideas, and many of your best passages, will come from it. Furthermore, if you put *every-thing* in a journal that is stored as a word-processing file, later you can write your paper with amazing speed by copying the entire journal file and using the word processor's cut-and-paste function to assemble a rough draft. Read the excerpts from my journal at the ends of Chapters 2–6 and 9–11 to see how the process works.

AVOIDING MISTAKES
IN CHOOSING A TOPIC

Before proceeding to a more detailed treatment of how to find a good research topic (in Chapter 2), let's single out some kinds of topics you should avoid. For just a moment, imagine that you are a college instructor who has to grade dozens of research papers every term. What kinds of topics are likely to bore you? Allowing for considerable variability among instructors, we can safely lump the undesirable topics under two main headings: topics that are trendy or too familiar and topics that lead to mere regurgitation of information. In turn, these two main headings fall under a single master heading: topics that are likely to strike the student writer as safe.

You can avoid the most common disasters in topic choice and topic development if you remember to choose a subject that is challenging to learn and to write about. Find and develop a genuine line of argument, and avoid the false safety of using unfocused summaries and background discussions to pad your paper. For example, you may think that a topic for which there are dozens of books and articles will yield so much information that the paper will practically write itself, but such a well-documented topic is usually too broad. Remember that your topic must be focused enough for you to develop a specific argument about it.

The following list describes some qualities you should strive for in a potential topic and its accompanying thesis sentence. But bear in mind that *if narrowed sufficiently and treated well, almost any topic can become the basis of an excellent paper.* If you are in doubt about your instructor's opinion of your topic, discuss it in detail with your instructor before you begin.

CRITERIA FOR A GOOD THESIS	
Arguable:	The thesis should express an idea that can be doubted.
Clear:	The thesis should use precise, unambiguous language, and thus it should contain no metaphors, similes, or other figures of speech.
Predictive:	The thesis should predict the paper's plan of development, usually by mentioning the paper's main subtopics in their order of appearance.
Unified:	The thesis should make a unified statement expressed as a single sentence.
Narrow:	The thesis should be about a topic that you can master thoroughly.
Original:	The thesis should be original (at least to some degree).

Of course, there are exceptions. For example, sometimes a paper's controlling idea is too complex to express in a single sentence that mentions all the subtopics.

But do not diverge from these criteria without your instructor's approval, because following them will help prevent common mistakes.

A RESEARCH WRITER'S BOOKSHELF

Essential Books

Dictionaries   Every writer should have at least one up-to-date desk-sized (not pocket-sized) dictionary. The following dictionaries are all good choices.

> *The American Heritage Dictionary of the English Language*, 3rd ed. (1992).
>
> *Merriam-Webster's Collegiate Dictionary*, 10th ed. (1993).
>
> *Random House Webster's College Dictionary*, 2nd ed. (1997).
>
> *Webster's New World Dictionary of American English*, 3rd college ed. (1988).

Guides to Style, Grammar, and Usage

> Strunk, William, and E. B. White. *The Elements of Style*. 3rd ed. (1979).
>
> Wilson, Kenneth G. *The Columbia Guide to Standard American English* (1993).

Wilson's is the standard reference work for detailed information about usage. *The Elements of Style*, though far from complete, is a familiar classic. Questions of grammar are best answered by one of the many good college handbooks on the market. Here are four leading examples.

> *Harbrace College Handbook*, 13th ed. (1998).
>
> *The Little, Brown Handbook*, 7th ed. (1998).
>
> *The St. Martin's Handbook*, 3rd ed. (1996).
>
> *Writing from A to Z*, 2nd ed. (1997).

Optional Books

Editing Guides

> Cook, Claire Kehrwald. *Line by Line: How to Improve Your Own Writing* (1985).

Useful Reference Works

> Bartlett, John. *Familiar Quotations*, 16th ed. (1992).
>
> *The Oxford Dictionary of Quotations*, rev. 4th ed. (1996).
>
> *Roget's II Desk Thesaurus* (1992).
>
> *Roget's International Thesaurus*, 5th ed. (1992).

Manuals of Research Format and Style

Biological Sciences and Medicine   *Scientific Style and Format: The CBE Manual for Authors, Editors, and Publishers*, 6th ed. (1994). *American Medical Association Manual of Style*, 8th ed. (1989).

Chemistry   *The ACS Style Guide: A Manual for Authors and Editors*, 2nd ed. (1997).

General   *The Chicago Manual of Style*, 14th ed. (1993). Turabian, Kate L. *A Manual for Writers of Term Papers, Theses, and Dissertations*, 6th ed. (1996).

Humanities   *MLA Handbook for Writers of Research Papers*, 5th ed. (1999).

Law   *The Bluebook: A Uniform System of Citation*, 16th ed. (1996).

Mathematics   *A Manual for Authors of Mathematical Papers*, 9th ed. (1990).

Physics   *AIP Style Manual*, 4th ed. (1990).

Psychology and the Social Sciences   *Publication Manual of the American Psychological Association*, 4th ed. (1994).

Sciences   *American National Standard for the Preparation of Scientific Papers for Written or Oral Presentation* (1979).

▪▪▪ EXERCISE 1

In ten minutes of freewriting, answer the question "What are the usual problems I run into when doing a research paper?" If you have never written a research paper, write about the problems you anticipate on the basis of your experiences in writing other kinds of papers.

▪▪▪ EXERCISE 2

Apply the criteria on page 9 to the following titles and theses. For each paired title and thesis, assign a letter grade; explain your reason for the grade.

1. *Title:*   Order in Puritan New England
   Thesis: This essay will examine the factors that led the Puritans to settle the New World and the factors that determined the society they developed.
2. *Title:*   A Critical Look at Genetic Recombination
   Thesis: Recombinants are a reality, but controls over present and future recombinants are not.

not a strong verb

3. *Title:*   Benjamin Franklin as Puritan Transformed

C— *Thesis:* Franklin typified the American of the late eighteenth century; he was an ideological descendant of the Puritans transformed by the open society of America during this period.

4. *Title:*   Anecdote Collections and Intellectual History in the Eighteenth Century

   Thesis: The anecdote collection is significant because it is the first literary mode to successfully combine biography with intellectual history.

5. *Title:*   Freud and the Gestalt School on Interpretation of Dreams

   Thesis: Freud's wish fulfillment theory contrasts with that of Gestalt's Fritz Perls, who emphasizes the dream as an attempt to complete an action or a thought, and these differences carry over into the methods of therapy: Freud uses the dream as a window, Perls as an actual tool of healing.

CHAPTER 2

FINDING AND NARROWING THE TOPIC

■ ■ ■ QUICK VIEW

Throughout the rest of this book, I will present detailed information about the research process in the main body of each chapter. Some chapters begin with a section like this one, called "Quick View," containing condensed and simplified advice that may enable some readers to skip parts of the chapter. In the main body of each chapter, I generally assume that you are writing a fairly long term paper in which you will aim to make a fresh contribution to knowledge about your research topic. However, you may be interested primarily in simply learning to carry out a basic library search, to formulate a clear thesis statement, to use sources appropriately, and to produce a *brief*, well-organized, and carefully revised and edited research paper appropriate for college credit. The "Quick View" sections in this text will focus on shorter papers and more modest goals.

But remember that even in a brief research paper, you still must aim for some degree of originality. Perhaps your instructor will not expect you to make a new contribution to knowledge, but he or she will at least expect you to find your own approach to the subject, to express your own thesis, and to impose your own patterns of argument and organization on the topic.

START WITH IDEAS AND QUESTIONS IN YOUR JOURNAL

To find your own approach, you need to use techniques such as freewriting, listing, and mapping, especially in the early stages of topic formulation (see Chapter 1). The best place to keep such prewriting materials is in an informal research journal. If you are using word processing, you will save a lot of time by storing your research journal on a disk that you use as a gathering place for all your research material, such as ideas, notes, and drafts. A research journal compiled in a word-processing file can later be copied and modified to produce a research paper draft very quickly.

Use the journal to talk privately to yourself about your research paper. Turn off the self-critical portion of your mind and jot down all the ideas and questions you have about your topic, no matter how dumb they may seem. For example, "Why does a cat purr?" may seem like a stupid question, but it could lead to a very sophisticated investigation of cat physiology. (Cats have a special fold in their vocal cords that enables them to purr, some researchers believe.) Allow one question to lead to another: "Why did the cat's larynx evolve in this way? What survival function does this adaptation serve?"

When you think you have found an interesting research question, try it out on some classmates. If it arouses their curiosity and interest, it will probably make a useful takeoff point.

Now try to write what you *think* the answer to your question might be. This answer is your first version of your *hypothesis*. It may change or get displaced by other hypotheses, but somewhere down the line, you will have found a satisfactory answer or will be able to say why a satisfactory answer cannot be given. The answer, or the statement that an answer cannot be given, will be your thesis.

OVERVIEW OF THE RESEARCH WRITING PROCESS

Since writing a research paper requires you to carry on many activities simultaneously, any step-by-step explanation is bound to oversimplify and falsify. It would be good if you could read this entire book at once to grasp the whole process from the outset. But since you are more likely to read it a chapter at a time, let's take a short look at the entire process.

The first principle to remember is that you should begin writing at once and keep writing until the paper is done. The most common mistake students make is to delay writing until they have gathered lots of source material and taken lots of notes. If you tend to have trouble getting started, see "Overcoming Writer's Block" in Chapter 9. If you doubt that it is possible or desirable to start drafting at once, see "The Advantages of Early Drafting" in Chapter 9.

In my own research journal and elsewhere in this book, I discuss the research writing process in terms of twenty work sessions that may range in length from just a few minutes to several hours. During one working session you may spend twenty minutes in the library hunting for sources; during another you may work on drafting for three straight hours. A schedule of twenty work sessions may involve some daily work geared toward producing a paper in two weeks, or it may involve two work sessions a week over a ten-week term.

A good rule of thumb is that the early tasks can usually be broken down into short working sessions; but the later drafting and revising of the paper will normally call for long, continuous work sessions. Set up your planning schedule accordingly. Starting with the paper's due date, work backward to set up a working schedule of deadlines for yourself.

You should write a working plan (such as an informal outline) at the beginning of the drafting process, then a more formal plan at the end of the drafting process, and finally a thorough outline at the end of the revising process. You may modify your plans as often as you need to if your paper doesn't develop as you thought it would (see "Alternative Ways of Outlining and Drafting" in Chapter 9).

STATE YOUR HYPOTHESIS BEFORE SOURCE HUNTING

Discovering what you want to say about your topic is a continuing process, so don't expect to reach a final topic formulation or thesis right away. Here's the important point: As soon as possible, try to express the controlling idea of your paper in a single sentence—the tentative thesis, or the hypothesis. Without a hypothesis to direct your search, you will waste time gathering irrelevant information.

The key to writing a good hypothesis is to apply the criterion suggested in Chapter 1:

> A good hypothesis or thesis must arouse some doubt.

This test rules out all statements that are purely informative; it forces you to be argumentative.

Your instructor may prefer that you begin with a *research question* rather than a hypothesis. If you think of your tentative thesis, your hypothesis, as the answer to a research question, you can imagine your audience of college-educated peers and anticipate the kinds of questions they might ask about a subject of your choice. Better still, sit down with some friends and list some questions.

Although a book like this one has to break the research writing process into stages, topic formulation and source hunting have to go on simultaneously, because a topic that at first seems narrow enough may turn out to be too broad once you begin to track down sources. After you have compiled a working bibliography that includes enough sources to let you write the paper (check this information with your instructor), and after you have scanned most of these sources, you should be able to arrive at a final version of your topic. But be prepared to develop and reformulate your topic even during the writing of the paper.

If you tend to choose very broad topics, review "Subject Areas and Narrow Topics" found on page 19 in this chapter. If you have difficulty finding any interesting topics at all, use your research journal to think aloud. Look around you. Try to find a topic that relates to an area you know something about but goes well beyond your current knowledge. For example, my sample paper in Chapter 8 deals with improvisation, which I know something about because I have played jazz for years. However, my paper focuses on improvisation in eighteenth-century music, an area about which I was curious but knew almost nothing.

Read at least the introductory portions of Chapter 4, "Finding Sources," in order to start your source hunting at once. And be flexible about choosing a topic that will work. It's better to revise your topic than to be stymied by a lack of (or overabundance of) source material. Remember: You cannot fully evaluate the scope of your topic until you have done some scanning and browsing in your library catalog and in well-chosen indexes.

FINDING EVIDENCE TO SUPPORT YOUR HYPOTHESIS

What do you do if you find too little evidence to support your hypothesis? One of my students, for example, wanted to write about the film version of John Steinbeck's *Grapes of Wrath*. After brainstorming in his research journal, he came up with this research question:

What effect did the film <u>Grapes of Wrath</u> have upon the living conditions of migrant workers in America during the Depression?

His initial hypothesis was that the film probably caused such a rise in sympathy for the migrant workers that the government passed all kinds of reforms. As he gathered source material and learned more about the film's reception, he grew more and more frustrated. He could not find evidence to support his hypothesis, and he felt that he might have to find a new topic. Instead, I urged him simply to reverse his hypothesis. He then argued, very successfully, that despite the film's popularity, it led to no significant social reforms. He later told me that having to reverse his hypothesis was one of the most useful experiences he had during the research writing process. So, be flexible! If the evidence does not support your original hypothesis, change your hypothesis.

In contrast, you may find too much evidence in support of your hypothesis. That is, you may find that the available sources so firmly support your initial hypothesis that there is really no need for your paper. Rather than let yourself feel useless because you are writing a rehash of readily available material, alter your hypothesis. Find some *aspect* of your original topic that arouses doubt.

As you scan source material, stay on the lookout for points of disagreement among experts. They may give you the beginnings of a topic and an argument.

In writing my paper on improvisation, for instance, I began with the hypothesis that improvisation died out in the eighteenth century because romanticism led to a cult of hero worship. I guessed that individual improvisation was destroyed by musicians' desires to accurately perform fully composed works by great romantic geniuses. I quickly found that the standard sources on improvisation already had expressed this hypothesis and that a full explanation was going to have to be considerably more complex. I began to alter and refine my hypothesis in an attempt to find a fresh slant. (To see how this topic evolved, read my Journal Excerpts at the end of this and subsequent chapters.)

MUST AN OBJECTIVE LIBRARY PAPER HAVE AN ARGUMENT?

In some disciplines, especially the sciences and the social sciences, *research* primarily means *empirical research:* the gathering of original data through experiments, surveys, and the like. Doing *library research* in these disciplines usually means carrying out an objective review of available literature on a topic. But a library research paper in these disciplines should not be thought of as a neutral summary, and it should not be organized as a chronological list of sources. Like a humanities research paper, it should argue in support of an original thesis; the argument, not the list of sources, should determine the paper's organization. A paper of this sort is a review article that aims to present an analysis of researchers' attempts to clarify a problem; it may draw connections, highlight difficulties and inconsistencies, and suggest directions for further research. Its scope may be comprehensive or selective.

Another type of paper in psychology and the social sciences, the *theoretical article*, advances a theory or criticizes previous theories. It uses published empirical studies only to illustrate theoretical points and therefore must have a strong, original argument.

TOPICS AND THE STAGES OF WRITING

It would be nice if research writing were a tidy, linear process, like this:

Find a subject area.

Narrow the subject area to a single topic.

Take notes on the narrow topic.

Organize the notes.

Write the rough draft.

Rewrite.

Edit and proofread.

But the average research paper never evolves this smoothly and easily. The most difficult part of the process is finding and narrowing the subject. Far from being a preliminary stage that you pass through quickly, it can extend through the whole process of creating the paper. It is not unusual to keep modifying your thesis and your subject as you go along. Sometimes you may find your true controlling idea late in the game, after you have written much of the preliminary draft. Then you must revise your draft to support your new thesis.

Your goal is to plan carefully so that you discard or redraft as little material as possible. But it helps to be aware that no matter how carefully you plan, you will make changes—sometimes drastic ones—as you go along. Common sense tells us that this must be so. You start with a topic and with questions about the topic. As you find sources dealing with your topic, some of your questions are answered, but other questions occur to you as you read. Furthermore, you find that some sources disagree with each other. This is a familiar part of learning: The more you find out about a subject, the more complexities you discover.

A curious dilemma arises here. You cannot take notes for your paper without some idea of what your main point will be. But you cannot formulate that main point until all the facts are in. You must know the whole before you can see how the parts fit together, but you cannot really know the whole before you know each part. In other words, you cannot know your thesis until you have gathered all your information, but you cannot gather all your information without a thesis to control your inquiry. This situation leads to the learning spiral.

THE LEARNING SPIRAL

The way out of the dilemma is to recognize that the process of learning takes the form of a circle or, more accurately, a spiral, in which each circular turn carries you to a higher level. You formulate questions; these questions send you to sources; the sources answer some questions but bring up others. You respond by making tentative statements, which you probe by arguing with them and questioning them.

Your curiosity, given a chance, will lead you to what you consider an interesting but manageable question, and your tentative answer to that question will be your hypothesis. The hypothesis will be your best early guess about what you want your paper to argue, and you will modify it as you go along. Therefore, throughout your work on the paper, you will be traveling around and around the circle shown in Figure 2.1.

As you gather arguments and pieces of information to prove or disprove your hypothesis, you may find that it is badly stated, too simple, or inaccurate in some way. You then may rephrase the hypothesis, and the rephrasing may alter

FIGURE 2.1 The Basic Research Writing Circle

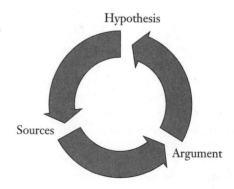

Hypothesis

Sources

Argument

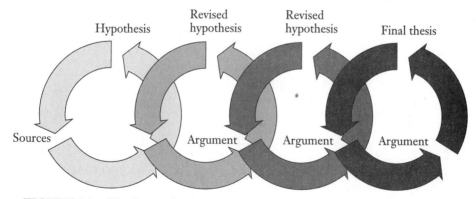

Hypothesis Revised hypothesis Revised hypothesis Final thesis

Sources Argument Argument Argument

FIGURE 2.2 The Research Writing Spiral

your view of the sources relevant to your study. You are *not merely* going around in circles, though, for each turn in the spiral advances your understanding of the subject and enables you to make more accurate statements about it (Figure 2.2).

SUBJECT AREAS AND NARROW TOPICS

Taking into account the circularity of this process, you would like to focus on a narrow topic as accurately as possible early in the writing process so that you will not have to revise or discard too much. In thinking about how to arrive at a sufficiently narrow topic, writers often use the term *subject area* to describe a general area of interest and the term *topic* to describe a narrow segment of the subject area. In fact, you can define a workable topic by thinking of it as the intersection between two subject areas.

The first sample paper in Chapter 8 analyzes some ethical problems raised by science's mapping of human genes. Its author, Todd Rose, found that medical ethics was an enormous subject area, and the Human Genome Project was a subject that had also generated many books and articles. But when he looked for sources in the intersection of the areas of medical ethics and the Human Genome Project, he found a much more manageable body of information.

Tracing the intersection between two subject areas may not always work, but it works often enough to be useful as a trick of the trade. Figure 2.3 gives three examples of this technique.

It is extremely difficult to know when a topic has been adequately narrowed. About the only way to be sure is to do a careful and thorough search for sources. If you are swamped with bibliographic items, your topic may be too broad. Scanning bibliographies and indexes may then suggest ways to narrow the topic further.

Another key to narrowing a topic is recognizing the topic's inherent subdivisions. "Spaceflight in the 1970s" is an example of a clumsy and illogical narrowing of a subject. Why should the topic be limited to the 1970s when the 1960s were an important era in spaceflight? The choice of a single decade seems arbi-

(a) Music + trade unions = topics dealing with the effects of unions on music

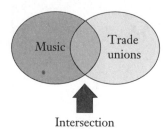

Intersection

Sample narrowed topic: the effects on American music of the American Federation of Musicians ban on studio recordings in 1942

(b) Jewish culture + drug abuse = topics dealing with drug abuse in Jewish culture

Intersection

Sample narrowed topic: reasons for low alcoholism rates in Jewish communities

(c) Spaceflight + nutrition = topics dealing with nutrition for astronauts

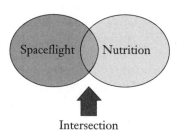

Intersection

Sample narrowed topic: devising menus for astronauts

FIGURE 2.3 Finding the Intersection Between Two Subject Areas

trary. If the topic becomes "Spaceflight After *Challenger 2*," the reader can see at once that the paper deals with (or at least takes into account) the setbacks to spaceflight since the shuttle disaster. The accident, because of its enormous impact on the space program, makes a natural dividing point.

Finally, be sure to remain consistent to your narrowed topic throughout your paper. If your topic is "Divorced Women Adjusting to Single Life," you have committed yourself to the adjustment problems of women. If you wish to discuss men's adjustment problems, you must show how they illuminate women's problems.

USING INDEXES AND SUBJECT HEADINGS TO FORMULATE A TOPIC

If you have only the vaguest idea of a subject area, you can use general indexes and outlines to zoom in on narrow topics. The reference volumes called the *Library of Congress Subject Headings* contain a comprehensive list of standard subject headings used by librarians in categorizing books; your library catalog uses these subject headings. By paying close attention to individual book listings as you browse, you can move from topic to topic by following the subject references that appear at the bottom of each card (or computer screen). (See "Library Catalogs" in Chapter 4.) If you are researching a medical topic, the reference work called *Medical Subject Headings, Tree Structure* will allow you to trace the connections between medical topics. (See "Library of Congress Subject Headings" in Chapter 4.)

To jostle your brain cells and stimulate your curiosity, turn to "Bibliographies, Indexes, Abstracts, and Electronic Databases" in Chapter 4 of this book and find a periodical index in a subject area that interests you. Then go to the library or go on-line and use the index to look up a specific topic. Scan the entries listed under it to find something that arouses your curiosity.

Let's say that in a literature class you have been given an assigned topic: imperialism. It so happens that you find political topics of this sort quite yawn inducing. But when you find the subtopic "imperialism in literature" in the *Humanities Index,* your eye is caught by the reference to Shakespeare's monster, Caliban, in *The Tempest* (see Figure 4.7 in Chapter 4). You've read and enjoyed *The Tempest,* but it never occurred to you that Caliban might symbolically represent the oppressed inhabitants of the New World. You jot down the citation to the article. When you track down the article to scan it, you find that it refers to a large body of source material dealing with just this interpretation. You decide to review the evidence for and against this interpretation—and you have found a topic that interests you and that will satisfy your assignment.

A TWENTY-QUESTION METHOD OF TOPIC FORMULATION

Ancient Greek and Roman writings on rhetoric are always worth looking at when you are trying to come up with ideas, because education in the ancient world was intended primarily to equip a student to argue about almost any topic under the sun. Aristotle came up with a useful list of standard questions to ask about any subject. They are really guides to what ancient rhetoric called *invention,* which means coming up with ideas.

Aristotle's list has been reformulated by Jacqueline Berke in her book *Twenty Questions for the Writer: A Rhetoric with Readings* (6th ed. [New York: Harcourt, 1995], 23). Berke's general questions, which follow, can help you generate specific questions about a subject, and sometimes your specific questions can lead to arguments. But notice that many of the questions call for purely expository or informative answers, not argumentative ones. As a convenience for readers of this book, each question in the left column is paired with an appropriate sort of writing in the right column.

Questions	*Types of Writing*
1. How can X be described?	Description
2. How did X happen?	Narration
3. What kind of person is X?	Characterization
4. What is my memory of X?	Personal experience
5. What is my personal response to X?	Personal experience
6. What are the facts about X?	Exposition
7. How can X be summarized?	Summary
8. What does X mean?	Definition
9. What is the essential function of X?	Functional analysis
10. What are the component parts of X?	Analysis
11. How is X made or done?	Process analysis
12. How should X be made or done?	Process analysis
13. What are the causes of X?	Causal analysis
14. What are the consequences of X?	Causal analysis
15. What are the types of X?	Classification
16. How does X compare to Y?	Comparison-contrast
17. What is the present status of X?	Description
18. How should X be interpreted?	Interpretation
19. What is the value of X?	Evaluation
20. What case can be made for or against X?	Argumentation

Only question 20 directly generates argumentation, and some of the questions may seem inappropriate for research writing. However, remember that description, narration, and exposition can be used to support an argument. (See "Describing, Narrating, Explaining, and Arguing" in Chapter 1.) Although a question like "What is my memory of X?" is clearly not going to lead to objective, argumentative writing, it may help you in the early stages of brainstorming. For example, the prewriting or idea-generating phase for a paper analyzing the television coverage of the 1991 Gulf War may begin with the question "What is my memory of the Gulf War?" Although the resulting first-person recollections may not be appropriate in a research paper, they may initiate observations, details, or examples that will later be useful for argumentation or development of the topic.

This book cannot give a general rule about the use of personal experience in research papers, since instructors' expectations may vary widely. But a good guideline in research writing is to keep yourself in the background and your topic in the foreground. Nevertheless, personal experience can sometimes be used effectively. A paper on native American dance, for instance, could begin with a vivid description of an actual performance; the introduction is a particularly appropriate place to use such material. Check with your instructor for guidance. (See also Chapter 11, "Editing," on the use of first-person pronouns.)

A FIVE-QUESTION METHOD OF TOPIC FORMULATION

Another way of developing new ideas about a topic was invented by the modern rhetorician Kenneth Burke (*A Grammar of Motives* [New York: Prentice-Hall, 1945]). When we discuss a topic involving human actions, Burke points out, we can teach ourselves about the topic by considering the following five aspects:

1. act
2. agent
3. scene
4. agency
5. purpose

Burke called his list a *pentad* because it invites five different ways of exploring a topic. You must examine *what happened* (act), *who did what* (agent), *where and when* the action occurred (scene), *how the action was carried out* (agency), and *what the motives were* (purpose). Burke's pentad closely resembles the six questions that are taught to beginning reporters: Who? What? Where? When? Why? and How? These, too, are designed to help the reporter write a complete report.

Lists of questions are especially useful when you are stuck, but they can help you at virtually every stage of the writing process, from topic formulation to revising and editing. New writers often check their final drafts, for example, by asking themselves, "Did I explain who did what? Did I say where it happened, when, why, and how?"

Whether you use a method involving questions, brainstorming, clustering, or any other technique is a matter of personal choice. The important thing is to record your thoughts at every stage of the research writing process. Do not make the mistake of passively gathering information (as notes, books checked out, or photocopies highlighted) in the belief that you can sort it out later. Remember:

> Value your first thoughts and *all* your questions. Begin writing before you begin researching, and write active responses to all the information you gather.

Later in the research process, you will find valuable draft material even in your most tentative early jotting.

One other reminder: If you record your topic-generating work on computer disks, make a backup copy of each disk after every work session.

HOW TO MAKE AN ASSIGNED TOPIC INTERESTING

In Chapter 1, I said that almost any topic could produce an excellent paper if it were handled correctly. The key is finding an interesting angle of approach. I will support my point here by providing an example by a gifted research writer.

The topic of animals in research, many readers might feel, is a *stale* subject (see "Avoiding Mistakes in Choosing a Topic" in Chapter 1). It has been in the news quite frequently, and most readers have probably decided where they stand on the issue and are not interested in hearing any more about it. So consider these issues as you read the following excerpt from "Human Morality and Animal Research: Confessions and Quandaries" by Harold Herzog. Herzog describes a research laboratory in which mice are intentionally killed for three different reasons: Mice running loose on the premises are killed as unsanitary pests, other mice are kept as food for predators, and still others are killed as research subjects.

> The laboratory in which I worked specializes in the study of snake behavior. Most of the research animals were garter snakes, which thrive on a diet of worms and small fish. We did, however, keep some rat snakes and small boa constrictors, which need mammalian prey in order to thrive, and these mammals were mice. . . . Animal-care committees do not typically regulate the use of mice as snake food. After all, many reptiles will only eat live prey. Not providing them with an adequate diet of live rodents would ultimately result in their starvation, a clear violation of our ethical responsibilities.
>
> In some experiments the role of a mouse as food or subject becomes clouded. Suppose Professor X wants to study the anti-predator strategies of mice. She plans to introduce live mice into a rattlesnake's cage and video-tape the encounter between predator and prey. Now from the point of view of the mouse, there is little difference between being dropped into a rattler's cage for the purpose of being eaten or for the purpose of a study of its defensive responses. From a legal point of view, however, these are quite different situations. If Professor X presents the mouse to the snake simply to provide her research animal with its weekly meal, she does not need to secure prior permission from the animal-care committee. If her motivation is to study how the mouse defends itself, she had best begin filling out the request forms. In this case, the moral and legal status of the animal hinges not on species, brain size, or even the amount of suffering it might be ex-pected to experience, but on its label—pest, food, or research subject. (*American Scholar* 62.3 [1993]: 343)

Notice how Herzog's fresh approach to the topic forces the reader to con-front the ethical complexities of using animals in research. The subject itself may be stale, but Herzog's strategy is startlingly original. He forces the reader to see how the stark fact of animal suffering—a fact we tend to respond to with compassionate but oversimplified judgments—becomes complex when it is viewed from several contradictory ethical perspectives. The contradiction between filling out paperwork for mouse-as-subject and not filling out paperwork for mouse-as-food is quite striking, but we would be wrong to conclude that Herzog is simplistically arguing that such paperwork should be abolished. On the contrary, he wants the reader to confront the complexity of human ethical decisions regarding animals, even when he uses a persuasive sentence such as the following one later in his piece, which seems designed to provoke animal rights activists: "It is even possible that more furry and feathered creatures die in the claws of cats owned by animal activists than in all the research laboratories in the United States" (345).

Herzog's persuasive strategy is effective partly because it is quite modest. He doesn't make grandiose claims or try to lay down universal moral principles about animal rights. Instead, he says, in effect, "Look: Here's a paradox about the way people behave in a typical research laboratory. What does this tell us about the ethical questions involved?" In finding a provocatively fresh way to handle a trite subject, in finding the subject's complexity, and in approaching it modestly but persuasively, Herzog illustrates beautifully the qualities of good research writing.

■■■ JOURNAL EXCERPTS

Finding and Narrowing the Topic

I kept a detailed research journal as I wrote the sample paper that appears in Chapter 8. I chose a topic outside my normal area of expertise to put myself in the position of a student. My intention was to write a research paper appropriate as an honors project or as a term paper for an upper-division course.

Completing this research paper took twenty working sessions spread over a period in which I was also writing several chapters of this book. Some of these working sessions were quite brief—perhaps a half hour spent scanning sources. Several working sessions, especially during the period from session 10 to session 15, involved several hours of drafting.

Finding and narrowing the subject lasted through more than a quarter of the sessions, though I had a fairly clear idea of the general purpose of my paper right from the very start. The journal entries that end Chapter 3, "Generating an Argument," reveal that developing the paper's argument was a slow process. Nearly all the various components of the writing process were spread out in time, except editing, which was confined to the last few working sessions.

Comments within square brackets were added later as a way of highlighting what was going on in the research journal. The journal's "Statement of Topic" section contains references to Library of Congress subject headings, periodical indexes, and topic bibliographies, terms that may be unfamiliar to you. If they are, read the following sections in Chapter 4: "Quick View," "Library of Congress Subject Headings," and "Step Three: Using Indexes."

Session 1

Hypothesis: I would like to show that the decline of musical improvisation as a skill after the classical period was related to the romantic cult of the author-genius.

Session 3

[I filled out my own "Statement of Topic" exercise to see whether it would clarify things. Here is the result.]

Statement of Topic

Topic: The Decline of Classical Improvisation

Library of Congress subject heading(s): Improvisation (Music); Embellishment (Music); Performance practice (Music)—18th Century; Performance practice (Music)—19th Century

Hypothesis: Improvisation, an important part of every musician's education during the eighteenth century, declined in the nineteenth century because the romantic cult of genius led to the increased prestige of composers rather than performers.

Most useful periodical index and/or topic bibliography: Vinquist and Zaslaw, *Performance Practice: A Bibliography*; RILM

Additional periodical index(es): Humanities Index; Music Index

Additional topic bibliography: Frederick Neumann, *Ornamentation and Improvisation in Mozart*, 289–292

Session 5

I now find that looking at several key sources has helped narrow the topic considerably, thereby cutting my huge initial bibliography of sources down to a manageable size.

I have a few quotations that relate to handbooks and instruction at this point, but *this has become my main research question:* How was improvisation taught?

▪▪▪ EXERCISE 3

Writing a Statement of Topic

To complete this exercise, fill in the spaces in Figure 2.4. To fill them in, you must carry out at least the initial stages of a search for sources. Read enough of Chapter 4, "Finding Sources," to be sure that you understand what a topic bibliography is, that you have found the periodical index that will be best for you, and that you know how to find the most useful Library of Congress subject headings related to your topic.

Notice that you must formulate two potential topics: a primary one and an alternate. The purpose of this twofold design is to remind you that a topic must remain tentative until a thorough source hunt has been carried out. Be flexible,

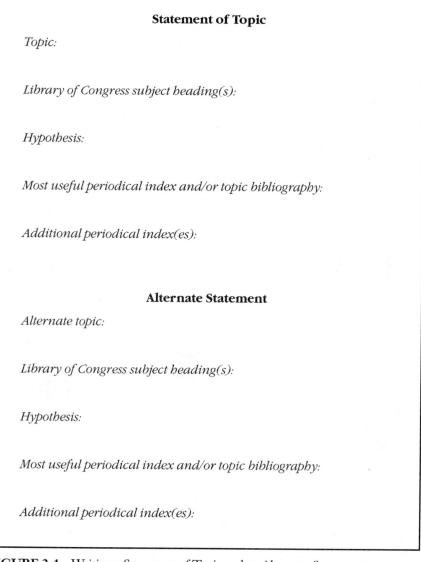

Statement of Topic

Topic:

Library of Congress subject heading(s):

Hypothesis:

Most useful periodical index and/or topic bibliography:

Additional periodical index(es):

Alternate Statement

Alternate topic:

Library of Congress subject heading(s):

Hypothesis:

Most useful periodical index and/or topic bibliography:

Additional periodical index(es):

FIGURE 2.4   Writing a Statement of Topic and an Alternate Statement

and always have an alternate plan in case the primary plan does not work. The backup topic may be closely related to the primary topic, or it may be entirely different. Put most of your effort into the primary topic.

Under "Topic," express your idea as a phrase, not a sentence. If you can do so, express the topic as a title.

Under the next heading, list as many useful Library of Congress subject headings as possible, but be sure to indicate which are most useful—that is, which will lead you to the most sources directly about your topic. (For an explanation of Library of Congress subject headings, see Chapter 4.)

Under "Hypothesis," write the answer to your primary research question. Remember that a hypothesis should arouse doubt, and it must be a single, complete sentence.

Under "Most useful periodical index and/or topic bibliography," list no more than two titles. The title(s) should tell your instructor where you have found the most citations to sources about your topic.

Under "Additional periodical index(es)," list any other indexes in which you have found some periodical articles.

This exercise will force you to formulate your topic clearly at an early stage in its development. The hypothesis may change later, but this early focusing of your efforts will still be useful.

■ ■ ■ EXERCISE 4
Prewriting

Begin your research journal by doing some prewriting on one or more topics of your choice, using any or all of the techniques discussed in Chapter 1.

■ ■ ■ EXERCISE 5
Research Questions and Hypotheses

Divide a page into two columns. In the left column, write a research question about one of your potential topics. In the right column, write some guesses about what you think the answer or answers might be. Continue this process with one or more topics until you have generated a set of questions to guide the first steps in your search for sources.

CHAPTER 3

GENERATING AN ARGUMENT

■ ■ ■ QUICK VIEW

If you are writing a very short research paper, you need to be especially careful to avoid any sort of padding; therefore, be sure to review the first section of this chapter, "Avoiding Passive Information Gathering." Remember that very brief portions of a short paper may narrate, describe, and explain, as long as these portions clearly support the main argument. That is, they must directly or indirectly serve to resolve the doubts aroused by the thesis statement.

For beginning research writers, the other crucial portion of this chapter is the section "The Three Bases of Persuasion." It explains how academic research writers present their arguments persuasively. It can help to prevent the dogmatic and one-sided tone that beginning researchers often mistake for a persuasive stance.

Consult other portions of this chapter as need arises. But first read and keep in mind the following two points.

1. Find common ground.
2. Make the argument go somewhere.

First, remember that your argument should not be entirely one sided. Your goal is not to overwhelm the reader with your undeniable logic. Real-life experience shows us how rare total persuasion really is. For instance, most spoken arguments end with both persons completely unpersuaded by the other person's point of view.

Think of argument, instead, as a process of showing an opponent or a doubter that your thesis deserves to be taken seriously and heard with respect. Acknowledge the existence of points of view other than your own, and show that you can treat them respectfully and fairly. Instead of aiming for a crushingly one-sided presentation of your case, consider as many sides as you can. (To get started, do Exercise 8 at the end of this chapter.) In this way you establish common ground, the area of agreement within which you and your opponents (or imagined opponents) can carry on a reasoned debate. The area of common ground may simply be an agreement upon the key question, the key pieces of evidence, and the key terms.

Second, remember that your argument must develop as the paper proceeds; it must go somewhere. Avoid giving away every key idea in the introduction. Consider using two versions of the thesis: an undeveloped thesis at the beginning and a developed thesis at the end (see "Generating a Topic Outline" and "The Developed Thesis" in Chapter 9). Developing your argument may require you to challenge and even refute the arguments of published sources. Refer to the section in this chapter called "Can I Really Challenge Experts?" for advice.

AVOIDING PASSIVE INFORMATION GATHERING

The most crucial but most difficult part of research writing is generating an argument. The processes of note taking, organizing, and explaining can become so comfortable and familiar that they block the process of arguing.

If you have a research topic that really interests you, you may find it fascinating as well as reassuring to highlight page after page of photocopied research material or to fill note card after note card with facts. Merely gathering information, however, can create a false sense that the research project is going somewhere. Piling up photocopies or note cards can become a way of putting off the difficult question: "What's the point of all this?" And if you have been assigned a topic that is not interesting to you, or if you have lost interest in your selected topic for some reason, an unsatisfying answer may come to mind: "The point is not to arrive at some new truth but simply to fulfill an assignment and to get a good grade."

Certain kinds of topics, such as surveys of past research, are particularly likely to encourage you to go through the motions passively. In addition, a paper organized chronologically is liable to lack argumentative impact, as is a paper that consists entirely of a string of examples.

If you adopt a familiar expository pattern for the paper as a whole, the pattern itself may lead you away from developing an argument. A comparison-contrast topic, for example, is likely to degenerate into a list of similarities and differences. In place of a meaningful thesis, the comparison-contrast paper may invite some yawn-inducing, general-purpose statement, such as "A and B are different, yet they have similarities, too."

USING EXPOSITION EFFECTIVELY

There are many reasons for writing, and getting a good grade or passing the time are two. In the broadest sense, one may write to fill space, to entertain, to inform, to persuade, to express feelings, to clarify thoughts—or just to try out a new pen. But when there is important information to convey or an important point to be made, writing tends to fall into the four primary types defined in Chapter 1: description, narration, exposition, and argument.

One thing our educational system attempts to do is move the student writer upward through the various modes; for an influential statement of this theory, see James Moffett's book *Teaching the Universe of Discourse* (Boston: Houghton, 1968). The simplest writing assignments usually involve telling a story (narration) or telling about a person or place (description). More demanding writing assignments generally stress the task of explaining something (exposition). College writing courses are expected to complete this movement from the simpler to the more complex modes by teaching you how to argue.

Since we have all been brought up on at least a partial diet of television, we are likely to be comfortable with narrative and expository modes, because television is a narrative and expository medium. But argumentation is a less familiar mode. It challenges the writer's ability to formulate a long, complex line of thought—an ability that television's split-second montages and sound bites are unlikely to foster. Worse still, some "talk shows" reduce argumentation to shouting.

Just as a squid defends itself by squirting ink, some insecure writers defend themselves from the anxiety of argumentation by expending ink—lots of it. They fall back on repeating and restating their opinion rather than offering fresh arguments that might persuade. However, creating a defensive cloud of ink is not a good strategy in the long run. The goal of effective argumentation is to express an idea with persuasive clarity, not to disguise it with murk.

ARGUING WITH YOURSELF

Where does a line of argument come from? It comes from your quarrels with yourself. As a research writer, you need an inner voice that constantly nags in your ear: "So what? What's the point?" If you keep asking yourself that question and keep answering it, you cannot help but begin to generate argumentative statements, even while you are taking notes or highlighting photocopied sources. Merely running the highlighting pen over a passage may be passivity disguised as a form of activity; but if you also write in the margin, "Supports my point about negative reactions," "How does he know this?" "Not proved," or "Compare Smith on this point," you are reading actively. Active rather than passive reading becomes automatic if you keep your research questions and your thesis constantly in mind as you gather information. Avoid letting mere information gathering take over as an end in itself. (See Chapter 6, "Gathering Information," especially the section "Active Reading.")

Every writer finds tricks for keeping self-doubts and self-criticism from blocking creativity. (Freewriting is one such trick.) But the research writer particularly needs a harmonious relationship between the creative and the critical aspects of the self. While one part of the research writer's mind is arguing to prove a thesis, the other part should be questioning, undermining, and doubting that same thesis. Even more urgently than most writers, the research writer needs to play both roles in a pro-and-con debate. The research writer has to cultivate a state of uncertainty in which one is actively testing different versions of the truth.

Consider a student paper on Jimmy Petrillo, longtime president of the American Federation of Musicians. The writer placed all her source notes in chronological order and then wrote the paper from these notes. The predictable result of this purely informative approach was a lack of focus. Chronological organization is not necessarily bad, but it can lead to a paper that avoids argument and thus seems purposeless. In revising, the student imposed an argumentative pattern on top of the chronology. Her argumentative thesis was, "Throughout his career, Jimmy Petrillo misunderstood the revolutionary implications of recording technology." Her opening phrase, "Throughout his career," allowed her to set up the study chronologically, but the main clause obliged her to give the study a focus, a line of argument relating to Petrillo and technology.

I learned this lesson from a well-known biographer. "Even a biographical sketch needs an argument," he insisted after reading a muddled piece I had written. When I showed him a revision, he read it (as was his habit) at lightning speed while talking to me in his office. "You've done a lot more research," he said several times as he read. "This is much better, though I didn't expect you to do this much new research." I smiled modestly. The truth was—though I didn't say so—the revision didn't contain a single item of information that hadn't been in the original draft! It was just that in the revised version the facts and details now supported a coherent argument. The chapter seemed to be better researched simply because it now had a point.

That revision taught me the need for focused argument in an extended piece of research. What I learned is that without an argument, a research paper will seem pointless and disorganized. Even a well-researched, informative paper will seem confusing and purposeless if the lines of its argument are not clear. I learned one other thing: Once I had imposed my own argument on the material, the assigned topic became my own. The material became more interesting to me once I found my own angle.

MAKING THE ARGUMENT DEVELOP

To be really effective, an argument should be more than just a thesis with supporting subsections. The argument should go somewhere; it should develop. It should undergo alterations and refinements as the paper proceeds.

Consider the following example: After a brief introduction, a research paper states its thesis: "Hollywood films have consistently misrepresented the American Indian." Then the body of the paper supplies a series of examples that merely support the main point, and the conclusion summarizes it. What is wrong with this approach?

There may be several things wrong, but what concerns me here is that the argument is static. It doesn't go anywhere. The writer states her main idea and then supports it merely (that's the key word) by piling up examples. As a result, the paper contains no surprises.

"But wait a minute," I hear you saying. "I thought that the paper was supposed to stick to the thesis sentence and support it. This writer's thesis makes a clear statement, and the examples support it. What's wrong with that?" Yes, the thesis should arouse clear expectations, and the paper should fulfill them. But if that's *all* it does, it may be boring. Ideally, the paper should fulfill and *surpass* the reader's expectations. Otherwise, there will be no surprises for the reader, no sense of discovery along the way. Here is the principle that solves the problem:

> The thesis sentence should clearly predict the paper's overall development, but it should state the controlling idea in a relatively undeveloped form.

In other words, the thesis statement should leave out some interesting subconcepts that the body of the paper develops. In the body, the thesis undergoes gradual transformation under the pressure of the examples and evidence that you bring to it. Then at the end of the paper, the thesis may be restated in a more complex, more developed form that reflects the complications raised in the body of the paper.

Presenting the argument this way makes it interesting for readers because they encounter a series of surprising modifications and developments of the thesis. And this technique helps the writer, too, because it counterbalances the writer's natural instinct to avoid hard work and serious thought whenever possible. After all, the writer thinks, the undeveloped thesis was hard enough to come up with. Who wants to complicate it and develop it further? Anyone, I would say, who wants to hold the interest of a reader. No one likes to read long, predictable lists, chronologies, or series of examples in support of an idea that has already been fully stated. Thus, it is usually desirable to have two thesis statements in a research paper: the undeveloped thesis at the beginning and the developed thesis at the end.

Let's return to the example. Despite some shortcomings, this statement could serve as an undeveloped thesis:

Hollywood films have consistently misrepresented the American

Indian.

The body of the paper might develop detailed analyses of several types of misrepresentation: Caucasian actors play Indian roles, Indian characters are stereotyped as villains or as noble savages, and Native American customs are inaccurately represented. The developed thesis at the end of the paper can touch upon these analyses.

Although there have been notable exceptions, most Hollywood

movies, through miscasting, ethnic stereotyping, and inaccurate

treatments of Native American customs, have done American Indians

a disservice by misrepresenting them to the American audience.

This developed thesis briefly mentions the complicating factors the writer has discussed in the body of the paper. (See also "Generating a Topic Outline" in Chapter 9 for another example.)

You should try to formulate a developed thesis before you begin drafting your paper, so that you have a clear pattern of development laid out in advance. Sometimes, though, you may arrive at your developed thesis while drafting, as a natural by-product of the learning that takes place during the writing process.

As this section has emphasized, the paper must go somewhere by advancing and complicating its thesis. But this guideline raises another question: What does it mean for an argument to "go somewhere"? In other words, how do arguments develop?

Four Types of Argument

As an aid in answering this question, think about how narrative plot lines usually develop. All the narratives we encounter in books, movies, and television shows are variations on a few basic story lines, such as the love triangle, the quest, and the initiation story. The same principle applies for arguments: There are really only a few basic types of argument. Just as handbooks on fiction writing list *master plots* such as the Cinderella story or the boy-meets-girl story, Aristotle long ago created a list of master plots for arguers. These master plots were known as the *topoi* (TOE-poy) in ancient Greece; we get the word *topics* from them. Aristotle actually provided a couple of sets of *topoi*: a short list of four master arguments and a long list of topics providing the twenty-questions approach to generating arguments discussed in Chapter 2.

While every good argument is fresh and unique, in his short list Aristotle mentioned only four basic lines of argument that he considered useful in virtually every subject area. Here are Aristotle's master arguments.

1. You can argue about what is possible (or impossible).
2. You can argue about what happened (or didn't happen).
3. You can argue about what will happen (or won't happen).
4. You can argue about how big or small something is.

The fourth category is really much broader than it appears, for into it Aristotle lumped all questions of degree—that is, any argument in which the central question is "How X is it?" For X substitute any relative term you like: In the following examples, "big," "important," "toxic," and "helpful" are the relative terms.

How big is the current neo-Nazi movement?

How important was Shakespeare's influence on *Moby Dick*?

How toxic to humans are lawn herbicides when used as directed?

How helpful is group therapy in treating bulimia?

How to Find Your Argument

Since your thesis statement is written as an answer to some doubt or uncertainty, finding a thesis can be thought of as a process of hunting for ambiguous and doubtful topic areas (see Chapter 1, "The Nature of Research Writing"). Thus, finding an appropriate thesis often means finding out what disagreements or ambiguities there are in a current research area. Usually, you can identify them only by surveying the existing literature, although sometimes you can tackle issues that no one has directly addressed yet.

For example, one of my students decided to write a paper about the Cincinnati suspension bridge designed by John Roebling, who later designed the historic Brooklyn Bridge. Gathering information was challenging in itself, but once he had found enough material for a research paper, he faced the problem of finding an argument. How could he prevent the paper from turning into a purely informative, nonargumentative report? As it turned out, the writer found his argument by noticing an ironic twist: The city of Cincinnati now proudly treats the bridge as an emblem of its civic greatness, but the historical record shows that the city did everything it could to block its construction. The student writer had found a fresh angle and an interesting thesis: "Ironically, the very bridge that Cincinnati now proudly hails as a civic landmark was originally opposed as an eyesore and as a dangerous avenue for an invasion from the south." By focusing on this irony, the writer gave his paper an argument and lifted it above the mere function of reporting information. Incidentally, this thesis also shaped his narrative portions by making him focus on irony as a theme.

Argument by Authority

A research paper makes extensive use of *argument by authority*—that is, it paraphrases and cites quotations from sources that support the writer's thesis. In using authoritative support, as in using other kinds of evidence, the research writer should avoid the *fallacy of selected instances*, in which only supporting evidence is cited and contradictory evidence is suppressed. A strong research paper cites the opposing evidence and argumentation and then successfully refutes it. An argument that appeals to authority is never the final word; the research writer can always move *behind* the authority, so to speak, to evaluate the authority's own use of evidence and argumentation.

The research writer is caught in a paradox. On the one hand, the use of authoritative support is practically the defining characteristic of the research paper; using supporting source material effectively is what library research is all about. On the other hand, the research writer is expected to treat source material critically and analytically; so in a sense, using independent judgment *against* the authorities is what library research is all about. How do you resolve this paradox? To put it quite simply:

> Refute the sources that are wrong and put to new uses the sources that are right.

This principle sounds simple to execute, but it's actually difficult and challenging. Digging out the nuggets of truth from the bedrock of falsehood in which they are buried is always difficult work. But that's the challenge (and the joy) of research writing.

Deductive Argument

Logicians divide arguments into two possible categories: deductive and inductive. A deductive argument can be stated as a syllogism: two premises supporting a conclusion. The premises make statements about the relationship between two categories and a third term. Consider this familiar example.

Premise 1: All men are mortal.

Premise 2: Socrates is a man.

Conclusion: Socrates is mortal.

The relationship between the two categories "men" and "mortals" can be diagrammed as shown in Figure 3.1. The conclusion then takes a third term (Socrates, in this example) and places it in relation to the diagrammed categories, as shown in Figure 3.2.

The syllogism is said to be logically valid if the conclusion necessarily follows from the premises; it is invalid if the conclusion does not necessarily follow from the premises. The previous valid example can be converted into an invalid syllogism as follows:

Premise 1: All men are mortal.

Premise 2: Socrates is mortal.

Conclusion: Socrates is a man.

Here we can see that the syllogism is invalid if we try to place the final term, Socrates, in one predetermined location in relation to the categories. Socrates

FIGURE 3.1 Relationship Between the Two Categories: "All men are mortal."

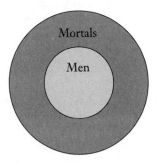

FIGURE 3.2 Relationship of the Third Term: "Socrates is a man."

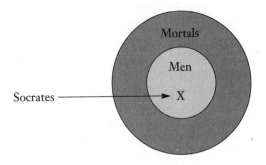

FIGURE 3.3 Invalid Syllogism: "Socrates is a man."

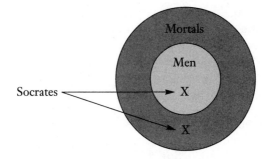

can in fact be placed in two possible locations, as shown in Figure 3.3. Thus, the syllogism is invalid. Socrates might be mortal but not a man.

Evaluating a Deductive Argument

When arguing deductively, writers must pay attention to the logical form of their argument and to the soundness of their premises. Remember that when you evaluate a deductive argument, you can challenge *only* its form or its premises; there is no other way a deductive argument can be flawed. In other words, if the conclusion is wrong, it must be based on faulty premises or on faulty reasoning from correct premises. So there are only two questions you can ask:

1. Does the conclusion logically follow from the premises?
2. Are the premises true?

Unfortunately, it is sometimes difficult to disentangle a syllogism from the words that have been used to package it. Writers (and scholarly writers are no exception) love to keep their premises out of sight, especially their weak premises! Arguing with a source can thus turn into a game of spotting the hidden premises, the unstated assumptions. You may be able to spot them without analyzing the writer's argument as a syllogism, but sometimes a syllogistic analysis can bring them to light. To analyze a passage of deductive argumentation, write down the conclusion first; then work backward, stating the premises that support it.

Read the following paragraph of argumentative prose. Look for its premises and its conclusions. Try to notice any hidden assumptions.

Increased deployment of nuclear power must lead to a more authoritarian society. Reliance upon nuclear power as the principal source of energy is probably possible only in a totalitarian state. Nobel Prize–winning physicist Hannes Alfven has described the requirements of a stable nuclear state in striking terms: Fission energy is safe only if a number of critical devices work as they should, if a number of people in key positions follow all of their instructions, if there is no sabotage, no hijacking of transports, if no reactor fuel processing plant or waste repository anywhere in the world is situated in a region of riots or guerilla activity, and no revolution or war—

even a "conventional one"—takes place in these regions. The enormous quantities of extremely dangerous material must not get into the hands of ignorant people or desperados. . . .

Nuclear power is viable only under conditions of absolute stability. The nuclear option requires guaranteed quiescence—internationally and in perpetuity. Widespread surveillance and police infiltration of all dissident organizations will become social imperatives, as will deployment of a paramilitary nuclear police force to safeguard every facet of the massive and labyrinthine fissile fuel cycle. (Denis Hayes, "Nuclear Power: The Fifth Horseman"; qtd. in Stuart Hirschberg, *Strategies of Argument* [New York: Macmillan, 1990], 146–147)

Take a moment to write down a syllogism containing what you believe to be the two premises and the conclusion of this argument. Now ask yourself: Are the premises true? Does the conclusion derive from the premises? If you wanted to make this argument more persuasive, how would you do so?

You can analyze this sample argument in a variety of ways; in fact, what often makes argumentation interesting and challenging is its ambiguity. In a room of thirty people, many will arrive at divergent interpretations of this passage. Nevertheless, most readers will probably agree that the underlying syllogism looks something like this.

Premise 1: Nuclear power is viable only under conditions of absolute stability.

Premise 2: An authoritarian society is required to produce absolute stability.

Conclusion: Therefore, nuclear power is viable only in an authoritarian society.

The conclusion does follow necessarily from the premises, so in this form the argument is logically valid. Both of the premises are dubious, however; they call for refutation or support.

Softening the premises by using qualifiers or less absolute terms (underlined in the example that follows) might make the entire argument more acceptable to some readers.

Premise 1: The use of nuclear power requires conditions of <u>relative</u> stability.

Premise 2: When stability is required, authoritarian measures are <u>often</u> imposed.

Conclusion: Therefore, the use of nuclear power <u>may often</u> lead to authoritarian measures.

But notice that Hayes does not soften his argument in this way. He uses absolute terms: "*must* lead," "possible *only* in a totalitarian state," "*only* under conditions," "*absolute* stability" (emphasis added). Thus, his argument is vulnerable to refutation because it overstates his case. In a research paper, you could refute Hayes by showing that his premises are flawed. At the same time, you could concede that Hayes's argument is valid when stated in less absolute terms.

Inductive Argument

While a deductive argument moves from general principles to a specific conclusion, the other main type of argument, inductive argument, moves from specific data to a general conclusion. If you produce four examples of governments that became more authoritarian after introducing nuclear power, you are arriving at a general conclusion (nuclear power encourages authoritarianism) by pointing to four specific items that support the general point.

One key difference between the two types of arguments is that deductive arguments can produce logical certainty, but inductive arguments can never produce more than probability. On inductive grounds, I am sure that the sun will rise tomorrow, because it always has risen in the past; but no matter how often the sun rises, there is always the tiny possibility that it will not rise tomorrow. Although I have a huge set of data to draw from—centuries and millennia of sunrises, and plenty of current data to show that no asteroid is heading this way to throw the earth out of kilter—my conclusion can never be more than highly probable. That's the nature of inductive argument. Deductive argument, on the other hand, is as certain as the premises upon which it is built. If Socrates is a man, and if men are mortal, then Socrates is certainly mortal.

Evaluating an Inductive Argument

In evaluating an inductive argument, you look at the set of data from which the conclusion is drawn. In evaluating or challenging a formal research study that argues by induction, you may need to address some subtle questions of statistical analysis or scientific method. The following are some key questions to ask:

1. Is the sample of data clearly described?
2. Is the sample large enough to support the conclusion?
3. Does the sample represent a typical cross section of the population or phenomenon studied?
4. Were scientific methods, such as the use of a control group, consistently employed?
5. Was the evidence presented and interpreted in an unbiased way?

In evaluating clinical studies, you may also ask, "Was bias eliminated through the use of double-blind techniques?" (For example, in clinical studies of a medication, members of a sample group are given a medication, but members of a control group are given a placebo, such as a sugar pill. "Double-blind technique" means that neither those administering the pills nor those taking them know which pills are which. This technique eliminates the effects of the potential biases of both the experimental subjects and the observers.)

To evaluate an inductive argument in an informal discussion with supporting examples, you can ask the following key questions.

> 1. Are the examples sufficient to support the conclusion?
> 2. Does the arguer discuss the supporting examples fairly and impartially?
> 3. Does the arguer overlook or misrepresent contradictory examples?

In most arguments, the two forms, inductive and deductive, are usually entangled with one another. The commercial that says "Nine out of ten doctors prescribe Blammo Pain Pills" is clearly using an inductive form of argument, since the implied conclusion ("Blammo is good stuff") is supported by a statistic ("nine out of ten"). But the underlying logic of this endorsement contains a bit of syllogistic reasoning, too. Here it is:

Premise 1: The good products are those recommended by a majority of doctors.

Premise 2: Blammo is recommended by a majority of doctors.

Conclusion: Blammo is a good product.

Extracting the implied deductive argument lets us see more clearly how weak the premises are. It also lets us see how the inductive and deductive arguments are intertwined. To determine whether premise 2 is really true, we need to study the inductive methods used to arrive at it. Premise 1 is liable to several objections; for instance, doctors routinely recommend products on the basis of name familiarity rather than quality.

CAN I REALLY CHALLENGE EXPERTS?

Often you must argue with the authorities you cite. Admittedly, it is daunting for a newcomer to challenge acknowledged experts. But experts make mistakes, and good instructors value students who think for themselves.

A word of warning: A frontal assault on, say, behavioral psychology in a research paper assigned by a Skinnerian behaviorist may be a bad idea. I am advising prudence here, not timidity. Check your ideas with your professor in advance. While I urge you to write for your own satisfaction, there is no point in spending a whole term or semester on a paper that may end up offending your instructor. On the other hand, your instructor may welcome your independence and may, by arguing with you in a friendly way, help you sharpen your argument. You should be able to find an argument that begins upon some common ground.

Authorities should be challenged politely and fairly. As you have seen, if you wish to refute an authority's argument, you must first analyze it to assess the validity of its deductive and inductive arguments. Furthermore, the authority's argument should never be distorted for the sake of refuting a fallacious misrepresentation, a strategy called "attacking a straw man." In paraphrasing the writer's premises, *state them as generously as possible*; refute the *strongest* version of his or her case that you can put together, not the weakest. Then apply the questions listed on pages 37, 39, and 40 to spot the weaknesses in your source's argument.

If you disagree with an argument but cannot refute it, you need to reconsider your own stance. You should not suppress viewpoints that challenge your own. Perhaps your hypothesis needs to be modified. Keep your mind open to the possibility that you are wrong. (See "Finding Evidence to Support Your Hypothesis" in Chapter 2 for an example of a student who totally reversed his initial hypothesis in response to what he learned while doing his research.)

Challenging Your Sources While You Read

Counterarguments and refutations should be written down, whenever possible, during the information-gathering stage. Often the dubious logic or flawed evidence in a source seems obvious at first reading, but it is easy to forget your refutation if you don't make note of it immediately.

Challenging Sources Near the End of Your Paper

Sometimes refutation is carried out at several places in the body of a research paper. It is often very persuasive, however, to wait until just before the end of the paper to raise key objections; then refute them and make your concluding statement. This pattern is as old as language itself, and it works.

THE THREE BASES OF PERSUASION

Strictly speaking, the research writer seeks to persuade by means of inductive and deductive logic. But in a broader sense, effective argumentation rests upon the following three means of persuasion identified by Aristotle:

1. The evidence must be convincing.
2. The speaker must be credible.
3. The audience's emotions (or at least its motives) must be engaged.

The credibility of the speaker depends upon what Aristotle called the speaker's character, or *ethos*. In research writing, the desired tone is one of impartiality, restraint, and self-effacement; the focus should be upon the topic, not the writer. (See Chapter 11, "Editing," on the use of first-person pronouns and on the effects of conciseness.) One hardly thinks of research writing as engaging the emotions; but if it is effective, it uses some degree of emotional persuasion. On the one hand, research writers seek an impartial tone; on the other hand, they use forceful language to help persuade their readers. There is an undeniable contradiction between these two principles, and it can be reconciled only by saying that the use of emotionally loaded language in research writing should be subtle and fair. It may legitimately take the form of what is sometimes called *semantic argument:* using the connotations of words to carry a subliminal emotional message. If you refer to a statement as a *concept*, you clearly respect it; if you call it an *idea*, your attitude seems neutral; if you call it a *notion*, you probably regard it as nonsense. But you should always avoid the use of obtrusively emotional or blatantly unfair language.

TOULMIN'S APPROACH TO ARGUMENT

In previous sections of this chapter I have treated argumentation by using traditional terms of rhetoric, particularly the rhetoric of Aristotle. Some readers may prefer to use the terms developed by Stephen Toulmin in his influential book *The Uses of Argument* (Cambridge: Cambridge UP, 1958).

Toulmin sees an argument as having three parts, which he calls the claim, the support, and the warrant. A *claim* is what the arguer is trying to prove; it is the hypothesis or thesis. Toulmin sorts claims into three categories:

1. *Claims of fact:* Something is or was the case.

2. *Claims of value:* Something is better than something else.

3. *Claims of policy:* Something should be done.

These categories are similar to Aristotle's four types of argument, described earlier (p. 34). The differences between the two schemes result from the social and philosophical differences between Aristotle's day and our own. Toulmin's scheme is typically modern in its insistence upon dividing questions of fact from questions of value. For Aristotle there was no dividing line; knowledge of the true and knowledge of the good were regarded as one and the same. For Toulmin, a single art of argumentation governs discourse in the several spheres of knowledge, value, and public policy; but Aristotle divided the art of rhetoric into three compartments: for public assemblies, for law courts, and for ceremonial displays. Thus, for Aristotle, arguing about what should or should not be done was appropriate only in the subdivision of rhetoric devoted to political or deliberative oratory.

By *support*, Toulmin means the evidence and appeals that you produce to persuade your audience. Evidence can include facts, interpretations of facts, evaluation of facts, and evaluation of interpretations. Appeals are directed at the needs and values of your audience.

By *warrant*, Toulmin means the expressed or unexpressed general assumption that provides a link between an argument's claim and its support.

Essentially, Toulmin's analysis is very similar to traditional rhetoric's analysis based upon the syllogism. In traditional rhetoric, a deductive argument might be expressed in a syllogism as follows:

Premise 1: Taxation without representation is tyranny.

Premise 2: Citizens of Washington, DC, pay U.S. taxes but are not represented by voting members of Congress.

Conclusion: Citizens of Washington, DC, are subjected to tyranny.

What makes Toulmin's method of analysis preferable for many modern readers is that it encourages us to notice that the warrant, or the most general assumption underlying the argument, is often left unstated. In other words, when we encounter an argument in a piece of writing, it will not be neatly presented with labeled premises and conclusion. Instead, an argument will usually look something like this:

> Citizens of Washington, DC, are being subjected to a form of tyranny, because they are being taxed without being represented by voting members of Congress.

Toulmin's terms make it easy for us to label the claim and the support.

> Claim: Citizens of Washington, DC, are being subjected to a form of tyranny.
>
> Support: They are being taxed without being represented by voting members of Congress.

Once you have identified the claim and the support in this fashion, ask, "What links the claim and the support?" The link is the unstated general principle: "Taxation without representation is tyranny." This is the argument's warrant. Identifying the warrant helps you see that the argument as a whole is based upon an appeal to the audience's shared values, and that the claim is implicitly directed at showing that a specific public policy is desirable. (That is, the citizens of Washington, DC, should have voting representatives in Congress.)

■ ■ ■ JOURNAL EXCERPTS

Generating an Argument

During sessions 2–6, I grappled with the common problem of having to discard my stale hypothesis and to find a new one.

Session 2

I am interested in exploring a possible paradox: that the cult of individual genius in the romantic era really killed the art of individual musical improvisation, at least as a part of standard musical education.

Session 4

Since the sources I have looked at so far have already thoroughly explored my thesis, how will I find a fresh line of argument?

Session 8

It's interesting to look back at my topic statement to test the accuracy of my early predictions about topic formulation and source hunting. I have widened my causal explanation (the part of the hypothesis beginning "because . . .") to include tasteless improvisation, the rise of amateur performance, the decline of the salon, the abandonment of thoroughbass methods, and the prestige of printed texts. Whew! The process has been exhausting, but these changes strike me as normal developments in the topic-formulating and information-gathering stages.

■■■ EXERCISE 6

Challenging Your Sources

Closely study the following opening paragraphs from an article by Margot Peters titled "The Phonological Structure of James Joyce's 'Araby'" (*Language and Style* 6 [1973]: 135–136). (*Phonology* means the study of speech sounds.) Notice that the article's thesis sentence is signaled by the words "We can conclude, therefore. . . ."

Read this passage resistantly and analytically; then answer the questions that follow it. (It is not necessary to have read Joyce's short story "Araby" to analyze the argument of this passage.)

James Joyce's "Araby" is certainly one of the most rigorously analyzed of modern short stories, yet its phonological patterning has gone largely unremarked. It is perhaps too obvious to note that Joyce, a word-magician, must be intensely conscious of the aural quality of his prose. Yet a closer look at "Araby," a story that strikes one even at first reading as possessing an almost poetic concentration of form, reveals a highly patterned sound system that goes beyond aesthetic effect to contribute significantly to the structure and meaning of Joyce's narrative.

The most striking phonological feature of "Araby" is the occurrence of many alliterative and assonant pairs within a relatively brief stretch of prose: *being blind, space of sky, silent street, side to side, pace and passed, morning after morning, street singers, single sensation, through a throng, prayers and praises, lamp or lighted, pressed the palms, O Love, O Love, round and round, room to room, pious purpose, sight of the streets, glaring with gas, station slowly, half its height, driven and derided, anguish and anger.* When the distribution of these alliterative and assonant pairs is examined, we discover that they occur regularly throughout the narrative until the moment the boy arrives at the bazaar. Here they stop (with the exception of the rather unremarkable *half its height*) until the final sentence, where we find not one, but two very striking pairs: *driven and derided* and *anguish and anger.* We can conclude, therefore, that these pairs are one of Joyce's principal means for conveying the shifting mood of the narrator, for their distribution coincides with the fluctuation of the boy's emotions: the exalted anticipation that has characterized his state of mind throughout the major part of the narrative receives an abrupt check when he arrives at the bazaar at "ten minutes to ten," and, passing through the turnstile into the darkened hall, finds that he has come too late. When the last light goes out, leaving him in darkness, the recognition of his folly sweeps over him, bringing with it a new emotion signalled again by the pairs: "Gazing up into the darkness I saw myself as a creature driven and derided by vanity; and my eyes burned with anguish and anger."

Questions for Analysis

1. In these paragraphs, how does the author support her main point, that "these pairs are one of Joyce's principal means for conveying the shifting mood of the narrator"? Raise as many objections to her argument as you can.

2. Does the author assert or imply that Joyce consciously used these word pairs? Do the paragraphs support the idea that Joyce consciously used these pairs? Express the implied argument as a syllogism, and evaluate its premises and conclusion.

3. Some alliterative word pairs crop up randomly in almost any selection of English prose. Flipping at random to the first paragraph of "Questioning and Analyzing" in Chapter 6 (p. 126), for example, I find *paragraph after paragraph*, *condense a complicated*, and *color coding*. Is it possible to tell when the alliteration has become more than just random use of everyday words or phrases? Explain a method of identifying passages in which alliteration has risen above or fallen below the random level. Do you see any indication that the writer of this excerpt has used such a method?

4. Do you see any signs that the author of the excerpt is forcing the evidence to fit her thesis? Explain.

5. Does the inductive evidence, the list of examples, adequately support the author's case? Why or why not?

■ ■ ■ EXERCISE 7

Generating Arguments from "Facts"

An argument can sometimes be implied without any direct statement of claim, support, or warrant. What implied arguments do you see in the following pairs of "facts"? (See Lewis H. Lapham, Michael Pollan, and Eric Etheridge, *The Harper's Index Book* [New York: Owl-Holt, 1987].) State each argument in a sentence or two; then analyze it by using syllogistic logic or Toulmin logic. (The statistics are all well documented and accurate; the quotation marks around the word *facts* are meant to suggest that a fact is only as good as the argument that supplies its context.)

1. (a) Reagan administration's 1985 budget for military bands: $154,200,000
   (b) Reagan administration's 1985 budget for the National Endowment for the Arts: $144,900,000

2. (a) cost of one *Miami Vice* episode: $1,500,000
   (b) cost of running the Miami police department's vice squad for one year: $1,161,741

3. (a) percentage of Iowa residents who say they listen to soul music "fairly often": 13

   (b) percentage of country and western music recordings purchased by
       minorities: 3
4. (a) number of United States astronomers: 3,650
   (b) number of United States astrologers: 15,000

■ ■ ■ EXERCISE 8
Generating Counterarguments

In your research journal, write down the hypothesis from your "Statement of Topic" (Exercise 3). (If you have revised it, write down the new, revised version.)

Divide a page into two columns. On the left, state your strongest supporting points (evidence, expert testimony, arguments, examples, and so forth). On the right, state the strongest points against your hypothesis (contradictory evidence, counterexamples, and so forth). Finally, try to refute the points that contradict your argument.

CHAPTER 4

FINDING SOURCES

■ ■ ■ QUICK VIEW

This chapter and the next two present the basic skills involved in finding library sources and gathering information. They present enough information to meet the essential needs of all but the most sophisticated postgraduate researchers. Unless you are thoroughly familiar with library research, I cannot recommend skipping any portions. But remember that this chapter boils down to *four basic steps:*

1. Use encyclopedias to get overviews of your subject.
2. Use library catalogs to find books and perhaps nonprint sources (such as recordings, films, and videotapes) related to your subject.
3. Use indexes that are appropriate to your subject.
4. Use search engines and directories to find on-line sources on the World Wide Web and the Internet.

You may use this book's index or scan the topic headings in this chapter to find answers to questions about each of these four steps.

HOW MANY SOURCES AM I LOOKING FOR?

At some point during your hunt for source material, you are likely to fall into one of two traps: You may doggedly pursue a topic that is simply not covered by enough sources, or you may compile a long working bibliography and then feel swamped by your source material. In either case, pause to set some realistic guidelines for yourself.

Most college research papers use about two sources per page, so a ten-page paper will, on the average, use about twenty sources. This number can vary drastically, though, from subject to subject and from discipline to discipline. Ask your instructor about the number of sources he or she expects. I once received a fifteen-page paper based on many short newspaper accounts of the Tonkin Gulf incident (which Lyndon Johnson used as a pretext to heighten United States involvement in Vietnam). It used two books and eighty brief newspaper stories without being too heavily documented. A paper of the same length about hand-carved carousel animals, on the other hand, might be based on two books and four articles simply because information on this topic is scarce.

So make a realistic estimate of the number of sources you will need, and strive for a balance between books and periodicals. If your list is either too short or too long after you have used this chapter to guide you through your source hunt, review Chapter 2, "Finding and Narrowing the Topic." Adjust the narrowness of your topic in accordance with the number of available (or required) sources.

One thing is certain about library research: It always takes longer than expected. So plan your work conservatively; set up your schedule to allow yourself plenty of extra time. Plan to finish the paper (and any intermediate assignments, such as a preliminary draft) at least a day or two ahead of the deadlines set by your instructor.

MAGIC SOLUTIONS

Whether you are writing a short research paper for freshman composition or a long research paper for an upper-division course, remember that most information searches use just *four major starting points:* encyclopedias, library catalogs, indexes to books and periodicals, and Internet resources. Some complications arise, as discussed in the following pages, but they are just side excursions from a four-step path that often leads directly to the information you need.

Sometimes, an information search can be completed at once, virtually at a single stroke. This *magic solution* is finding a recent list of sources on exactly the topic you are investigating. There is nothing wrong with finding such a list and using it as a launching platform for your paper. In fact, it would be foolish to spend hours searching through indexes to compile a list that somebody else has already compiled.

A magic solution of this sort can take the form of either a subject guide or a topic bibliography. Any list of sources on a single topic (such as the list of works cited at the end of an article) can serve as a core list of likely sources for your paper. A subject guide (or reference guide), on the other hand, is a list of sources especially compiled for researchers. Subject guides are less common, though there are hundreds of them. At several points in this chapter, I emphasize the importance of looking for subject guides and topic bibliographies. *Before* plunging into long searches through other indexes, scan the library catalog, the *Bibliographic Index*, and the Internet as possible sources of topic bibliographies. (See p. 89.)

> **reference guide** A handbook providing instructions on how to carry out library research.

> **subject guide** A handbook providing instructions on how to carry out library research in a specific academic discipline or in a specific subject area.
>
> **topic bibliography** A list of works dealing with a specific topic.

Although you may find a good subject guide or topic bibliography, your instructor may want you to search beyond its list of sources, if only to get some experience with standard search techniques. Check with your instructor to be sure.

STARTING A BIBLIOGRAPHICAL CARD FILE

Although you may print out many bibliography entries directly from a library catalog or a database, you should nevertheless compile your working bibliography by transferring entries to note cards, preferably 4 × 6 inches or larger. Compiling a bibliography is the one part of the research process for which note cards are indispensable. Cards require a bit of extra work in the short run, but in the long run they will save you a lot of time, because you can easily rearrange them. You can shuffle them by call number, for example, to make your trips to the library stacks more efficient. You can shuffle them alphabetically when typing your final bibliography. You can make notes on them about library availability, the usefulness of sources, and the location of notes or photocopies. I always record information such as the location of my notes, since I can easily forget where I filed the notes (on other cards? on a marked photocopy? on a word-processing disk? under what heading?). Record the nearby locations of copies of works unavailable in your university library, and shuffle sources unavailable locally into a separate pile so that you can request interlibrary loans early in the research process.

As you begin compiling your bibliography, you may feel that you can work from a pile of printouts, sheets of source references written in longhand, and photocopies of bibliographies. However, it is easy to become bewildered by the accumulating mass of material. Since the working bibliography is the key to your whole research project, organize it well. Start a card file at once.

There is one final and persuasive reason for using a card file. You are going to find your sources listed differently in different indexes. Indexers are human, and they make mistakes; or they follow different indexing conventions and thus punctuate, underline, and even spell differently. For example, one indexer may accurately copy an ampersand (&) in a title; another indexer may write it out as the word *and*. You want your final bibliography to be precisely correct in every detail.

> You should copy the final version of a bibliography entry directly from the source itself, never from an index or a bibliography.

Therefore, verify each bibliography card when you look at the source for the first time. At that time, correct your bibliography card and mark it as final. (I like to put a check mark in the upper right-hand corner of each card after verification.)

Does this procedure sound finicky and pedantic? It isn't, really. Remember one of the primary purposes of documentation in research writing: It enables another researcher to retrace your steps. If you record an incorrect title such as *Dictionary of Social Sciences* (the correct title is *Dictionary of the Social Sciences*), a researcher searching a computerized library catalog by title may be completely defeated or misdirected. Incorrect volume or page numbers may make an article impossible to find.

As you compile your bibliography, remember to expand the abbreviations that printed indexes commonly use in recording journal titles. (However, if you plan to type the final draft of your paper in a scientific format, such as that described in the *CBE Manual*, record the abbreviated titles, too. You will need the full titles to find the journal articles in the library, but you will need the abbreviated titles for your bibliography.) Indexes abbreviate journal titles to save space; a guide to abbreviations generally appears in the front of each index. In the *MLA International Bibliography*, for example, *RMR* stands for *Rocky Mountain Review of Language and Literature*, and you should spell out this title in unabbreviated form.

Notice that some journals use acronyms as their actual titles. The title *Publications of the Modern Language Association of America* long ago became the easier-to-write *PMLA*. When in doubt about whether a series of letters is an abbreviation or an actual title, look at the journal's title page.

Don't worry about mastering the details of bibliographical format just yet, since they are covered in Chapter 7 and Chapter 8. Simply be sure that you record all the information you will need. To avoid backtracking later, each time you record a source reference, write down the items of information listed later in this chapter, or as many of them as may apply (see "Items to Record When Copying Citations"). The three lists cover all the information you will need in citing the types of sources most commonly used in a research paper. (For lists covering unusual types of sources, see Chapters 7 and 8.) If an item of information is not given, leave that space blank; fill it in later when you examine the source. If you don't carry this book with you when you do your library research, make a photocopy of the lists and keep it with your bibliography cards. For model bibliography cards to imitate, see Chapter 6, "Gathering Information."

PRELIMINARIES

Ask Your Instructor and the Reference Librarian

Before you begin your information search, discuss your topic with your instructor. Ask for advice about finding information on your topic. Particularly in upper-division courses, college instructors may know about specific sources or lists of sources not found in this book. For example, when I teach courses about eighteenth-century British literature, I direct my students to an annual bibliography called *The Eighteenth Century: A Current Bibliography*, because it is much more detailed and informative than the *MLA International Bibliography* for topics related to the period 1660–1800. But it is too narrow in its focus to deserve inclusion in a general list, such as the one later in this chapter.

By all means, ask the reference librarian for advice, too. But read this chapter first.

Find a Local Authority

Finding a local authority is another step that should precede or accompany a library information search, and its value is too frequently overlooked. An instructor may be able to direct you to someone with special expertise. A glance at your college catalog may show which faculty member specializes in your topic. Word-of-mouth inquiries may turn up an expert in an unexpected place. (In my university, a modern language professor is an authority on twentieth-century cartoons.) A local institution may be able to help you locate source material. (I teach near an air force base, and students have sometimes received expert advice by calling the base to ask about topics such as human factors engineering and artificial intelligence.) A bit of creative work with a telephone directory can sometimes help you turn up information through courteous telephone inquiries. You might also be able to use a directory of associations to find an organization of people interested in your topic. (See "Special Ways of Finding Sources" in Chapter 12.)

> **primary sources** The original works or writings that constitute the body of evidence upon which a research study is based. Depending upon the academic discipline, primary-source material might include literary works, musical compositions, works of art, case studies, interviews, government reports, and experiments.
>
> **secondary sources** Writings about the primary sources used in a research study. Depending upon the academic discipline, secondary source material might include critical analyses of literary works, studies of musical compositions, descriptions of works of art, evaluations of and commentaries upon case studies, review articles, analyses of government reports, and textbook summaries of experiments.

STEP ONE: Using Encyclopedias

General Encyclopedias

Usually, the articles in encyclopedias such as the *Encyclopedia Britannica* or the *Encyclopedia Americana* are not appropriate to use as sources for college research papers; your instructor will expect you to find sources that are more scholarly and more specialized. You may think that general encyclopedias are reliable guides to the whole body of human knowledge, but in fact, they often contain erroneous and out-of-date information.

Nevertheless, general encyclopedias can be useful in several ways, and you should not make the mistake of bypassing them. First, they can give you a good overview of your subject, preparing you for more specialized research. Second, they can give you a start in compiling a preliminary bibliography. Third, they can help you identify standard and highly influential sources, precisely because their bibliographies are limited. Fourth, they can provide basic information that will guide you in your search for information. For example, in studying wolf habitat, you will find that you need to know the wolf's taxonomic name, *canis lupus*, to find articles in a standard index, the *Zoological Record*.

ENCYCLOPEDIA AMERICANA

COLUMBIA ENCYCLOPEDIA (5th ed.; on-line)   A one-volume encyclopedia. Precisely because of its brevity and limited scope, it is useful for finding short bibliographies of standard works about a subject.

ENCARTA (on-line; CD-ROM)   Excellent multimedia material.

NEW ENCYCLOPEDIA BRITANNICA (on-line as *Britannica Online*)   Use the Micropaedia first; the Macropaedia is an encyclopedia of articles in depth. The Propaedia contains an outline of knowledge and the list of contributors.

Specialized Encyclopedias and Dictionaries

Specialized encyclopedias and dictionaries can perform many of the same functions as general encyclopedias. They often provide excellent bibliographies; in my hunt for sources for my paper on improvisation, one of the best topic bibliographies I found was at the end of the article on improvisation in the *New Grove Dictionary of Music and Musicians*. The articles in specialized encyclopedias are often very scholarly, thorough, and up to date—fully worthy of being included in your bibliography and used as sources of summaries, paraphrases, and quotations in the body of your paper.

Remember that the list of specialized encyclopedias that follows is wide ranging, not selective. The quality of such works varies widely, and you need to evaluate your sources carefully. Usually, by the time you have researched a topic carefully, you will have learned who the reputable authorities are (see "Evaluating Sources" in Chapter 6). If you need further advice, you can find reviews of encyclopedias by using an index to book reviews.

An article in an encyclopedia should be listed in your bibliography by author, just like any other article. But usually encyclopedia articles are signed only with initials, and you must consult a list of contributors to get the author's full name.

For the sake of conciseness, the following list omits reference guides to specific disciplines or topics; many of them exist, and they can save you hours of work. Consult your instructor about the reference guide appropriate for your subject. (I have made a few exceptions by including subject guides in areas for which there are few or no cumulative indexes—in women's studies, for example.)

Throughout the lists, initial articles (*a, an, the*) have been omitted except when needed to distinguish between two similar works (for example, *Encyclopedia of Education* and another called *The Encyclopedia of Education*). When two reference works have identical titles, I distinguish them by editor, publisher, and/or date.

To works or groups of reference works useful in more than one field, I provide *see also* cross-references. I generally list only the name of the related subject area, but in some cases I name specific works, particularly if their titles do not clearly indicate their interdisciplinary usefulness.

The list of reference works is selectively annotated. Annotated entries (marked *) are designed primarily to single out the following types of references:

1. works that are broadly useful in more than one major or discipline
2. works that require special search techniques
3. works that pose special difficulties for the researcher
4. works that are easily confused with other, similar references

Anthropology
ENCYCLOPEDIA OF ANTHROPOLOGY

Archaeology
CAMBRIDGE ENCYCLOPEDIA OF ARCHAEOLOGY
DICTIONARY OF CONCEPTS IN ARCHAEOLOGY
DICTIONARY OF IRISH ARCHAEOLOGY
LAROUSSE ENCYCLOPEDIA OF ARCHAEOLOGY

Architecture
ARCHITECTURE THROUGH THE AGES
DICTIONARY OF ARCHITECTURE AND BUILDING
DICTIONARY OF ARCHITECTURE AND CONSTRUCTION
ENCYCLOPAEDIA OF ARCHITECTURAL TERMS
ENCYCLOPAEDIA OF ARCHITECTURE
ENCYCLOPAEDIA OF WORLD ARCHITECTURE
ENCYCLOPEDIA OF AMERICAN ARCHITECTURE
ENCYCLOPEDIA OF ARCHITECTURE: DESIGN, ENGINEERING
    AND CONSTRUCTION
ENCYCLOPEDIA OF BUILDING TECHNOLOGY
ENCYCLOPEDIA OF MODERN ARCHITECTURE
HISTORY OF ARCHITECTURE (B. Fletcher)
MACMILLAN ENCYCLOPEDIA OF ARCHITECTS
MACMILLAN ENCYCLOPEDIA OF ARCHITECTURE AND TECHNOLOGICAL
    CHANGE

Art
ART THROUGH THE AGES
BRITANNICA ENCYCLOPEDIA OF AMERICAN ART
DICTIONARY OF AMERICAN ART
DICTIONARY OF ART TERMS
DICTIONARY OF ART TERMS AND TECHNIQUES
ENCYCLOPEDIA OF PAINTING

ENCYCLOPEDIA OF THEMES AND SUBJECTS IN PAINTING
ENCYCLOPEDIA OF WORLD ART
HARPER'S ENCYCLOPEDIA OF ART
MCGRAW-HILL DICTIONARY OF ART
NEW INTERNATIONAL ILLUSTRATED ENCYCLOPEDIA OF ART
OXFORD COMPANION TO ART
OXFORD COMPANION TO THE DECORATIVE ARTS
OXFORD COMPANION TO TWENTIETH CENTURY ART
OXFORD ILLUSTRATED ENCYCLOPEDIA OF THE ARTS
THAMES AND HUDSON ENCYCLOPAEDIA OF GRAPHIC DESIGN
    AND DESIGNERS

Astronomy

CAMBRIDGE ATLAS OF ASTRONOMY
CAMBRIDGE ENCYCLOPEDIA OF ASTRONOMY
ENCYCLOPEDIA OF ASTRONOMY
ENCYCLOPEDIA OF ASTRONOMY AND ASTROPHYSICS
INTERNATIONAL ENCYCLOPEDIA OF ASTRONOMY

Biography

AMERICAN MEN AND WOMEN OF SCIENCE (on-line)
AMERICAN MEN OF SCIENCE
BAKER'S BIOGRAPHICAL DICTIONARY OF MUSICIANS
BIOGRAPHICAL DICTIONARY OF AFRO-AMERICAN AND AFRICAN
    MUSICIANS
BIOGRAPHICAL DICTIONARY OF IRISH WRITERS
CONTEMPORARY AUTHORS
CONTEMPORARY DRAMATISTS
CONTEMPORARY NOVELISTS
CONTEMPORARY POETS (1st ed. James Vinson; 5th ed. Tracy Chevalier)
*DICTIONARY OF AMERICAN BIOGRAPHY   The standard biographical reference work on Americans. Lists only deceased persons. Updated with supplements. Indexes to biographical subjects, contributors, occupations, and other topics.
DICTIONARY OF AMERICAN NEGRO BIOGRAPHY
DICTIONARY OF CANADIAN BIOGRAPHY
THE DICTIONARY OF CANADIAN BIOGRAPHY
DICTIONARY OF LITERARY BIOGRAPHY
*DICTIONARY OF NATIONAL BIOGRAPHY   The standard biographical reference work on British subjects and colonial Americans. Lists only deceased persons. Lengthy, authoritative, documented articles.
DICTIONARY OF SCIENTIFIC BIOGRAPHY
DICTIONARY OF TWENTIETH-CENTURY WORLD BIOGRAPHY
ECONOMIST DICTIONARY OF POLITICAL BIOGRAPHY
GREAT LIVES FROM HISTORY
INTERNATIONAL DICTIONARY OF WOMEN'S BIOGRAPHY
MCGRAW-HILL ENCYCLOPEDIA OF WORLD BIOGRAPHY

McGraw-Hill Modern Men of Science
McGraw-Hill Modern Scientists and Engineers
Notable American Women, 1607–1950
Notable American Women: The Modern Period
Twentieth Century Authors

Biology

Dictionary of Biochemistry and Molecular Biology
Dictionary of Biology (M. Abercrombie)
Dictionary of Biology (E. B. Steen)
Cambridge Encyclopedia of Life Sciences
Encyclopaedia of Mammals
Encyclopedia of Bioethics
Encyclopedia of the Biological Sciences
Facts on File Dictionary of Biology
Grzimek's Animal Life Encyclopedia
Grzimek's Encyclopedia of Evolution
Grzimek's Encyclopedia of Mammals
Larousse Encyclopedia of Animal Life
Macmillan Illustrated Animal Encyclopedia
Magill's Survey of Science: Life Science Series
Oxford Companion to Animal Behavior

Business

Dictionary for Business and Finance
Dictionary of Banking
Dictionary of Banking Terms
Dictionary of Business and Economics
Dictionary of Business and Finance
Dictionary of Business and Management
Dictionary of Finance
Dictionary of Personnel and Human Resources Management
Encyclopaedia of Personnel Management
Encyclopedia of American Business History and Biography
Encyclopedia of Banking and Finance
Encyclopedia of Business Information Sources
Encyclopedia of Management
New Palgrave Dictionary of Money and Finance
VNR Dictionary of Business and Finance   (See also Economics.)

Chemistry

Encyclopedia of Biochemistry
Encyclopedia of Chemical Technology
Encyclopedia of Chemistry
Glossary of Chemical Terms
Hawley's Condensed Chemical Dictionary
Van Nostrand Reinhold Encyclopedia of Chemistry

Van Nostrand's International Encyclopedia of Chemical
Science (*See also* Science and Technology.)

Classical Studies

Dictionary of Classical Mythology
New Century Classical Handbook
Oxford Classical Dictionary
Oxford Companion to Classical Literature (*See also* Folklore.)

Communications

Communication Serials
Dictionary of Communication and Media Studies
Encyclopedia of American Journalism
Encyclopedia of Television
International Encyclopedia of Communications
Longman Dictionary of Mass Media and Communication
World Press Encyclopedia

Computer Science

Computer Dictionary and Handbook
Dictionary of Computer Terms
Dictionary of Computing
Encyclopedia of Artificial Intelligence
Encyclopedia of Computer Science
Encyclopedia of Computer Science and Engineering
Encyclopedia of Computer Science and Technology
Encyclopedia of Software Engineering

Dance

Concise Oxford Dictionary of Ballet
Dance Encyclopedia
Dictionary of Ballet Terms
Encyclopedia of Dance and Ballet

Drama

Encyclopedia of World Theater
McGraw-Hill Encyclopedia of World Drama
New York Times Theater Reviews, 1920–1970
Oxford Companion to American Theatre
Oxford Companion to the Theatre
Reader's Encyclopedia of World Drama
Theater Dictionary

Economics

Dictionary of Economics (F. Livesy)
Dictionary of Economics (D. Rutherford)
Dictionary of Economics and Business
Encyclopedia of American Economic History

FORTUNE ENCYCLOPEDIA OF ECONOMICS
McGRAW-HILL DICTIONARY OF MODERN ECONOMICS
McGRAW-HILL ENCYCLOPEDIA OF ECONOMICS
MIT DICTIONARY OF MODERN ECONOMICS
NEW PALGRAVE: A DICTIONARY OF ECONOMICS
PENGUIN DICTIONARY OF ECONOMICS   (*See also* Business.)

Education

DICTIONARY OF EDUCATION (ed. C. V. Good)
A DICTIONARY OF EDUCATION (ed. P. J. Hills)
A DICTIONARY OF EDUCATION (ed. D. Rowntree)
ENCYCLOPAEDIA OF EDUCATIONAL MEDIA COMMUNICATIONS
    AND TECHNOLOGY
ENCYCLOPEDIA OF EARLY CHILDHOOD EDUCATION
ENCYCLOPEDIA OF EDUCATION
THE ENCYCLOPEDIA OF EDUCATION
ENCYCLOPEDIA OF EDUCATIONAL RESEARCH
ENCYCLOPEDIA OF HIGHER EDUCATION
INTERNATIONAL DICTIONARY OF EDUCATION
INTERNATIONAL ENCYCLOPEDIA OF EDUCATIONAL TECHNOLOGY
INTERNATIONAL ENCYCLOPEDIA OF HIGHER EDUCATION
INTERNATIONAL ENCYCLOPEDIA OF TEACHING AND TEACHER
    EDUCATION
WORLD EDUCATION ENCYCLOPEDIA

Electronics

ENCYCLOPEDIA OF ELECTRONICS (ed. S. Gibilisco and N. Sclater)
IEEE STANDARD DICTIONARY OF ELECTRICAL AND ELECTRONICS
    TERMS
MODERN DICTIONARY OF ELECTRONICS   (*See also* Computer Science.)

Engineering

DICTIONARY FOR HUMAN FACTORS/ERGONOMICS
ENCYCLOPEDIA OF ENGINEERING MATERIALS
ENCYCLOPEDIA OF ENGINEERING MATERIALS AND PROCESSES
ENCYCLOPEDIA OF ENVIRONMENTAL SCIENCE AND ENGINEERING
ENCYCLOPEDIA OF FLUID MECHANICS
ENCYCLOPEDIA OF MATERIALS SCIENCE AND ENGINEERING
McGRAW-HILL DICTIONARY OF ENGINEERING
McGRAW-HILL DICTIONARY OF SCIENCE AND ENGINEERING
McGRAW-HILL ENCYCLOPEDIA OF ENGINEERING   (*See also* Environ-
    mental Science.)

Environmental Science

ATLAS OF ENDANGERED SPECIES
DICTIONARY OF ECOLOGY AND ENVIRONMENTAL SCIENCE
DICTIONARY OF ECOLOGY AND THE ENVIRONMENT
DICTIONARY OF ECOLOGY, EVOLUTION, AND SYSTEMATICS

DICTIONARY OF ENVIRONMENTAL SCIENCE AND TECHNOLOGY
ENCYCLOPEDIA OF COMMUNITY PLANNING AND ENVIRONMENTAL
    PROTECTION
ENCYCLOPEDIA OF ENVIRONMENTAL INFORMATION SOURCES
ENCYCLOPEDIA OF ENVIRONMENTAL SCIENCE AND ENGINEERING
ENCYCLOPEDIA OF ENVIRONMENTAL STUDIES
GRZIMEK'S ENCYCLOPEDIA OF ECOLOGY
MCGRAW-HILL ENCYCLOPEDIA OF ENVIRONMENTAL SCIENCE

Ethnic Studies

BLACK MUSIC AND MUSICIANS IN THE NEW GROVE DICTIONARY OF
    AMERICAN MUSIC AND THE NEW HARVARD DICTIONARY OF MUSIC
BLACK WOMEN IN WHITE AMERICA
BLACK WRITERS
DICTIONARY OF BLACK CULTURE
DICTIONARY OF INDIAN TRIBES OF THE AMERICAS
DICTIONARY OF NATIVE AMERICAN MYTHOLOGY
ENCYCLOPEDIA OF AFRICAN-AMERICAN CIVIL RIGHTS
ENCYCLOPEDIA OF AFRICAN AMERICAN RELIGIONS
ENCYCLOPEDIA OF NATIVE AMERICAN RELIGIONS
HARVARD ENCYCLOPEDIA OF AMERICAN ETHNIC GROUPS
NEGRO ALMANAC
REFERENCE LIBRARY OF BLACK AMERICA   (*See also* Biography;
    Geography.)

Film

DICTIONARY OF FILMS
ENCYCLOPEDIA OF ANIMATED CARTOONS
ENCYCLOPEDIA OF FILM
*HALLIWELL'S FILM GUIDE (formerly *Filmgoer's Companion*)   Halliwell's
    amusing comments and his entries on cinema trivia should not mislead
    the user into regarding this reference work as trivial. It is an accurate
    general reference work on cinema. New editions are issued at frequent
    intervals.
OXFORD COMPANION TO FILM

Folklore

DICTIONARY OF BRITISH FOLK-TALES IN THE ENGLISH LANGUAGE
DICTIONARY OF CELTIC MYTH AND LEGEND
DICTIONARY OF CELTIC MYTHOLOGY
DICTIONARY OF MYTHOLOGY, FOLKLORE, AND SYMBOLS
DICTIONARY OF NATIVE AMERICAN MYTHOLOGY
DICTIONARY OF SUPERSTITIONS
FUNK AND WAGNALL'S STANDARD DICTIONARY OF FOLKLORE,
    MYTHOLOGY AND LEGEND
LAROUSSE ENCYCLOPEDIA OF MYTHOLOGY
LAROUSSE WORLD MYTHOLOGY

MYTHOLOGY OF ALL RACES
OXFORD COMPANION TO AUSTRALIAN FOLKLORE   (*See also* Ethnic
  Studies; Popular Culture.)

Geography

COLUMBIA LIPPINCOTT GAZETTEER OF THE WORLD
GOODE'S WORLD ATLAS
ILLUSTRATED ENCYCLOPEDIA OF MANKIND
LAROUSSE ENCYCLOPEDIA OF WORLD GEOGRAPHY
MODERN GEOGRAPHY: AN ENCYCLOPEDIC SURVEY
NATIONAL ATLAS OF THE UNITED STATES OF AMERICA
TIMES ATLAS OF THE WORLD
TIMES INDEX-GAZETTEER OF THE WORLD
WEBSTER'S NEW GEOGRAPHICAL DICTIONARY

Geology and Earth Sciences

CAMBRIDGE ENCYCLOPEDIA OF EARTH SCIENCES
CLIMATES OF THE CONTINENTS
DICTIONARY OF EARTH SCIENCES
DICTIONARY OF GEOLOGY
ENCYCLOPEDIA OF EARTH SCIENCES
ENCYCLOPEDIA OF EARTH SYSTEM SCIENCE
ENCYCLOPEDIA OF MINERALS
ENCYCLOPEDIA OF THE SOLID EARTH SCIENCES
MAGILL'S SURVEY OF SCIENCE: EARTH SCIENCE SERIES
MCGRAW-HILL DICTIONARY OF EARTH SCIENCES
MCGRAW-HILL ENCYCLOPEDIA OF OCEAN AND ATMOSPHERIC
  SCIENCES
MCGRAW-HILL ENCYCLOPEDIA OF THE GEOLOGICAL SCIENCES
TIMES ATLAS OF THE OCEANS

History

CAMBRIDGE ANCIENT HISTORY
CAMBRIDGE MEDIEVAL HISTORY
COLUMBIA DICTIONARY OF EUROPEAN HISTORY SINCE 1914
DICTIONARY OF AMERICAN HISTORY
DICTIONARY OF THE MIDDLE AGES
ENCYCLOPEDIA OF AMERICAN HISTORY (ed. R. B. Morris)
ENCYCLOPEDIA OF AMERICAN SOCIAL HISTORY
ENCYCLOPEDIA OF HISTORIC PLACES
ENCYCLOPEDIA OF LATIN-AMERICAN HISTORY
ENCYCLOPEDIA OF WORLD HISTORY
HARPER ENCYCLOPEDIA OF MILITARY HISTORY: FROM 3500 B.C. TO
  THE PRESENT
LAROUSSE ENCYCLOPEDIA OF ANCIENT AND MEDIEVAL HISTORY
LAROUSSE ENCYCLOPEDIA OF MODERN HISTORY FROM 1500 TO THE
  PRESENT DAY

MODERN ENCYCLOPEDIA OF RUSSIAN AND SOVIET HISTORY
NEW CAMBRIDGE MODERN HISTORY
NEW ILLUSTRATED ENCYCLOPEDIA OF WORLD HISTORY
OXFORD COMPANION TO AMERICAN HISTORY
OXFORD COMPANION TO CANADIAN HISTORY AND LITERATURE
TIMES ATLAS OF WORLD HISTORY

Law

BLACK'S LAW DICTIONARY
DICTIONARY OF INTERNATIONAL AND COMPARATIVE LAW
DICTIONARY OF MODERN LEGAL USAGE
ENCYCLOPEDIA OF CRIME AND JUSTICE
ENCYCLOPEDIA OF PUBLIC INTERNATIONAL LAW
ENCYCLOPEDIA OF THE AMERICAN JUDICIAL SYSTEM
GUIDE TO AMERICAN LAW
OXFORD COMPANION TO LAW
PARRY AND GRANT ENCYCLOPEDIC DICTIONARY OF INTERNATIONAL
    LAW

Linguistics

DICTIONARY OF GRAMMATICAL TERMS IN LINGUISTICS
DICTIONARY OF LANGUAGE AND LINGUISTICS
DICTIONARY OF LINGUISTICS AND PHONETICS
ENCYCLOPEDIA OF LANGUAGE AND LINGUISTICS
ENCYCLOPEDIC DICTIONARY OF SEMIOTICS
INTERNATIONAL ENCYCLOPEDIA OF LINGUISTICS
LINGUISTIC ATLAS OF ENGLAND
LINGUISTIC ATLAS OF THE UNITED STATES AND CANADA
LONGMAN DICTIONARY OF APPLIED LINGUISTICS
OXFORD COMPANION TO THE ENGLISH LANGUAGE

Literature

CASSELL'S ENCYCLOPEDIA OF WORLD LITERATURE
COLUMBIA DICTIONARY OF MODERN EUROPEAN LITERATURE
CONTEMPORARY AUTHORS
DICTIONARY OF CONCEPTS IN LITERARY CRITICISM AND THEORY
ENCYCLOPEDIA OF CONTEMPORARY LITERARY THEORY
ENCYCLOPEDIA OF LITERATURE AND CRITICISM
ENCYCLOPEDIA OF WORLD LITERATURE IN THE 20TH CENTURY
*HANDBOOK TO LITERATURE   The standard desk reference for literary
    terms. Contains useful summaries of literary periods and parallel chro-
    nologies of English and American literature.
LITERARY HISTORY OF ENGLAND (A. C. Baugh)
LITERARY HISTORY OF THE UNITED STATES
*MASTERPLOTS   Synopses of over two thousand literary works.
OXFORD COMPANION TO AMERICAN LITERATURE
OXFORD COMPANION TO CANADIAN LITERATURE

OXFORD COMPANION TO CHILDREN'S LITERATURE
OXFORD COMPANION TO CLASSICAL LITERATURE
OXFORD COMPANION TO GERMAN LITERATURE
OXFORD COMPANION TO SPANISH LITERATURE
OXFORD COMPANION TO THE LITERATURE OF WALES
OXFORD GUIDE TO BRITISH WOMEN WRITERS
NEW PRINCETON ENCYCLOPEDIA OF POETRY AND POETICS

Mathematics

ENCYCLOPAEDIA OF MATHEMATICAL SCIENCES
ENCYCLOPAEDIA OF MATHEMATICS
ENCYCLOPAEDIA OF STATISTICAL SCIENCES
ENCYCLOPEDIA OF MATHEMATICS AND ITS APPLICATIONS
ENCYCLOPEDIC DICTIONARY OF MATHEMATICS
PRENTICE-HALL ENCYCLOPEDIA OF MATHEMATICS
VNR CONCISE ENCYCLOPEDIA OF MATHEMATICS

Medicine, Nursing, Health Sciences

AMERICAN MEDICAL ASSOCIATION ENCYCLOPEDIA OF MEDICINE
COLUMBIA ENCYCLOPEDIA OF NUTRITION
DORLAND'S MEDICAL DICTIONARY
ENCYCLOPEDIA AND DICTIONARY OF MEDICINE, NURSING, AND ALLIED
    HEALTH
ENCYCLOPEDIA OF IMMUNOLOGY
HARRISON'S PRINCIPLES OF INTERNAL MEDICINE
MARSHALL CAVENDISH ENCYCLOPEDIA OF FAMILY HEALTH
NUTRITION AND HEALTH ENCYCLOPEDIA
OXFORD COMPANION TO MEDICINE
*PHYSICIAN'S DESK REFERENCE   The standard guide to medications.
    Updated annually.

Music

CONCISE OXFORD DICTIONARY OF OPERA
DICTIONARY OF OPERA
ENCYCLOPEDIA OF JAZZ
ENCYCLOPEDIA OF JAZZ IN THE SEVENTIES
ENCYCLOPEDIA OF JAZZ IN THE SIXTIES
ENCYCLOPEDIA OF OPERA
ENCYCLOPEDIA OF POP, ROCK AND SOUL
ENCYCLOPEDIA OF ROCK
ENCYCLOPEDIA OF THE BLUES
GUINNESS ENCYCLOPEDIA OF POPULAR MUSIC
NEW COLLEGE ENCYCLOPEDIA OF MUSIC
NEW GROVE DICTIONARY OF AMERICAN MUSIC
*NEW GROVE DICTIONARY OF MUSIC AND MUSICIANS   The standard
    reference work on music; detailed and scholarly articles by more then
    two thousand contributors. Supersedes the old *Grove Dictionary of Music*

and Musicians; provides extensive coverage of musical traditions excluded from the old *Grove,* such as the African-American musical tradition.
NEW GROVE DICTIONARY OF OPERA
NEW HARVARD DICTIONARY OF MUSIC
NEW OXFORD COMPANION TO MUSIC
OXFORD COMPANION TO MUSICAL INSTRUMENTS
OXFORD COMPANION TO POPULAR MUSIC
OXFORD DICTIONARY OF OPERA

Philosophy

CONCISE ENCYCLOPAEDIA OF WESTERN PHILOSOPHY AND
  PHILOSOPHERS
A DICTIONARY OF PHILOSOPHY (ed. A. Flew)
A DICTIONARY OF PHILOSOPHY (ed. A. R. Lacey)
DICTIONARY OF PHILOSOPHY (ed. D. D. Runes)
DICTIONARY OF PHILOSOPHY AND PSYCHOLOGY
DICTIONARY OF PHILOSOPHY AND RELIGION, EASTERN AND WESTERN
DICTIONARY OF THE HISTORY OF IDEAS
ENCYCLOPAEDIA OF PHILOSOPHY
ENCYCLOPEDIA OF ETHICS
HARPERCOLLINS DICTIONARY OF PHILOSOPHY   (*See also* Religion.)

Physical Education

BIOGRAPHICAL DICTIONARY OF AMERICAN SPORTS
ENCYCLOPEDIA OF PHYSICAL EDUCATION, FITNESS, AND SPORTS
ENCYCLOPEDIA OF SPORTS
OXFORD COMPANION TO SPORTS AND GAMES
OXFORD COMPANION TO WORLD SPORTS AND GAMES

Physics

ENCYCLOPAEDIC DICTIONARY OF PHYSICS
ENCYCLOPEDIA OF PHYSICS (ed. R. M. Besancon)
ENCYCLOPEDIA OF PHYSICS (ed. R. G. Lerner and G. L. Trigg)
HANDBUCH DER PHYSIK (in English, French, and German)
MAGILL'S SURVEY OF SCIENCE: PHYSICAL SCIENCE SERIES   (*See also*
  Science and Technology.)

Political Science

AMERICAN POLITICAL DICTIONARY
BLACKWELL ENCYCLOPAEDIA OF POLITICAL INSTITUTIONS
BLACKWELL ENCYCLOPAEDIA OF POLITICAL SCIENCE
BLACKWELL ENCYCLOPAEDIA OF POLITICAL THOUGHT
COLUMBIA DICTIONARY OF EUROPEAN POLITICAL HISTORY SINCE 1914
DICTIONARY OF AMERICAN FOREIGN AFFAIRS
DICTIONARY OF AMERICAN POLITICS (E. C. Smith and A. J. Zurcher)
DICTIONARY OF MODERN POLITICS
DICTIONARY OF POLITICAL ANALYSIS (J. C. Plano, R. E. Riggs,
  and H. S. Robin)

DICTIONARY OF POLITICAL ANALYSIS (G. K. Roberts)
DICTIONARY OF POLITICAL SCIENCE
DICTIONARY OF POLITICAL SCIENCE AND LAW
DICTIONARY OF POLITICS (F. Elliott)
DICTIONARY OF POLITICS (W. Laqueur)
DICTIONARY OF TWENTIETH-CENTURY HISTORY: 1914–1990
DICTIONARY OF 20TH-CENTURY WORLD POLITICS
DORSEY DICTIONARY OF AMERICAN GOVERNMENT AND POLITICS
ENCYCLOPEDIA OF AMERICAN FOREIGN POLICY
ENCYCLOPEDIA OF AMERICAN POLITICAL HISTORY
ENCYCLOPEDIA OF ARMS CONTROL AND DISARMAMENT
ENCYCLOPEDIA OF THE UNITED NATIONS AND INTERNATIONAL
    RELATIONS
OXFORD COMPANION TO POLITICS OF THE WORLD
WORLD ENCYCLOPEDIA OF PEACE
WORLD ENCYCLOPEDIA OF POLITICAL SYSTEMS AND PARTIES
WORLDMARK ENCYCLOPEDIA OF THE NATIONS   (*See also* Biography.)

Popular Culture

ARTS AND ENTERTAINMENT FADS
ENCYCLOPEDIA OF BAD TASTE
ENCYCLOPEDIA OF POP CULTURE
FOLKLORE, CULTURAL PERFORMANCES, AND POPULAR
    ENTERTAINMENTS
HANDBOOK OF AMERICAN POPULAR CULTURES

Psychology

ENCYCLOPEDIA OF DEPRESSION
ENCYCLOPEDIA OF MENTAL HEALTH
ENCYCLOPEDIA OF PSYCHOLOGY (ed. R. J. Corsini)
ENCYCLOPEDIA OF PSYCHOLOGY (ed. H. J. Eysenck, W. Arnold,
    and R. Meili)
ENCYCLOPEDIC DICTIONARY OF PSYCHOLOGY (ed. R. Harre
    and R. Lamb)
ENCYCLOPEDIC DICTIONARY OF PSYCHOLOGY (ed. T. F. Pettijohn)
INTERNATIONAL ENCYCLOPEDIA OF PSYCHIATRY, PSYCHOLOGY,
    PSYCHOANALYSIS AND NEUROLOGY
OXFORD COMPANION TO THE MIND
PSYCHIATRIC DICTIONARY   (*See also* Philosophy.)

Religion

ATLAS OF THE ISLAMIC WORLD SINCE 1500
DICTIONARY OF AMERICAN RELIGIOUS BIOGRAPHY
DICTIONARY OF COMPARATIVE RELIGION
DICTIONARY OF JUDAICA
ENCYCLOPAEDIA OF BUDDHISM
ENCYCLOPAEDIA OF ISLAM

ENCYCLOPAEDIA OF RELIGIONS
ENCYCLOPEDIA JUDAICA
ENCYCLOPEDIA OF AMERICAN RELIGIONS
ENCYCLOPEDIA OF RELIGIONS IN THE UNITED STATES
ENCYCLOPEDIC DICTIONARY OF RELIGION
*INTERPRETER'S DICTIONARY OF THE BIBLE   Scholarly and authoritative;
   a standard reference work.
NEW CATHOLIC ENCYCLOPEDIA
NEW STANDARD JEWISH ENCYCLOPEDIA
OXFORD COMPANION TO THE BIBLE   (*See also* Ethnic Studies;
   Philosophy.)

Science and Technology

ACADEMIC PRESS DICTIONARY OF SCIENCE AND TECHNOLOGY
CRC HANDBOOK OF CHEMISTRY AND PHYSICS
DICTIONARY OF THE HISTORY OF SCIENCE
ENCYCLOPAEDIA OF THE HISTORY OF TECHNOLOGY
ENCYCLOPEDIA OF PHYSICAL SCIENCE AND TECHNOLOGY
MCGRAW-HILL DICTIONARY OF SCIENTIFIC AND TECHNICAL TERMS
MCGRAW-HILL ENCYCLOPEDIA OF ENERGY
MCGRAW-HILL ENCYCLOPEDIA OF SCIENCE AND TECHNOLOGY
   (CD-ROM)
VAN NOSTRAND'S SCIENTIFIC ENCYCLOPEDIA

Social Sciences

DICTIONARY OF THE SOCIAL SCIENCES (ed. J. Gould and W. L. Kolb)
DICTIONARY OF THE SOCIAL SCIENCES (H. F. Reading)
A DICTIONARY OF SOCIOLOGY
DICTIONARY OF SOCIOLOGY
DICTIONARY OF SOCIOLOGY AND RELATED SCIENCES
ENCYCLOPEDIA OF HUMAN BEHAVIOR
ENCYCLOPEDIA OF SOCIAL WORK
ENCYCLOPEDIA OF SOCIOLOGY (ed. E. F. Borgatta)
ENCYCLOPEDIA OF SOCIOLOGY (pub. Guilford, CT: DPG Reference,
   1981)
INTERNATIONAL ENCYCLOPEDIA OF THE SOCIAL SCIENCES
NEW DICTIONARY OF THE SOCIAL SCIENCES
SOCIAL SCIENCE ENCYCLOPEDIA   (*See also* Anthropology.)

Urban Studies

ENCYCLOPEDIA OF URBAN PLANNING   (*See also* Environmental Science.)

Women's Studies

ENCYCLOPEDIA OF AMAZONS
ENCYCLOPEDIA OF CONTINENTAL WOMEN WRITERS
A HISTORY OF THEIR OWN: WOMEN IN EUROPE FROM PREHISTORY
   TO THE PRESENT

HISTORY OF WOMEN IN THE WEST
WOMEN'S STUDIES ENCYCLOPEDIA   (*See also* Biography; Ethnic Studies;
   Literature.)

STEP TWO: Using Library Catalogs

Finding a library book or nonprint source (such as a film or a recording) requires you to carry out two steps: (1) look it up in the library catalog, and (2) use the call number to locate it. Some aids to this search are given in the following sections.

Knowing Where to Look

Before beginning your search, be sure that you know the locations of the following features of the library you are using.

1. *The library catalog.* It usually takes the form of a set of computer terminals linked to a remote computer.

2. *The general collection.* Also known as the "stacks," the general collection houses the main holdings of the library that are available for general use.

3. *The periodicals collection.* Magazines and journals are sometimes shelved in a separate section of the library for easy access.

4. *The current-periodicals section.* Recent issues of periodicals are often separately shelved in a browsing room so that scholars can read recent issues or skim to find sources that have not yet been indexed.

5. *Special collections.* Many libraries have collections of rare books or materials relating to a special subject such as a local person or institution. Music recordings or films may be housed in special collections, too. Researchers often must get special permission to use these portions of the library.

6. *Reserve room.* Particularly in academic libraries, books that are in frequent demand, perhaps because of a course requirement, are kept in a separate reserve room. They are available to all library users but for a limited checkout period.

7. *Browsing section.* Recently acquired books are often shelved temporarily in a browsing section for library users who like to see what's new in their areas of interest.

8. *Reference collection.* Books of general information that are frequently consulted, such as dictionaries, are kept in a separate collection near the reference desk. They cannot be checked out, because they are needed constantly. Most of the general reference works described in this chapter will be found in the noncirculating reference collection. Particularly important are the encyclopedias and the indexes, key resources in the four-step strategy for finding sources. A couple of other crucial items are generally kept in the reference collection: the individual library's list of

serial holdings, which lists the periodicals that the library carries; and the *Library of Congress Subject Headings,* a list of key phrases to use when doing subject searches. The reference section also is likely to house some computerized workstations for access to computerized indexes.

9. *Microfilm collection.* Even libraries of modest dimensions may hold surprising amounts of information on microfilm. A complete set of a major newspaper such as the *London Times* or the *New York Times* can be stored in a small space.

10. *Oversized books.* To save space, many libraries house oversized books in one or more separate sections of shelves. Unwary beginners may assume that volumes missing from the call number sequence in the main collection are unavailable, but they may be oversized books shelved nearby.

How Library Holdings Are Organized

To carry out a successful search for source material, you need to know just a bit about how library materials are inventoried and shelved. Although a library may store books and periodicals in various special locations such as a reference section, browsing room, or reserve room, virtually all the library holdings, no matter what their locations, are inventoried by means of call numbers. (A catalog entry for any book that is not in the main collection will normally carry a location code along with the call number.) American libraries use two systems of assigning call numbers: the Library of Congress system and the Dewey decimal system. Most university research libraries use the Library of Congress system.

You need not memorize the lists of call letters and numbers given in the following pages, but notice a couple of useful things. First, notice the letter that matches your subject area. When you are searching card catalogs and indexes, you will find that most of the books you need will have call numbers beginning with this letter. Also notice any exceptions, because they may guide you to seemingly unrelated areas where shelf browsing may turn up unexpectedly useful items. For example, a researcher writing a paper on fiction about eighteenth-century criminals would search primarily in the PR section, books on British literature; but items might turn up in CT, biography, or in H, criminology, or in D, Old World history.

Finally, notice that bibliography and library science are assigned to the Z classification in the Library of Congress system and to the 0 section in the Dewey decimal system. Thus, books about books will often be found in these sections. Many magic solutions—the subject guides and topic bibliographies—will be found in this information-rich section of the classification system.

LIBRARY OF CONGRESS SYSTEM

The Library of Congress system classifies books by assigning a different letter to each major subject area. A second letter subdivides the major subject area. In the list here, subdivisions of P are shown as examples.

Call Numbers Beginning	Assigned to These Books
A	General works
B	Philosophy, psychology, religion
C	History and auxiliary sciences
D	History: general and Old World
E–F	History: North and South America
G	Geography, maps, anthropology
H	Social sciences
J	Political science
K	Law
L	Education
M	Music
N	Fine arts
P–PA	General philology, linguistics
PA Supplement	Byzantine and modern Greek literature; medieval and modern Latin literature
PB–PH	Modern European languages
PJ–PM	Languages and literatures of Asia, Africa, Oceania; American Indian languages; artificial languages
PN	General literature
PQ	French, Italian, Spanish, and Portuguese literatures
PR	English literature
PS	American literature
PT	German literature
Q	Science
R	Medicine
S	Agriculture
T	Technology
U	Military science
V	Naval science
Z	Bibliography, library science

The system is consistent and universal. Hence, once you have found a book's call number, you can find the book shelved under that number in *any* library using the Library of Congress system (assuming that the library has purchased the book).

DEWEY DECIMAL SYSTEM

The Dewey decimal system classifies books by using the following numbering system.

Call Numbers Beginning	Assigned to These Books
000–090	Generalities
100–190	Philosophy and psychology
200–290	Religion
300–390	Social sciences
400–490	Language
500–590	Natural sciences and mathematics
600–690	Technology (applied sciences)
700–790	The arts
800–890	Literature and rhetoric
900–990	Geography and history

Shelf Browsing

One of the main purposes of the classification systems is to make sure that related items are shelved near each other. Upon finding a long series of similar call numbers, many a researcher simply heads for the stacks to see what's there—to do some shelf browsing, in other words. The Library of Congress classification system exists, in part, to make shelf browsing possible. It is especially helpful when you are looking for material in books whose contents have not been analyzed or indexed. For example, the *MLA International Bibliography* indexes the contents of collections of essays, so it would list an essay on *The Tempest* that has been published in a collection on various topics. The *MLA International Bibliography* does *not* index chapters in books, however, so a researcher might want to shelf browse to scan the contents of single-author books on Shakespeare's plays.

I found one of the best quotations in my research paper on improvisation by shelf browsing in books close to one I had found through the library catalog. But shelf browsing should always be just an additional search strategy, never the primary one. Often the best books on a subject have been checked out, and the remaining ones are there on the shelf precisely because they are the worst sources in the field.

Library of Congress Subject Headings

One problem in the source-gathering process may not have occurred to you unless someone has pointed it out: You cannot effectively search for a topic unless you know the phrases that indexers have used to catalog it. To complicate matters, such phrases (called subject headings) vary from nationality to nationality and from place to place. What the British call ergonomics, for instance, Ameri-

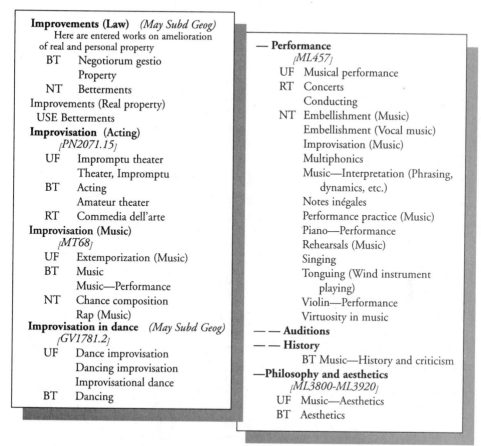

Improvements (Law) *(May Subd Geog)*
    Here are entered works on amelioration
of real and personal property
    BT   Negotiorum gestio
            Property
    NT   Betterments
Improvements (Real property)
  USE Betterments
Improvisation (Acting)
    [PN2071.15]
    UF   Impromptu theater
            Theater, Impromptu
    BT   Acting
            Amateur theater
    RT   Commedia dell'arte
Improvisation (Music)
    [MT68]
    UF   Extemporization (Music)
    BT   Music
            Music—Performance
    NT   Chance composition
            Rap (Music)
Improvisation in dance *(May Subd Geog)*
    [GV1781.2]
    UF   Dance improvisation
            Dancing improvisation
            Improvisational dance
    BT   Dancing

— Performance
    [ML457]
  UF   Musical performance
  RT   Concerts
        Conducting
  NT   Embellishment (Music)
        Embellishment (Vocal music)
        Improvisation (Music)
        Multiphonics
        Music—Interpretation (Phrasing,
           dynamics, etc.)
        Notes inégales
        Performance practice (Music)
        Piano—Performance
        Rehearsals (Music)
        Singing
        Tonguing (Wind instrument
           playing)
        Violin—Performance
        Virtuosity in music
— — Auditions
— — History
        BT Music—History and criticism
—Philosophy and aesthetics
    [ML3800-ML3920]
  UF   Music—Aesthetics
  BT   Aesthetics

FIGURE 4.1 Two Sample Portions of Pages from the *Library of Congress Subject Headings*

cans now usually call human factors engineering. For topics in African-American culture, the Library of Congress assigned the subject heading "Negro" in the 1950s, "black" in the 1960s, and "African-American" in recent years.

    Therefore, before you begin a library catalog search, you need to make sure that you are searching for appropriate subject headings. Fortunately, the Library of Congress supplies an abundantly cross-referenced guide in several volumes: the *Library of Congress Subject Headings*. If you are not sure whether "satire" is an appropriate subject heading, the guide will supply cross-references to "comedy," "lampoon," and so on.

    Figure 4.1 reproduces pages from the *Library of Congress Subject Headings*. Notice that "Improvisation (Music)" is cross-referenced to the broader term "Music" and its subheading, "Music—Performance." (The long dash before "Performance" indicates that "Performance" is a subheading under the broader heading "Music," which is listed on an earlier page.)

    Notice the useful features illustrated by the sample pages. Under a major subject heading or major subheading (shown in bold type) is the Library of

Congress call number, which guides your shelf browsing. For instance, "Improvisation (Music)" is followed by the call number MT68; "Performance" is followed by ML457. Abbreviations guide you to related subject headings. "UF" stands for "use for," which tells you that the Library of Congress uses "Music— Performance" rather than "Musical performance" as a subject heading for classification purposes. "BT" stands for "broader term" and "NT" stands for "narrower term"; these cross-references guide you to more general or more specific headings. Finally, "RT" stands for "related term," guiding you to another part of the *Library of Congress Subject Headings*.

Besides using the printed volumes of headings, you can find appropriate Library of Congress subject headings in two other ways.

1. If you already know the name of one book on your subject, when you look up this book in a library catalog, you will find that the catalog entry lists the subject headings under which the book has been classified. Record these headings, because they can guide your search. See the discussion of library catalogs later in this chapter for an example of how paying attention to subject headings helped me find a good bibliography on my topic.

2. All recently published books and many older books carry Library of Congress cataloging information on the copyright page. Look at the copyright page of this textbook and notice the subject headings under which it has been cataloged. Other similar books will carry the same headings.

For topics in medical science, an alternative subject-heading system (medical subject headings, or MeSH) is commonly used. There are several guides to these headings, all compiled by the National Library of Medicine: *Medical Subject Headings, Annotated Alphabetic List; Permuted Medical Subject Headings*; and *Medical Subject Headings, Tree Structure*. (The last guide displays the subject headings in outline or tree structure form, so that you can trace your way from specific headings to more general ones, and vice versa.)

Library Catalogs

For most college researchers, searching the library catalog is the heart of the research project. But do not think that once you have searched for a topic and compiled a list of sources, your source gathering is done. A library catalog search is simply the second of the four main steps. In addition, be sure to use several subject headings as you search. Consider the following list, which illustrates how limited your search would be if you used a single subject heading to look for sources in a single library catalog.

LIMITATIONS OF A CATALOG SEARCH
USING ONE SUBJECT HEADING

1. You may have used an inappropriate subject heading.
2. You may have used an appropriate but excessively narrow subject heading.

3. You may be searching the holdings of a single, small library, and other holdings may be available nearby.

4. You may have missed recent works that have not yet been cataloged by the library.

5. Since library catalogs list the titles of periodicals but not their contents, you have certainly missed all the current periodical literature available on your topic.

You can avoid the first two limitations by collecting appropriate subject headings, using the *Library of Congress Subject Headings* and the subject headings found in library catalog entries and on copyright pages. Although most undergraduate research papers can be written with the use of one library's holdings, sometimes you can avoid the third and fourth limitations by searching WorldCat, a union catalog, or a trade bibliography (see "Finding Books Outside Your Library" in Chapter 12) or by using a computerized catalog to search the holdings of more than one library. The fifth limitation will be covered in step 3 of the four-step strategy.

Now that computers have become such common tools in library research, you will probably compile a substantial part of your list of sources by printing out bibliographical entries directly from the computerized library catalog. Don't be afraid of computerized information sources; software designers are constantly making them easier to use.

Do remember, however, that computers are precise and unforgiving. A student once reported to me that our university library had not one copy of *A Tale of a Tub*. Knowing that our library had more than one copy of Swift's satiric masterpiece, I asked the student to search the computerized catalog while I watched. He typed "T=A Tale of a Tub," and the computer displayed the message, "No matching entries found." The problem here was the initial article; catalogs ignore *a*, *an*, and *the* when alphabetizing titles. Another student told me that our library had no works at all by Jonathan Swift. Again I went to the library with the student and watched as she typed "A=Johnathan Swift." And the computer said, again, "No matching entries found" because of the misspelling of Swift's first name.

In the past few years, though, library computer software has become much more user-friendly. My university's new computerized catalog ignores initial articles if you type them. And if you misspell an author, title, or subject, the software's "browse" function automatically lists spellings close to the one you typed.

Although you will probably print your entries on a printer attached to a computer terminal or workstation, many libraries now have terminals that also let you record your entries on your own computer diskette. You can later edit these entries to conform to the standard bibliographic formats commonly used in college research papers.

Because it is so easy, a computerized search is likely to create a false sense of security. Remember that a catalog search is simply a single step and that the catalog search may require you to try quite a few alternative strategies.

Computerized library catalogs may be searched by key words, subject, author, or title. You may also search for a specific call number, although this search technique is of little value unless you are scanning an unfamiliar library to see whether it has a specific book you've already identified.

Particularly valuable is the key word or word search technique: Select "word search" (or a similar menu item), and enter one or more words. The computer will find entries containing the words whether they appear in a book title, a subject tracing, a series title, or some other portion of the entry. This technique can turn up information that you might otherwise overlook. Bear in mind, though, that if you search for very general key words in the holdings of a large library, you will turn up an unusably large number of entries. Furthermore, word searches are usually much slower than other searches.

Whenever you are searching for a word, phrase, or subject heading, remember this useful tip:

> It's usually best to search for the shortest possible term first.

Here's why: A computer looks for a string of characters, called a "search string" or a "character string." It looks only for the string you type. Thus if you type "bibliography," it will find only entries containing that string. But if you type "bibliograph," it will find entries containing any of the following words: *bibliography, bibliographic, bibliographical*. Thus, the shorter the character string is, the more likely the search will include related terms that you may not have thought of. Note, however, that searching for shortened, or truncated, character strings is not possible on some computerized indexes, although others search for truncated strings automatically. Finally, some indexes require you to enter a "wild card" character to perform truncations; so you might type something like this: "bibliograph*." In such a system, typing "wom*n" (or something similar) may let you search for both "women" and "woman." Learn the wild cards that your library system uses.

Some computerized library catalogs offer a "limit" function for refining a search. You can limit a search by date (say, only sources after 1985), by type of material (say, only books), by keyword, and by other limiting factors. This feature is occasionally useful. In searching for books on improvisation in classical music, for example, I was able to speed up my search by entering "not jazz" as a limiting factor, which told the computer to omit any books with "jazz" in the catalog entry.

Many computerized catalogs and indexes offer some version of Boolean logic, which is a method of formulating search strings to operate selectively. You need to pay close attention to this feature. At my library, for example, the standard interface offers three main choices once you've entered a string of words to search for: (1) "Find this exact phrase," (2) "Find any of these words," and (3) "Find all of these words." These three options naturally produce radically different results!

When you find an entry you want to print out, be sure that you print from what is commonly called the "full record," which contains all the information

```
        SUBJECT: [music - - performance]                OhioLINK

      Type all or part of the Library of Congress SUBJECT HEADING.

         for example - - - >  COMPUTERS

         for example - - - >  London England

         for example - - - >   lincoln, abraham [last name first]


              [Press the ESC key to begin a different search.]

      . . . . then press the RETURN key
```

FIGURE 4.2   Menu Screen for "Subject Search"

you will need later when you compile your final bibliography: title, publisher, place and year of publication, series name, and so on (see the full lists of information on pp. 103–104). Some catalogs and databases normally display a "short record" screen that may not contain all the information you will ultimately need. If you have trouble getting full record displays, check with a librarian.

As an example of a library catalog subject search, I'll discuss some of the things I did for my research paper. Since the first goal was to find a topic bibliography or subject guide that would save me the trouble of scanning pages of standard indexes, I immediately looked for bibliographies on improvisation. I had already used the *Library of Congress Subject Headings* to learn that "Improvisation (Music)" is an appropriate subject heading. Unfortunately, a search for books under that subject heading turned up no subject guides.

Next, I decided to try a more general heading. The *Library of Congress Subject Headings* showed me that "Improvisation (Music)" is a subheading under "Music—Performance" (refer to Figure 4.1). On the library terminal's menu screen, then, I chose "Subject Search" and typed "music—performance." (See Figure 4.2.)

In response, the terminal displayed a screen that offered nineteen subjects under this general heading (see Figure 4.3). Before plunging into the 108 entries under "Music Performance," I spotted menu item 7, "Music Performance Bibliography." I thought that a good subject guide might be lurking there, so I chose menu item 7. In response, the terminal displayed a list of five bibliographies (see Figure 4.4).

I chose the five bibliographies, one by one, and found among them two useful subject guides. The first one looked outdated, but I thought that it still

You searched for the SUBJECT: music performance
19 SUBJECTS found, with 184 entries; SUBJECTS 1-8 are:

1. Music Performance .... 108 entries
2. Music Performance 15th Century .... 1 entry
3. Music Performance 16th Century .... 1 entry
4. Music Performance 19th Century .... 1 entry
5. Music Performance 500 - 1400 .... 1 entry
6. Music Performance Auditions .... 1 entry
7. Music Performance Bibliography .... 5 entries
8. Music Performance Congresses. .... 3 entries

FIGURE 4.3 "Music Performance" Screen

You searched for the SUBJECT: music performance
5 entries found, entries 1 - 5 are:

Music Performance Bibliography
1. An annotated bibliography of written material pertinent to
2. An annotated bibliography of written material pertinent to
3. Performance practice; a bibliography
4. Performance practice; a bibliography
5. Performance practice, medieval to contemporary

FIGURE 4.4 "Music Performance Bibliography" Screen

AUTHOR	Vinquist, Mary.
TITLE	Performance practice: a bibliography. Edited by Mary Vinquist and Neal Zaslaw.
PUBLISH INFO	New York, W.W. Norton [1971]
DESCRIPT'N	114 p. 20 cm.
SERIES	The Norton Library, N550
SUBJECTS	Music - - Performance - - Bibliographly
	Music - - Interpretation [Phrasing, dynamics, etc.] - - Bibliography
ALT NAME	Zaslaw, Neal Alexander, 1939–
LC NO	ML128.L3 V55
DEWEY NO	016.78073
OCLC #	207828.
ISBN	0393021483 [cloth ed.] 039300550X [pbk]
LCCN	7512803B / MN

FIGURE 4.5   First Bibliography: Vinquist

might guide me to some of the older, standard sources on improvisation. (See Figure 4.5.) The second bibliography looked much more promising. It was fairly recent and it was annotated, which meant that it contained short summaries of the sources it listed. (See Figure 4.6.)

Does it seem odd that the entries for Vinquist's and Jackson's books do not have subject headings for "Performance practice," even though the *Library of Congress Subject Headings* lists this as a standard subject heading? The reason is that catalogers are human beings who must make choices. Not every book is cataloged under every conceivable subject heading that might apply to it. Thus, the cataloger chose to classify these as books about "Music—Performance—Bibliography" and "Music—Interpretation (Phrasing, dynamics, etc.)—Bibliography" but not as books about "Performance practice." You may decide for yourself whether this is a cataloging error. But the important point is this: It took some patient work at trying alternative search strategies to find two books of the sort I needed. It was not possible simply to enter a subject heading and walk away with a list of sources, confident that I had found every book on my subject.

Another important point to remember is to search first for magic solutions. Vinquist's and Jackson's books are good examples of subject guides: bibliographies on relatively narrow subjects, compiled to provide convenient lists of sources for researchers. Taken together, they saved me many hours of research. They were certainly worth the effort it took to find them.

Remember that the information universe is not a fast-food restaurant. You cannot drive up, order your sources, and drive away. You must be patient and try a variety of search strategies. See the entries in my journal at the end of this

AUTHOR	Jackson, Roland John, 1925–
TITLE	Performance practice, medieval to contemporary: a bibliographic guide / Roland Jackson
PUBLISH INFO	New York : Garland, 1988.
DESCRIPT'N	xxix, 518 p. ; 23 cm.
SERIES	Music research and information guides ; vol. 9. Garland reference library of the humanities vol. 790.
NOTE	Includes indexes.
SUBJECTS	Music - - Performance - - Bibliography. Music - - Interpretation [Phrasing, dynamics, etc.] - - Bibliography
LC NO	ML 128.P235 J3 1988.
DEWEY NO	016.78/07/3 19.

FIGURE 4.6   Second Bibliography: Jackson

chapter for an object lesson in the false sense of confidence that a computer search can create.

When can you be sure that you have found every useful source on your topic? Never. All right then, speaking realistically, when should you stop searching? You should stop when you have mastered the material in this chapter and have thoroughly applied it to your research. After you have found a reasonable number of sources related to your topic, have thoroughly explored the four main information avenues (encyclopedias, library catalogs, indexes, and the Internet), and have searched diligently to make sure that you are not duplicating someone's efforts, there will come a moment when you realize that you have done enough.

What If the Book I Need Is Not in the Library?

If your library does not own the book, you have two main options: Search other libraries in the area or make an interlibrary loan request. If you have a full quarter or semester in which to write the paper, an interlibrary loan will work as long as you move quickly to identify the key sources unavailable in your library. Interlibrary loans usually take from one to three weeks.

> If your library owns the book but it is checked out, have the library's circulation department put a "hold" on the book, *immediately.*

The most common mistake students make is to get discouraged and to delay before requesting missing materials. In most academic libraries a hold request means that the library will hold the book for you as soon as it is returned, and you will be notified of its arrival. Some libraries will mail out a request for the book's early return. Hold requests can be made in person; at many libraries they can also be made by telephone or directly through the computerized library catalog.

If your library owns the book and it is missing but not checked out, you have several options. Check the reshelving areas to see whether the book is awaiting reshelving. Wait a day or two and check the stacks again. Ask the circulation department to search for the missing item and to notify you if it is found. Check nearby shelf spaces, and check related call numbers, since occasionally a book in, say, the PR section (English literature) will be misshelved among the PS (American literature) holdings. Check to see whether the book is shelved in some special collection or in the oversized collection. (See "Knowing Where to Look" earlier in this chapter.)

STEP THREE: Using Indexes

To find articles in periodicals, you must first consult a bibliography or index. Pages 84–95 provide a comprehensive list of bibliographies and indexes, including printed and computerized ones. Because the information technologies are changing so rapidly, the list contains computerized databases and abstract services, too. Twenty years ago, a researcher had to pore through printed volumes of indexes to find periodical articles; today, a researcher can use indexes electronically, either from a modem or from a library terminal. Increasingly, the electronic services do more than just index articles by author, title, and subject; they now often provide short abstracts of the article and sometimes provide even the article's full text.

Indexes fill the gap left by library catalogs. That is, they list periodical articles and sometimes books and book chapters as well, and thus they allow you to survey the most specialized and the most current publications on a topic.

To use an index efficiently, remember that anything published in a series, usually at regular intervals, is considered a serial or periodical publication. Academic researchers commonly distinguish among three types of periodicals:

1. Magazines, which are usually published weekly or monthly, are aimed at a wide audience and often are "slick"—that is, produced on glossy paper with some color illustrations.
2. Journals, which are often published quarterly (four times a year), are aimed at a narrow, scholarly audience and usually resemble books, in that they are published on durable, nonglossy paper.
3. Newspapers, which are usually published daily or weekly, are aimed at a wide audience, and are published on nondurable newsprint paper.

Like periodicals themselves, indexes come in a bewildering variety of types. They may, like the *Readers' Guide to Periodical Literature*, index only articles published in periodicals; or they may, like the *MLA International Bibliography*, index books as well. Like the *Readers' Guide*, they may consign book reviews to a separate section at the end of each volume; or they may, like the *MLA International Bibliography*, choose not to index book reviews at all.

Since indexes vary drastically in scope and purpose, they also vary in their degree of usefulness. For instance, the *Readers' Guide* covers popular magazines quite well but scholarly journals hardly at all; thus, its usefulness for college research is limited. The *Business Index* covers thousands of periodicals and is often useful to the college researcher; the *Business Periodicals Index* covers only several hundred periodicals and is oriented toward the general-interest reader. Some indexes allow the researcher to find material by subject headings but not by the name of the author; others do just the reverse. In general, most indexes allow subject searches, some allow title searches, and a few allow author searches.

To decide what index will be appropriate for you, first find your subject area in the list of indexes on pages 84–95, paying particular attention to the annotations. Be sure to check "general" as a subject area, since many of the best all-purpose indexes are listed under this heading.

> When you try one or more indexes, pay close attention to the index's explanation of its scope, its purposes, and the search techniques appropriate for it.

This explanation will appear in the front pages of the index (if it is printed) or in the opening screens or "help" screens (if it is computerized).

You will probably be doing subject searches, but remember to consider alternative search strategies. If you find a magic solution for your subject, search under the author's name to see whether other relevant works pop up. When using computerized indexes, consider combining key words to produce highly focused searches. Use "martial arts" and "learning" (or similar sets of terms), for example, to find articles that discuss whether karate has positive effects on a child's performance in school. Try many key word combinations.

When you find an item in an index, print out or record the index entry in full. Later, you will have to locate the periodical by call number. To find the call number in some libraries, you must look up the titles of periodicals in the main library catalog; in other libraries, you must locate periodicals by finding them in a separate list of serials, which may be a bound volume or a catalog. In either case, the entry will show which volumes of the journal your library holds. Note that the library's holdings of some periodicals may be divided in several locations: Some printed volumes may be in the main stacks, some recent issues in the periodicals browsing room, and some older issues in the microfilm collection. So be sure to note the location of the periodical holdings that contain the particular source you plan to track down.

Using Printed Indexes

Probably at least part of your source list will come from a printed index. The speed of computerized searching may make you impatient with leafing through printed volumes, but avoid the temptation to record less than full bibliographical information. You may feel that you are saving time by taking a shortcut, such as writing down just a list of call numbers or titles of books, or the titles and dates of magazines without page numbers. But later, you will have to retrace your steps to fill in an incomplete entry, or you will end up tracking down an item more than once because you failed to recognize it the second time you found it cited. If an index page contains several useful items, photocopy it to save time and effort.

It would be convenient if all indexes used the Library of Congress subject headings; unfortunately, they do not. Thus you must solve again the problem you faced in searching the library catalog. Fortunately, there are "families" of indexes published by individual companies that use their own consistent systems of subject headings. An example is the family of Wilson indexes, whose subject headings usually coincide with those of the Library of Congress.

Many printed indexes such as the *Readers' Guide to Periodical Literature* are published several times a year to provide up-to-date coverage. At the end of each year (or sometimes at longer intervals), a one-volume *cumulation* is published for the sake of easy handling. When you carry out a subject search in an index, it is usually best to begin with the most recent issues and move backward through the cumulative volumes, since later sources often cite earlier ones.

Figure 4.7 reproduces a page from the *Humanities Index*. I chose the *Humanities Index* as an example because it is useful in many academic disciplines, because it is a member of the Wilson family of indexes, and because it is available in both printed and computerized forms. Like other Wilson indexes, the *Humanities Index* uses bold type to highlight subject headings, and indentations make the pages easy to scan. If you select a subject heading that the *Humanities Index* does not use, it provides a "see" cross-reference; thus after the entry "Impurity ritual" comes the cross-reference "*See* Purity, Ritual." If the *Humanities Index* uses several related headings, it provides a "see also" cross-reference; thus "Imprisonment" is followed by "*See also* Prisons."

Look at the entry under "Imperialism in art" to see how the *Humanities Index* presents information. First it lists the title, "Signs from the imperial quarter: illustrations in Chums, 1892–1914," and then it gives the author's last name and initials. Next, it lists the journal or magazine's abbreviated title, *Child Lit;* to find the spelled-out title, consult the list of abbreviations in the front of each index volume. Next comes the volume number (16), then a colon, and then the page numbers (31–55); note that most indexes use this volume number/colon/ page numbers format. Finally, it lists the year, 1988; the issue may also be identified by date, month, season, or year, depending on how often the issues are published.

Although computerized indexes are more efficient, printed indexes have some advantages. They are more widely available, and they are more likely to provide complete retrospective coverage. Many computerized index services have data extending back only ten years or so. In rapidly changing fields, this chronological limitation may not matter; but in the humanities a researcher may wish to extend a search well into the past.

HUMANITIES INDEX

Imperialism—*cont.*

Canaanites in a promised land: the American Indian and the providential theory of empire. A. A. Cave. *Am Indian Q* 12:277–97 Fall '88

The costs and benefits of British imperialism 1846–1914. P. K. O'Brien. *Past Present* no120:163–200 Ag '88

Discourses on colonialism: Bernal Díaz, Las Casas, and the twentieth-century reader. R. Adorno. *MLN* 103:239–58 Mr '88

Empire, trade and popular politics in mid-Hanoverian Britain: the case of Admiral Vernon. K. Wilson. il *Past Present* no121:74–109 N '88

James H. Blount, the South, and Hawaiian annexation. T. S. McWilliams. *Pac Hist Rev* 57:25–46 F '88

Local imperatives and imperial policy: the sources of Lord Carnarvon's South African confederation policy. R. L. Cope. *Int J Afr Hist Stud* 20 no4:601–26 '87

Northcliffe the imperialist: the lesser-known years, 1902–1914. J. D. Startt. *Historian* 51:19–41 N '88

Revisionism and Wilhelmine imperialism. R. Fletcher. *J Contemp Hist* 23:347–66 Jl '88

Sport, cultural imperialism, and colonial response in the British empire. B. Stoddart. *Comp Stud Soc Hist* 30:649–73 O '88

Star wars: an imperial myth. K. Kuiper. *J Pop Cult* 21:77–86 Spr '88

The subjugation of the Zulus and Sioux: a comparative study. J. Gump. maps *West Hist Q* 19:21–36 Ja '88

Third World pirating of U.S. films and television programs from satellites. D. A. Boyd. bibl *J Broadcast Electron Media* 32:149–61 Spr '88

Imperialism in art

Signs from the imperial quarter: illustrations in Chums, 1892–1914. R. H. MacDonald. bibl il *Child Lit* 16:31–55 '88

Imperialism in literature

Cahiers d'écolier and Ollier's fiction; tr. by N. J. Meyerhofer. I. Axmann. *Rev Contemp Fict* 8:126–30 Summ '88

Caliban in the Third World: Shakespeare's savage as sociopolitical symbol. A. T. Vaughan. *Mass Rev* 29:289–313 Summ '88

Caribbean and African appropriations of The tempest. R. Nixon. *Crit Inq* 13:557–78 Spr '87

Carnival and the canon. S. Slemon. bibl *Ariel* 19:59–75 Jl '88

Error as a means of empire in The faerie queene 1. J. Knapp. *ELH* 54:801–34 Wint '87

Fictional formations and deformations of national culture. M. N. Layoun. *South Atl Q* 87:53–73 Wint '88

Magic realism as post-colonial discourse. S. Slemon. *Can Lit* no116:9–24 Spr '88

A symposium of new approaches to Commonwealth literature. *J. Commonw Lit* 23 no1:143–81 '88

Imprisonment   *See also* Prisons

Imprisonment in motion pictures   *See* Prisons in literature

Improvisation (Music)

See also Chance composition

Form and function of the classical cadenza. J. P. Swain *J Musicol* 6:27–59 Wint '88

Jazz as a process of organizational innovation. D. T. Bastien and T. J. Hostager. bibl *Commun Res* 15:582–602 O '88

Sea-changes: Boulez's Improvisations sur Mallarmé. J. McCalla. *J Musicol* 6:83–106 Wint '88

"A special kind of courtesy": action at a bluegrass festival jam session. M. Kisliuk. il *Drama Rev* 32:141–55 Fall '88

Impurity, Ritual   *See* Purity, Ritual

In the shadow of Vesuvius [film]   *See* Motion picture reviews—single works

In vitro fertilization   *See* Fertilization in vitro

Inaccuracy, Scientific   *See* Errors, Scientific

FIGURE 4.7   Sample Page from the *Humanities Index*

```
Current Database: Humanities Index


                    DISC SEARCH MENU              Version 2.5.1

                    Search Compact Disc


       1.  Single subject search . . . . . . . . . . . . [Browse]

       2.  Multiple subject search . . . . . . . . . . . [Wilsearch]

       3.  Command language disc search . . . . . . . . [Wilsonline]

       4.  QUIT


   Press ENTER on HIGHLIGHTED selection or press the number of desired choice

   FI = HELP      F3 = Change Database/Disc       ESC = To Quit
```

FIGURE 4.8 Disc Search Menu

Using Computerized Indexes

The disadvantage of using a printed version of an index such as the *Humanities Index* is that you must leaf through the volumes year by year to do a thorough source hunt. A computerized index lets you search all the recent years of the index at a stroke. In this section I'll describe how I might carry out a source hunt for articles on improvisation in the computerized *Humanities Index*, which is available on CD-ROM (*c*ompact *d*isc, *r*ead-*o*nly *m*emory) and on-line.

The first screen (shown in Figure 4.8) is a "Disc Search Menu" that offers a choice of types of searches. "Single subject search" will let me search for entries under a single subject heading and browse among them. "Multiple subject search" will let me combine subject headings to do more selective or specialized searches. But in this index, as in many others, a single-subject search will find *only items that the indexers have cataloged using a list of standard subject headings.* Thus, if I type "herring," I will find articles on fish but not a single article by or about someone named Herring, even though there are several of them in the database.

A multiple-subject search lets me combine subjects to perform more complicated searches. I might use "improvisation" and "trumpet" to see whether there are any articles specifically on trumpet improvisation, for example. The multiple-subject search also lets me search for the names of authors and even the names of specific journals, though you would not guess this from the menu screen. If I remember that Stephen Jay Gould wrote something in 1992 in the *New Yorker,* for example, I can search for it by specifying the magazine title, the author, and the year.

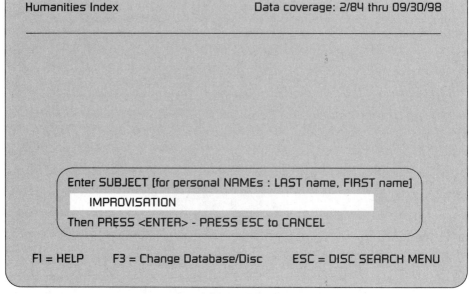

FIGURE 4.9   Single Subject Search Screen

The "Command language disc search" is somewhat difficult; an instruction manual and various "help" screens (indicated on the bottom line of the menu under function key 1 (F1) will guide me through the search. If a single-subject search or multiple-subject search turns up too many items, a command language search can help limit the number of sources retrieved. It can combine terms to perform Boolean searches. For example, a command to find "improvisation not jazz" asks the computer to find all the entries with the word *improvisation* in them but to omit any entries with the word *jazz*.

If I choose "Single subject search," a second screen is displayed (see Figure 4.9). At the top it shows the chronological limits of the index I am searching: "2/84 thru 09/30/98." Thus for sources before 1984, I will need to search elsewhere: either on another disc, if one is available, or in the printed volumes of the index. Notice that the menu at the bottom of the screen lets me ask for help (F1, or function key 1), shift to other discs or databases (F3), and quit the program (ESC, or escape key).

Now I type "improvisation," and I am shown a list of subject headings and the number of entries under each heading (see Figure 4.10). This screen is known as a "browse" screen. It lists the standard subject headings used by the indexers and shows how many sources are indexed under each heading. An asterisk shows that there are no sources under that heading. Arrow keys allow me to move a highlight bar up and down the subject headings. I next highlight "Improvisation (Music)" and hit the key <Enter>. Now the individual entries are displayed one at a time; I scroll through them by using the <PgUp> and <PgDn> keys.

Figure 4.11 shows the screen when I choose entry 10. (This source for my paper on improvisation was later cut.) Notice that related subject headings are

```
┌─────────────────────────────────────────────────────────────────────┐
│ Humanities Index              Data Coverage: 2/84 thru 09/30/98       │
│                                                     READY             │
│ ──────────────────────────────────────────────────────────────────── │
│ Press ENTER to see entries for HIGHLIGHTED subject - FB to see related subject │
│                                                                       │
│        ENTRIES   SUBJECT                                              │
│           *      IMPRINTS, FICTITIOUS [IN BOOKS]                      │
│           3      IMPRISONMENT                                         │
│           *      IMPRISONMENT IN LITERATURE                          │
│           *      IMPRISONMENT IN MOTION PICTURES                     │
│           *      IMPROMPTU THEATER                                   │
│           1      IMPROVEMENTS [LAW]                                  │
│           6      IMPROVISATION [ACTING]                              │
│           4      IMPROVISATION [DANCING]                             │
│          20      IMPROVISATION [MUSIC]                               │
│           *      IMPULSIVENESS IN LITERATURE                         │
│           *      IMPURITY, RITUAL                                    │
│           *      IMVO ZABANTSUNDU [NEWSPAPER]                        │
│           *      IN                                                   │
│                                                                       │
│ F1 = HELP      ESC = MENU      ^ = Move UP      PgUP = Previous 12 subjects │
│ F3 = Change Database/Disc      v = Move DOW     PgDn = Next 12 subjects │
└─────────────────────────────────────────────────────────────────────┘
```

FIGURE 4.10   Screen After Typing "Improvisation": A Browse Screen

```
┌─────────────────────────────────────────────────────────────────────┐
│ Humanities Index              Data Coverage: 2/84 thru 09/30/98       │
│                                                     READY             │
│ ──────────────────────────────────────────────────────────────────── │
│        SUBJECT is IMPROVISATION [MUSIC]              10 of 20 Entries │
│        #10                                                           │
│             AUTHOR:   Swain, Joseph P.                              │
│              TITLE:   Form and function of the classical cadenza    │
│             SOURCE:   The Journal of Musicology [ISSN 0277-9269] v 6 p27-59 │
│                       Winter '88                                     │
│                                                                       │
│        SUBJECTS COVERED:                                             │
│ SUB Concertos/Analysis                                               │
│ SUB Cadenza                                                          │
│        Composition [Music]                                          │
│        Music/Theory/18th century                                    │
│        Beethoven, Ludwig van:1770-1827                              │
│        Mozart, Wolfgang Amadeus:1756-1791                           │
│                                                                       │
│        PgDn for Next Entry or ESC to STOP DISPLAY                   │
│                                                                       │
│ ESC = STOP Displaying Entries - Resume BROWSING Subjects   F1 = HELP │
│ F2  = BROWSE a NEW Subject   F4 = PRINT this Entry   F5 = Go to an Entry │
│ F6  = PRINT all Entries from HERE to the print limit               │
└─────────────────────────────────────────────────────────────────────┘
```

FIGURE 4.11   Entry 10 of the "Improvisation (Music)" List

displayed, just as they would be in a computerized library catalog. They can guide me in further searches. Some are marked "SUB" to indicate that they are subject headings that I can look up separately in the "browse" screen to find related materials. The menu at the bottom of the screen invites me to browse by hitting <F2>. The menu also allows me to print just this entry (F4) or this and all the remaining entries under "Improvisation" (F6).

Remember that a computerized search through a periodical index is not necessarily any more final or definitive than a computerized library catalog search. Also keep in mind that indexes in subject areas seemingly unrelated to your paper topic may prove to be quite useful. For example, if you are writing a paper on karate, you might not think to look in *ABI/Inform*, which is a business index. But karate schools are businesses, after all, and you will find sources there. Use your imagination; it takes only a few minutes to try a source hunt on another computerized index.

What If the Article I Need Is Not in the Library?

Periodical sources have one great advantage over book sources: Books can leave the library, but periodicals can't. Thus you will usually find the periodical articles you will need. If a particular volume is missing, it may be in use; check the reshelving areas, especially near the photocopier. If you don't find it, wait a day or two and try again. If your library does not own the periodical or the particular volume you're seeking, use your interlibrary loan service to request a copy, or consult a union list of serials to find a nearby library that has the journal you need (see "Finding Books Outside Your Library" in Chapter 12). Another strategy to use if (and only if) the article you are searching for is well known and likely to have been reprinted is to consult the *Essay and General Literature Index* to see whether the article has been reprinted in a collection (see p. 89).

Computerized Indexes to Microforms

A few information services supply electronic indexes to materials that are separately available on microfilm or microfiche. *NewsBank* is an example. When using such an index, you perform a subject search on the electronic index. Then you request the microform from the librarian, using an identifying item number.

Bibliographies, Indexes, Abstracts, and Electronic Databases

Indexes available for on-line or CD-ROM searches are labeled, but since computer searching is a rapidly evolving field, no book can offer completely up-to-date lists and descriptions of databases. At least the lists will suggest the rapidly expanding range of computerized indexes. Note that a parenthetical description such as "on-line" does *not* mean that the index is available *only* on-line. Most of the electronic indexes are based on printed counterparts.

Finally, remember to look for topic bibliographies on your specific subject before spending a lot of time scanning one of the general bibliographies. (See "Library Catalogs" earlier in this chapter for examples of topic bibliographies.)

Agriculture

AGRICOLA (on-line)
BIBLIOGRAPHY OF AGRICULTURE (on-line; CD-ROM)   (*See also* Biology; Environmental Science.)

Anthropology

ABSTRACTS IN ANTHROPOLOGY
ANTHROPOLOGICAL INDEX ONLINE (on-line)
ANTHROPOLOGICAL LITERATURE

Architecture

ARCHITECTURAL INDEX
ARCHITECTURAL PERIODICALS INDEX (on-line)
AVERY INDEX TO ARCHITECTURE

Art

AMERICAN ART DIRECTORY
ARTBIBLIOGRAPHIES MODERN (on-line)
*ART INDEX (on-line; CD-ROM)   Surprisingly broad coverage, including subjects such as architecture, film, and city planning.
DESIGN AND APPLIED ARTS INDEX
INDEX TO ART PERIODICALS
RILA [RÉPERTOIRE INTERNATIONAL DE LA LITTÉRATURE DE L'ART] (on-line)   (*See also* Humanities.)

Astronomy

ASTRONOMY AND ASTROPHYSICS ABSTRACTS

Biography

*BIOGRAPHY AND GENEALOGY MASTER INDEX (on-line)   The most comprehensive index to persons living and deceased, since it indexes several hundred biographical reference works. The best starting point.
*BIOGRAPHY INDEX (on-line)   Indexes several thousand periodicals, including the *New York Times* obituaries. Also indexes books in English. Indexes persons living and deceased by name, occupation, and topic.
CURRENT BIOGRAPHY
*DIRECTORY OF AMERICAN SCHOLARS   Sometimes helpful in evaluating sources. Lists scholarly credentials and publications.
INDEX TO BLACK AMERICAN WRITERS IN COLLECTIVE BIOGRAPHIES
*INTERNATIONAL WHO'S WHO   The standard reference work on living persons worldwide. Note that there are many subsidiary volumes, such as the *International Who's Who in Education,* that may provide information on your sources or on specific subject areas (such as the *International Who's Who of Women* for a paper in women's studies).
NATIONAL CYCLOPEDIA OF AMERICAN BIOGRAPHY

WHO'S WHO

*WHO'S WHO IN AMERICA (on-line)   The standard reference work on living Americans. Note that there are many subsidiary volumes, such as *Who's Who in American Education,* that may provide information on your sources or on specific subject areas (such as *Who's Who in American Politics* for a paper in political science). Note also that for deceased persons there are volumes titled *Who Was Who, Who Was Who in America,* and so on.

Biology

BIOETHICSLINE (on-line)

BIOLOGICAL ABSTRACTS (on-line; CD-ROM)

BIOLOGICAL AND AGRICULTURAL INDEX (on-line; CD-ROM)

BIORESEARCH ONLINE

BIOSIS (on-line)

BIOSIS PREVIEWS (on-line)

CURRENT CONTENTS: LIFE SCIENCES

*ZOOLOGICAL RECORD (on-line)   Indexes information by zoological taxonomy. Thus for a paper on wolf habitat, you need to know that the wolf is *canis lupus,* listed among carnivora, mammalia. (*See also* Science and Technology.)

Business

ABI/INFORM GLOBAL (on-line; CD-ROM)

ACCOUNTANTS' INDEX

*AMERICAN BUSINESS INFORMATION (on-line)   Information on over nine million U.S. businesses, updated semiannually.

*BUSINESS INDEX (microfilm; CD-ROM)   An index to about two thousand business, legal, and general-interest periodicals. (*See also* General.)

*BUSINESS PERIODICALS INDEX (on-line; CD-ROM)   An index to several hundred business periodicals.

BUSINESS PUBLICATIONS INDEX AND ABSTRACTS

*DISCLOSURE GLOBAL ACCESS (on-line)   Financial reports of over 11,000 companies.

PERSONNEL LITERATURE

PERSONNEL MANAGEMENT ABSTRACTS

*PREDICASTS (on-line; CD-ROM)   Indexes covering American, European and world business.

WALL STREET JOURNAL INDEX   (*See also* Economics; General, *NewsBank.*)

Chemistry

ANALYTICAL ABSTRACTS (on-line)

CHEMICAL ABSTRACTS (on-line)   (*See also* Science and Technology.)

Classical Studies

L'ANNÉE PHILOLOGIQUE

Communications

BIBLIOGRAPHIC ANNUAL IN SPEECH COMMUNICATION
COMMUNICATION ABSTRACTS
INDEX TO JOURNALS IN COMMUNICATION STUDIES
JOURNALISM ABSTRACTS   (*See also* Business; Humanities; Psychology.)

Computer Science

COMPUTER ABSTRACTS
COMPUTER AND CONTROL ABSTRACTS (on-line as *Inspec*)
COMPUTER AND INFORMATION SYSTEMS ABSTRACTS JOURNAL
COMPUTER DATABASE (on-line)
COMPUTER LITERATURE INDEX
MICROCOMPUTER ABSTRACTS (on-line)
MICROCOMPUTER INDEX (on-line)   (*See also* Engineering; Physics, *Inspec;*
   Science and Technology.)

Dissertations in All Fields

AMERICAN DOCTORAL DISSERTATIONS
COMPREHENSIVE DISSERTATION INDEX
*DISSERTATION ABSTRACTS INTERNATIONAL (DAI) (on-line;
   CD-ROM)   Indexes dissertations in several volumes: A. humanities and
   social sciences; B. sciences; C. worldwide.
WORLDCAT

Drama

CUMULATED DRAMATIC INDEX, 1909–1949
PLAY INDEX   (*See also* Literature.)

Economics

CHASE ECONOMETRICS (on-line)
*ECONLIT (CD-ROM)   Indexes periodicals, books, and collections of lit-
   erature in economics, with selected abstracts. Comprises the *Index of
   Economic Articles* and the index of the *Journal of Economic Literature*.
INDEX OF ECONOMIC ARTICLES
INTERNATIONAL BIBLIOGRAPHY OF ECONOMICS
JOURNAL OF ECONOMIC LITERATURE
KEY TO ECONOMIC SCIENCE   (*See also* Business.)

Education

BRITISH EDUCATION INDEX
EDUCATION ABSTRACTS (on-line)
EDUCATIONAL DOCUMENTS ABSTRACTS
EDUCATION INDEX (on-line; CD-ROM)
*ERIC (EDUCATIONAL RESOURCES INFORMATION CENTER). CURRENT
   INDEX TO JOURNALS IN EDUCATION (on-line; CD-ROM)   Indexes
   current journals in education.

*ERIC (EDUCATIONAL RESOURCES INFORMATION CENTER). RESOURCES IN EDUCATION (on-line; CD-ROM) Indexes resources other than journal articles, such as pamphlets and microforms. (*See also* General, *NewsBank;* Psychology, *Child Development Abstracts and Bibliography.*)

Electronics

ELECTRICAL AND ELECTRONICS ABSTRACTS (*See also* Engineering; Physics; Science and Technology.)

Engineering

ANNUAL REVIEWS OF INDUSTRIAL AND ENGINEERING CHEMISTRY
EI COMPENDEX PLUS (on-line)

Environmental Science

CURRENT CONTENTS: AGRICULTURE, BIOLOGY, AND ENVIRONMENTAL SCIENCE (on-line)
ECOLOGY ABSTRACTS (on-line)
ENVIRONMENT ABSTRACTS (CD-ROM)
ENVIRONMENTAL PERIODICALS BIBLIOGRAPHY (on-line)
ENVIRONMENT INDEX
GREEN INDEX
POLLUTION ABSTRACTS (on-line)
SELECTED WATER RESOURCES ABSTRACTS (*See also* Science and Technology.)

Ethnic Studies

AFRICAN-AMERICAN INDEX
AMERICAN INDIAN INDEX
ETHNOARTS INDEX
HISPANIC-AMERICAN PERIODICALS INDEX (on-line)
INDEX TO BLACK NEWSPAPERS
*INDEX TO BLACK PERIODICALS (1983–) Continues *Index to Periodical Articles by and About Blacks* (1973–1983), *Index to Periodical Articles by and About Negroes* (1960–1972), *Index to Selected Periodicals* (1954–1959), *Index to Selected Negro Periodicals* (1950–1954), *Guide to Negro Periodical Literature* (1941–1946).
INDEX TO LITERATURE ON THE AMERICAN INDIAN
SAGE RACE RELATIONS ABSTRACTS (*See also* Biography; Social Sciences.)

Film

ANNUAL INDEX TO MOTION PICTURE CREDITS
FILM LITERATURE INDEX
INTERNATIONAL INDEX TO FILM PERIODICALS
INTERNET MOVIE DATABASE (on-line)
NEW YORK TIMES FILM REVIEWS
RETROSPECTIVE INDEX TO FILM PERIODICALS, 1930–1971
SCREEN SITE (on-line)

Folklore

CENTENNIAL INDEX (*See also* Literature, *Annual Bibliography of English Language and Literature* and *MLA International Bibliography.*)

General

ANNUAL MAGAZINE SUBJECT INDEX

*ARTICLEFIRST (on-line) Indexes articles from thousands of journals.

*BIBLIOGRAPHIC INDEX (on-line) An all-purpose bibliography of bibliographies. Every topic search should scan the recent volumes of this index, because it is brief, easy to use, and relatively comprehensive. (It lists bibliographies in books and articles as well as bibliographies published separately.) Indexes about two thousand periodicals.

*BOOK REVIEW DIGEST (on-line) Condensed reviews from about a hundred English and American periodicals. Good for reviews of literary works; more thorough coverage of general-interest books is provided by *Book Review Index* after 1965.

*BOOK REVIEW INDEX (CD-ROM) Indexes reviews from over four hundred periodicals after 1965. For scholarly books in the humanities, more thorough coverage is provided by *Index to Book Reviews in the Humanities.*

*BOOKS IN PRINT (on-line; CD-ROM) A bibliography of American books currently available. Indexed by author, title, and subject. Especially useful for finding current books that may not yet have been acquired or cataloged by your library. Limited to books published in the United States.

COMBINED RETROSPECTIVE INDEX TO BOOK REVIEWS IN SCHOLARLY JOURNALS, 1886–1974

*CUMULATIVE BOOK INDEX (on-line; CD-ROM) An international bibliography of books published in English. Indexed by author, subject, and title. Continues *United States Catalog: Books in Print (1898–1928).* Sometimes useful to the general researcher who wants to verify bibliographical information about a book not available locally.

CURRENT BOOK REVIEW CITATIONS

DIRECTORY OF ON-LINE INFORMATION RESOURCES

DISSERTATION ABSTRACTS INTERNATIONAL (on-line; CD-ROM)

*ESSAY AND GENERAL LITERATURE INDEX (on-line; CD-ROM) An author-subject index of essays and articles published in collections. Especially useful for finding republished essays when the journal containing their original appearance is unavailable locally.

*GALE DIRECTORY OF DATABASES Semiannual directory formed by the merger of *Computer-Readable Databases, Directory of On-Line Databases,* and *Directory of Portable Databases.*

GUIDE TO U.S. GOVERNMENT PUBLICATIONS

GUIDE TO U.S. GOVERNMENT SERIALS AND PERIODICALS

*INFOTRAC (on-line; CD-ROM) An information service offering many databases, including *Expanded Academic ASAP* (index plus full-text database in humanities, sciences, and social sciences, from 1994 on, with access to *Backfile* [1980–1993]), *General BusinessFile ASAP,* and *Health*

Reference Center, plus other databases. *Expanded Academic ASAP* indexes nearly one million articles and provides full-text articles from more than five hundred journals. *National Newspaper Index* is a general-purpose index of citations to articles from five leading U.S. newspapers. *General Periodicals Index ASAP* indexes one thousand periodicals and provides full-text articles from seven hundred of them.

*INTERNATIONAL INDEX (1907–1965)   Replaced first by the *Social Sciences and Humanities Index* (1965–1974) and then by the *Social Sciences Index* (1974–) and *Humanities Index* (1974–).

*LEXIS-NEXIS ACADEMIC UNIVERSE (on-line)   A full-text database of news, reference, business, and legal information.

*MONTHLY CATALOG OF UNITED STATES GOVERNMENT PUBLICATIONS (on-line as *GPO Access*)   The printed volumes are indexed by author, subject, title, and keywords; various search techniques are available on CD-ROM. A source of hidden treasures. I list this catalog under the "General" heading because Uncle Sam is one of the world's largest publishers. Government publications may cover anything from copyright laws to recipes for making pickles. Government publications are cataloged by a potentially confusing system of what are called SuDocs (Superintendent of Documents) numbers, so seek help from a reference librarian if you have trouble locating a source. See the annual *Guide to U.S. Government Publications* for an explanation and list of SuDocs numbers.

*NEWSBANK (on-line; CD-ROM)   General information service that contains *Newsfile*, a selective database of newspaper articles from more than five hundred cities in the United States. *Global NewsBank* contains selected material from hundreds of international sources. Articles on business are supplied in *Business NewsBank*.

NEWSPAPER ABSTRACTS (on-line)

*NEWSPAPER INDEXES: A LOCATION AND SUBJECT GUIDE FOR RESEARCHERS   A useful guide to indexes of newspapers not covered by the major indexes.

*NEW YORK TIMES INDEX (on-line)   Useful in finding authoritative treatment of news events. But because of the broad coverage provided by the *New York Times,* the index also covers general-interest topics. Also useful in finding the date of an event as a guide to tracing stories in non-indexed newspapers.

NINETEENTH CENTURY READERS' GUIDE TO PERIODICAL LITERATURE, 1890–1899

*PAIS (formerly PUBLIC AFFAIRS INFORMATION SERVICE BULLETIN) (on-line; CD-ROM)   Indexes articles relating to political science, economics, and the social sciences. Broadly useful.

*PERIODICAL ABSTRACTS (on-line)   Author-title-keyword index to over sixteen hundred periodicals from 1986 to the present; updated monthly. Covers business, general interest, and scholarly journals. Provides twenty-five-word abstracts and citation information. Indexes movie and book reviews.

*POOLE'S INDEX TO PERIODICAL LITERATURE   The only comprehensive subject index to British and American periodicals of the nineteenth century. Unsystematic subject headings make it somewhat difficult to use; try a variety of phrases.

READERS' GUIDE ABSTRACTS (CD-ROM)

*READERS' GUIDE TO PERIODICAL LITERATURE (on-line; CD-ROM) An all-purpose index to general-interest magazines. Very useful in finding magazine articles but less so in finding scholarly journal articles.

Geography

GEOREF (on-line; CD-ROM)   (*See also* Social Sciences.)

Geology and Earth Sciences

BIBLIOGRAPHY AND INDEX OF GEOLOGY

BOSSGEOBASE (on-line)

CURRENT CONTENTS: PHYSICAL, CHEMICAL, AND EARTH SCIENCES (on-line)

EARTH SCIENCE DISC (CD-ROM)

GEOINDEX (on-line)   (*See also* Geography; Science and Technology.)

History

AMERICA, HISTORY AND LIFE (on-line; CD-ROM)

C.R.I.S.: THE COMBINED RETROSPECTIVE INDEX SET TO JOURNALS IN HISTORY, 1838–1974

HISTORICAL ABSTRACTS (on-line; CD-ROM)

INTERNATIONAL BIBLIOGRAPHY OF HISTORICAL SCIENCES

RECENTLY PUBLISHED ARTICLES. AMERICAN HISTORICAL ASSOCIATION (*See also* Humanities.)

Humanities

*ARTS AND HUMANITIES CITATION INDEX (on-line; CD-ROM)   (*See* "Using Citation Indexes" in Chapter 12.)

ARTS AND HUMANITIES SEARCH (on-line)

BRITISH HUMANITIES INDEX

COMBINED RETROSPECTIVE INDEX TO BOOK REVIEWS IN HUMANITIES JOURNALS, 1802–1974

CURRENT CONTENTS: ARTS AND HUMANITIES (on-line)

*HUMANITIES INDEX (on-line; CD-ROM)   A subject and author index to several hundred periodicals in classical studies, folklore, history, language, literature, philosophy, and theology. Broadly useful because of its interdisciplinary scope.

*INDEX TO BOOK REVIEWS IN THE HUMANITIES   Indexes books by author. Covers over four hundred periodicals. After 1970, its focus became primarily literary; many journals in history and the social sciences were dropped.

LANGUAGE AND LANGUAGE BEHAVIOR ABSTRACTS

*PCI WEB (on-line)   Electronic index to about twenty-four hundred journals in the humanities and social sciences. (*See also* Social Sciences.)

Law

CANADIAN LEGAL LITERATURE
CONGRESSIONAL UNIVERSE (on-line)
CRIMINAL JUSTICE ABSTRACTS
CURRENT LAW INDEX
INDEX TO LEGAL PERIODICALS AND BOOKS (on-line; CD-ROM)
LEGALTRAC (CD-ROM; *see also* General, *INFOTrac.*)
NCJRS (on-line)   (*See also* General, *LEXIS-NEXIS Academic Universe.*)

Linguistics

BIBLIOGRAPHIE LINGUISTIQUE/LINGUISTIC BIBLIOGRAPHY
LINGUISTICS AND LANGUAGE BEHAVIOR ABSTRACTS (on-line)
MLA INTERNATIONAL BIBLIOGRAPHY (Vol. 3) (on-line; CD-ROM)   (*See also* Literature.)

Literature

ABSTRACTS OF ENGLISH STUDIES
AMERICAN LITERATURE ABSTRACTS
*ANNUAL BIBLIOGRAPHY OF ENGLISH LANGUAGE AND LITERATURE (on-line)   British counterpart to the *MLA International Bibliography*. Since it often picks up items missed by the *MLA International Bibliography*, a thorough researcher should use the two works in conjunction. Unfortunately, the *Annual Bibliography of English Language and Literature* runs several years late.
CONTEMPORARY LITERARY CRITICISM
LANGUAGE AND LITERATURE
*MLA INTERNATIONAL BIBLIOGRAPHY (on-line; CD-ROM)   The standard bibliography for finding books and articles on literature in the modern languages, linguistics, and folklore. About two thousand periodicals are indexed, along with books and collections of articles. Entries on literature are arranged by language, nationality, and historical period; there is also an author index. A subject index was introduced in 1981. Lengthy review articles are indexed; reviews of individual works are not. Since the *MLA International Bibliography* often picks up items missed by the *Annual Bibliography of English Language and Literature*, a thorough researcher should use the two works in conjunction.
*NEW CAMBRIDGE BIBLIOGRAPHY OF ENGLISH LITERATURE   A selective bibliography of writings by and about British authors from the beginnings to about 1950. Though selective rather than comprehensive, it is nevertheless the most extensive bibliography of English literature up to the mid–twentieth century.
*SHORT STORY INDEX   An index to short stories in periodicals and collections.
*YEAR'S WORK IN ENGLISH STUDIES   An excellent place to find short reviews and summaries of scholarly works about literature. Annual, but

runs several years late. (*See also*, in "Specialized Encyclopedias and Dictionaries," Biography, *Dictionary of Literary Biography*.)

Mathematics

INDEX OF MATHEMATICAL PAPERS
*MATHEMATICAL REVIEWS (on-line as *MATHFILE*)   Indexed annually. (*See also* Science and Technology.)

Medicine, Nursing, Health Sciences

CANCER-CD (CD-ROM)
*CUMULATIVE INDEX TO NURSING AND ALLIED HEALTH LITERATURE (CINAHL) (on-line; CD-ROM)
CURRENT AWARENESS IN HEALTH EDUCATION
CURRENT CONTENTS: CLINICAL MEDICINE
CURRENT CONTENTS: CLINICAL PRACTICE
HEALTH INDEX (CD-ROM; *see also* General, *INFOTrac*.)
*INDEX MEDICUS   The standard hard-copy index to medical literature. Annual cumulations of monthly issues are published as *Cumulated Index Medicus*.
INTERNATIONAL NURSING INDEX
*MEDLINE (on-line; CD-ROM)   The most useful general index for biomedical literature. Coverage equivalent to *Index Medicus* plus literature in nursing and dentistry.
MEDOC: A COMPUTERIZED INDEX TO U.S. GOVERNMENT DOCUMENTS IN THE MEDICAL AND HEALTH SCIENCES

Music

MUSIC ARTICLE GUIDE
*MUSIC INDEX (CD-ROM)   An annual, cumulative, subject-author index of over 350 music periodicals, plus *Dissertation Abstracts International*, Section A: The Humanities and Social Sciences. Unlike *RILM Abstracts*, it indexes trade journals and magazines devoted to individual instruments. It includes reviews of books, performances, and recordings.
*RILM ABSTRACTS [RÉPERTOIRE INTERNATIONAL DE LITTÉRATURE MUSICALE ABSTRACTS] (on-line)   An annual cumulation of abstracts of writings about music. Cumulative subject-author indexes are compiled at four-year intervals. They index journals (approximately 3500), festschrifts, books, collections of essays, reviews, dissertations, and editions of music. The cumulative indexes to printed *RILM Abstracts* use a highly abbreviated and initially puzzling system of classification, which is explained in the front matter of each volume. Each cumulative index also contains an "International Thesaurus" in seventeen languages to provide interlingual cross-referencing.

Philosophy

PHILOSOPHER'S INDEX (on-line; CD-ROM)   (*See also* Humanities.)

Physical Education

ABSTRACTS OF RESEARCH PAPERS
PHYSICAL EDUCATION INDEX   (*See also* Education.)

Physics

CURRENT PAPERS IN PHYSICS
CURRENT PHYSICS INDEX
INSPEC (on-line)
PHYSICS ABSTRACTS (on-line)
SCIENCE ABSTRACTS
SCISEARCH (on-line)   (*See also* Science and Technology.)

Political Science

ABC POL SCI: ADVANCE BIBLIOGRAPHY OF CONTENTS, POLITICAL
   SCIENCE AND GOVERNMENT
C.R.I.S.: THE COMBINED RETROSPECTIVE INDEX TO JOURNALS
   IN POLITICAL SCIENCE, 1886–1974
INTERNATIONAL BIBLIOGRAPHY OF POLITICAL SCIENCE
INTERNATIONAL POLITICAL SCIENCE ABSTRACTS   (*See also* General,
   PAIS.)

Popular Culture

ABSTRACTS OF POPULAR CULTURE

Psychology

ANNUAL REVIEW OF PSYCHOLOGY
CHILD DEVELOPMENT ABSTRACTS AND BIBLIOGRAPHY
*PSYCHOLOGICAL ABSTRACTS   The standard source of abstracts on psy-
   chological topics. Cumulated author and subject indexes.
*PSYCINFO (on-line); PSYCLIT (CD-ROM)   Indexes sources on psycho-
   logical topics. More than 1.5 million records, 1887–present.   (*See also*
   Social Sciences.)

Religion

*CATHOLIC PERIODICAL AND LITERATURE INDEX   Continuation
   (1968–) of *Catholic Periodical Index* (1930–1966).
CHRISTIAN PERIODICAL INDEX
INDEX TO BOOK REVIEWS IN RELIGION
NEW TESTAMENT ABSTRACTS
*RELIGION INDEX ONE: PERIODICALS (on-line; CD-ROM)
   Continuation (1977–) of *Index to Religious Periodical Literature*
   (1949–1972).
RELIGION INDEX TWO: MULTI-AUTHOR WORKS
RELIGIOUS AND THEOLOGICAL ABSTRACTS

Science and Technology

*APPLIED SCIENCE AND TECHNOLOGY INDEX (on-line; CD-ROM)   A
   subject index to several hundred periodicals in technology, engineering,
   and industrial arts. Diverse coverage; broadly useful.

CURRENT CONTENTS: LIFE SCIENCES (on-line)

ENERGY RESEARCH ABSTRACTS

*GENERAL SCIENCE INDEX (on-line; CD-ROM)   A subject index to general-science periodicals. Diverse coverage; broadly useful.

HISTORY OF SCIENCE AND TECHNOLOGY (on-line)

INDEX TO SCIENTIFIC AND TECHNICAL PROCEEDINGS

INDEX TO SCIENTIFIC BOOK CONTENTS

INDEX TO SCIENTIFIC REVIEWS

*INDUSTRIAL ARTS INDEX   Covers 1913–1957. Divided in 1958 and became the *Applied Science and Technology Index* and the *Business Periodicals Index.*

*SCIENCE CITATION INDEX (on-line; CD-ROM) (See "Using Citation Indexes" in Chapter 12.)

TECHNICAL BOOK REVIEW INDEX

Social Sciences

ANTHROPOLOGICAL INDEX

APPLIED SOCIAL SCIENCES INDEX AND ABSTRACTS

BOOK REVIEW INDEX TO SOCIAL SCIENCE PERIODICALS

C.R.I.S.: THE COMBINED RETROSPECTIVE INDEX TO JOURNALS IN SOCIOLOGY, 1895–1974

CURRENT CONTENTS: SOCIAL AND BEHAVIORAL SCIENCES (on-line)

INDEX TO SOCIAL SCIENCES AND HUMANITIES PROCEEDINGS

INTERNATIONAL BIBLIOGRAPHY OF SOCIOLOGY

LONDON BIBLIOGRAPHY OF THE SOCIAL SCIENCES

SAGE FAMILY STUDIES ABSTRACTS

*SOCIAL SCIENCES CITATION INDEX (on-line; CD-ROM) (See "Using Citation Indexes" in Chapter 12.)

*SOCIAL SCIENCES INDEX (on-line; CD-ROM)   An author and subject index to several hundred English-language periodicals in the social sciences. Diverse coverage of fields: human ecology, economics, law, political science, in addition to psychology and sociology. Broadly useful.

SOCIAL WORK ABSTRACTS PLUS (SWAB +) (CD-ROM)

SOCIOLOGICAL ABSTRACTS (on-line; CD-ROM)

Urban Studies

URBAN AFFAIRS ABSTRACTS   (*See also* General, *NewsBank*)

Women's Studies

*CONTEMPORARY WOMEN'S ISSUES (on-line)   Full-text, interdisciplinary database, 1992–present.

INDEX TO WOMEN OF THE WORLD FROM ANCIENT TO MODERN TIMES

WOMEN STUDIES ABSTRACTS

WOMEN'S STUDIES: A GUIDE TO INFORMATION SOURCES

WOMEN'S STUDIES INDEX

| INTERNET | ## STEP FOUR: Searching the Internet

The Internet and its most popular component, the World Wide Web, have produced the most dramatic revolution in information technology since the invention of the printing press. The Web is especially exciting because it organizes knowledge in a new and highly accessible way. Simply clicking on a link can carry you in a flash from one information source to another source on the other side of the world. The Web offers far more than mere speed and convenience. It offers a truly new way of doing research—one that mimics the way the human mind actually works!

In this chapter, steps one, two, and three all rely on traditional search techniques based on print technology: The researcher must methodically and painstakingly search through alphabetized catalogs and indexes organized by means of headings. The Web, on the other hand, lets the researcher learn in a more natural, more casual way, through a process of association. Although libraries may organize knowledge systematically, most people learn unsystematically, simply by letting one thing lead to another. Curiosity about sports may lead to curiosity about ancient Roman circuses, which may lead to curiosity about Pompeii, and so on. The Web encourages this kind of learning by using the *hypertext link* (highlighted text or image that automatically sends you to another Web site or page) as its organizing principle.

The Internet is a worldwide network of interconnected computers; the World Wide Web is simply that portion of the Internet that uses *hypertext mark-up language* (or *HTML*) to present information in the form of *Web sites* that contain individual *Web pages*. Each Web page has a unique address to distinguish it from every other Web page in the world; this is its *universal resource locator* (or *URL*).

To the researcher, the Web offers some remarkable advantages. Its simple point-and-click method of linking documents requires no special expertise. It rewards the simplest form of searching, which is trial and error. It is fast and worldwide in scope. It enables the researcher to make copies of text, pictures, sound, and even video. It is just plain fun.

Why, then, did I put Internet and Web searching *last* among the four steps in finding sources? Frankly, I did it to counteract the researcher's natural tendency to go to the Web *first* and to stop after searching the Web! Most university teachers will confirm this point:

> College students now tend to over-rely on the Web for information while neglecting to master the traditional library search techniques that often yield superior results.

By placing Web searching last, I'm pointing out that your research will definitely not be complete and thorough if you skip steps one through three.

But as I've already said, it is often best to start by briefly searching the Web, as long as you backtrack at some point to carry out the other search steps. Research is rarely a tidy, step-by-step process, and there is no single "best" search pattern.

Using Web Search Engines

We have seen the advantage of finding Library of Congress subject headings: Once you have found an appropriate subject heading for your topic, you will find other works indexed under the same heading. You will even be able to shelf browse to find related works in a cluster in the library stacks.

The World Wide Web is organized entirely differently. There is no standard system of subject headings, although most search engines organize sites into a few content categories. Instead of being systematically indexed, the Web is designed to accommodate an infinite number of hypertext links between Web sites, so that once you have found a relevant site, it may send you, via hypertext links, to related sites.

Instead of searching by subject headings, Web search engines use the relatively less efficient method of searching for words and strings of words. As we saw while looking at library catalogs, *word* searches are much less focused—and often much slower—than *subject* searches.

Search engines use massive computing power to compensate for the relatively slow, unfocused, unselective nature of word searches. Search engines constantly examine the Internet and the Web, compiling files of word strings for retrieval. The result is that a Web search is more like a floodlight than a flashlight: It lights up a lot of material, but much of it is irrelevant.

Although there are differences between search engines, most of them return search results as a prioritized list. If you search for "Appalachian story teller," the search engine will give you a list of sites. The list itself will probably have the following characteristics.

1. There will be thousands, perhaps tens of thousands, of "hits." (You may think, at first, that you are swamped with information.)

2. Many of the "hits" will be repetitious. (The search engine may generate an entry for every page of a site with hundreds of pages.)

3. The search engine may rank the "hits" in order of "relevance," usually expressed as a percentage. (The search engine may simply check to see how many of your search words appear in the document, how frequently, how close to each other, and how close to the top of the page.)

4. Many of the "hits" will be irrelevant. (In the example given, the search engine may include many sites related to Edward *Teller*, for example.)

5. The Web site most useful to you may be buried on the sixth page of "hits." (If you are a typical Web cruiser, you may have clicked the mouse and moved on, long before reaching page six!)

Most search interfaces use Boolean logic, so that when you type "Appalachian story teller," the engine will list every site containing one or more of those words. But if you type "Appalachian and story and teller," the engine will retrieve only those sites containing *all three words*. Unfortunately, methods of refining a search vary from engine to engine. AltaVista, Excite, Infoseek, and WebCrawler, for example, are configured to find sites matching *any* of the words in a string of words, whereas HotBot and Lycos are configured to find only sites matching *all* the words in a search string. Helpful tips on how to make a search engine find what *you* want it to find are given at Search Engine Watch (<http://www.searchenginewatch.com/facts/powersearch.html>).

Perhaps it's most accurate to say that the average search engine's grasp is wide but clumsy. It is impossible to search the Web as systematically, narrowly, and efficiently as one can search a library catalog using Library of Congress subject headings. However, the sheer size of the Web, coupled with the massive computing power of the search engine, makes it likely that a useful site will turn up; furthermore, the search engine's results may be augmented by the use of a directory (see "Search Engines and Directories"). Once you find a good site, that site's links can quickly lead you into a fairly comprehensive survey of related materials on the Web.

> *Advice:* Try all the search engines. Try a variety of words and word strings. Use Boolean logic to limit and focus your search.

Search Engines and Directories

Search engines mechanically roam the Internet to compile lists of Web pages. Directories, on the other hand, are compiled by humans who analyze Web sites and assign them to categories. AltaVista, Excite, GoTo, HotBot, Insfoseek, Lycos, Northern Light, and WebCrawler are examples of search engines, while LookSmart, Snap, and Yahoo are examples of directories. Some search engines are hybrids: That is, they have directories built into them. The term *search engine* is commonly used to denote all three types of service—search engines, directories, and hybrids.

> **POPULAR SEARCH ENGINES AND DIRECTORIES**
>
> *AltaVista*
> A popular "all-purpose" search engine. You may search in any language.
>
> *AOL NetFind*
> Although operating under its own brand name, this search engine is powered by Excite (see next entry).

Excite
A "full Web" engine, it searches every word of every page on the Web. It also includes an extensive set of pre-selected Web sites and Usenet postings.

GoTo
A popular "all-purpose" search engine that attempts to make the search process simple.

HotBot
Another "full Web" engine and part of the Lycos Network, it searches every word of every page on the Web.

Infoseek
A popular "all-purpose" search engine; advanced features enable you to search for specific titles, URLs, or links.

LookSmart
Really a human-compiled Web directory rather than a search engine. LookSmart indexes, categorizes, and reviews selected Web sites.

Lycos
Once merely a popular "all-purpose" search engine, this is now an Internet "hub" offering a variety of services, including searches.

MSN Search
A popular "all-purpose" search engine.

Netscape Search
Like AOL NetFind, Netscape Search is powered by Excite (see previous entries).

Northern Light
Features a large index and the ability to cluster documents by topic. Also offers its own collection of full-text documents not available through other search engines.

Snap
A human-compiled Web directory that aims to challenge Yahoo's pre-eminence in this field (see Yahoo entry).

WebCrawler
A popular search engine operated by Excite, but with a smaller index, WebCrawler is useful when Excite produces too many results.

Yahoo
Really a human-compiled Web directory rather than a search engine, Yahoo indexes, categorizes, and reviews Web sites. Its organization and selectivity make it among the most popular search engines on the Web.

Searching for Internet Material Not on the Web

Much valuable research information is available on the Internet but not on the Web. For example, an agency may decide to make a huge database available by means of *file transfer protocol* (or *FTP*) without constructing a Web site for it. This sort of material can be found by using *Archie*, a search engine that looks for FTP sites by file name. Other non-Web-based information servers include *WAIS* (*Wide Area Information Server*), *Gopher* (a menu interface to the Internet using its own search engine, *Veronica*), and *Telnet* (which allows telephone access to remote computers). Access to these older types of Internet resources may vary from library to library, so speak to someone in your library's reference department about them.

Evaluating the Internet as a Source of Information

Although search engines make it easy to find source material on the Internet and the World Wide Web, such material should be used with special care. The Web is really just a giant public bulletin board upon which anyone can post material. In addition to valuable information, it contains lots of biased, mistaken, badly edited, and sometimes even stolen material.

Would you base an important personal decision—say, a decision about medical care—by gathering advice from a public bulletin board covered with graffiti? Of course not. Similarly, you should not hope to base a research paper solely upon Web sources. The key to using the Web is knowing which sources are worth using.

Think of the world of information as a marketplace of ideas. Printed books and articles have proven some degree of merit by successfully competing in the marketplace. A journal article, for example, normally has been evaluated by expert readers before it appears in print, and usually its writer has revised it several times in response to expert evaluations known as peer reviews. A typical book has undergone an even more searching process of evaluation. The book that you are holding in your hands, whatever its merits and demerits, has benefited from twelve peer reviews of its two editions; the reviewers supplied literally hundreds of pages of helpful criticisms and suggestions.

But peer reviews are only part of the story. Publishers and editors spend money to bring out books and articles, so they, too, take a hard, critical look at the material submitted to them. After publication, magazine and newspaper reviewers may evaluate the book. Finally, the ultimate judge in the competitive marketplace is the consumer who buys the book or subscribes to the journal.

Most Web sources do not pass any of these competitive tests. (Of course, Web versions of reputable published sources—*Britannica Online* and *Time Magazine Online*, to cite a couple of random examples—are fully as credible as their print counterparts.) Anyone who wants to can post a personal Web page, however, and virtually no marketplace mechanisms are at work to ensure even a minimum level of quality. The Web is like Kansas City in the 1930s: fast-paced, free and exciting, but dangerous for the unwary.

Before evaluating specific Web sites, keep in mind the *general* advantages and disadvantages of Web sources:

ADVANTAGES OF WEB RESOURCES

Can be found quickly and easily

Can be printed out or stored on disk

Contain multimedia

May be frequently updated, current

May contain topic bibliographies

Are linked to related material

May be based on credible print sources (indexes, databases, electronic journals)

DISADVANTAGES OF WEB RESOURCES

Must be found with search engines that are powerful but unfocused

Lack peer reviews

Lack advantages conferred by competitive marketplace

Are unpredictable in quality and reliability

May be misinformed or deceptive

Evaluating Individual Web Sites

You should apply to Web sites the same principles of evaluation that you use in judging other kinds of source material. (See "Evaluating Sources" in Chapter 6 for specific tips.) But because the average college researcher is now likely to use the Web quite early in the research process, let's discuss some basic rules of thumb and visit a few actual Web sites.

1. Learn to distinguish between different types of Web sites. Jan Alexander and Marsha Tate discuss advocacy pages, business/ marketing pages, informational pages, news pages, and personal home pages, while offering a series of programmed lessons on evaluating Web sites. Visit <http://www.science.widener.edu/ ~withers/webeval.htm>.

2. If you plan to use material from a specific Web site, evaluate it thoroughly. Esther Grassian at UCLA supplies an excellent checklist of criteria. Visit <http://www.library.ucla.edu/libraries/ college/instruct/web/critical.htm>.

3. Apply your skills of critical thinking to Web sites. Robert Harris at Southern California College provides a clear and lively introduction. Visit <http://www.sccu.edu/faculty/R_Harris/ evalu8it.htm>.

4. Remember that you may always safely use Web sites to find topic bibliographies. Even if a topic bibliography is incomplete or inaccurate, you can correct it later and supplement it by using standard indexes. (Using "Save as" to save a bibliography on a floppy disk is a great way to speed the source-hunting process, though you should *never* hand in final versions of listings from such a bibliography without verifying and correcting them by looking at the actual sources.) See the inside front cover of this book for some examples of helpful, scholarly Web sites.

5. A research paper based *solely* on Web sources is virtually *never* adequately researched. Good college research judiciously blends carefully chosen material from books, periodical articles, and other sources, including on-line resources. (Rare exceptions: Some topics, such as those involving popular culture or very recent trends or fads, may be *best* supported by means of Web resources.)

AFTER STEP FOUR: What Next?

As you have seen, the four-step strategy soon branches out into substrategies. Before the search process becomes too complex, begin collecting not just citations but also actual sources. Gathering source material early in your search will let you accomplish several goals. It will give you some idea of how many sources will actually be available to you through your library. Skimming the sources and studying their lists of citations will help you identify key subtopics and will thus help you develop your argument. You will also begin to recognize key authorities, an important part of evaluating your source material. (To tell a good source from a bad one, review "Evaluating Sources" in Chapter 6.) Make short evaluative notes directly on your bibliography cards so that you remember which sources looked most useful and, perhaps, which ones deserve to be challenged. Although new material sometimes shows up unexpectedly even at the last moment, once you have identified the major works by the major sources, you can feel fairly confident that the source-gathering stage is nearing its end.

During the early stages in the source-hunting process, one of the most important functions of examining actual sources is to network from source to source; that is, through studying the source citations in your source material, you can build a working bibliography by following the network of citations. If you get swamped by too much source material turned up through networking, return to the topic-narrowing stage as often as you need to. Review your source material to find narrower aspects of your original topic.

The preceding lists of encyclopedias and indexes are quite extensive, and they will probably guide you to all the information you will need. But if you feel lost—and particularly if you need a more detailed overview of the entire library research process—some general reference works can provide help. A thorough and well-written guide to library research is Thomas Mann's *Oxford Guide to Library Research* (New York: Oxford UP, 1998). And, again, don't feel shy about asking a librarian for help.

ITEMS TO RECORD WHEN COPYING CITATIONS

When you find a source, be sure to record all the information you will later need to complete your bibliography entry. It is frustrating to have to revisit the library simply to record some tiny bit of information, such as a volume number, that you forgot to write on a photocopy.

Use the following checklists to make sure that your citations are complete. For sources other than books, periodicals, and Web sites, see the checklists in Chapter 7 (pp. 176–179).

Book Citations

1. author's name (in full)
2. title of the part of a book if you are using only a part (for example, a story, a chapter, or an article in a collection)
3. title of the book (including the subtitle)
4. name of the editor, compiler, or translator, if any
5. edition (if an edition is identified on the title page or copyright page) (see *edition* on p. 170.)
6. volume number, in Arabic numerals
7. name of the series, if any (check the Library of Congress data in the library catalog if you are unsure) and the number of the book in the series
8. city of publication and the name of the publisher
9. year of publication
10. page numbers
11. supplementary information, such as the total number of volumes in a multivolume work or the original version of a translated work
12. library call number and location for personal use

Article Citations

1. author's name (in full)
2. title of the article in a periodical
3. title of the periodical
4. volume number, in Arabic numerals
5. issue number, for journals only, if each issue of the journal begins with page 1

6. name or number of the series, if any (for example, "ns" for "new series," "os" for "old series"; "3rd ser." for a numbered series)

7. date: the issue's month or season and year for quarterly journals; the issue's day, month, and year for weekly periodicals; the issue's month and year for monthly periodicals; the edition, if any (such as "late ed.") for newspapers (see *edition* on p. 170)

8. page numbers; section and page numbers for newspapers

9. name of a computerized information service and the item's identification number

Web and Internet Citations

1. author's name, in full (if given)

2. title of the material, in quotation marks, if it is an article, short story, or similar short work within a scholarly project, database, or periodical; or title of newsgroup posting, in quotation marks, followed by "Online posting"

3. title of a book (underlined)

4. name of the editor, compiler, or translator (if relevant and not already cited), preceded by the appropriate abbreviation (such as "Trans.")

5. publication data for print version of the source

6. title of scholarly project, database, periodical, or site (underlined); for untitled site, a description such as *Home page*

7. name of scholarly project's or database's editor (if available)

8. version number; or, for a journal, the volume number, issue number, or other identifying number

9. date of electronic publication, of update, or of posting

10. for a newsgroup posting, the name of the list

11. the number range or number of pages, paragraphs, or other sections, if they are numbered

12. name of sponsoring institution (if given)

13. date when the researcher accessed the material

14. electronic address, or URL, in angle brackets

List only the information that applies to the site you are using.

INTERPRETING TITLE PAGES, COPYRIGHT PAGES, AND COMPUTER SCREENS

Writing an accurate bibliography entry can be tricky when the title page or copyright page contains ambiguous or confusing information. Although the details of bibliography format will be covered later in Chapters 7 and 8, right now you need to know how to interpret a book's publication data so that you can copy down the right information.

LOUIS ARMSTRONG

An American Genius

JAMES LINCOLN COLLIER

New York   OXFORD UNIVERSITY PRESS   1983

FIGURE 4.12   Example of a Title Page

Let's look at an example. Figure 4.12 reproduces a title page. This title page has all the information you need to write a complete bibliography entry. As a rule, when the title page unambiguously supplies all the necessary information, base your entry on it. This title page lists the title, author, city of publication, publisher, and date. A bibliography entry for this book, set up in the MLA format, should look like this:

Collier, James Lincoln. Louis Armstrong: An American Genius. New York: Oxford UP, 1983.

Now let's look at a more difficult example. Figure 4.13 reproduces another title page. We see that the author is Elizabeth Bishop, the title is *The Complete*

Elizabeth Bishop

The Complete Poems

1927-1979

Farrar · Straus · Giroux

NEW YORK

FIGURE 4.13 Example of a Title Page Without a Copyright Year

Poems 1927–1979, the city of publication is New York, and the publisher is Farrar, Straus, and Giroux. But what is the copyright date? When you turn to the copyright page, a bewildering series of dates confronts you (see Figure 4.14). Which one should you list? When was the book published, 1979 or 1983? Or should you list the date of the fifteenth printing, 1994? And what are all the other dates?

Sometimes you have to analyze the copyright data in conjunction with other information to arrive at the right answer. The facts are that when Elizabeth Bishop died in 1979, Alice Helen Methfessel was the executor of her estate, and on Bishop's behalf she renewed the copyright registration of Bishop's works. So

Most of the poems in this volume originally appeared in *The
New Yorker*. Others were first published in *Direction, Harper's
Bazaar, The Kenyon Review, The Nation, New Directions,
The New Republic, The New York Review of Books, Partisan Review,
Ploughshares, Poetry, The Quarterly Review of Literature, Saturday
Review, Shenandoah*, and *Vassar Review*.

Library of Congress Cataloging in Publication Data
Bishop, Elizabeth.
The complete poems, 1927–1979.
Includes indexes.
I. Title
PS3503.I785   1983   811'.54   82–21119

FIGURE 4.14   Copyright Page from Bishop's Book

1979 is the date when she secured legal protection of Bishop's writings; 1983 is
the copyright date of *this specific collection*. The other dates are individual copy-
rights for poems that appeared singly in various magazines and collections. The
date of the fifteenth printing, 1994, should be ignored, because a printing is
an unaltered republication of a book that has already been published and
copyrighted.

Fortunately, you can usually avoid using deduction and detective work to
determine the facts of a book's publication. Most books contain Library of
Congress publication data, and you can safely assume that the Library of Congress has assigned the correct date. Notice that the very bottom of the Bishop

```
*  *  *  *  *  *  *  *  Full Record Display  *  *  *  *  *  *  *  *
DATABASE: WorldCat                    LIMITED TO:
SEARCH: au:bishop elizabeth

Record 91 of 177 _____ [Page 1 of 2]

ACCESSION:  16597160
   AUTHOR:  Bishop, Elizabeth, 1911-1979
    TITLE:  The complete poems 1927-1979
    PLACE:  New York
PUBLISHER:  Farrar, Straus and Giroux
     YEAR:  1983
 PUB TYPE:  Book
   FORMAT:  287 p. ; 25 cm
_____
HINTS: Another page: type F or B. Another record: type record number.
       See which libraries own this item . . . . . . . . . . . . . type LIB.
       Return to Record list . . . . . . . . . . . . . . . just press Enter.

ACTIONS: Help  Search  Print  LIBraries  Forward  Back  BYE
RECORD NUMBER [or Action]:  ▭
```

FIGURE 4.15 *WorldCat* Information for the Bishop Book

copyright page has a block of Library of Congress information, and the last line contains the date, 1983. An MLA bibliography entry for Bishop's book should look like this:

> Bishop, Elizabeth. <u>The Complete Poems 1927–1979</u>. New York: Farrar, 1983.

As it happens, some copies of this book have a slightly different title page. Above the publisher's name in some books appear the words "A Noonday Book." They indicate that the book has been issued under an *imprint*, which is a specialized subdivision of a publishing house. A copy of the book with the Noonday title page should look like this:

> Bishop, Elizabeth. <u>The Complete Poems 1927–1979</u>. New York: Noonday-Farrar, 1983.

When you are unsure how to list a book, you can always check to see how expert catalogers have treated it: Look it up in a reliable library catalog. As an example, Figure 4.15 shows the computer screen from one of the copies of the Bishop book listed in the worldwide database *WorldCat*. It confirms the accuracy of the first entry listed for this book.

Finally, let's look at a complex example. Penguin Books has published an edition of James Joyce's collection of short stories, *Dubliners*. The title page contains nothing but author, title, and publisher. The copyright page is shown in Figure 4.16, and it is a source hunter's nightmare.

PENGUIN BOOKS
Published by the Penguin Group
Penguin Books USA Inc.
375 Hudson Street, New York, New York 10014, U.S.A.
Penguin Books Ltd, 27 Wrights Lane, London W8 5TZ, England
Penguin Books Australia Ltd, Ringwood, Victoria, Australia
Penguin Books Canada Ltd, 10 Alcorn Avenue,
Toronto, Ontario, Canada M4V 3B2
Penguin Books (N.Z.) Ltd, 182–190 Wairau Road, Auckland 10, New Zealand

Penguin Books Ltd, Registered Offices:
Harmondsworth, Middlesex, England

First published in the United States of America by
B. W. Huebsch 1916
Viking Compass Edition published 1958
Reprinted 1959 (twice), 1960 (three times), 1961 (twice),
1962 (three times), 1963 (twice), 1964 (twice), 1965 (twice), 1966, 1967
Revised Edition published 1968
Reprinted 1968, 1969 (three times), 1970, 1971 (twice),
1972 (three times), 1973, 1974 (twice), 1975, 1976
Published in Penguin Books 1976

25 27 29 30 28 26 24

Copyright © Estate of James Joyce, 1967

ISBN 0 14 00.4222 9

Library of Congress catalog card number: 25-23228

Printed in the United States of America
Set in Linotype Times Roman

Except in the United States of America,
this book is sold subject to the condition
that it shall not, by way of trade or otherwise,
be lent, re-sold, hired out, or otherwise circulated
without the publisher's prior consent in any form of
binding or cover other than that in which it is
published and without a similar condition
including this condition being imposed
on the subsequent purchaser.

FIGURE 4.16 Copyright Page from the *Dubliners* Published by Penguin Books

Penguin likes to include its branch offices in its copyright notices. So what is the city of publication for this edition? Here is a guideline: No matter where the book was actually produced, if the title page doesn't list a city, treat the publisher's *home office* as the city of publication. Harmondsworth, England, then, is the city to use for this example. (The English county name, Middlesex, should be omitted.)

Anyone studying Joyce's *Dubliners* would like to know, or to be reminded of, the date of the first edition of this famous book. Unfortunately, the copyright page of the Penguin edition omits this information and instead gives the date of the first *American* edition. By reading the prefatory section, "A Note on the Text," which appears on page 5, we can discover that the British edition was published in London by the Grant Richards firm in 1914. Of the many dates given, the crucial one is 1968, because that is when the Revised Edition appeared—a version of the text substantially different from all preceding ones. Again, ignore all the reprint dates, because, unlike an edition, a reprint is unaltered. But note that *this specific printed version of the revised edition* first appeared as a Penguin book in 1976. Thus, a careful, accurate bibliography entry in the MLA format should look like this, with the year for the first edition tucked in as supplementary information after the title:

> Joyce, James. <u>Dubliners</u>. 1914. Harmondsworth, Eng.: Penguin, 1976.
>   Rev. ed. 1968.

Again, a large library database such as *WorldCat* can confirm the accuracy of this entry, and trade bibliographies can confirm publication dates (see "Finding Books Outside Your Library" in Chapter 12). Sometimes there is no way to be sure about a book's publication facts without checking an outside source.

■■■ JOURNAL EXCERPTS
Finding Sources

Session 2

So far I have conducted all my source hunting by modem, using the following databases, among others.

Humanities Index (on CD-ROM): 1984 to the present.   I found an article on the function and form of the classical cadenza.

OhioLINK.   This database covers the combined resources of the Ohio network of cooperating libraries, comprising about 31 million volumes. I noticed that the most relevant LC (Library of Congress) headings are "Improvisation (Music)," "Embellishment (Music)," and "Performance practice (Music)—18th Century." In a collection of essays on music from Haydn to Schubert I found an essay on improvisation in Mozart's concerti. I found a major book by Neumann on improvisation and ornamentation in Mozart; its three-page bibliography will bear looking at.

WorldCat.   This database is even larger than OhioLINK, and the results of my search were overwhelming. The label "improvisation" turned up 4195 sources! I had to limit the search several times. First, I used Boolean logic by adding "not jazz" to the search word, to cut out all sources with the word *jazz* in the title or elsewhere in the database record. To eliminate sources that deal with improvisation in the theater, I added "and music" as a further limiting term. The fully limited search produced 445 items, which I was able to scan—and print out selectively—in a little less than two hours.

I feel relatively confident that my printout, which I am marking in red to indicate primary sources, direct-hit secondary sources, and bibliographies, has given me 90 percent of the book sources I will need. It will be interesting to see later what key sources, if any, the computer search failed to turn up.

Session 9

My preliminary bibliography now contains twenty-seven sources. The actual number is smaller and less intimidating, however, when I consider that eight of these sources are sections of two encyclopedia articles; thus, the actual number of sources is twenty-one. I have eliminated at least as many other sources (probably twenty to thirty) as too specialized or too hard to find.

Source	Place Where I Found It Cited
8 *New Grove* articles	List of encyclopedias earlier in this chapter
4 books, 2 articles	*OhioLINK*
2 books, 1 article	Vinquist's topic bibliography
2 books	*New Grove* bibliography
1 book, 1 encyclopedia article	Keller (found shelf browsing)
1 article	Ferand's bibliography
1 article	Neumann's bibliography in *Ornamentation and Baroque*
1 book	*WorldCat*
1 article	*RILM* abstracts
1 article	*Arts and Humanities Search* database
1 article	*Humanities Index* database

Of the twenty-seven sources, all but four were available in my local university library; I made four interlibrary loan requests. There was nothing useful on the Web.

This list confirms that the best places to begin are the library catalog, general reference works, and topic bibliographies. My references often came from books and articles as I found them.

It's also interesting to see that shelf browsing turned up a couple of good items. Although Keller's book aims to teach modern performers how to perform a thoroughbass accompaniment, it contained one of the best potential quotations in my notes so far, expressing the idea that thoroughbass made composition easy.

It's interesting to compare my feelings now and this list with my initial | INTERNET | optimism after I scanned *WorldCat* and came up with 445 items. I felt then that I had probably found most of the major sources. Yet my tabulation shows that *WorldCat* turned up only one of my sources.

Why was the *WorldCat* computer search not as useful as I thought it would be? For one thing, I remember that I found but did not print out Ferand's collection, because it was clearly a book of scores rather than a written text. Only later did I realize that it had a written introduction (which turned out to be among my best sources). In fairness, what *WorldCat* did very well was turn up lots of primary sources—early handbooks on improvisation—which I decided were too numerous to handle in a short paper.

■■■ EXERCISE 9

Finding Sources

In "Treasure Hunt, Part 1" some questions about specific sources let you measure your performance against answers your instructor will supply. "Treasure Hunt, Part 2" presents some open-ended questions dealing with the source material you will actually be using for your paper. Specific answers cannot be given to questions of this sort, but the skills needed to answer the questions are parallel to those covered in "Treasure Hunt, Part 1."

The questions in Part 1 get increasingly difficult, so don't worry if you slow down toward the end. Answers may vary in accordance with the library resources available to you.

Be sure to study this chapter before you plunge into the library research.

Treasure Hunt, Part I

1. You're interested in finding out how soon atomic fusion may become a feasible source of electric power.
   (a) Under what Library of Congress subject heading will you find information on fusion as a potential source of power?
   (b) What other headings might be useful?
2. Name a couple of ways of finding Library of Congress subject headings.
3. You want to find out whether the medication Allegra produces any side effects. Where should you look to find a quick answer?
4. Track down a biographical article on the American writer W. D. Snodgrass. Then answer the following questions.
   (a) What reference work is generally the best starting point for a search for biographical information?
   (b) Where did you find one or more biographical articles on Snodgrass?
   (c) When was Snodgrass born? Where? How many children has he had? Where did he attend college?
   (d) What major literary prize has Snodgrass won?
   (e) Name something written by him.
5. What index is most likely to be useful in finding nontechnical articles on the design of antilock braking systems?
6. You know that within the past two years an American book has been published on the subject of education for the blind, but your library does not have it. You do not know its title.
   (a) Where should you look to find the title?
   (b) How can you obtain a copy of it?

7. You are interested in the subject of educating autistic children. Your instructor remembers reading, in the late 1970s, a fascinating review in the *New York Review of Books* about a book by Lorna Selfe. The review criticized the education given to a young girl named Nadia, who was autistic but artistically gifted. You would like to find both the book and the review.
   (a) You need to find an index that covers the *New York Review of Books*. How can you find the name of such an index?
   (b) List some indexes that will enable you to find the review.
   (c) What is the name of the book?
   (d) Who wrote the review?
   (e) You are not sure that you understand what autism is. Where can you find a brief but authoritative definition of the term?

8. You have decided to write a paper on the rather obscure ancient Roman writer Apuleius. You would like to find out what scholars have cited Apuleius during the past few years. Where might you look to find an answer to this question relatively quickly? Check the index and note the number of citations to Apuleius in a sample year.

9. You would like to find out about computer software that translates texts from one human language into another. Describe some search strategies. See whether you can identify the most useful index to articles on computer translation. What subject heading does it use for this topic? (Note: This question does *not* ask you to find the best index for articles on *computer* languages.)

Treasure Hunt, Part 2

1. Under what Library of Congress subject heading have you found information on your paper topic? What other headings have also been useful?

2. In dealing with your topic, what subject headings have been most useful for searching in indexes to periodicals?

3. You want to find a concise, authoritative definition of a technical term that you plan to use in your paper. What specialized dictionary or dictionaries can provide such a definition?

4. Track down a biographical article on one of the writers whose work you plan to use in your paper. (You may not be able to do this if the writers are all obscure. But you may be surprised at how much information you can gather even about little-known authors.)
   (a) What reference work is generally the best starting point for such a search?
   (b) Where did you find a biographical article?
   (c) Evaluate the writer's academic qualifications: education, specialization, publications, prizes and fellowships, and so on.
   (d) Does this information affect your opinion of the writer's expertise?

5. Look for topic bibliographies or research guides on your subject.
   (a) What index lists nothing but topic bibliographies? Did it contain any that looked at all useful for your paper?

    (b) If you have found no topic bibliographies or research guides, then what index or indexes will be most useful in helping you find periodical articles?

6. You want to find out if there are any useful books on your topic that are not among the holdings of your library. Where can you search for this information?

7. To evaluate one of the books you are using for your paper, try to track down a review of it. Then answer the following questions.
    (a) Name some standard methods of finding reviews.
    (b) Did these methods work for you? Why or why not? If you found a review, think about using the review itself as a source in your paper.
    (c) Did the review change your view of the book?
    (d) Did the review challenge or disagree with your book?
    (e) Might the review contribute to your argument in any way? How?

▪▪▪ EXERCISE 10

Evaluating a Web Site

Write a 250-word evaluation of a Web site containing information relevant to your topic. Consider authorship, accuracy, currency, and coverage, plus any other factors you consider relevant.

CHAPTER 5

WRITING A SHORT PLAN

■ ■ ■ QUICK VIEW

A short plan may take the form of a prospectus, an abstract, or an outline. A prospectus may contain a preliminary bibliography, which is simply an accurate list of the sources you plan to use for your paper, or an annotated bibliography, which is a list of sources with short summaries and/or evaluative remarks. The preliminary biography is useful as an early step in consolidating your planning, before you have had a chance to study your sources closely. If time permits, however, do an annotated bibliography, because it will force you to analyze your sources carefully before you go any farther.

A PROSPECTUS AND ITS ADVANTAGES

The short plan most commonly used by writers is the prospectus. A prospectus is a forward look (the word comes from the Latin root words *pro-*, meaning "for," and *specere*, meaning "look"). It is a proposal, just like a written estimate from a body shop or a contractor. A prospectus is sometimes called a "research proposal," but I generally avoid this term because it suggests the complicated, formal type of document that is usually submitted with an application for a research grant.

In a prospectus you explain what you hope to prove in your research paper. You also list sources you have found, to show that your paper is both feasible and useful: feasible, because there are enough sources to support a research paper of the length you propose; and useful, because there are no sources that have definitively proved exactly the hypothesis you have formulated.

A prospectus is especially valuable if your paper is going to be long and complex, but it is useful as a preliminary step toward a research paper of any length. Although it may look like an extra step at the beginning, writing a prospectus can save a lot of time later and can also improve the final draft.

In the academic world a prospectus or research proposal is a way of making sure that large projects (theses and dissertations) are carefully planned and carried out. But the prospectus is useful for small projects as well. If you hand in a neatly done prospectus to an instructor who has not required or requested one, he or she will be impressed by the care you've taken. If the prospectus is done well, the instructor is apt to approve your topic after offering various suggestions and warnings. Furthermore, you may get some tips on additional sources or ways of finding sources. You have nothing to lose by writing a prospectus, and you may gain something: You will learn about the instructor's expectations (certainly) and about your subject (maybe). Even if your instructor does not like your prospectus and discourages you, you have learned something and can remedy the problem before the paper is written.

Let's be frank. The prospectus can serve to create an instructor's goodwill and a predisposition to judge your paper favorably. The prospectus works this magic by enrolling the teacher as a collaborator in the research project. Once an instructor has approved a prospectus that you have revised in response to objections and suggestions, the instructor has become a participant. And collaboration casts the instructor in the flattering roles of approver, helper, and planner, roles dear to every teacher's heart. Do the prospectus well, write a paper that lives up to the prospectus, and your paper will succeed.

FORMATS FOR A PROSPECTUS

There is no universally accepted format for a prospectus, but common sense suggests that a good prospectus should have three main parts:

1. thesis statement
2. explanation of purpose
3. preliminary bibliography

Since a generic title such as "Research Proposal" or "Prospectus" conveys no information and arouses no interest, combine it with a descriptive title. This is what student Lisa Hewitt did to get the following prospectus title:

Prospectus: Negative Effects of Infant Day Care

Use the most precise statement of your research hypothesis that you have been able to formulate. If necessary, review the criteria for good thesis statements. (See "Research as New Knowledge" and "Avoiding Mistakes in Choosing a Topic" in Chapter 1 and "State Your Hypothesis Before Source Hunting" in Chapter 2.) Here is Lisa Hewitt's hypothesis.

Although long-term effects have not yet been studied, day care in the
first two years of an infant's life has several negative effects on infant-
parent attachment.

Next, write an explanation of the purpose of your research paper. There are
three ways to do this.

1. Write a condensation.
2. Write a paragraph on each component subtopic of the hypothesis.
3. Write a first-person narrative.

Perhaps the most elegant method is to write a condensation, normally fifty
to two hundred words long, of the entire paper as you envision it. The trouble is
that most of us find it very difficult, if not impossible, to condense something
that has not yet been written. The paper may take all kinds of unexpected
turns that a preliminary abstract cannot predict. However, if you are the unusual
writer who can foresee all or most of your potential lines of argument, you may
be able to write a condensation. Work from the material that you have compiled
so far.

In the second method you break down the hypothesis into its component
subtopics and write a paragraph on each of them. Thus Lisa Hewitt's hypothesis
(given earlier) could lead to a series of paragraphs on (1) the uncertain evidence
concerning long-term effects, (2) the firmer evidence concerning the effects of
day care during an infant's first two years, and (3) the negative effects that have
been most convincingly demonstrated.

In the third method, perhaps the least elegant but easiest, you write the
statement of purpose as a first-person narrative in which you talk about the paper
and describe how you plan to develop your thesis. This method produces a
looser, less analytic project description. But for that very reason, many students
feel more comfortable with it.

Next, compile the preliminary bibliography. Do not list reference tools such
as indexes and subject guides, but include every other source that you think you
might use in the paper. At this stage it is better to include too much than to risk
leaving out sources. The key goal of a preliminary bibliography is thoroughness.
Selectivity can come later, unless your instructor specifically asks for a selective
bibliography.

Check with your instructor to see whether your prospectus, if one is assigned, must conform to a standard format. The sample prospectus in Figure 5.1
shows the MLA format for documentation, since MLA format is the one most
commonly used in college research writing. For the actual paper reprinted in
Chapter 7, Lisa Hewitt converted the documentation of Figure 5.1 to APA format, which is the format appropriate for her field. Compare the two bibliographies to see how they differ.

Whatever standard format you use, all the information in the individual
bibliography entries should be absolutely accurate. Proofread your preliminary

Hewitt 1

Prospectus:

Negative Effects of Day Care on Infant Development

Thesis:

    Studies have shown that the negative emotional and intellectual effects of day care are great among children under the age of two. For this reason, and because these years are crucial to later develop-ment, mothers should seriously consider staying at home for at least the first two years of their babies' lives.

Description of project:

    A selective review of recent research on infant development in day care versus home care shows that negative effects upon infant-parent attachment have been well documented. Infants placed in day care at an early age tend to form less secure emotional bonds with mothers.

    Other characteristics of children enrolled in day care at early ages include uncooperativeness, increased aggressiveness toward peers and parents, and more frequent illness.

    Long-term effects of infant day care have not been adequately studied, primarily because of the inherent limitations of the Strange Situation Test.

Preliminary Bibliography:

Barglow, Peter, Brian E. Vaughn, and Nancy Molitor. "Effects of
    Maternal Absence due to Employment on the Quality of Infant-
    Mother Attachment in a Low-Risk Sample." Child Development
    58 (1987): 945–54.

    This empirical study assesses the effects of maternal absence
    upon fifty-four low-risk infants receiving at-home substitute care

FIGURE 5.1   A Sample Prospectus

initiated at least four months before the first birthday. Using the
Ainsworth Strange Situation Test to compare these infants at
twelve to thirteen months of age with a control group of fifty-six
infants whose mothers remained at home, the authors conclude
that firstborn children of mothers working full-time are more
likely to develop "insecure-avoidant" infant-mother attachments.

Belsky, Jay. "The 'Effects' of Infant Day Care Reconsidered." Early
Childhood Research Quarterly 3 (1988): 235–72.

This review article reexamines research on the effects of day
care upon infants by arguing that the infant-mother attachment
cannot be studied in isolation but must be seen in relation to
other variables, such as the quality and location of day care, the
characteristics of the infant and its family, and the adaptive
functions of insecure-avoidant attachment.

Belsky, Jay, and Michael J. Rovine. "Nonmaternal Care in the First
Year of Life and the Security of Infant-Parent Attachment." Child
Development 59 (1988): 157–67.

Combining and analyzing evidence from two longitudinal studies
of the development of 149 healthy firstborn infants, the authors
conclude that infants receiving twenty or more hours of substitute care per week are more likely to develop insecure infant-
mother (and, in the case of sons, infant-father) attachments.

Gamble, Thomas J., and Edward Zigler. "Effects of Infant Day Care:
Another Look at the Evidence." American Journal of Orthopsychiatry 56 (1986): 26–42.

This review article points out that the Ainsworth Strange Situation Test is the best available instrument to assess infant-parent

FIGURE 5.1 A Sample Prospectus *(continued)*

attachment, but only if it is used to assess attachment in children before the age of twenty months. Research shows that
other variables such as the infant's gender and the degree of
stress experienced by child or parent can affect the development
of infant-parent attachment.

King, Donna, and Carol E. MacKinnon. "Making Difficult Choices Easier: A Review of Research on Day Care and Children's Development." Family Relations 37 (1988): 392–98.

This review article analyzes research on day care since 1980,
emphasizing that many variables affect the quality of the day
care experience, including the child's age of entry, amount of
time spent in day care, quality of day care, physical setting, and
caregiver training. The authors point out that longitudinal
studies have not yet confirmed or falsified the prediction that insecure attachments lead to negative outcomes in later child
development.

Rubenstein, Judith L., Frank A. Pedersen, and Leon J. Yarrow. "What
Happens When Mother Is Away: A Comparison of Mothers and
Substitute Caregivers." Developmental Psychology 13 (1977):
529–30.

This empirical study compares the effects of maternal and substitute care upon sixty-five black infants in a low-income urban
area. Caregiver behaviors in an at-home setting were sampled by
three observers who regulated their data collecting by observing
ten cases in pairs before and during the study. The authors
found that mothers provide more positive emotional responses,

FIGURE 5.1   A Sample Prospectus *(continued)*

more social play, and more variety of play objects and social
stimulation.

White, Burton L. "Viewpoint: Should You Stay Home with Your
Baby?" <u>Young Children</u> Nov. 1981: 11–17.

Because current research on the effects of day care is inconclu-
sive, children should receive parental care rather than substitute
care. However, part-time care in a family day care setting or in a
carefully chosen day care center may be acceptable when a family cannot or will not provide adequate care.

Wingert, Pat, and Barbara Kantrowitz. "The Day Care Generation."
<u>Newsweek</u> Winter/Spring 1990 [special ed.]: 86–92.

This article summarizes the current debate over day care in
three major areas of concern: the effects of infant day care on
infant-parent attachment, the high turnover rate among day
care workers, and the effects of day care upon children's health.
The authors portray Jay Belsky as "a lightning rod for controversy" (92).

Zinsmeister, Karl. "Brave New World: How Day-Care Harms Children." <u>Policy Review</u> 44 (1988): 40–48.

Summarizing common arguments against day care, Zinsmeister
emphasizes Belsky's findings that day care for infants weakens
the infant-parent attachment.

FIGURE 5.1   A Sample Prospectus *(continued)*

bibliography very carefully. It will probably be the first piece of work you hand
in that really shows how careful and precise you can be, so try to make a good
first impression.

The following list summarizes the qualities a prospectus should have:

TIES OF A GOOD PROSPECTUS

ospectus should identify a topic that is sufficiently narrow,
ing, and unusual to arouse the curiosity of your hypothetical
e.

sis should be unified, should address a real question that
doubt, and should clearly predict a plan of development.

The explanation of purpose should be stylistically effective (though plain and direct) and mechanically correct.

The bibliography should be accurate and reasonably complete.

Above all, the prospectus should clearly provide a starting point for a college-level research paper.

AN ABSTRACT

An abstract is a condensation of an entire book, article, or paper, usually in fifty to two hundred words. It is more difficult to write an abstract before you have completed your paper than after you have completed it.

If you have made substantial progress in formulating your topic, generating your thesis and subtopics, and gathering at least some preliminary source material, you should be able to write a short list of the main topics you plan to discuss and the sources you plan to use. Write them down and devote a sentence or two to each of your topics. The result will be an abstract. Devote a sentence or two to summarizing and/or evaluating each source, and the result will be an annotated bibliography.

Some kinds of abstracts come more naturally than others, because of their structure. For example, a review article in psychology may be organized around a statement about the sources reviewed. See Chapters 7 and 8 for more information on how specific disciplines prefer abstracts to be organized. The APA (American Psychological Association) and CBE (Council of Biology Editors) formats require an abstract as one of the preliminary sections of the finished research paper. Abstracts are generally not used in the MLA format unless a journal editor or conference organizer specifically requests one.

USING A SHORT PLAN TO GUIDE YOUR RESEARCH

The main reason for writing a prospectus or other type of short plan at this point is to pull your ideas together as concretely and as specifically as possible. You need to have your controlling purpose firmly in mind, and you need to see whether the sources you have found will enable you to carry out your plan.

The most familiar type of short plan is an outline. However, I will not discuss this underappreciated (perhaps *dreaded* is a more accurate word) method of organization until Chapter 9, "Writing the Rough Draft," because I think that most writers turn out better, fresher work if they *draft* their way toward a pattern of organization that works for them. For most writers, the formal outline works best as a tool used to guide the revising process. If you feel that you work best with a fully developed formal outline in hand, skip forward now and read the sections of Chapter 9 that relate to outlines and how to use them.

An informal outline, though—which may be nothing more than a list of things you intend to discuss—is something that you have probably already started to work on if you have been keeping a research journal. If you haven't yet done so, begin a list of subtopics. Update it and reorganize it periodically. Before long, you will need it to help you control the drafting process. At this point, I am assuming that you have identified most of your sources but have not yet closely studied them. The prospectus is designed to guide you in the next phase of the writing process, which is the highly selective task of gathering information.

■ ■ ■ JOURNAL EXCERPTS

Writing the Prospectus

[What follows are the first portions of the prospectus I drew up at the end of session 6. My preliminary bibliography now included most of the sources I later used in the final draft, so I will omit it here (see Chapter 8).]

Prospectus:

The Decline of Musical Improvisation in the Time of Mozart

Hypothesis:

Although several well-recognized causes contributed to the decline of improvisation, ultimately it died out because musicians came to rely on printed texts--especially instructional treatises and printed scores--rather than on the direct transmission of skills from masters to apprentices.

Description of project:

In the first section of the paper I will describe the decline of improvisation, using Bach, Mozart, and Beethoven as key examples of the transition. I will provide an extended definition of improvisation and distinguish between two main senses in which the word improvisation is used: It can mean either mere ornamentation or fully extemporaneous composition.

After limiting my discussion to extemporaneous composition, I will use baroque and classical keyboard instruction manuals to illustrate how improvisation was taught. I will single out the decline of the thoroughbass technique and the decline of apprenticeship as key causes of the broader decline of the art of improvisation.

■■■ EXERCISE 11

Writing a Prospectus

Use the research material you have already compiled—ideas, journal entries, statement of topic, and preliminary list of sources—to write a prospectus on the basis of this chapter's instructions and examples. Keep the title, thesis, and statement of purpose shorter than two double-spaced pages. The length of the preliminary bibliography (or annotated bibliography) may vary; check with your instructor. Assume that some sources in the preliminary bibliography will probably not be used and that other sources may be added. Assume that your hypothesis and purpose may change as you get deeper into your research.

CHAPTER 6

GATHERING INFORMATION

■ ■ ■ QUICK VIEW

Since this chapter discusses the heart of the research process, I can't suggest that you skip to specific parts of it. Instead, I'll give a short summary of the chapter.

Avoid getting slowed down during the information-gathering stage. Read selectively and actively, questioning your sources.

Evaluate your sources. Use one of several suggested methods for getting secondhand evaluations of sources. Use the list of questions in "Evaluating Sources" later in this chapter to guide your firsthand evaluation of sources.

Find an information-gathering style that works for you, whether it involves note cards, photocopies, word-processing files, or a combination of these. Keep three kinds of files: journal, notes, and bibliography. Use topic headings to organize your notes.

In note taking, quote freely but paraphrase sparingly. In drafting, quote sparingly but paraphrase freely.

Practice writing various sorts of notes, including summaries. Learn to spot the qualities of a good paraphrase and to apply the two tests that prevent plagiarism in a paraphrase.

Consider the advantages of using word processing, computerized databases, and computerized card files. Use downloads and photocopies to save time and to produce more accurate treatments of source material.

ACTIVE READING

Although research is hard work, it is tempting to prolong the information-gathering stage in order to delay the more stressful drafting stage. With strong motivations for delay, a researcher can easily fall into the trap of gathering information without thinking enough about what the information is for.

Avoid the trap. Gathering sources and taking notes on them is not enough; your information gathering should remain highly focused. At every moment, you must be working toward developing the argument of your paper. Chapter 3 discussed the need for argumentation, but it is time to bring up this point again. If you hope to develop an argument, you must be an active reader, which means that you must question and analyze what you read.

Questioning and Analyzing

Highlighting paragraph after paragraph of source material is a common— and often useless—way of trying to be an active reader. Highlighting can help you read actively only if you highlight selectively and later analyze the high- lighted portions carefully. A good way to condense a complicated source is to highlight only the main ideas and then review them by marking them to indicate their relative degrees of importance: perhaps three stars next to the article's main idea, two stars for important subpoints, and one star for key examples. Color coding is another way of organizing your responses: green marks in the margin next to key passages, red marks next to quotable ones, and so on.

However, selective highlighting may accomplish only one of the two main jobs of the active reader: analyzing. The other main job is reading critically or resistantly, which means that as you read, you should be questioning your sources, noting inconsistencies, finding connections, raising objections, and thinking of possible ways of supporting or refuting the source's points. If you use photocopies, record your critical ideas in the margins next to the passages you are challenging. If you use note cards, record your questions or remarks beneath the passages you are summarizing, paraphrasing, or quoting. (In this book the term *note card* refers to a card used to record information drawn from sources. The term *bibliography card* refers to a card used to record the author, title, and publication data of a source.)

It is important to record your questions and objections right away. Since you will have dozens of other things to think about as you work on your paper, you may later forget some of your most original and independent thoughts. In writ- ing my paper on improvisation, for instance, I found that I constantly felt over- whelmed by the experts, so it was reassuring to note some logical fallacies in their arguments when I looked at their writings carefully. In trying to establish your own argument, you have to find a new approach to a subject "owned" by the experts; every researcher thus feels a bit like David going up against Goliath. Counterarguments are too precious to forget. Store each one for future use.

An Example of Active Reading

In an introductory science course, Mark Gibson was given the assignment of writing a library research paper in which he had to take one side or the other in a current scientific controversy. He decided to investigate cold fusion, a topic much written about in recent years. His research question was, "Is cold fusion possible?" His initial hypothesis was that the early reports of successful cold fusion reactions had been based on flawed experiments. Much of the literature that he found on cold fusion was either oversimplified or too technical, but then he found an article that seemed to address his research question quite directly in nontechnical language. It was called "Pariah Science: Whatever Happened to Cold Fusion?" and it appeared in the *American Scholar* (63 [1994]: 527–541). A contributor's note identified the author, David Goodstein, as vice provost and professor of physics at the California Institute of Technology. The author of *States of Matter* and the creator of the PBS television series *The Mechanical Universe*, Goodstein is clearly a reputable authority with a gift for making difficult issues comprehensible. Figure 6.1 reproduces a few pages from Goodstein's article. Passages that Mark analyzed closely show his handwritten comments in the margins.

Notice how Mark responds to the text by identifying key statements, raising objections, exploring implications and unstated assumptions, outlining subpoints, highlighting quotable passages, spotting points for further research, and summarizing the article's argument. On the article's page 540, Mark notices and focuses carefully on the article's key point: The crucial question is whether the excess heat supposedly generated by cold fusion can be produced reliably and predictably by experimenters. The reliable production of excess heat, it turns out, may depend upon the amount of deuterium that is loaded into the palladium reactor plates. Thus, Goodstein begins his article by stating clearly that cold fusion is impossible, but he ends it by suggesting that cold fusion may be possible after all. Mark notices this pattern and makes marginal comments drawing attention to it.

Although Mark's first goal is to understand a fairly difficult subject, some of his comments show that he is reading skeptically and resistantly. One comment explores an ambiguous implication in the article: Goodstein doesn't directly say whether he is one of "those who believe that there is serious science going on here" or whether he regards cold fusion research as "crackpot" science. Finally, Mark's last comments suggest that he may be able to make the potentially huge topic of cold fusion more manageable by focusing just on the question of deuterium saturation levels; he has made a note to find sources dealing with the Japanese and American studies mentioned at the end of Goodstein's article.

EVALUATING SOURCES

As you make photocopies and take notes, you should constantly try to see which sources on your topic are most reliable. This process of constant evaluation is another aspect of reading critically. Remember to record your evaluations; for research writing your job is to record information *and* to weigh and sift it. You can record evaluative comments about the virtues and shortcomings of your sources on bibliography cards, on note cards, on photocopies, or in your research journal. Some of these comments may later lead to useful arguments.

Another reason to record evaluations is to save time. Especially in the early stages of information gathering, you are likely to be looking at many sources in a hurry, trying to see whether they are credible and relevant to your topic. Write down your responses to remind yourself why you decided to use or not to use a particular source. Avoid backtracking.

PARIAH SCIENCE
Whatever Happened to Cold Fusion?

DAVID GOODSTEIN

The Fourth International Conference on Cold Fusion took place on the island of Maui, in Hawaii, December 6–9, 1993. It had all the trappings of a normal scientific meeting. Two hundred and fifty scientists took part, mostly from the U.S. and Japan (hence the site in Hawaii), but also a sprinkling from Italy, France, Russia, China, and other countries. More than 150 scientific papers were presented on subjects such as calorimetry, nuclear theory, materials, and so on. The founders of the field, Stanley Pons and Martin Fleischmann, both of the University of Utah, were in attendance and were treated with the deference due their celebrity status. Pons and Fleischmann carry out their research today in a laboratory built for them in Nice, on the French Riviera, by Technova, a subsidiary of Toyota. At the meeting it was announced that the Japanese trade ministry, MITI, has committed $30 million over a period of four years to support research on what was delicately called "New Hydrogen Energy," including Cold Fusion.

Contrary to appearances, however, this was no normal scientific conference. Cold Fusion is a pariah field, cast out by the scientific establishment. Between Cold Fusion and respectable science there is virtually no communication at all. Cold Fusion papers are almost never published in refereed scientific journals, with the result that those works don't receive the normal critical scrutiny that science requires. On the other hand, because the Cold Fusioners see themselves as a community under siege, there is little internal criticism. Experiments and theories tend to be accepted at face value, for fear of providing even more fuel for external critics, if anyone outside the group is bothering to listen. In these circumstances, crackpots flourish, making matters worse for those who believe that there is serious science going on here.

Inadequate peer review for cold fusion research.

Is Goodstein objective?

527

So some cold fusion research is well done? Does Goodstein believe there is "serious" science in this field?

FIGURE 6.1 Annotated Pages from Goodstein's Article

There are two kinds of source evaluations: independent and secondhand. Chapter 4, "Finding Sources," discussed several methods of secondhand evaluation; and by the time you have reached the information-gathering stage, you have probably already used some of them. For example, by now you should have asked a knowledgeable authority, such as your instructor or an expert on your

PARIAH SCIENCE

leaves tritium behind, and *c* the one where the helium 4 remains intact. In conventional nuclear physics, fusion results about half the time in *a*, half the time in *b*, and one millionth of the time in *c*. To account for the observations reported, with some consistency, by various researchers in Cold Fusion, fusion inside a metal would nearly always result in reaction *c* (without, however, emitting a gamma ray). One in every hundred thousand or so reactions would result in *b*, and the probability of a reaction *a* would be smaller by yet another factor of a hundred thousand. These are the conditions needed to explain why Cold Fusion cells can generate power at the rate of watts, for periods of days or months, while, far short of killing Pons and Fleischmann, still yield barely detectable traces of neutrons, and only tiny amounts of tritium.

Does metal alter fusion reaction? No. Three reasons: (1) distance (2) time (3) energy release

It is plausible that the nuclear reaction might be altered radically when it takes place among the atoms in a metal, rather than in a rarefied atmosphere? The answer, quite simply, is no. For one thing, the atomic nucleus is so small compared to the distances between atoms in a metal that for all practical purposes, the nucleus is always in a near vacuum. For another thing, events occur so quickly in the nuclear fusion reaction that the metal is simply unable to respond. If you like orders of magnitude, the fastest anything can happen in a metallic crystal is nine orders of magnitude slower than the typical time in which the nucleus created by fusing deuterium plays out its drama of fusion and breakup. When the nucleus is doing its thing, the atoms of the crystal are far away and frozen in time. Finally, the energy released in the nuclear reaction is so large that the crystal has no means to absorb it, unless it is spread out instantaneously, over vast distances, by some mechanism not now known (presumably, the same mechanism would have to account for why no gamma ray is emitted). According to everything we know about the behavior of matter and nuclei, Cold Fusion is impossible. This is what I meant when I said that Cold Fusion is an experiment whose result is contrary to prevailing theory.

Quote: cold fusion is impossible.

In spite of all that, scientists are aware that they must be prepared, from time to time, to be surprised by a phenomenon they previously thought to be impossible. There are two recent examples that seem relevant to Cold Fusion. One is called High Temperature Superconductivity, and the other is called the Mössbauer Effect.

But the "impossible" can happen. 2 examples.

533

FIGURE 6.1 Annotated Pages from Goodstein's Article *(continued)*

PARIAH SCIENCE

Heat from chemical reaction, not fusion?

Another objection that had been raised was that, if heat was generated in these experiments, it was the result of some uninteresting chemical process rather than the result of nuclear fusion. Chemical processes that generate heat are not uncommon in electrolysis experiments. The strongest argument for nuclear fusion (given the near absence of the neutrons and tritium) was that the amount of heat generated was far too large to be due to any chemical process. That would be true, the critics replied, if the chemicals were being generated at the same time as the heat. But all these Cold Fusion cells had long dormant periods during which energy was being pumped in and no excess heat was being produced. The heat finally liberated in the Cold Fusion episodes might just have been chemical energy stored up during the dormant periods. The cells were not producing more energy than was being put into them; they were just storing up energy and releasing it in bursts. Not only would that be much less exciting than a discovery of controlled nuclear fusion, it also wouldn't be of much help in our struggle against the oil barons. Now this argument could be countered as well: there were what appeared to be very careful experiments in which the total amount of energy consumed during the dormant periods was minuscule compared to the amount of heat liberated during the active periods.

No-heat excesive.

But may be stored chemical energy.

Identify "careful" experiments.

Lack of controls.

Finally, one of the most damaging criticisms of Pons and Fleischmann was that they had failed to do control experiments. Nuclear fusion (if it occurred) should only have been possible (if it were possible) when electrolysis was done in heavy water, made of deuterium. It should not be possible using ordinary water, made of ordinary hydrogen. Now many groups, including Franco's, had done the necessary control experiments and obtained the necessary confirming results (no heat in the controls).

Inconsistent results with controls.

Unfortunately, other groups reported that they did observe excess heat in experiments done with ordinary light water. Franco dutifully reported these results at the Rome seminar, expressing only muted disapproval ("In my opinion, these results have not been consolidated," he said).

All of this was much less important than the fact that Cold Fusion experiments, if they gave positive results at all, gave them only sporadically and unpredictably. When Bednorz and Mueller announced the discovery of high-temperature superconductivity in 1986, no one carped

539

FIGURE 6.1 Annotated Pages from Goodstein's Article *(continued)*

about control experiments because, once the recipe was known, any competent scientist could make a sample and test it and it would work immediately. If, at their press conference, Pons and Fleischmann had given a dependable recipe for producing excess heat, they very likely would be Nobel Prize winners now (as Bednorz and Mueller are) rather than intellectual outcasts from the community of scientists. The essential key to the return of Cold Fusion to scientific respectability is to find the missing ingredient that would make the recipe work every time.

Quote: Key is consistent ability to produce heat.

Experiments done in the U.S. and in Japan, which were reported at the Maui meeting, indicate that the missing ingredient may have been found. In all the various Cold Fusion experiments, the first step is to load deuterium into the body of metallic palladium. The issue is how much deuterium gets into the metal. The ratio of the number of atoms of deuterium in the metal to the number of atoms of palladium is called x. It turns out, by means of electrolysis, or by putting the metal in deuterium gas, that it is rather easy to get x up to the range of about 0.6 or 0.7. That is already a startlingly high figure. If there are almost as many deuterium atoms as palladium atoms in the material, the density of deuterium (a form of hydrogen) is essentially equal to that of liquid hydrogen rocket fuel, which can ordinarily exist only at extreme low temperatures. In other words, palladium (and certain other metals including titanium) soak up almost unbelievable amounts of hydrogen or deuterium if given the chance. This is far from a new discovery. However, according to the experiments reported at Maui, x=0.6 or 0.7 is not enough to produce Cold Fusion. Both the American and Japanese groups showed data indicating there is a sharp threshold at x=0.85. Below that value (which can only be reached with great difficulty and under favorable circumstances) excess heat is never observed. But, once x gets above that value, excess heat is essentially always observed, according to the reports presented at Maui and recounted by Franco Scaramuzzi in his seminar at the University of Rome.

Find Sources.

The missing key: deuterium levels. So cold fusion is possible after all?

Above deuterium threshold, results are consistent.

The audience at Rome, certainly the senior professors who were present, listened politely, but they did not hear what Franco was saying—that much became clear from the questions that were asked at the end of the seminar and comments that were made afterward. If they went

540

FIGURE 6.1   Annotated Pages from Goodstein's Article *(continued)*

topic, for guidance in finding information. You should have looked at some standard encyclopedia articles to get an overview of your topic, and in doing so, you may have found a list of standard sources. You may have identified the author of an encyclopedia article as an authority in the field. As you compiled your preliminary bibliography and scanned your sources, you probably noticed that certain names cropped up repeatedly, and you recognized these names as standard authorities.

Book reviews are excellent sources of secondhand evaluations. A researcher often does not have time to track down reviews, but a crucial, central source may deserve this extra effort. A book review can yield surprising dividends, such as objections and refutations that can help you develop your argument. You can find book reviews by using the *Book Review Index*, the *Book Review Digest*, the *Readers' Guide to Periodical Literature* (where reviews are indexed separately at the end of each volume), and other, more specialized indexes. (See "Bibliographies, Indexes, Abstracts, and Electronic Databases" in Chapter 4)

Even better than individual book reviews are *review articles*, when you can find them. Scholarly publishers often invite authorities to review a set of sources on a single topic, and a review article of this sort enables a beginning researcher to survey a broad range of scholarship in a single brief reading. For example, in a course on literary research methods, I ask my students to identify the best available biography of John Keats, the most comprehensive discussion of all the known Keats manuscripts, the most fully annotated edition of Keats's poems, and the definitive edition of Keats's letters. This assignment can take hours to carry out unless the student has paid close attention to what I've said about the need for a rapid and comprehensive overview of a subject area. Then the answer is quite simple: Frank Jordan's *English Romantic Poets: A Review of Research*, 4th edition (New York: MLA, 1985), which I place on reserve for the class, announces by its very title that it is a collection of review articles. The article on Keats scholarship is by Jack Stillinger, and a glance at any library catalog will reveal that Stillinger is one of the most important Keats scholars of the twentieth century. In a concise article of about fifty pages (with subheadings that allow one to scan it selectively in about thirty minutes), Stillinger elegantly summarizes Keats scholarship to 1985 and identifies all the books I mentioned. For evaluations of Keats scholarship since 1985, one may consult the review of research known as *Year's Work in English Studies*. (See "Bibliographies, Indexes, Abstracts, and Electronic Databases—Literature" in Chapter 4.)

Not all questions about sources can be handled neatly by means of secondhand evaluations, but you can always use the other approach: evaluating the source independently. Chapter 3, "Generating an Argument," described several ways of evaluating and challenging a source's argument. Here is a list of additional questions to ask when independently evaluating potential sources.

> ### QUESTIONS TO ASK WHEN EVALUATING SOURCES
> 1. Is the author well qualified as an expert on this topic?
> 2. Is the author frequently cited by other authorities?

3. Does the author cite the most important research?

4. Do the author's credentials (as revealed by a search for a biographical article in, say, *Contemporary Authors* or one of the *Who's Who* volumes) suggest that he or she is a reputable authority on this topic?

5. Do the author's other publications (as revealed in a library catalog or in periodical indexes) suggest that he or she is an expert on this topic?

6. Is the work current and up to date?

7. Am I using the latest available edition?

8. Has the work been published by a reputable printing house or journal?

Remember that no secondhand evaluations are absolutely reliable; the ultimate test is your own independent judgment. In my classes on research I routinely use exercises in evaluating wretched works by good authors. As an example, I use a book written by a world-renowned scholar and published by a world-famous university press—a book so ill informed, so fraught with errors, and so badly conceived that it truly did not deserve to be printed. It shall remain nameless here; the moral of the story is simply that in evaluating this book, some students are taken in by the author's credentials and the prestige of the university press, but others carefully examine its contents and find thoughtful reviews by experts who point out the blunders. Even in relying upon secondhand evaluations, these students are critical readers. Emulate them.

NOTE-TAKING METHODS

It is impossible to identify one best way to take notes for a research paper, because people vary in their learning styles and because the tools of research change at an incredible pace. You must decide for yourself what methods and tools work best for you. This section, however, offers some general guidelines that may help you find a successful research style as quickly as possible.

Your information-gathering method should represent a compromise between two potentially conflicting goals. On the one hand, you want a method that is systematic and orderly enough to prevent you from making time-wasting mistakes. On the other hand, you want a system that is flexible and adaptable enough to allow you to change your ideas and plan of organization as the paper develops, grows, and changes.

If you tend to be systematic anyway, you will be comfortable using the traditional one-idea-per-note-card method of compiling information. But to avoid being locked in by your tendency for structure, also be sure to keep a free-form research journal in which you try some free associating, listing, and other unstructured approaches to your topic. If you tend to be disorganized, you may feel comfortable filling your research journal with random lists of bright ideas and questions. But you need to be especially careful to develop some systematic habits by keeping your notes organized and by making yourself write a series of tentative outlines to keep yourself on task.

THREE TYPES OF FILE:
Journal, Notes, Bibliography

To help your research paper develop, you need a private space in which you can mull over the topic, express frustrations, jot down bright (and dumb) ideas, and generally grapple with the job without feeling that you are writing for anyone but yourself. The *research journal*—which can be kept on sheets of paper, on index cards, or in a word-processing file—fills this need. Don't think that the research journal is just time-consuming busywork that will lengthen your job; it is guaranteed to improve the speed and quality of your work, even if it sometimes *seems* to take a little extra time. Keeping the journal will help give your paper its creative edge, that extra something that makes your paper more than just another rehash of source material.

The key advantage of keeping a journal is that *no one is listening*. You can be yourself. This genuineness will find its way into the more public, more formal writing that you're doing for the research paper itself.

Your *notes* are primarily your borrowings from sources. They may take the form of note cards, marked photocopies, and files on computer disks. No matter how you organize them, your method of handling notes should ensure that they meet several goals. They should be (1) accurate, (2) easy to retrieve, and (3) easy to organize and reorganize during the drafting process.

Although most research writing manuals urge you to record your notes by writing on cards, recording one idea per card, many students end up having to work with a combination of materials, including books, photocopies, disk files, and printouts. If your research paper is going to be complex, you should consider transferring all your notes to note cards, because they are easiest to handle during the drafting stage. But if your paper is going to be short and fairly manageable, you may prefer to work directly from marked photocopies.

Your list of sources is the one part of the research project that you really must record on index cards, for the reasons discussed in Chapter 4, "Finding Sources." Keep your *bibliography cards* in a separate file. One good way to keep your cards clearly separated is to use 4 × 6-inch cards for notes and 3 × 5-inch cards for bibliography entries.

USING TOPIC HEADINGS
TO ORGANIZE YOUR NOTES

Topic headings are the key to making notes easy to retrieve and to reorganize. Just as a Library of Congress subject heading allows you to retrieve a book on your topic, subject headings of your own allow you to retrieve and organize your research material during drafting. Either during the note-taking stage or later, you should record a subject heading above each quotation, fact, paraphrase, or summary. Leave blank space above and below the heading so that you can rephrase it later if you need to. (I prefer to leave some blank space at the top of each card so that I can assign subject headings later; I find that pausing to think of descriptive phrases slows me down during the note-taking process.)

Notes on cards should be written in ink rather than in pencil. You are using cards to make the information easy to sort and shuffle; but as you shuffle cards written in pencil, they will become illegible. Subject headings, however, may be written in pencil to make them easy to revise later.

Be sure to label cards by recording the author (plus a short title if necessary) and page number at the top of each card. You will still want to add subject headings later; an author/page number heading by itself is not very helpful during the organizing and drafting stages.

AVOIDING PLAGIARISM:
Quoting, Paraphrasing, and Summarizing

When you *quote* from a source, you copy its exact words, enclosed by quotation marks to indicate the borrowing. When you *paraphrase*, you express the content of a passage in your own language, using about the same number of words as the original. When you *summarize*, you express the content of the source using far fewer words than the original.

Most notes are quotations and paraphrases, but summary notes can be very useful. For instance, a source such as an article that is only marginally relevant to your topic may end up being discussed in just a sentence or two of your paper. A note summarizing the entire article can be directly incorporated into your paper, and it can also be used in compiling an annotated bibliography, if your instructor should assign one. Summary notes should be written immediately after you finish reading an article for the first time. If you must use many brief sources for your paper, summary notes can save you a lot of time later in figuring out who argued what.

Should You Quote or Paraphrase?

Most writing manuals urge research writers to take notes by paraphrasing source material rather than recording direct quotations, for two reasons: First, writing down direct quotations can lead to passive information collecting, whereas paraphrasing encourages active, critical reading by forcing you to put everything in your own words. Second, since a paraphrase is expressed in your own words, it is easy to fit it into the body of your paper; thus, paraphrasing during note taking will speed up the drafting process later. Both reasons are valid. If you are confident in your skill of paraphrasing, use that skill during your note taking, if you like—though I suggest that you first review this chapter's section on paraphrasing techniques (pp. 138–143).

I think that it is both safer and more efficient, however, to record direct quotations, not paraphrases, during the note-taking stage. Here's why: Although paraphrased notes may save time during drafting, they slow the note-taking process. Writing a quotation is easy and quick, but writing a paraphrase can be slow and difficult, especially if the vocabulary of the original source contains many words for which synonyms do not readily come to mind. Also, you later will probably discard some of your notes, either because the direction of your argument has shifted or because you have found better source material. Would you rather discard a direct quotation that cost you only a moment's work or a paraphrase that cost you a laborious five minutes of searching for words and phrases?

Besides speed and efficiency, there is one more important reason for using quotations rather than paraphrases during note taking. Let's say that you have paraphrased a few passages from a newspaper article that you consulted in the library on a microfilm reader. The article had only a few useful items in it, so you didn't print out a hard copy. Later, in drafting your paper, you discover that your paraphrase is clumsily expressed. So you paraphrase your paraphrase to make it more graceful—and in the process, you commit inadvertent plagiarism, because in your new paraphrase you unwittingly use phrases identical to phrases in the original source. Make no mistake about it: Once you have paraphrased a source, you are committed to using your paraphrase. If you tinker with it later, you have no way of knowing how closely your changes will approximate the now-unavailable original.

Contrast this situation with what happens if you have recorded a direct quotation from the same source. During drafting you can tinker with your paraphrase as much as you like to make it fit better in your paper. This revising may slow the drafting process just a bit. But this disadvantage is more than offset by the advantages of avoiding plagiarism and gaining speed during note taking and flexibility during drafting.

But remember that the final draft will use quotations very sparingly. Here is a rule of thumb for adjusting the ratios of notes and paraphrases in the two stages of writing your paper.

During Note Taking	*During Drafting*
Quote freely.	Quote sparingly.
Paraphrase sparingly.	Paraphrase freely.

Now, here are some guidelines about what to record when you are taking notes and what to quote in your final paper.

What to Record During Note Taking
1. For detailed notes on crucial sources
   a. Thesis sentence
   b. Most important topic sentences
   c. Evidence or opinion supporting your argument

    d. Evidence or opinion contradicting your argument

    e. Any passage you intend to argue with or analyze

    f. Any passage that is strikingly well expressed or colorful

    g. Quotation marks around words or phrases that are borrowed

    h. Words acknowledging borrowing of ideas you've paraphrased ("Smith argues," "Jones points out," and the like)

    i. Author and page number (plus short title if you are using more than one source by that author)

2. For summaries of brief or less crucial sources

    a. Entire argument of source

    b. Any passage in which the main ideas are relevant to your topic but the details are not

    c. Author and page numbers (plus short title if you are using more than one source by that author)

What to Quote in the Paper Itself

1. Well-written, striking passages

2. Passages you intend to refute or analyze at length

What Not to Quote in the Paper Itself

1. Passages that are not striking and well written

2. Long passages that you do not refute or analyze at length

Developing the Skill of Paraphrasing

If you follow my advice, you will be doing most of your paraphrasing during the drafting stage. But since you will still probably need to do at least some paraphrasing during the note-taking stage, now is the best time to discuss this subject. If you find yourself struggling with paraphrasing later when you are drafting your paper, return to this section and review it.

The Uses and Advantages of Paraphrases   The main reason a research writer paraphrases is to assimilate source material into a consistent, flowing body of prose that is clearly under the writer's control. A research paper overloaded with quotations is like lumpy pudding; it needs more blending. Most readers are distracted by the stylistic shifts that occur when too many quotations appear in succession. If your draft contains many quotations, check with your instructor. Avoid even the appearance of padding or excessive borrowing.

The advantages of paraphrasing are fourfold.

WHAT A GOOD PARAPHRASE CAN DO

1. A paraphrase may be better expressed than the original.

2. A paraphrase can highlight some features of the original source's argument while subordinating unwanted distractions.

> 3. A paraphrase can compare and contrast rival theories and interpretations.
> 4. A paraphrase can point out connections between sources that the reader might not notice otherwise.

In virtually every academic discipline, the modern preference (in contrast to the abundant quoting that was common fifty years ago) is for the smooth incorporation of research material by means of paraphrase and summary. Remember, though, to *quote only colorful or strikingly well written passages, unless you must quote for some other special reason.*

A good paraphrase has three qualities.

> **WHAT A GOOD PARAPHRASE MUST DO**
>
> 1. A good paraphrase will accurately convey the content of the original passage without any significant distortion of meaning.
> 2. A good paraphrase will clearly acknowledge the source of the borrowed material and the nature of the borrowing.
> 3. A good paraphrase will *entirely recast* the language of the original source.

Occasionally, you may not be able to find substitutes for phrases in the original. In such rare cases, borrowed phrases that are *routine and not unique or expressive* need not be set off with quotation marks. But in all other cases, follow this principle:

> A paraphrase should borrow neither the words nor the overall structure of the original.

Paraphrasing Techniques   A few fortunate writers have a natural ability to paraphrase concisely and gracefully, but most find it hard to develop this skill. A good paraphrase can't be created mechanically or written haphazardly; it must be worked over. One approach is to read a passage carefully; then turn aside and try to express its meaning in your own words. This method will work well if you practice it, but remember that it is incomplete *unless you pause to compare your paraphrase with the original word by word and phrase by phrase.* You may be surprised at how many words and phrases from the original you have unconsciously borrowed. These are all bits of unintentional plagiarism.

To avoid plagiarism, practice the following alternative technique. Since a paraphrase must use new words and new sentence structures, go through the original passage and substitute synonyms for all the key words. Then shift phrases and clauses so that the paraphrase has a new structure as well as new word choices. This method calls for some hard work, but it is worth practicing. It will, at least at first, produce some really clumsy paraphrases; later, though, it will make you an expert paraphraser.

Let's apply some paraphrasing techniques to a specific passage. I've intentionally chosen an abstract statement to show how complex the process of paraphrasing can become. Bear in mind that the meaning of this or any other sentence normally is clarified by a surrounding context that makes paraphrasing a bit easier than it may seem here. Here is the original passage, from page 32 of David H. Miles's "Lukacs' *Theory of the Novel*" (*PMLA* 94 [1979]: 22–35).

> Hegel, as we know, attributed the passing of classical Greek realism to the rise of Christianity, in particular to the profound inwardness of the Gospels.

Now, here is a paraphrase that a student produced by reading the original and then expressing the idea in his own words.

> As David H. Miles points out, Hegel attributed the passing of ancient
>
> Greek realism to the coming of Christian belief, especially the deeply
>
> inward belief expressed in the Gospels.

This paraphrase violates Miles's intellectual property rights. The student writer has only lightly retouched the original wording without properly acknowledging the indebtedness. Notice that giving credit to Miles does not eliminate the plagiarism; the writer says that he has borrowed from Miles, but he doesn't indicate the *nature* or the *extent* of the borrowing. There are no quotation marks to indicate the passages that were stolen (probably accidentally), but the phrases "attributed the passing of" and "Greek realism to the" are direct thefts. Of course, quotation marks should not enclose such routine and unquoteworthy language as "attributed the passing of," but the student *should not have borrowed the language in the first place*. The words should have been entirely recast. Also notice that the overall sentence structure of the original has been left intact in the paraphrase, and some borrowed words have simply changed grammatical form. "Inwardness" has become "inward," for example.

Although one can argue that "Greek realism to the" is such routine phrasing that it is not worth anything and thus can hardly be stolen, remember the following rule of paraphrasing.

> If identical wording can be avoided, it should be—always.

Accidental borrowings are the sign of sloppy scholarship, at best, and academic dishonesty at worst. Even if an example of plagiarism is inadvertent and innocent, it must be treated as a serious offense. Why? Because those who intentionally plagiarize almost always defend their dishonesty by claiming that it is inadvertent! Most plagiarists cite the sources from which they have stolen so that they can then argue that the borrowings were unintentional. ("Surely if I had meant to steal, I would have covered my tracks!" is the usual argument.)

Unless you are very experienced at handling sources, you should not trust your ability to avoid unintentional plagiarism. Instead, systematically double-check each paraphrase to make sure that it passes both of the following tests:

> **TEST 1 FOR PARAPHRASING**
>
> The key terms in the original sentence have been replaced by synonyms.

Here is a list of synonyms for the Miles quotation.

attributed = ascribed, identified the cause of

passing = end, demise

classical = ancient

rise = advent, coming

Christianity = Christian faith

profound = deep

inwardness = introspection

Gospels = Gospels

Note that some *individual* words, such as *Gospels* here, may be irreplaceable. But you can still generally avoid any duplication of phrases, which are strings of two or more words.

If you merely substitute the listed synonyms without changing the structure of the sentence, you get something like this:

> Hegel identified the cause of the demise of Greek realism as the
>
> coming of the Christian faith, and more specifically the deeply
>
> introspective faith expressed in the Gospels.

Now, closely compare this paraphrase with the original phrasing by Miles.

> Hegel, as we know, attributed the passing of classical Greek realism to the rise of Christianity, in particular to the profound inwardness of the Gospels.

Notice that the paraphrase does not directly borrow phrases, but the structure of the sentence is still taken directly from Miles. This dependence upon Miles's syntax makes the word substitution paraphrase a form of borderline plagiarism. To make the paraphrase completely the writer's own, the word order must be changed.

Notice, too, that the word substitution paraphrase is longer and clumsier than Miles's sentence. The paraphrase retains one of the original passage's flaws, which is the ugly pileup of little connectors: cause *of,* demise *of, as* the coming, *of* the Christian faith, *in* the Gospels.

> **TEST 2 FOR PARAPHRASING**
>
> The sentence structure of the original has been recast.

Whenever possible, the paraphrase should also improve the style of the original. Thus, you should apply the editing principles discussed in Chapter 11. In the sample paraphrase we've been discussing, the writer should aim for a reduction in the number of weak preposition connectors.

Recasting means presenting the main items in a different order. Here is a condensed version of the word substitution paraphrase, with the sentence's main ideas numbered.

1	2	3	4
Hegel	identified	the cause of the demise	of Greek

5	6
realism	as the coming of the Christian faith,	especially the

7	
introspective faith	expressed in the Gospels.

To recast it, we put the items in a different order. In recasting, we may have to change a few words; so it is wise to check to make sure that the changes do not result in inadvertent echoes of the original. Here is a recasting of the paraphrase.

1	2	5	6
Hegel	felt that	the coming of the Christian faith,	especially

7	3
the introspective faith	expressed in the Gospels,	caused the

4	
demise	of Greek realism.

Now the sentence structure and the word choices are all new; only the idea has been borrowed from Miles. Furthermore, the paraphrase does what it is supposed to do: It improves the original, since it has promoted the crucial historical event (the coming of Christianity) to the position of grammatical subject. It also contains only three prepositions instead of five.

Still, something is missing in the paraphrase. What is it? If you focus on the ethics of using sources, its omission should be glaring.

In this final version of the paraphrase, the crucial element has been inserted.

```
Hegel felt that the coming of the Christian faith, especially the

introspective faith expressed in the Gospels, caused the demise of

Greek realism (Miles 32).
```

The element that was missing was acknowledgment of indebtedness to Miles, along with a page number that will allow another researcher to retrace your steps.

In the example we just analyzed, a parenthetical reference to Miles is enough, because it is clear that the writer is expressing an idea by Hegel that Miles refers to. But writers should avoid puzzling the reader by sprinkling parenthetical citations into a passage in which they paraphrase extensively without indicating the nature of their borrowings. Here is an example of confusing parenthetical citations.

> Scientists and social scientists are being drawn together by the rapidly growing new field of research known as psychoneuro-immunology, or PNI for short (Gelman and Hager 89). American medical scientists generally are coming to accept the idea that positive thinking can advance the healing process (Cowley et al. 90). Popular books by Arthur J. Barsky, Joan Borysenko, Blair Justice, Robert Ornstein, and David Sobel argue that readers can achieve good health by doing things that make them feel good (Monmaney).

These parenthetical citations leave many questions unanswered. Are Gelman and Hager the inventors of the term *psychoneuroimmunology* or of the abbreviation *PNI*? Or did they write something about the field's drawing scientists and social scientists together? Did Cowley and coauthors assert that positive thinking can advance the healing process? Or did they point out that American medical science is starting to accept this idea? And what is the connection between Monmaney and the list of authors of popular books on this subject?

Because a paraphrase is a more ambiguous type of borrowing than a direct quotation, a paraphrase often has to be explained by a brief, clear statement about the nature of the borrowing. Here is the same paragraph, with in-text acknowledgments (they are underlined to highlight them) that clarify the nature of the borrowing.

> Gelman and Hager point out that scientists and social scientists are being drawn together by the rapidly growing new field of research known as psychoneuroimmunology, or PNI for short (89). The idea that positive thinking can advance the healing process "is becoming a truism in American medicine" (Cowley et al. 90). Several popular books by Arthur J. Barsky, Joan Borysenko, Blair Justice, Robert Ornstein, and David Sobel argue that readers can achieve good health by doing things that make them feel good, says reviewer Terence Monmaney.

If every sentence begins with a phrase such as "Smith argues" or "Jones points out," however, the result is monotony. In the preceding example, I tried to avoid this problem in a couple of ways: by moving the reference to Monmaney to the end of the sentence (with no page reference because the source is only one page long) and by introducing a direct quotation in the middle sentence. I liked the conciseness of the word *truism*, but I felt that quoting the word by itself might seem to indicate that the word was being used sarcastically or in some other special sense. Thus, I quoted an entire phrase.

The sources for this paragraph, typed in the MLA format, would look like this in a list of works cited.

> Cowley, Geoffrey, Lisa Brown, Judy Howard, and Ellen Blum Barish. "Learning to Harness the Power of Positive Thinking." <u>Newsweek</u> 7 Nov. 1988: 90–91.
>
> Gelman, David, and Mary Hager. "Body and Soul." <u>Newsweek</u> 7 Nov. 1988: 88–97.
>
> Monmaney, Terence. "A Reader's Guide to Thinking Well." <u>Newsweek</u> 7 Nov. 1988: 97.

SAMPLE JOURNAL ENTRIES, NOTES, AND BIBLIOGRAPHY CARDS

Before we look at some sample notes, let me suggest that you *not* do what some manuals suggest: Do *not* use a special numbering or lettering system to organize your notes. For example, do *not* label your notes with numbers and letters tied to an outline of your paper, because your outline may change. Topic headings are the most flexible way to label notes. Now let's look at some samples from each of the three essential types of files: journal, notes, and bibliography. (I'll display all three types as note cards for the sake of consistency, even though I prefer to use actual cards only for bibliography entries. See p. 134.)

Figure 6.2 shows a sample journal card on which I did some thinking aloud. Figure 6.3 is a note card that uses the one-idea-per-card method. The advantage of using such simple card entries is that every fact, example, or idea can later be shuffled and rearranged during the drafting process.

Figure 6.4 reproduces another type of note card. This note card doesn't summarize an idea or a fact; instead, it serves as a reminder. While reading Collins's article in the *New Grove Dictionary of Music and Musicians*, I ran across an anecdote about Bach's amazing abilities as an improviser; I had seen the same anecdote some years earlier, so I made a note to look it up again, thinking that it might make a good introduction to the paper. Notice that the parenthetical documentation (to Collins, page 42) provides all the information I need to find the original passage in my photocopy of the encyclopedia article. Thus a note card can be a quite brief reminder guiding the retrieval of information from another source, such as a book, photocopy, or word-processing file.

Figure 6.5 shows a sample note card with an analytic comment. Notice that this card raises a question about the source and suggests a possible way of refuting it.

A sample bibliography card is shown in Figure 6.6.

Figure 6.7 reproduces another bibliography card that illustrates other functions. This card contains a check mark in the upper right-hand corner to show that I have verified all of its details for bibliographical accuracy. The brackets

Handbooks versus apprenticeship

Doesn't the very existence of "handbooks" on improvisation in the eighteenth century say something about a shift away from a master-apprentice style of teaching?

Today's jazz improvisation textbooks take the place of the informal apprenticeship system that operated when the big bands were schools for improvisers.

FIGURE 6.2   Sample Journal Card

Libby 50

Nineteenth-century church organists improvised

Improvisation later remained "a required part of the church organist's training" in the nineteenth century, especially in France (Libby 50).

FIGURE 6.3   Sample Note Card Giving One Idea Only

indicate that only the author's middle initial appears on the title page. After noting how the Library of Congress catalog entries list Ferand, I supplied the rest of his middle name, because this information often helps distinguish writers with similar names.

I also made evaluative comments on the card in Figure 6.7. Use such comments on your bibliography cards, because they help you remember which

Collins 42

Bach's Musical Offering—anecdote

Collins (42) mentions the famous story about Bach's Musical Offering that I encountered long ago in an American Scholar article. It might make an interesting introductory anecdote.

FIGURE 6.4 Sample Note Card for Guiding Later Retrieval

decline of composer-improviser

"With the decline of the salon as a center of musical performance, in which improvisation was more at home than in the increasingly formal atmosphere of the concert hall, and of the composer-performer, in whom the art had usually reached its peaks, improvisation gradually died out" (Libby 50).

But this strikes me as puzzlingly circular: improvisation declined because great composers no longer improvised?

FIGURE 6.5 Sample Note Card with Analysis

sources are best. This card also contains the call number (preceded by my school's initials, WSU) to help me locate the book quickly and to remind me that the book is available on campus.

Kopetz, Barry E. "Bach's Fantasia in G: An
    Interpretive Analysis." <u>Instrumentalist</u> 48.1 (1993):
    25–30.

FIGURE 6.6 Sample Bibliography Card

✔

Ferand, Ernest T[homas]. <u>Improvisation in Nine Centuries of</u>
    <u>Western Music: An Anthology with a Historical</u>
    <u>Introduction</u>. Köln: Volk, 1961.

WSU M2 .M94512 no. 12

Ferand's "Historical Introduction" (pp. 5–21) is superb—
perhaps my key source. Gives a fuller explanation of the
decline of improvisation than any of the other sources.

FIGURE 6.7 Sample Annotated Bibliography Card

NOTES ON DISKS

If your typing skills are good, you may prefer to take notes on computer disks rather than on index cards. Since I can type 90 words per minute, I can type notes much faster than I can write them by hand, so I do most of my note taking at the keyboard of my personal computer. However, taking notes on disks ties you to your desk, unless you have a laptop computer that you can carry to the library. Perhaps you will want to use notes on disk just for material that you can take home, such as books. Or perhaps you will want to use notes on disk to condense, summarize, and record details from long photocopied articles. Personal computers give the research writer many note-taking options.

Word-Processing Files

Word processing is the simplest way to record notes on disk. Chapter 9, "Writing the Rough Draft," discusses ways of using notes on disk to speed the writing of your draft. Record all your notes in one long file, and build your paper around this file; or keep separate files for each source, each topic heading, or each note, later pasting these into your draft, one at a time.

Computerized "Card Files"

Some of the most popular types of software let you paste from one application to another. If you know how to use spreadsheet or database software, you might want to record notes, data, or bibliography entries in such applications, especially if your data require sorting or statistical analysis.

Database software lets you design your own way of storing information. You can create a custom template for note cards with as many custom-designed fields, or information slots, as you like. For example, you can create a simple card format with a 50-character field for the subject heading, a 25-character field for the author's last name, and a 1000-character field for notes. The database will then let you search for all the records filed under the name "Williams," or it will alphabetize the records by subject heading, or it will find all the records with the word "plasma" in them.

I have found database software to be very useful for compiling bibliographies, indexes, and lists of all types, including mailing lists. But database software is of limited use in routine note taking.

There are some bibliography databases on the market that can simplify the process of compiling a list of works cited. You simply enter the author's name, the title, and the publication data; the database formats the information (usually in MLA, APA, or another standard format, but not always) and prints the bibliography. Try entering and printing some sample entries before you commit yourself to entering an entire bibliography into this kind of database.

USING THE WEB AND THE PHOTOCOPIER RESPONSIBLY TO AVOID PLAGIARISM

In the 1960s, the indispensable research tool was the packet of note cards; in the 1970s, it was the photocopier; by the 1980s, it was the personal computer; and now it is the modem or high-speed link to the information superhighway. All these tools allow you to have exact quotations from or duplicate copies of your sources at your fingertips. So let us examine the advantages and disadvantages of mechnaical copies, both photocopies and downloads.

When used carelessly or irresponsibly, photocopying leads to sloppy scholarship, even plagiarism. Some college research writers take inadequate notes, do very little planning, use tons of photocopied material, and hurriedly produce papers that are nothing more than badly stitched quilts of clumsily borrowed or plagiarized material.

The information superhighway is going to make the mechanical duplication of information still simpler and the potential for abuse still greater. Once upon a time, plagiarists using photocopied material had to at least retype the stolen passages; today they can use a scanner to digitalize such passages and paste them into a paper.

If you realize that copying source material is only the beginning of the information-gathering process, then you know that you must still select, paraphrase, analyze, challenge, refute, and reinterpret the material you find. Don't let the Web or photocopier lure you into doing sloppy or hasty work. Use these tools responsibly for their practical advantages.

The photocopier's chief advantage is speed. A researcher can quickly skim through sources and make photocopies to study closely later. Another advantage is privacy. Many people who like research don't like working in libraries. Whenever possible, they check out books and make photocopies to use at home—either to mark them in the ways discussed in this chapter or to transfer notes directly to a partial draft or to a research journal. Now that copy cards make it unnecessary for researchers to carry around bags of dimes or quarters, quick information raids into the library have become even more convenient. Just carry a card for photocopies and a disc for downloads!

Another advantage of using the photocopier is the retrievability of copied material. No matter how good you may be at taking notes, in the writing of every paper there are times when your notes omit something crucial. A photocopy lets you return to the original to find what you need. Note cards, on the other hand, force you to return to the library.

In the writing of my paper on improvisation, the advantages of instantly retrievable photocopies were brought home to me repeatedly. For example, at one point in my preliminary draft, I said that Bach taught third-year Latin. A peer evaluator doubted that Bach ever did this. Sure enough, when I consulted my photocopy, I found that my source said that Bach was well enough educated to be *able* to teach third-year Latin; I had misinterpreted this to mean that he had actually taught it. This sort of mistake will creep into even the most careful summaries and paraphrases. Believe me, the mistakes can become even worse, and harder to correct, when you paraphrase notes that are themselves paraphrases from some reading you did weeks earlier. Photocopies may not prevent all such errors, but at least they let you check and recheck your work conveniently.

The final and most persuasive advantage of working from a downloaded file or photocopy is that it reduces labor and prevents mistakes caused by transferring material from card to draft to revised draft. When you take notes from a photocopy directly to a word-processing file, you can check it once very carefully for accuracy. Subsequent pastes and cuts will not introduce typographical errors if you work carefully.

USING INTERVIEWS

Conducting a successful interview is an art. The most important part of the interview is your preparation for it. Carefully record the date and the name of the interview subject, and use a list of questions prepared in advance. Improvise new questions during the interview if your subject brings up something unexpected and interesting.

The nonfiction writer John McPhee is a master at capturing the living voices of his interview subjects, and he never uses a tape recorder. For most of us, however, the recorder is essential for ensuring complete accuracy. We aim never to misquote a printed source, so we should expect no less of ourselves in handling an interview. But since a large tape recorder can be distracting and even intimidating, use an inconspicuous microcassette recorder. And be sure to get your subject's permission to use a recorder.

College and university audiovisual departments often have special recorders, called transcribers, that are activated by a foot pedal. A transcriber automatically backs up a few seconds' worth of tape each time you use the pedal. Thus, you can sit at a word processor and transcribe portions of an interview without having to interrupt yourself by rewinding or adjusting the recorder.

Since you will be quoting your own tape recording or your own notes, you will not document the interview by supplying page numbers or other information. Your bibliography will contain a description of the interview but no information about the interviewee. (See Chapter 7, p. 179.) Nevertheless, during the interview, be sure to collect accurate information about the subject's credentials. In that way, the first time you cite or quote from the interview, you will be able to identify the speaker in a way that clarifies his or her qualifications: "John Doe, a spokesman for Nabisco, said that. . . ." Subsequently, document your source merely by using his or her name in your sentence.

▪▪▪ JOURNAL EXCERPTS
Gathering Information

Session 4

As I expected, the *New Grove Dictionary of Music and Musicians* article on improvisation is superb. It has clarified my thoughts on the subject and has also raised new problems. I need to change my hypothesis to make it fresh.

Session 8

Today I recorded Keller's passage about how "composition was made easy" by thoroughbass, and his words really stuck in my memory. Keller's words might be interpreted to mean that thoroughbass made the *physical* element of improvisation easy. This brings up an entirely new subpoint that not one of my sources (so far) discusses: Thoroughbass helped keyboard players improvise because it made them *feel* the intervals between the notes.

Session 17

It occurred to me more than once that I didn't make clear why apprenticeship would be more successful than another form of teacher-pupil relationship. So I remembered the episode of Quantz's cold: Quantz was the music teacher of Frederick the Great, and he had to be so polite that he could only *cough* to indicate Frederick's musical mistakes. I managed to slip this anecdote in to suggest the limitations, at least in royal or aristocratic households, imposed upon music teachers—limitations that would not apply when they instructed their own apprentices. Maybe the anecdote is not enough to carry this point; but at least it's vivid and funny.

■ ■ ■ EXERCISE 12

Summarizing, Paraphrasing, and Quoting

Here is a paragraph from Edward Rothstein's "Memoirs of a Middle-Class Pianist" (*American Scholar* 48 [1979]: 227–235). The quoted paragraph is from page 229 of the article. After reading Rothstein's paragraph, do the writing requested in items 1–5. Then answer questions 6–10.

> By the middle of the nineteenth century, the piano was as common in the bourgeois household as aspirations for a good marriage. With that class it entered fully into the age of industry and commerce. Pianos had become so numerous, so much in demand, that they were no longer made to order; their construction had itself become an industry. In England, during the instrument's infancy, the Broadwood firm was already producing an average of 400 pianos a year. (They later provided Beethoven with one, which he praised.) By the 1850s that figure grew to 2,300. In Paris, where the Pleyels and Erards had set up shop, Eduard Fétis wrote in 1847, "There is not a home, even of the smallest bourgeois, where one does not find a piano." There were 60,000 instruments in the city.

1. Pretend that you are writing a research paper on the growth of mass production during the nineteenth century. Summarize the paragraph in a single sentence. Cite your source just as you would in writing a research paper in the MLA format.

2. Pretend that you are writing a research paper on the rising living standards of the middle class during the nineteenth century. Summarize the entire paragraph in a single sentence. Cite your source just as you would in writing a research paper in the MLA format. Compare the summary with the one you wrote for question 1.

3. Closely paraphrase the third sentence in the paragraph. Cite your source just as you would in writing a research paper in the MLA format.

4. Write a sentence or two expressing some idea of your own but incorporating one or more of Rothstein's statistics. Cite your source just as you would in writing a research paper in the MLA format.

5. Write a sentence in which you quote a highly effective phrase or sentence by Rothstein. Cite your source just as you would in writing a research paper in the MLA format.

Questions 6–10 ask you to evaluate some unedited examples drawn from student work. Consider the accuracy, style, and mechanics of the examples given.

6. How satisfactory or unsatisfactory is the following sentence as an answer to question 1, and why?

   In response to a rapidly growing middle-class market for pianos, by the mid-1800s many piano manufacturers stopped building these instruments and shifted to mass producing them instead (Rothstein 229).

7. How satisfactory or unsatisfactory is the following sentence as an answer to question 2, and why?

   Rothstein notes that by the middle of the nineteenth century, the piano was a staple in the bourgeois household (229).

8. How satisfactory or unsatisfactory is the following sentence as an answer to question 3, and why?

   The demand for pianos became so great that they were no longer made to order but were becoming mass produced (Rothstein 229).

9. How satisfactory or unsatisfactory is the following sentence as an answer to question 4, and why?

   In England, the bourgeois class encouraged the production of pianos. 400 (Rothstein 229) pianos were produced each year.

10. How satisfactory or unsatisfactory is the following sentence as an answer to question 5, and why?

    The piano has become "as common . . . as aspirations for a good marriage" by the middle of the nineteenth century, according to Edward Rothstein.

■■■ EXERCISE 13

Evaluating a Print Source

1. Without looking at the book itself, write a short paragraph evaluating the book *Jonathan Swift* by A. L. Rowse. First, write a few sentences based on the evaluation questions listed on pages 132–133. Then find some reviews of Rowse's book. Look up the reviewers in a library catalog and/or index to see which reviewers are authorities on Swift. (*Hints:* Be sure to find out who wrote the standard, authoritative modern biography of Swift. It is a substantial piece of work, three volumes long. Look for a review by this scholar.)

To find indexes to book reviews, see Chapter 4, "Bibliographies, Indexes, Abstracts, and Electronic Databases." Look under "General." If you use the *Readers' Guide to Periodical Literature*, notice that book reviews are listed separately at the end of each volume.

2. A book titled *The Nurture Assumption: Why Children Turn Out the Way They Do* has excited considerable controversy. You want to find a review by a reputable authority, written in nontechnical terms, to help you decide whether or not the book's arguments are valid. A review was published in *The New Leader* in November 1998. Who wrote it? Did the reviewer praise or condemn the book? Why?

▪▪▪ EXERCISE 14

Using the Research Journal

Turn in your research journal (or portions of it) for comments and suggestions from your instructor.

CHAPTER 7

RESEARCH PAPER FORMATS:
MLA and APA

■ ■ ■ QUICK VIEW

I recommend using the MLA (Modern Language Association) format in drafting your paper, even if you are required to prepare the final typescript in one of the other three formats covered in this chapter and Chapter 8: the APA (American Psychological Association) format, the CBE (Council of Biology Editors) citation sequence format, or the Chicago (footnote-style) format. The MLA format is the best for drafting because it places nearly all references to sources inside parentheses within the body of your paper. It is easy to convert these notes to other formats later. If you reorganize your paper by using the MLA format, the parenthetical citations will stay right with the text that they document.

The other formats can cause problems during drafting. The CBE citation sequence method, for example, requires you to give each source a number and to cite the source by that number in the body of your paper. If you attempt to draft your paper by using this format, you'll have to renumber all your sources each time you incorporate material from a new source. If you reorganize your paper during drafting, you can get confused about which citations go with which quotations. Almost inevitably, errors will creep in. The APA format is somewhat better for drafting purposes; but again, confusion can arise, particularly if you use more than one source published in a single year by a single author.

This chapter assumes that you will be using the MLA format as a foundation or platform format for your paper. For the APA, CBE, and Chicago formats, this chapter and the next explain the *changes* you'll have to make to convert your paper to these formats. To keep the discussion simple, Chapters 7 and 8 will concentrate on the *main features* and *common problems* in each format. Mechanical details (punctuation and the like) are covered in Chapter 13, which discusses common mechanical mistakes.

> If you'll be using the MLA format for your final draft, read on, but skip all of this chapter's subsections following page 193.
> If you'll be using the APA format for your final draft, read pages 193–223, and then return to this spot.
> If you'll be using the CBE citation sequence format for your final draft, read pages 224–244, and then return to this spot.
> If you'll be using the Chicago format for your final draft, read pages 244–267, and then return to this spot.

OVERVIEW OF RESEARCH PAPER FORMATS

From a student's point of view, in the best of all possible worlds there would be a single format for all college research papers. But in the real world, unfortunately, there are many formats, because each academic discipline has special needs and preferences. For example, it makes sense to cite sources by author and date, as the APA format requires, in a field in which conclusions are often cited but quotations are less frequent. In the humanities direct quotations are more common, so it makes sense for the MLA format to use page numbers instead of dates. Perhaps eventually, all the disciplines will agree upon some interdisciplinary standards for inconsequential details such as margin size.

Chapters 7 and 8 cover the most commonly used formats for college research papers as they are described in the four most widely used research manuals.

1. *The MLA Handbook for Writers of Research Papers* (5th ed., 1999)

2. *Publication Manual of the American Psychological Association* (4th ed., 1994)

3. *Scientific Style and Format: The CBE* [Council of Biology Editors] *Manual for Authors, Editors, and Publishers* (6th ed., 1994)

4. *The Chicago Manual of Style* (14th ed., 1993)

The first is generally used in the humanities; the second, in psychology and the social sciences; the third, in biology, zoology, botany, and the medical sciences; the fourth, in many disciplines. In addition, there are citation sequence formats resembling the CBE format for many individual disciplines, such as the ACS (American Chemical Society) format for chemistry, the AMS (American Mathematical Society) format for mathematics, and the AIP (American Institute of Physics) format for physics. Your instructor may want you to consult a style manual appropriate for your subject, although the CBE citation sequence format is appropriate for most scientific papers. (See "A Research Writer's Bookshelf" at the end of Chapter 1 for the names of style manuals for specific disciplines.)

The Chicago Manual of Style is a hefty volume that presents not just one format but a range of choices in preparing texts for academic publication. The main characteristic of what is commonly called the "Chicago style" is the use of footnotes or endnotes to cite sources. Rather than attempting to summarize the many options given in *The Chicago Manual of Style*, I will summarize the basic footnote format and use my own sample paper to illustrate it (see Chapter 8).

Although the four formats differ in some minor details such as page layouts and the kinds of abbreviations that are preferred, the primary differences involve source citations. Here is a summary of the formats' main features. (Notice that the *CBE Manual* offers two choices of format.)

Manual	*Format*	*Characteristic*
MLA	Parenthetical documentation with "Works Cited" list	All sources are cited in parentheses within the body of paper by author's name and page number, with a "Works Cited" list at the end. Footnotes or endnotes are used only for special explanations or detailed bibliographic information. (See the sample paper by Jill Colak on pages 180–192.)
APA	Parenthetical documentation with author-date citations	All sources are cited in parentheses within the body of the paper by the author's name and the date of publication. (See the sample paper by Lisa Hewitt on pages 205–216.)
CBE	1. Parenthetical documentation with name-year citations	Similar to the APA format.
	2. Documentation using superscripts to cite numbered sources	Sources are numbered in their order of appearance, so the style is known as the citation sequence format. (See the sample paper by Todd Rose on pages 231–243.)
Chicago	Documentation using endnotes or footnotes to cite sources	Chicago lists many possible variations. (See my sample paper on pages 249–266.)

The key to understanding modern documentation formats is to recognize that they attempt to do away with the unnecessary distractions of elaborate source citations. In the MLA and APA formats, you are encouraged to do most of your documentation in the body of the paper so that the reader's attention is not diverted by constantly traveling to the bottom of the page or to a separate set of endnotes.

ALL FORMATS: The Functions of Documentation

In research writing, *documentation,* or the citing and listing of sources, performs several functions. It acknowledges what you have borrowed, and it helps your readers find your sources and see how you've used them.

Acknowledging Borrowing

The primary function of documentation is to acknowledge that you are indebted to the sources you used. A book or an article is the intellectual property of the persons who wrote and published it. To fail to give credit where credit is due is plagiarism. Plagiarism is a particularly serious and offensive kind of theft because it injures many: the writer who labored honestly to create the source material, the publisher or person who holds copyright over that material, the instructor who is deceived by the plagiarism, and the nonplagiarizing students who have worked honestly to earn academic credit that the plagiarist steals. (Accidental plagiarism is a less serious matter, but you should take pains to avoid it.) (See "Developing the Skill of Paraphrasing" in Chapter 6.)

Helping Your Reader Find Your Sources

In addition to giving fair credit, documentation enables your reader to retrace your steps. Thus, you must scrupulously indicate every borrowing: every quotation, fact, table, idea, or key phrase you drew from a source. Complete and accurate bibliographical information for this purpose is essential. There is one exception to reporting sources: Common knowledge should not be documented (see p. 158).

Helping Your Reader Know the Territory

A less obvious function of documentation is that it sometimes welcomes a newcomer to a field of research. At some point in a research project, you may encounter a source that surveys the existing knowledge about a subject. Perhaps a review article compares standard discussions of a topic; perhaps a book or an article supplies a note that directs you to standard sources. A *see* or *see also* note of this sort may not indicate any borrowing at all; it may simply provide helpful hints for other researchers. As a newcomer to the field, you breathe a sigh of relief and gratitude upon encountering this kind of documentation; and you may choose to offer similar help to your readers. Although your real audience—an instructor—may already know the standard sources for a topic, *see also* documentation may be appropriate for your paper since your hypothetical audience is usually a group of your peers. When you are using parenthetical documentation, a helpful list of standard sources, if you include one, should be put in an endnote. (See "Documentation Using Endnotes or Footnotes" in Chapter 12.) If you wonder whether you should include documentation of this sort, ask your instructor. And remember that bibliographical documentation that helps your reader is not used merely to pad a list of works cited.

Helping Your Reader See How
You Have Used Your Sources

Yet another function of documentation is to allow your reader to evaluate how you have used your sources. For example, an instructor can tell at a glance when you rely too heavily upon a single source. Let's say that a page of text has a

series of parenthetical citations like these examples in the MLA format: "...
(Wilson 12)...(Wilson 12)...(Wilson 13)...(Wilson 14)...(Wilson 15)."
It's clear that you have based the discussion entirely upon Wilson and have
merely repeated Wilson's discussion, point by point. True, you may sometimes
need to rely on a crucial source in this way, particularly if you are challenging or
refuting it. However, if clusters of such documentation occur throughout a paper,
it is unlikely that you have organized the passages around your own independent
line of argument.

An independent argument, by its very nature, tends to result in the piecemeal
blending of source material. If you are in charge of your paper's argument and
organization, your documentation will naturally tend to look more like this:
"...(Wilson 12)...(Smith 254)...(Jones 37)...(Wilson 24)." Thus I suggest
that you do what your instructor may do: Scan the documentation of your paper
as a way of spotting passages in which you may have overrelied upon a single
source. See whether you can reorganize these passages and assimilate other
source material. But do not simply sprinkle in other source material as a way of
covering your tracks, because this carries you a step toward dishonest, plagiaristic
use of the crucial source material. You should assume that your instructor will
check your sources and will spot your overreliance upon one source; therefore,
any attempt to cover your tracks will only make matters worse.

A research writer aims to show the reader exactly how a source has
been used. Signal words are used constantly to indicate what sort of borrowing
is taking place. If you are summarizing an entire article in your own words,
you might say "Harrington's article argues that...." If you are paraphrasing
just one sentence by Harrington, you might say "At one point Harrington
suggests...."

Signal phrases become especially important in the rare event that you must
use a single source for a long stretch. The reader should never be misled—
through the accidental or intentional omission of signal words—into believing
that a long passage is your argument when it is really a summary or paraphrase
of someone else's. Announce the fact that you are summarizing at length; insert frequent signals of your indebtedness: "Wilson points out that...(12).
Furthermore, Wilson claims...(14). Yet surely Wilson is wrong in concluding
that...(24)."

Notice that these signals give the reader still more information about how
you are using Wilson's material. When you are not directly quoting, clauses such
as "Wilson points out" show that you are either paraphrasing or summarizing;
the page numbers help the reader decide whether you are condensing Wilson's
discussion or paraphrasing it at length. A clause such as "Wilson claims" performs yet another function: Through the word *claims*, it hints at skepticism and
suggests that you are subjecting Wilson's argument to a critical examination.
Finally, "Surely Wilson is wrong" signals that you disagree with Wilson and are
about to refute his argument.

Frequent references to an author's name can, of course, create some monotony. But it is best to overdocument the paper this way during its drafting; later
you can eliminate excessive, repetitive source citations (see "Consolidating Parenthetical Citations" later in the chapter). Remember this rule:

> When in doubt, overdocument. Ask your instructor about the documentation later if you are still unsure.

Occasionally, a student asks, "Do I have to cite a source even if I first had an idea and later found it expressed in one of my sources?" The answer is yes. An idea, like a quotation, is the intellectual property of the person who published it. But your citation need not imply indebtedness where none really existed. You can state the idea in your own words first and then cite the source in a way that suggests confirmation rather than borrowing: "Nelson confirms this point in his analysis of the case . . . ," or "Nelson agrees, pointing out that . . . ," or "Nelson reaches the same conclusion in his review article. . . ."

PLAGIARISM AND COMMON KNOWLEDGE

Familiar sayings and well-known quotations are examples of common knowledge, and you should not document them. Unfortunately, it is hard to say just what *common knowledge* really is, despite the attempts made by cultural critics such as E. D. Hirsch, whose book *Cultural Literacy* (Boston: Houghton, 1987) tries to describe (as his book's subtitle puts it) "What Every American Needs to Know."

"Needs to know" perhaps. But what does the average college-level reader *actually* know? Among the items in Hirsch's list of items of common knowledge is "X chromosome." In an informal survey conducted among university faculty members in many disciplines, nearly all of them knew that the X and Y chromosomes determine human gender, but a surprisingly large number could not remember whether the XX combination was male or female.

To decide whether an item is common knowledge, the *MLA Handbook* urges you to apply *common sense*—which is an even more difficult concept to define. How are you to get out of this muddle?

When drafting your paper, apply my general rule: When in doubt, document—and then check with your instructor. The definition of *common knowledge* within a specific academic discipline is best decided by an expert in that discipline.

Here is another general rule: If you spot facts that can easily be verified in a readily available reference work, these facts should not be documented. The date of the attack upon Fort Sumter is not something that the average person is likely to know, but it is so easy to look up that documenting it would be inappropriate in virtually any context. Similarly, it is naive to document the birth date of Robert Frost by citing a specific biography when there are dozens of reference volumes that can supply the information. The sea-level melting point of iron is another example of a fact that you should not document.

Unfortunately, though, what may seem unusual to you may be common knowledge to your instructor or your readers.

MLA

> The best rule of thumb I can give you—and it is not infallible but must be used judiciously—is that if a fact is readily available through standard reference works, it should not be documented.

This guideline, however, is *not* a license to plunder an encyclopedia article by copying or paraphrasing long sections of material and using them without documentation, because they are common knowledge. Certainly, some facts found in an encyclopedia article need not be documented; but any time you use any source extensively, you should cite it in a way that shows clearly just how you used it.

MLA FORMAT: General Appearance

The following sections present the details you will need to use the MLA format for your research paper. But to get an overview of its main features, read this checklist. It shows at a glance the basic stylings your paper should have.

MLA FORMAT: CHECKLIST OF MAIN FEATURES

1. Do not type a separate title page; imitate the sample paper's first-page format (see p. 180).
2. Use a one-inch margin on all sides of the paper.
3. Double-space everything, including block quotations.
4. Type your name and the page number, each page, top right.
5. Indent block quotations ten spaces.
6. Cite sources in parentheses, using the basic citation forms.
7. Title the bibliography "Works Cited," and list the bibliographic information in the order given on pp. 168–179. Capitalize the first letter of the main words in titles.
8. Use hanging indentation in the "Works Cited."
9. Use endnotes or footnotes only for special purposes or when specifically requested.

Note: The fifth edition of the *MLA Handbook* (1999) contains greatly expanded discussions of mechanics and the use of electronic sources. However, one change the editors made alters the general appearance of every element of a paper: *Type one space* (not two) *after a period.* (The *Handbook* does acknowledge, however, that using two spaces is also correct, though it is not preferred. Simply be consistent.)

Nearly all of the guidelines that follow (and the mechanical details covered in Chapter 13) are designed to make college research papers easy to handle and to read. If you follow these guidelines, you show courtesy toward an instructor who often must read dozens or even hundreds of papers at a time. In addition, following these conventions shows that you know something about college writing. Any instructor accustomed to teaching research writing will tell you that when a paper stands out from the rest because of its nonstandard and perhaps inconvenient format, it often is marked by serious flaws. Follow the conventions so that the paper's appearance avoids setting off warning bells.

Headings

Research papers in the MLA format aim for as much continuity as possible, so headings are seldom used. If for some reason you think that you need headings for the sections of your paper, check with your instructor about them. But be careful to avoid the abrupt topic shifts that section headings can create. The best way to use headings effectively is to draft your paper as a smooth, continuous line of argument; then after you are done, insert section headings at natural breaking points. (Note that writers whose final drafts will be in APA or CBE format may use headings freely, since the sciences and the social sciences use standard patterns of organization signaled by section headings.)

Margins and Spacing

Two simple and unchanging rules govern the appearance of a paper in MLA format.

1. Set all four margins to one inch. (With some word processors you may need to set the top margin to less than one inch to accommodate a header.)

2. Double-space between lines, throughout the paper. This rule includes the spacing after headings and within indented block quotations. The rare exception is for footnotes: Single-space within footnotes, but double-space between them. Quadruple-space before the first footnote on a page.

Unfortunately, many word processors create nonstandard spacing when you choose double spacing from their format menus.

> The only way to be sure that you are using proper double spacing is to print out some sample text and measure the line intervals. The bottom edges of double-spaced lines should be a third of an inch apart. If necessary, adjust your word processor's line spacing accordingly.

On some pages, you may adjust the bottom margin to more than one inch to prevent widows and orphans. A *widow* is a paragraph's last line appearing by itself at the top of a page; an *orphan* is a paragraph's first line appearing by itself at the bottom of a page. Most word processors automatically control page breaks to avoid the occurrence of widows and orphans, because they are considered awkward and unsightly.

Title Page

Papers in MLA format do not normally have a separate title page. Follow the first-page format of the sample paper on pp. 180–192. Choose your title carefully. Avoid vague and general words ("A Study of," "An Analysis of") that add nothing to the title's meaning. Avoid using a title that identifies only the main subject without specifying the paper's subtopics or angles of interest. Thus, rather than using "Swift and *Gulliver's Travels*," use "Characterization in *Gulliver's Travels*." Or instead of "The Early Years of the French Revolution," use "The Role of the Intelligentsia in the French Revolution's Early Years." Remember that first impressions are important. A vague title often makes the instructor suspect that the paper will not state and develop a clear thesis.

Header

Near the top of each page, a half inch from the edge, type a header with your name and the page number. Most word processors allow you to enter a header that will automatically be inserted on each page and that will contain automatically generated page numbers.

Quotations

For guidance on quoting, summarizing, and paraphrasing material during the early stages of working on your paper, see Chapter 6, "Gathering Information." For guidance on smoothly blending quotations into your paper, see Chapter 9, "Writing the Rough Draft." This section deals primarily with quotations in relation to the paper's layout and general appearance.

Selecting Quotations A glance at the layout of your finished paper should show that most of your source material has been presented as paraphrase and summary. Quotations should be brief. Be especially careful to avoid including lots of block quotations, because they may clash with your style and may look like padding. A few block quotations are permissible when the quoted material is crucial or when you analyze it at length. To be included in your paper, a quoted passage should pass the following *quotability test*.

> A quotation should be, in the words of the *MLA Handbook*, "particularly interesting, vivid, unusual, or apt" (sec. 2.7.1).

There is no way to avoid harshness in stating an inevitable consequence of this rule: Much, perhaps most, of what you read while doing research will be unquotable. Scan your paper to see whether all your quotations pass the quotability test; if some of them don't, or if they clash with your own style, replace them with paraphrases. There are exceptions to the quotability test: If you analyze or refute a passage at length, fairness may require you to quote the original.

It is certainly acceptable to quote only the striking phrases in a passage, blending them into a sentence of your own devising:

> In the music he presented to Frederick the Great, Bach incorpo-
> rated many "ingenious musical acrostics" (Bettmann, "Bach at
> Potsdam" 86).

But too many fragmentary quotations in a row are distracting, especially if they require ellipses. The following bits of quotation reveal that the original passage has been clumsily dismembered:

> But Bettmann feels that the "extraordinary fugal ingenuity" of Bach's
> work struck "not so much [. . .] deaf as [. . .] insensitive ears."
> Obviously, Bach's "ingenious musical acrostics" were musical
> elements that Frederick "would never take the time to puzzle out"
> ("Bach at Potsdam" 86).

It would be better to paraphrase or, if quotation is really necessary, to give the passage in its entirety, as a block quotation, without carving it up. Here is Bett-mann's original phrasing, which is surely elegant enough to deserve being quoted in full.

> Yet such extraordinary fugal ingenuity fell, in the case of King Frederick, not so much on deaf as on insensitive ears. Seen in retrospect, it now seems clear that the king would never take the time to puzzle out the ingenious musical acrostics that Bach had so painstakingly devised for him. ("Bach at Potsdam" 86)

There are occasional exceptions to the rule against piling up fragmentary quotations. In closely analyzing poetry, for example, you may need to quote words or individual phrases.

Paraphrasing is the only sure way to escape the potential conflict between two rules that contradict each other.

> 1. Avoid block quotations.
> 2. Avoid awkward piecemeal quotations.

When you quote, arrive at a reasonable compromise between the two principles. Scan your paper to assess the quotability, length, and frequency of your quotations.

For punctuation of parenthetical documentation after quotations, review "Quotation Marks" in Chapter 13 and "Setting Up Block Quotations" (next).

Setting Up Block Quotations   Quotations longer than four typed lines should be set off as block quotations, indented ten spaces, without quotation marks at the beginning or end (unless the quotation marks are part of the quoted material). Parenthetical documentation should *follow* the last item of punctuation in a block quotation.

If the block quotation is drawn from a single paragraph, all the lines should be indented ten spaces, or one inch. If the block is drawn from more than one paragraph, reproduce the original paragraph indentations; but do not indent the first line of the block unless it was indented in the original. Use *three* spaces (or a fourth of an inch) for indentations inside block quotations.

Setting Up Quotations of Poetry In a brief quotation of poetry, use one or more slash marks (with a space before and after each mark) to indicate line divisions: "Had we but world enough, and time, / This coyness, Lady, were no crime." Four or more lines of quoted poetry should be set off as a block and not enclosed by quotation marks. If the original contains unusual patterns of indentation, reproduce the poem's layout as accurately as you can. You may use a left indentation of less than ten spaces or one inch to avoid awkward spillover continuations of lines.

ALTERING QUOTATIONS

1. You may use an ellipsis mark [. . .] to show that you have omitted a passage within a quotation.

2. You may interpolate an additional word to clarify an ambiguity: "At this time she [Earhart] was unaware of the impending storm."

3. You may underline a word or passage to call it to the reader's attention. If you do so, indicate your alteration with the phrase *emphasis added*, either in square brackets within the quotation or in parentheses after it.

4. You may use the comment *sic* (Latin for "thus" or "just so"), without quotation marks or underlining, to indicate that you have quoted accurately, even though the spelling, grammar, or logic of the original seems incorrect. *Sic* should be placed either in square brackets inside a quotation or in parentheses after a quotation. (*Sic* should never be used to correct British or archaic spellings. For example, *colour* is standard modern British spelling, and *shew* is a standard eighteenth-century alternative spelling for *show*.)

5. You may alter the last item of punctuation in a quotation to make it fit its new context. For example, a period may become a comma. But exclamation points and question marks should be retained, and a sentence containing a question or an exclamation should continue without further punctuation: " 'What's the matter with the whole human race!' thinks Perkins as he recalls how his best ideas have been rejected."

MLA FORMAT: Parenthetical Documentation

Basic Form

The MLA format is by far the most convenient format for drafting, because almost all citations occur in one of several simple forms. Master them and you have nearly mastered the MLA parenthetical documentation format. Here are four basic examples.

(13)

(Wilson 13)

(Wilson, "Renegades" 13)

(Wilson, Immigration 24)

The first example gives only a page number; it is appropriate if you mention Wilson in your sentence and if your bibliography lists only one work by him. The second example is appropriate if your sentence does not mention Wilson by name. The third and fourth are appropriate if your bibliography contains two works by Wilson, and you need to distinguish between them. The third example cites an article; the fourth example cites a book. Note the form's simplicity; except for *et al.* (which means "and others" and is not underlined), no abbreviations such as *ed.*, or *trans.*, *ibid.*, or *op. cit.* are used in parenthetical citations.

The simplicity of MLA parenthetical documentation makes it an ideal platform format for drafting.

Common Exceptions to the Basic Form

There are several exceptions to the basic forms given, but most of the exceptions make matters still simpler. The following subsections describe the most common ones.

Citing an Entire Work   If you mention Wilson in your sentence by name and are citing his *entire* book or article, no page number (and therefore no parenthetical citation) is needed. If Wilson's work is a one-page article, then the page number is already listed in the bibliography, and again no parenthetical citation is necessary as long as you mention Wilson in your sentence.

Citing a Nonprint Source   If Wilson is the subject of a taped personal interview, then no page number *can* be given, and no parenthetical citation is necessary as long as you give credit to Wilson in your sentence. Similarly, you cannot cite page numbers for a film, video, or Web page, so you should mention the source, by title, in your sentence. If a Web page is very long, you may include the paragraph number, thus: ("Sharks" par. 22).

Citing Authors with Identical Last Names   If there are two Wilsons in your list of works cited, add a first initial, like this:

(H. Wilson 56)

If two authors share the same first initial, use the full first name for both.

Citing a Multivolume Work If your paper cites several volumes of a multivolume book, give volume and page numbers after the name.

(Wilson 2: 124)

But if your paper cites only one volume of a multivolume work, give just the page number.

(Wilson 124)

Citing a Multiauthor Work Use all the authors' names when there are two or three authors.

(Wilson and Smith 24)

(Wilson, Smith, and Jones 35)

When there are four or more authors, you may list all the authors' names.

(Wilson, Jones, Howard, and Smith 67)

Or you may use the abbreviation *et al.* (not underlined) after the first author's name.

(Wilson et al. 67)

Note that *et al.* is the abbreviation for the Latin phrase *et alii*, "and others." Because *et* is a word, not an abbreviation, it is not followed by a period.

Citing a Work Listed by Title An unsigned encyclopedia article is a common example of an anonymous source that will be alphabetized by title in the list of works cited. Use the title or a shortened version of it (see "Using Shortened Titles" later in the chapter).

("Abacus")

No page number should be given, since the article's alphabetized placement in a reference work makes that information unnecessary.

Citing a Work by a Corporate Author Pamphlets and government documents often are written or compiled by corporate authors. Although you may use the corporate author's name (or a shortened version of it) in parenthetical citations, it is usually best to mention the corporate author directly in your sentence so that the citation in parentheses can be shortened to include only page numbers.

> In its report <u>Combating Discrimination in the Schools</u>, the National
>
> Education Association found that legal remedies for discrimination are
>
> often overlooked (13).

Citing a Literary Work   Literary works are commonly available in many different editions, and your reader may be using an edition that differs from the one you are citing. Thus it is helpful to give some information in addition to, or in place of, page numbers. Chapter, act, scene, stanza, canto, and line numbers are standard examples, although it is not appropriate to give line numbers to short poems that can be scanned at a glance.

In citing prose works, give the page number followed by additional information. Book 3, Chapter 2 of Henry Fielding's *Joseph Andrews* would be cited like this:

> (169; bk. 3, ch. 2)

In citing poetry (including plays in verse), leave out the page number and cite the passage by using standard divisions. Byron's *Don Juan* would be cited by canto and line number like this:

> (5.24)

If you cite only line numbers, do not use the abbreviations *l.* or *ll.*, because they can be mistaken for numbers. Instead, use the word *line* or *lines* in the first citation and use only numbers from that point forward.

Citing a Secondary Quotation   Sometimes, you may wish to quote someone who has been quoted by one of your sources. The best way to do this is to name the original writer or speaker in your sentence and to indicate that the statement was quoted in the source you are using.

> Nabokov once described the lack of good butterfly hunting as
>
> "calamitous" (qtd. in Boyd 387).

Notice that you use the abbreviation *qtd.*

One good thing about this method is that you needn't worry about giving full bibliographical data for the original quotation—which is information that your secondary source may not have supplied. Another thing to notice is that this method is scrupulously *honest*. When you are using the MLA format, it is *never* acceptable to cite the original source in a way that might lead the reader to conclude that you have consulted it instead of a secondary quotation. Even if you track down the original and cite it, you should say *see also* and then cite the secondary quotation. Remember that documentation is meant to allow the reader to retrace your steps.

If you plan to convert your paper to the APA format later, note that this format takes a different approach to citing sources that have been cited within other sources (see p. 201).

Using Shortened Titles   Parenthetical citations should be kept as short as possible. Thus, when your source has a long and cumbersome title, you should shorten it. Generally, the shortened title should begin with the first word after *the*, *a*, or *an*, so that the reader will not have to hunt for it in the list of works cited but will find it readily in its alphabetized location. Thus, in my paper, Frederick Neumann's *Ornamentation and Improvisation in Mozart* became simply *Ornamentation* in the parenthetical citations.

The short title must clearly distinguish the source from other sources. For a while, I intended to use some material from another book by Neumann entitled *Ornamentation in Baroque and Post-Baroque Music*, which would have forced me to use shortened titles such as *Ornamentation and Improvisation* and *Ornamentation in Baroque.*

Shortened titles are written just like full titles. Thus, you may safely use identically worded short titles such as *Improvisation* and "Improvisation" as long as one is underlined and one is quoted. The underlining tells the reader that the title is for a book, and the quotation marks tell the reader that the title is for an article.

Placement of Parenthetical Documentation

Parenthetical documentation normally comes at the end of a sentence. Occasionally, you may wish to place the parentheses somewhere else in the sentence, particularly if you wish to distinguish borrowed material from common knowledge or the expression of your own ideas.

> Bach later reworked these improvisations and published them less than two months later, at his own expense (Bettmann, "Bach at Potsdam" 86), as the Musical Offering, one of his greatest works.

Notice that the parentheses should be placed at a normal pause in the sentence, immediately before the punctuation that marks the end of the borrowed material.

If a parenthetical citation becomes so long that it badly interrupts the flow of the sentence—as it may, for example, if several sources must be cited—then you should type a superscript number in place of the parentheses and shift the citation to an endnote. (See "Documentation Using Endnotes or Footnotes" in Chapter 12.)

Consolidating Parenthetical Citations

If several quotations from the same page of a source occur within one of your paragraphs, and if no other sources are quoted within the series of quotations, consolidate the citations into a single parenthetical reference following the last quotation. The *MLA Handbook* does not explicitly say that you may consolidate citations to *paraphrased* material in the same fashion, but as long as the paraphrases are clearly signaled ("Smith argues . . . Smith further points out"), this procedure is fair and efficient. The general trend of MLA documentation conventions is to streamline the citations as much as possible.

To further consolidate parenthetical citations, you may cite more than one source within parentheses. Separate the citations with a semicolon, and cite the multiple sources in the order in which they are quoted or paraphrased.

(Smith 24; Wesson 52)

Again, turn the citation into an endnote if it becomes disruptively long.

MLA FORMAT: The List of Works Cited

In accordance with the trend toward streamlining, the MLA format normally uses a list of works cited, not works consulted. Only sources actually cited in the paper should be included in this list. Call it "Works Cited," not "Bibliography."

Occasionally, an instructor may prefer a bibliography called "Works Consulted," "Selected Bibliography," or "Annotated Bibliography." Check to be sure which type your instructor expects.

General Principles

Avoiding Mistakes in Imitating Examples   The complexities of listing various types of special sources are fully covered in the *MLA Handbook*. If, like most students, you choose to scan the handbook's examples for guidance in handling problem cases, be careful not to accidentally model your entries after the examples given in the handbook's Appendix B.

Usual Format for All Sources   Remember that bibliography entries for *all* sources normally contain at least three elements: author, title, and publication data.

Listing Multiple Sources by a Single Author   Use the author's full name in the first entry. In subsequent entries, replace the author's name with three unspaced hyphens. After the hyphens you may add abbreviations such as *ed.* or *trans.* where they are appropriate. But since the three hyphens always stand for *exactly* the same name as given in the previous entry, give the full name again if the same author reappears as a coauthor or coeditor in subsequent entries.

Listing Books

Rather than attempting to cover all the exceptions and special cases discussed in the *MLA Handbook*, I will describe a *simple* entry for each of the common types of sources: books and articles. This section focuses on books, and the next section focuses on articles. The examples given cover most of the sources you are likely to use, and the simplicity of the examples should reassure you that applying the MLA bibliography format is really not difficult in most cases. Throughout, I will focus on avoiding common mistakes.

A basic book entry contains just three items of information: author, title, and publication data.

Morwood, William. <u>The Lazy Gardener's Garden Book</u>. Garden City,

NY: Doubleday, 1970.

The following discussion about specific items in bibliographic entries should help you to avoid some common mistakes students are apt to make.

- *Author.* Give the author's name exactly as it appears on the book's title page. It is helpful to supply additional information in square brackets, thus: Abrams, M[eyer] H.

- *Place of publication.* If more than one city is given on the title page, list only the first. If no city is given on the title page, consult the copyright page; but be sure to list the city of the company that *published* the book rather than the city of the *printing* firm that produced it. Supply an abbreviation for state or country only if the city is ambiguous (Cambridge, Eng., as opposed to Cambridge, MA) or relatively unfamiliar (Gnawbone, IN). Use two-letter U.S. Postal Service abbreviations for the names of states. In accordance with the MLA's general policy of streamlining, avoid duplicating unnecessary information, such as the name of a state clearly indicated in the publisher's name (use "Bloomington: Indiana UP" rather than "Bloomington, IN: Indiana UP"). If no place of publication is given, write *n.p.* ("no place"); since this abbreviation starts a new portion of the bibliography entry, it should be capitalized, as *N.p.*

- *Publisher.* Abbreviate the publisher's name, using the following rules.
  1. Omit articles (*a, an, the*) and generic terms (such as *Co., Ltd., Press,* and *Books*). However, always include the abbreviation *UP* when citing a university press.
  2. Shorten a person's name to the surname; for instance, list *W. W. Norton and Company* as *Norton.* If several persons' names are given, list only the first; thus, list *Farrar, Straus and Giroux, Inc.* as *Farrar.*
  3. Whenever possible, use common abbreviations (*Assn.* for *Association, Soc.* for *Society,* and so on).
  4. Use acronyms such as *MLA* if they are likely to be familiar to your readers.

See also the list of standard abbreviations in the *MLA Handbook* (sec. 6.5).

Sometimes, the title page indicates that a book has been published under an *imprint.* For example, Oxford University Press publishes paperback editions of some of its more popular works under the Galaxy imprint. Indicate an imprint, if there is one, by putting the imprint name before the publisher's name, with a hyphen connecting the two items: "Galaxy-Oxford UP."

■ *Date of publication.* Give the date listed on the title page. If the title page does not have a date, use the latest copyright date given on the copyright page. If the title page indicates that you are using a new or revised edition (it may say something like "Revised Edition" or "6th Edition"), then list the date of that edition. But usually one must ignore all the dates given for reprints or impressions, because these terms indicate that the text was issued again without alterations. The copyright page of my Penguin paperback edition of *Candide*, for example, says that the book was "reprinted 1951, 1952, 1953, 1954, 1956 (twice), ... 1986 (twice), 1987, 1988 (twice)." All of this information is irrelevant; what counts is the line that says "This edition copyright 1947 by John Butt." The date of publication is 1947, even though my copy was printed decades later. If no date is given, write *n.d.* ("no date").

BIBLIOGRAPHY: CONFUSING TERMS

imprint (1) The publisher's name usually found at the foot of the title page. (2) The special label assigned to a publisher's series or subdivision. For example, Harcourt published a series of books under its Harbinger imprint. The foot of the title page of a Harbinger book carries the following information.

A Harbinger Book
Harcourt, Brace & World, Inc.
1962

In an MLA-style bibliography, this information should be recorded as follows: "Harbinger-Harcourt, 1962."

edition (1) When used to describe a book, *edition* primarily means a specific version of a printed text, distinct from other versions. Every printed book is an example of an *edition* in this sense. An edition is often identified by a number or by descriptive words (2nd edition, Revised Edition). (In contrast, the terms *printing, impression,* and *reprint* indicate that the text was issued again in an essentially unaltered state.) (2) When used to describe a book or set of books, the word *edition* can also mean a text prepared for publication by a specific editor or group of editors, and an edition in this sense may be known by a specific name: the Revised Standard Edition of the Bible, the Yale Edition of the Works of Samuel Johnson. (3) When used to describe a newspaper, the word *edition* refers to the particular version of the newspaper identified on the masthead. For example, some newspapers have a morning edition, late edition, and overseas edition.

reprint (1) A republished book. This term is confusing primarily because one must distinguish between a printing, a reprint, and an edition. For example, the copyright page of an Oxford University Press book might carry the following notice: "First published by Oxford University Press, 1960. This reprint, 1967." In a bibliography, the publication date would be listed as 1960, because the reprint of 1967 is textually unchanged and is issued by the same publisher. (If textual changes had been made, the title page and/or copyright page would refer to a revised edition or second edition—the key word being *edition*.) On the other hand, a book first published in 1902 by one publisher and reissued by a different publisher in 1962 is a reprint in a different sense and must be treated differently in a bibliography, since the reprinted book may differ significantly from the original. In a bibliography, give the original publication date and then the publication data of the reprint: "1902. New York: Octagon, 1962." (2) A reprinted article or portion of a book, usually republished in an anthology or collection. In a bibliography, list the original publication information first and then the publication information of the reprint. (Compare *edition*.)

A Book in a Numbered Edition

Erikson, Erik H. <u>Childhood and Society</u>. 2nd ed. New York: Norton, 1964.

An Edited Book in a Series

Schakel, Peter J., ed. <u>Critical Approaches to Teaching Swift</u>. AMS Studies in the Eighteenth Century 21. New York: AMS, 1992.

A Book by a Corporate Author

Committee for a Study of the Health Care of Racial/Ethnic Minorities and Handicapped Persons. <u>Health Care in a Context of Civil Rights</u>. Washington, DC: National Academy, 1981.

A Translation

Dostoyevsky, Fyodor. <u>Crime and Punishment</u>. Trans. Sidney Monas. New York: New American Library, 1968.

A Work in an Anthology

Herbert, George. "The Flower." <u>The Norton Anthology of English Literature</u>. Ed. M. H. Abrams et al. Vol. 1. New York: Norton, 1993. 1384–85. 2 vols.

An Introduction, Preface, Foreword, or Afterword (See also "Titles" in Chapter 13.)

> Mitchell, William J. Introduction. Essay on the True Art of Playing Keyboard Instruments. By Carl Philipp Emanuel Bach. Trans. and ed. William J. Mitchell. New York: Norton, 1949. 1–23.

A Republished Book

> Nabokov, Vladimir. Lolita. 1955. New York: Vintage-Random, 1989.

The Bible Usually, you should cite scripture sources in parentheses within the text of your paper, using the MLA abbreviations for books of the Bible. (See *MLA Handbook* sec. 6.7.1.) But if your instructor specifically requires you to include the Bible in your bibliography, use the title page information to create a standard MLA bibliography entry, omitting the "author" position.

> The New Oxford Annotated Bible with the Apocrypha. Revised Standard Version. Expanded ed. Ed. Herbert G. May and Bruce M. Metzger. Oxford: Oxford UP, 1977.

If you are listing a specific edition of the Bible because you have cited its notes or other editorial apparatus, cite the editor(s) first.

> May, Herbert G., and Bruce M. Metzger, eds. The New Oxford Annotated Bible with the Apocrypha. Revised Standard Version. Expanded ed. Oxford UP, 1977.

Listing Articles

Articles are normally found in periodicals, but college researchers often use articles collected in books and encyclopedia articles. Let's look at all three cases.

Articles in Periodicals

A Journal Article Journals are specialized periodicals that are usually published quarterly. A basic journal article entry in the list of works cited contains just six items of information: author, article title, journal title, volume number, date of publication, and page numbers.

> Swain, Joseph P. "Form and Function of the Classical Cadenza." Journal of Musicology 6 (1988): 27–59.

Here are some details to help you avoid common mistakes.

- *Title of the journal.* If the journal's title begins with *a, an,* or *the,* omit the first word. Thus, the journal *The American Scholar* should be listed as *American Scholar.* If there is a subtitle, omit it.
- *Name of the journal editor.* This information should never be included in citations to journal articles.
- *Place of publication.* This information should never be included in citations to journal articles unless there are two journals with the same name, in

GUIDE TO CONVERTING ROMAN NUMERALS

Here are the basic Roman numerals and the Arabic numeral each represents.

I (or i) =   1
V (or v) =   5
X (or x) =   10
L (or l) =   50
C (or c) =   100
D (or d) =   500
M (or m) = 1000

To convert a Roman numeral to an Arabic numeral, simply add the Roman numerals, as long as they are arranged in descending order from left to right:

CLXXVI = 100 (C) + 50 (L) + 20 (XX) + 5 (V) + 1 (I) = 176

But when ascending order occurs (for example, XL, which ascends from X [10] to L [50]), subtract the smaller numeral from the larger:

XL = 50 (L) − 10 (X) = 40

So volume CXCIV is volume 194:

100 + (100 − 10) + (5 − 1) = 194

The good news is that Roman numerals are being abandoned in the numbering of volumes. Besides being clumsy, they are ambiguous; for example, it is easy to misread the Roman numeral two (II) for the Arabic numeral eleven (11).

which case the place name should be enclosed within square brackets, without underlining, immediately after the periodical's name.

■ *Volume number.* Use Arabic numerals, not Roman numerals. If each issue of the journal begins with page one, indicate the issue number: "5.2" means volume 5, issue number 2, in a journal that paginates each issue separately. This exception, unfortunately, can cause unnecessary trouble for researchers. The MLA editors' apparent purpose in omitting the issue number in citations to continuously paginated journals is to streamline article entries as much as possible. But the gain in streamlining is offset by the extra effort researchers must make to notice the pagination system of each journal they consult. Perhaps future editions of the handbook will change this guideline. But for now, be aware of this exception, and note the pagination system of the journals you use.

■ *Date of publication.* Give just the year, not the month or season of the issue (though you will often find this information cited in indexes and bibliographies).

The most complex journal article entry possible in the MLA format should contain all of the following information.

1. author's name (in full)
2. title of the article, in quotation marks
3. name of the periodical (in full, but omitting subtitle, if there is one)
4. series number (if any) or name (if any)
5. volume number(s) and issue number(s)
6. date of publication
7. page numbers
8. supplementary information

An Article in a Weekly, Monthly, or Bimonthly Periodical Most magazines are nonspecialized periodicals published weekly or monthly. A basic entry to a magazine article in the list of works cited omits the volume number and instead gives just the date.

> Kantrowitz, Barbara. "The Metaphor Is the Message." Newsweek
> 14 Feb. 1994: 49.

Here are some details to help you avoid common mistakes.

- *Title of periodical.* If the periodical's title begins with *a*, *an*, or *the*, omit the first word. If there is a subtitle, omit it.
- *Volume number.* Do not list the volume number of a monthly or weekly periodical, even if it is given.
- *Date of publication.* Use the day-month-year format. *May*, *June*, and *July* should be written in full; names of other months should be abbreviated to the first three letters. (*September* may be abbreviated as *Sep.* or *Sept.*) For a bimonthly periodical, give the month(s) and year: "July–Aug. 1993."
- *Page numbers.* In many magazines, articles are distributed on nonconsecutive pages. In such cases, write just the first page number with a plus sign, without any intervening space: 7+.

The most complex monthly or weekly periodical article entry possible in the MLA format should contain all of the following information.

1. author's name (in full)
2. title of the article, in quotation marks
3. name of the periodical
4. date of publication
5. page numbers
6. supplementary information

An Article in a Newspaper   Since newspapers are commonly divided into sections, a basic entry to a newspaper article in the list of works cited gives the article's section designation as well as the page number.

> Stryker, Mark. "Bebop College." Dayton Daily News 22 Oct.
>   1993: 1C–2C.

Here are some details to help you avoid common mistakes.

- *Place of publication.* If the newspaper's title does not indicate the place of publication, include the city's name in brackets: "*Daily Progress* [Charlottesville, VA]." No city of publication should be given for national newspapers such as *USA Today.*

- *Section.* Give the section designation as it actually appears in the newspaper. The *Dayton Daily News,* for instance, numbers its pages A1, A2, . . . , B1, B2, . . . , and so on; in the previous example, I thus used the newspaper's style of pagination. If page numbers without letters had appeared at the top of each page, I would have written "sec. c: 1–2."

- *Edition.* Some newspapers publish more than one edition per day. Indicate the edition, if one is listed on the masthead, immediately after the date: "*New York Times* 6 Mar. 1994, natl. ed.: 16."

The most complex newspaper article entry possible in the MLA format should contain all of the following information.

1. author's name (in full)
2. title of the article, in quotation marks
3. name of the newspaper
4. date of publication
5. edition (if any); for example, "late ed."
6. section and page numbers
7. supplementary information

Articles in Books

An Article in a Collection   If the article has not been published before its appearance in the collection, use this format. (On Valparaiso U, see pg. 248.)

> Buszin, Walter E. "Criteria of Church-Music in the Seventeenth and
>   Eighteenth Centuries." Festschrift Theodore Hoelty-Nickel: A
>   Collection of Essays on Church Music. Newman W. Powell, ed.
>   Valparaiso, IN: Valparaiso U, 1967. 14–21.

If the article has been republished in the collection after having appeared first in another book or periodical, give the original publication data if available; then write "Rpt. in" ("Reprinted in") and give the new publication information.

> Walker, Ralph S. "Ben Jonson's Lyric Poetry." <u>Criterion</u> 13 (1933–34): 430–48. Rpt. in <u>Seventeenth-Century English Poetry</u>. Ed. William R. Keast. New York: Galaxy-Oxford UP, 1962. 178–92.

Notice that without the original publication data, the reader might falsely assume that Walker's article was first published in 1962.

Do not become confused by the mixture of formats. Notice that the first part of the citation follows the normal format for a journal article; the second part follows the normal format for a portion of a book.

More than One Article from a Single Collection College researchers often use more than one source from a collection of articles by different writers. Typical examples of such collections include anthologies of critical articles; readers, which are collections of sources on a single topic; and festschrifts, which are collections of articles published to celebrate the retirement of a distinguished scholar. The *MLA Handbook* offers a convenient system for streamlining the citations to multiple sources within such a collection. The collection as a whole is given a full entry, listed under its editor's name; the individual articles are listed only by author, title, and page number, with cross-reference to the editor's name. Each entry is listed in its usual alphabetic location.

> Buszin, Walter E. "Criteria of Church-Music in the Seventeenth and Eighteenth Centuries." Powell 14–21.
> Gehring, P. "The Aesthetics of Improvisation." Powell 77–89.
> Powell, Newman W., ed. <u>Festschrift Theodore Hoelty-Nickel: A Collection of Essays on Church Music</u>. Valparaiso, IN: Valparaiso U, 1967.

A common mistake for this type of entry is to get confused about how to cite the source parenthetically. Cite the *author* you are quoting, not the editor of the collection. A quotation from Buszin should be followed by the parenthetical documentation "(Buszin 17)." The reader will find Buszin in the list of works cited, will note the cross-reference to Powell, and will find the full publication data listed under Powell's name. (Compare this styling with the format suggested on p. 175 if Buszin's is the *only* article you use from Powell's collection.)

An Article in a Reference Work List an encyclopedia article as you would an article in a collection, but do not cite the editor of the entire reference work. If the article is initialed, consult the list of contributors to find the author's full name. If the article is unsigned, begin the bibliography entry with the title. If the reference work is arranged alphabetically, omit the page number, since your reader does not need it to find the article. If the reference work is well known, omit full publication data, but give the edition (if it is stated) and the year.

> "Improvisation." <u>Encyclopedia Americana</u>. 1985 ed.

Listing Internet Sources

List only the information that applies to the Internet site you are using.

1. author's name, in full (if given)

2. title of the material, in quotation marks, if it is an article, short story, or similar short work within a scholarly project, database, or periodical; or title of newsgroup posting, in quotation marks, followed by "Online posting"

3. title of a book (underlined)

4. Name of the editor, compiler, or translator (if relevant and not already cited), preceded by the appropriate abbreviation (such as "Trans.")

5. publication data for print version of the source

6. title of scholarly project, database, periodical, or site (underlined); for untitled site, a description such as *Home page*

7. name of scholarly project's or database's editor (if available)

8. version number; or, for a journal, the volume number, issue number, or other identifying number

9. date of electronic publication, of update, or of posting

10. for a newsgroup posting, the name of the list

11. the number range or number of pages, paragraphs, or other sections, if they are numbered

12. name of sponsoring institution (if given)

13. date when the researcher accessed the material

14. electronic address, or URL, in angle brackets

Personal Web Site

Padgett, John B. <u>William Faulkner on the Web</u>. 23 June 1998. U of Mississippi. 6 Jan. 1999 <http://www.mcsr.olemiss.edu/~egjbp/faulkner/faulkner.html>.

Professional Web Site

Aphra Behn Society. Ed. Carole Meyers. Nov. 1998. Emory U. 7 Jan. 1999 <http://prometheus.cc.emory.edu/behn/index.html>.

Scholarly Project

<u>Electronic Text Center</u>. Ed. David Seaman. 1992. U of Virginia. 4 Jan. 1999 <http://etext.lib.virginia.edu/>.

Book On-Line

Adams, Henry. <u>The Education of Henry Adams</u>. Ed. Scott Atkins. Boston: Houghton, 1918. <u>Electronic Text Center</u>. Ed. David Seaman. Feb. 1996. U of Virginia. 4 Jan. 1999 <http://xroads.virginia.edu/~HYPER/hadams/ha_home.html>.

Article in a Journal On-Line

O'Brien, John. "Union Jack: Amnesia and the Law in Daniel Defoe's Colonel Jack." <u>Eighteenth-Century Studies</u> 32.1 (1998): 65–82. 8 Jan. 1999. <http://direct.press.jhu.edu/journals/eighteenth-century_studies/v032/32.lobrien.html>.

Article in a Magazine On-Line

Hallowell, Christopher. "Playing the Odds: Health Insurers Want to Know What's in Your DNA." <u>Time</u> 11 Jan. 1999. 15 Jan. 1999 <http://cgi.pathfinder.com/time/magazine/articles/0,3266,17689,00.html>.

Article in a Reference Database On-Line

Parrish, Stephen Maxfield. "William Wordsworth." <u>Britannica Online</u>. Ver. 98.2. Apr. 1998. <http://www.eb.com>.

Posting to a News Group Discussion List

Enfield, John. "The Omnivore Hypothesis." Online posting. 12 May 1998. Anthropology On-Line Seminar. 12 Jan. 1999 <http://www.anthro.unc.edu/anthro/OMNIVORE.txt>.

E-Mail Message

Limouze, Henry. "Bach's Training in Latin." E-mail to the author. 2 Feb. 1997.

Listing Other Kinds of Sources

A Television or Radio Program   List the following information.

1. episode title (if appropriate), in quotation marks
2. program title, underlined
3. series title (if appropriate), neither underlined nor in quotation marks
4. network
5. local station's call letters and city
6. broadcast date

If you are referring primarily to the work of a person (such as the director), his or her name may precede the series title. For guidance in including other information, see the *MLA Handbook* (sec. 4.10.1).

Here is an example.

"Elizabeth Bishop: One Art." Writ., prod., and dir. Jill Janows. <u>Voices and Visions</u>. PBS. South Carolina Educational Television Network

and the New York Center for Visual History. WPTD, Dayton.
5 Apr. 1988.

A Recording   List the following information.

1. name of person (performer, conductor, composer, or the like, depending upon what aspect of the recording is being cited)
2. title, underlined
3. artist(s)
4. manufacturer
5. year of issue (*n.d.* if date is unknown)

A comma should follow the name of the manufacturer; a period should follow each of the other items. For guidance in including other information, see the *MLA Handbook* (sec. 4.10.2).

Ma, Yo Yo. <u>Don Quixote</u>. By Richard Strauss. Cond. Seiji Ozawa. CBS
Masterwork. 1985.

A Film or Videotape   List the following information.

1. title, underlined
2. director (preceded by "Dir.")
3. distributor
4. year

Other information may follow the year; see the *MLA Handbook* (sec. 4.10.3). The following example names the original distributor and date of release, followed by the videotape distributor and release date. Supplementary information, such as the names of performers ("perf."), is placed before the name of the distributor.

<u>Dr. Strangelove: Or, How I Learned to Stop Worrying and Love the
Bomb</u>. Dir. Stanley Kubrick. Writ. Stanley Kubrick, Peter George,
and Terry Southern. Perf. Peter Sellers, George C. Scott, Sterling
Hayden, Keenan Wynn, Slim Pickens. Hawk, 1963. Videocassette.
RCA/Columbia, 1983.

A Personally Conducted Interview   List the following information.

1. name of interviewee (in full)
2. kind of interview (for example, telephone interview or personal interview)
3. date

Here is an example.

Turney, Norris. Personal interview. 14 July 1992.

Sample Paper: MLA Format

Colak   1

Jill Colak

Martin Maner

English 401

22 November 1998

Clegg as the Romantic Hero:

Denying Culpability in <u>The Collector</u>

At one point in her captivity, Miranda Grey tells a fairy tale to
her captor, Clegg. It entails an ugly monster's capture of a beautiful
princess. Much like the "Beauty and the Beast" fairy tale, it ends
with the monster letting the princess go and being transformed into
a handsome prince (Fowles 199). Although Miranda tells this romantic story to encourage Clegg to release her, <u>The Collector</u> remains, in
a sense, a dark parody of a romantic fable. The final step is missing:
there is no release, no miraculous transformation of the monster, and
no "happily ever after." Despite this, many critics want to see Clegg
as a Romantic hero, or at least to find explanations for his behavior
which would make him less culpable for the crimes he has committed. However, these readings deny the fact that Clegg, of his own
free will, imprisoned and psychologically abused an innocent person,
and that he was solely responsible for her death.

John Neary and Simon Loveday both see Clegg as a species of
the Romantic hero. Neary suggests that Clegg is "a kind of fairy-tale
hero, an ugly stepson who contains a hidden, beautiful self" (48).
This is how Clegg would like to see himself. In his dreams, he pictures Miranda being attacked and imagines himself running up to
rescue her, her knight in shining armor (14). After he has captured
her, and Miranda has tried to get him to understand that he is com-

mitting a crime, he says, "I was very happy . . . it was more like I had done something very daring, like climbing Everest" (28). Clegg has cast himself in the role of Romantic hero and has captured the maiden; now all that is left is for him to wait for the transformation when she will love him and he will become a prince.

Unfortunately for Clegg, there are some very important factors missing from his fairy tale scenario. In "Beauty and the Beast," the beast is forgivable for two reasons. First, he has been placed under a spell that turned him into a beast, and so he is not fully responsible for his reprehensible behavior. Second, he releases his captive beauty of his own free will, because he loves her. Neither reason for forgiveness applies to Clegg. Miranda dies of pneumonia while still his prisoner, and Clegg has never been under any supernatural spell. However, many critics seem to believe that Clegg behaves the way he does because of predetermining factors in his upbringing.

In fact, Fowles wants readers to think that Clegg's behavior is the result of a poor education and other societal influences. He writes in The Aristos that "Clegg, the kidnapper, committed the evil; but I tried to show that his evil was largely, perhaps wholly, the result of a bad education, a mean environment, being orphaned: all factors over which he had no control" (qtd. in Neary 46). If there is a spell on Clegg in The Collector fable, Fowles would have us believe that it has been cast by society and class.

Bruce Woodcock agrees with Fowles's assertion that Clegg is not only a product of his society, but also a reflection of its values (30). According to Woodcock, Clegg's actions result not from his social class, but from his masculinity:

Colak 3

> All men may not act out the fantasies Clegg has in the
> manner in which he does, just as all men may not be actual
> rapists; but potentially they can and are because of the re-
> lation of social power and dominance they maintain over
> women. (34)

These frightening assertions reveal a rather dark opinion of mankind. They are, actually, in complete agreement with Clegg's belief
that "a lot of people who may seem happy now would do what [he]
did or similar things if they had the money and the time" (20).
Clegg's view of the world as being peopled by serial kidnappers kept
in check only through lack of funds seems symptomatic of his mad-
ness. On the other hand, having critics and authors espouse the
same view is even more disturbing.

Bruce Bawer reacts to Fowles's assertion that Clegg's evil is a
product of his environment:

> How can Fowles possibly use such a figure as a symbol of
> the ordinary man? It simply doesn't wash. And it's offen-
> sive, as well: does Fowles really think that somewhere in
> every working-class soul there lurks a desperately sick kid-
> napper? Does he really think that human evil is primarily
> the result of "poor education" and "mean environment,"
> and that aptitude and intelligence are to be found exclu-
> sively, or even primarily, in the privileged classes? (63)

The misreading produced by using Clegg as a symbol of the ordinary
man results from Fowles's use of this novel as a platform for discussing class. Because of the plot in this particular novel, the discussion
of class becomes blurred, and Fowles's message is turned into something uncomfortable and ugly.

Robert Campbell describes the kidnapping as "a kind of symbolic revenge by the working-class protagonist on middle-class values" (47). This symbol is full of flaws. There are, of course, the offensively limited characterizations of the lower class that Bawer noted. In addition, there is the fact that Clegg does not take anything from the middle class; he takes everything from Miranda. There is nothing laudable in gaining power over an innocent victim who has no more control over her class situation than does Clegg. For Clegg, Miranda is something he aspires to, some thing he thinks he deserves but has been denied by class and society.

The relation of class to Clegg's behavior is clearly overstated by Fowles, and presumably Woodcock's comparison of Clegg's behavior to men in general is merely metaphorical. In search of more satisfactory explanations, critics have delved into Clegg's mental world to find reasons for his behavior. As a candidate for psychoanalysis, Clegg provides ample opportunity for speculation.

Instead of generalizing Clegg's behavior as a symptom of class, Andrew Brink sees his relationships with the women from his childhood as the source of his warped attitude towards women now. Brink notes, "Deprivation of his actual mother and impingement by his aunt have made him both crave and despise mothers [and all women], producing impotence and rage" (149). In the convenient post-Freudian habit of blaming bad behavior on poor parenting, Brink excuses Miranda's victimization by blaming the women who came before her.

While blaming Clegg's behavior on his mother and aunt may be irresponsible, it is not nearly as reprehensible as blaming it on Miranda. Some critics actually claim, as Clegg does, that Miranda is, to

Colak 5

some extent, responsible for her own fate. From his earliest descriptions of Miranda, Clegg makes it clear that she would have nothing to do with him under normal circumstances. This is not something he has learned about her through experience, but something he believes because of the society in which he lives. Clegg has never even attempted to speak to Miranda before he abducts her. He simply assumes that she will automatically shun him because of class differences, and this is why he believes he must kidnap her. Since she would not give him a chance in an ordinary situation, he feels he must create a situation in which she will have no choice but to give him a chance.

This, after all, is Clegg's original plan: to provide an opportunity for Miranda to fall in love with him. All that comes later, Clegg feels, is due to mistakes that she makes or things she does to him. As part of Clegg's dementia, this view makes sense. However, when critics begin to take the same vein in their discussions of Miranda, it seems discordant. For instance, Sherril E. Grace compares The Collector story to the Bluebeard tales. In these tales, the recurring theme is that a cruel man locks up or kills each of his wives for having an overdeveloped sense of curiosity. When discussing the Bartok opera based on Bluebeard, Grace writes of the doomed heroine, "The opening of doors dooms her from the start" (253). This is, in fact, what seals Miranda's fate, according to Clegg. Arnold E. Davidson explains that Clegg "uses what he insists on calling [Miranda's] whorishness" to rationalize his cruelty in her last weeks (30). She metaphorically opens doors to his psyche when she discovers that he is impotent. The Bluebeard stories and The Collector have clear

Colak 6

parallels, and they are equally guilty of blaming the victim for crimes perpetrated against her.

The fact that Clegg blames Miranda for things he does to her is one of the most revolting aspects of his character. When he says, after she attempts to seduce him, "all I did later was because of that night" (109), it is tempting to ask what the reason was for all he did before. Shyamal Bagchee, on the other hand, claims that Miranda "precipitates her tragic end by her planned assault on Clegg's sense of masculinity" (227). Bagchee seems to overlook the fact that Miranda's intention was not an assault, but a desperate effort to get Clegg to release her. As Miranda contemplates the seduction, she writes, "Perhaps I really should kiss him. More than kiss him. Love him. Make Prince Charming step out" (254). Miranda thinks that by giving Clegg what she imagines he wants, she will allow him to play the role he has cast for himself. He will be able to prove his chivalry with resounding finality.

Bagchee continues her attack on Miranda by suggesting that her attempt to educate Clegg is part of "a desire to play a mild version of the godgame" (233). This reading comes from a tendency of critics to read Miranda's journal as an accurate reflection of her thoughts and opinions, while neglecting to realize that everything she writes must be infected with the fact that she is a prisoner living in constant fear. For while Clegg allows Miranda to tell him what to do and what to get for her, he also keeps her tightly bound to himself. He is always putting her through a form of psychological torture. Despite this fact, critics read Miranda's diary as the thoughts of an ordinary spoiled girl, and not those of a prisoner. If Miranda says that she is so superior to Clegg, and seeks to teach him, why would we

Colak   7

see that as conceit and not a rational reading of the situation? Miranda is superior to Clegg; she knows, for one thing, that she would never hold an innocent person captive. Perhaps she does not know exactly why; this is simply part of her reality. This is the reason she wants to teach him. She wants him to realize that what he has done is wrong. It is only a logical conclusion that if he knew what she knows, he would know that it is wrong and would then release her.

The shocking insensitivity with which many critics view Miranda, when compared with their relatively sympathetic readings of Clegg, reveals that Clegg's rationalizing and projection of blame throughout his narrative have actually convinced some critics. Perry Nodelman, for instance, writes that "for Miranda, sex and even love are always like rape--and so Clegg's collecting her is something like love, for her as well as for him" (342). Similarly, Thomas C. Foster writes that "indeed, Miranda is looking to be dominated by a man" (35). Foster further suggests that Miranda's identification with Anne Frank instead of with a more aggressive or successful captive was a "possibly fatal" mistake she made (36). Foster's reasoning seems to overlook the fact that Clegg used Gestapo tactics and that her identification with Frank was appropriate. It was not as if (as Foster seems to imply) Miranda ever stopped plotting her escape.

Bagchee actually sympathizes with Clegg while she points out Miranda's mistakes:

> Miranda seals her own fate by being herself. With each successive escape attempt she alienates and embitters Clegg the more. Clegg is not predisposed to hating Miranda. In fact it is amazing how much trouble from Miranda he is willing to put up with. (225)

Colak   8

She congratulates Clegg for his perseverance with his unruly prisoner while she blames Miranda for trying to escape. But Miranda's actions turn out to be mistakes only because she misjudges her captor. She should hardly be held responsible for the reactions of someone as irrational as Clegg.

Much is made over the class split between Miranda and Clegg, but actually their greatest difference is the valley that divides sanity from insanity. Still, some critics persist in seeing Clegg as a victim of society, someone whose development was halted or twisted by an unfortunate upbringing; others overlook particulars of his life and simply see his behavior as the result of happenstance. John Neary explains:

> Frederick Clegg embodies the most blindly deterministic aspects of such a world view [where impartial chance reigns], and it is this fact, ironically, that to a large degree makes his actions forgivable. Again and again the character tells us, and he at least partially convinces us, that he has stumbled into his involvement with Miranda by a series of accidents--by hazard--rather than by real choice. (46; emphasis added)

It is bizarre to assert that a person who kidnaps a stranger, holds her captive, and then allows her to die of pneumonia because it was too risky for him to call a physician is forgivable. However, Neary reveals how he can earnestly make such an assertion when he claims that Clegg "convinces us" that he is more of a bumbling kidnapper than a cold and calculating one. Clearly Neary has been taken in by Clegg's explanation of things.

Colak   9

This idea that "in <u>The Collector</u> things happen by chance, by absurd combinations of events" (Bagchee 224), while it seems popular, is simply untrue. Like many of the other critical readings attempting to forgive Clegg, this reading only reflects Clegg's own sentiments. Clegg's narrative reads very much like a plaintive explanation. For instance, when he asserts that "it's how I was made. I can't help it," he reveals an attitude not of one unable to change, but someone who is unwilling to (292). He is trying to convince not only the reader, but also himself, that he has not done anything wrong, or that if he has, it was somehow beyond his control.

Clegg is not so insane that he is unaware that he has committed a crime. If he were that insane, the whole exercise of projecting the blame onto others and rationalizing his motives would probably be unnecessary. Yet statements such as "anyone would have seen it" (294) and "there was always the idea that she would understand" (14) indicate that he wants confirmation of his innocence. The entire tone of his narrative reveals a guilty conscience trying to achieve absolution by convincing himself that there is nothing to be guilty for.

Clegg knows that what he has done is wrong. In his grief after Miranda's death, he thinks to himself, "perhaps it was my fault after all that she did what she did and lost my respect, then I thought it was her fault, she asked for everything she got" (297). He can only sustain his own guilt until he finds something else to blame. David H. Walker agrees, explaining that "here Clegg conveniently dispels latent remorse with the memory of Miranda's sexual advances. He can now regard his detention and maltreatment of her as a punishment" (55). He remembers only her affront to him, not the fact that it never would have occurred without the kidnapping.

His suicide plans also last only until he can rationalize himself out of guilt. After a good night's sleep, he reminds himself that he did not, after all, actually kill Miranda. She died of pneumonia, and as Clegg points out, "a doctor probably could have done little good. [. . .] It was too far gone" (303). Naturally Clegg neglects the fact that he could have saved her life by getting the doctor at any time during the course of her illness. It was not too far gone when it was still a cold.

Clegg is clearly culpable for his actions, yet critics deny this fact. Nodelman even compares Clegg's amount of freedom to Miranda's: "Imprisoned both by their attitudes and by the cruel logic of the situation, neither Clegg nor Miranda possesses any relative degree of freedom" (344). They may both lack the freedom to abandon class roles and attitudes, but the situation they are in is Clegg's creation. He controls the situation that denies Miranda her freedom.

In a novel that is so much about the deprivation of free will, denying that Clegg had any is tragically ironic. Clegg is the catalyst of this novel, not society, not chance, not the sudden inheritance of wealth. Kidnapping is not something that just happens to the kidnapper. It is something he plans, and in Clegg's case, the kidnapping was meticulously planned and executed. Nor can he avoid responsibility for Miranda's death; she tells him herself that "not fetching a doctor is murder" (119).

Even the view that chance rules the world is something Clegg uses to excuse his actions. When he is remembering the moment of the abduction, he writes, "perhaps I wanted to give fate a chance to stop me. [. . .] I felt I was swept on, like down rapids, I might hit

Colak   11

something, I might get through" (23). Fate did not stop him, but that does not mean that what follows was meant to be.

From the very conception of his plan, from the very first time he dreams of himself as Miranda's heroic savior, he is aware that what he is doing is wrong. His dream when he "ran up and rescued her" continues, "then somehow I was the man that attacked her" (14). He is aware not only that his actions are wrong, but also that he commits them by choice. His language reveals that even in daydreaming about his plan he is making conscious decisions. He writes, "That was the day I first <u>gave</u> myself the dream that came true" (14; emphasis added). Thinking about his fantasy was a conscious act, just as all of his building, preparation, and acquisition of gear were conscious acts. Clegg may have had a sad beginning, but it hardly excuses his criminal activity. Things did not just happen in <u>The Collector</u>; Clegg made them happen. No matter how hard you try to find a Romantic hero in Clegg, there will never be anything more there than a monster. There was no spell cast on Clegg that he did not cast himself.

Colak   12

Works Cited

Bagchee, Syhamel. "The Collector: The Paradoxical Imagination of John Fowles." Journal of Modern Literature 8 (1980–81): 219–34.

Bawer, Bruce. "The Mysteries of John Fowles." The Aspect of Eternity. Saint Paul: Graywolf, 1993. 51–76.

Brink, Andrew. "Female Sacrifice in the Novels of John Fowles." Obsession and Culture: A Study of Sexual Obsession in Modern Fiction. Madison: Fairleigh Dickinson UP, 1996. 139–65.

Campbell, Robert. "Moral Sense and The Collector: Novels of John Fowles." Cambridge Quarterly 25 (1983): 45–53.

Davidson, Arnold E. "Caliban and the Captive Maiden: John Fowles' The Collector and Irving Wallace's The Fan Club." Studies in Humanities 8.2 (1981): 28–33.

Foster, Thomas C. Understanding John Fowles. Columbia: U of South Carolina P, 1994.

Fowles, John. The Collector. Boston: Little, 1963.

Grace, Sherrill E. "Courting Bluebeard with Bartok, Atwood, and Fowles: Modern Treatment of the Bluebeard Theme." Journal of Modern Literature 11 (1984): 245–62.

Loveday, Simon. "The Collector." The Romances of John Fowles. New York: St. Martin's, 1985. 11–28.

Neary, John M. "John Fowles' Clegg: A Metaphysical Rebel." Essays in Literature 15 (1988): 45–61.

Nodelman, Perry. "John Fowles's Variations in The Collector." Contemporary Literature 28 (1987): 332–46.

Walker, David H. "Remorse, Responsibility, and Moral Dilemmas in Fowles's Fiction." Critical Essays on John Fowles. Ed. Ellen Pifer. Boston: Hall, 1986. 54–75.

MLA

Woodcock, Bruce. "Bluebeard and the Voyeurs: The Collector." Male

Mythologies: John Fowles and Masculinity. Sussex, Eng.: Har-

vester; Totowa, NJ: Barnes, 1984. 27–44.

CRITIQUE Jill Colak's paper is an excellent example of a research paper on a literary work, although it is somewhat unusual in one respect: Jill focuses more upon the literary critics than upon the work itself. (Research papers about literature often blend analysis of a work with analysis of the critics, and the proportions of these two components may vary.) In the process of analyzing the critics, however, she also illuminates *The Collector* in a very interesting way, showing that no accurate reading of the novel should attempt to relieve Clegg of moral responsibility for his own actions. In a more general sense, she shows how critics often sidestep moral issues in their attempts to explain the actions of fictional characters.

One might challenge Jill's argument by pointing out that *any* attempt to explain a criminal's behavior can *sound* like an attempt to excuse it, even if that is not the writer's intention. When Jill challenges a Freudian reading, for example, she makes it sound as though the psychoanalytic reader aims to excuse rather than to explain, which is a popular misconception about psychoanalysis rather than an accurate depiction of it. The notion that the psychoanalytic reader is guilty of "blaming bad behavior on poor parenting" is not really supported by the quotation she supplies.

Taken as a whole, however, Jill's argument is persuasive, because she finds many examples of critics whose arguments, intentionally or not, seem to excuse Clegg. Only a reader who has examined all the writings cited by Jill can say whether or not she overstates her case, but certainly the quotations she provides are persuasive evidence of the critics' persistent tendency to misread the novel. She quotes from them accurately and fairly, and her condemnations are usually stated calmly, in noninflammatory, perhaps even understated, language: she finds the misreadings "irresponsible" and "disturbing."

Jill's paper is also well constructed and well written. She uses an effective framing device for her introduction and conclusion: she analyzes the analogy (a faulty one, she points out) between romantic fairy tales and *The Collector.* In the body of the paper, she provides clear transitions to lead the reader through her sequence of subtopics. The result is that the paper "reads" effortlessly. One's attention remains fixed upon the novel and the critics, rather than upon Jill, who has placed herself in the background. Her style is clear, concise, and unforced.

Above all, what is most praiseworthy is Jill's willingness to challenge the authorities and to engage them in argument.

APA FORMAT: General Appearance

The following sections present the details you will need to use the APA format for your research paper. But to get an overview of its main features, read this checklist. It shows at a glance the basic stylings your paper should have.

APA FORMAT: CHECKLIST OF MAIN FEATURES

1. Provide a title page and an abstract; imitate the sample paper's format (see pp. 205–216).

APA

2. Use a one-inch margin on all sides of the paper.

3. Double-space most text. You may use single or triple spacing in some portions of your paper to make the typescript more readable.

4. Provide a manuscript page header on each page at the top right.

5. Indent block quotations five spaces.

6. Cite sources in parentheses, using the basic citation forms. Use MLA format to capitalize titles in parenthetical documentation.

7. Title the bibliography "References" for works cited or "Bibliography" for works consulted. Capitalize only the first letter of titles, subtitles, and proper names. List the date in parentheses after the author's name.

8. Use normal paragraph indentation in the bibliography, not hanging indentation. (However, the APA's Web site [<http://www.apa.org/journals/faq.html>] now suggests that hanging indentation is acceptable unless the paper is being submitted for publication. Find out which method your instructor prefers. I have used hanging indentation in the sample paper and bibliography examples because this format makes bibliographies easier to consult.)

Remember that this discussion focuses upon the *differences* between APA and MLA format; details shared by the two formats are not discussed, so you should consult the section on MLA format to answer questions not covered here. Be sure to review "All Formats: General Appearance" in Chapter 13, since the MLA and APA manuals agree upon such matters as avoiding hyphenation at the end of a line and using justification only on the left margin.

Verb Tenses in the MLA and APA Formats

In the MLA format, the present tense is used in references to works cited: "Johnson argues that. . . ." In contrast, the APA format draws a subtle distinction between *empirical studies* and the *results or conclusions* drawn by those studies. An empirical study as a whole is regarded as a specific event, and so the past or perfect tense should be used: "Williams and Haroldson *conducted* an experiment. . . ." But the results or conclusions of the study are regarded as proven hypotheses, and so the results are expressed in the present tense: "Williams and Haroldson conducted an experiment which showed that alcoholics *are* more likely to experience stress-related illnesses."

Differences Between Journal Articles and Student Papers

The *Publication Manual of the American Psychological Association* focuses primarily upon preparing manuscripts for publication in APA journals. Only a very brief portion of the manual, Appendix A, deals specifically with the preparation of student papers, theses, and dissertations. It acknowledges that there may be many variations in student paper formats from one institution to another. Check to see whether your department or college has its own guidelines.

Whereas a journal article normally contains a list of works cited, titled "References," a student paper may contain a list of works consulted, titled "Bibliography." Published articles normally do not contain appendixes containing raw data, questionnaires, and verbatim instructions to experimental subjects, but student papers may. Tables, figures, and footnotes appear at the end of a manuscript submitted for publication; in student work, such material often appears within the body of the paper.

Types of Research Papers in Psychology and the Social Sciences

Student papers will generally be expected to emulate one of three major types of published research.

1. *Reports of empirical studies.* These reports give the results of original research projects; they present the stages in the research process by dividing it into four main sections. (See "Headings and Subheadings," next.)

2. *Review articles.* Reviews critically evaluate previous research by defining a research problem, summarizing previous studies, analyzing relations and contradictions in earlier findings, and suggesting directions for further research. Review articles should be organized analytically, not chronologically.

3. *Theoretical articles.* These articles use previous research literature to advance a theory, to analyze flaws in an existing theory, or to show one theory's superiority over others. They refer to empirical studies only to illustrate theoretical points. Like review articles, theoretical articles should be organized analytically, not chronologically.

Headings and Subheadings

Headings and subheadings are used freely in APA format. An empirical study normally has four main sections: *introduction, method, results,* and *discussion.* The introduction is not given a heading, but each of the three subsequent sections begins with a heading. The method section is often divided into three subsections: *participants, apparatus,* and *procedure.* The results and discussion sections, if they are brief, may be combined into a section labeled "Results and Conclusions" or "Results and Discussion."

Most theses and dissertations and some long student papers may contain preliminary pages: title page, approval page, acknowledgment page, table of contents, list of tables and figures, and abstract. Preliminary pages should be numbered with lowercase Roman numerals.

Review papers and theoretical papers may use as many subheadings as are needed to improve the paper's readability. The APA format allows the use of the following five levels of headings, with a different format for each level:

Level 5:

CENTERED UPPERCASE HEADING

Level 1:

Centered Uppercase and Lowercase Heading

Level 2:

<u>Centered, Underlined, Uppercase and Lowercase Heading</u>

Level 3:

<u>Flush Left, Underlined, Uppercase and Lowercase Heading</u>

Level 4:

<u>Indented, underlined, lowercase paragraph heading with a period.</u>

Most papers will require fewer than five levels of heading. Follow these guidelines:

One Level: Use level-1 headings.

Two levels: Use level-1 and -3 headings.

Three levels: Use level-1, -3, and -4 headings.

Four levels: Use heading levels 1 through 4.

Five levels: Introduce a level-5 heading above the other four.

Margins and Spacing

Set all margins to at least one inch. The first page may have an extra-wide top margin. Theses and dissertations should have a left margin of at least 1½ inches to allow for binding.

Papers for publication should be double spaced throughout. But student papers may use other types of spacing to make the typescript more readable. Here are some suggestions.

POSSIBLE USES FOR SINGLE SPACING

Table titles and headings

Figure captions

List of references (with double spacing between items)

Footnotes

Block quotations

POSSIBLE USES FOR TRIPLE OR QUADRUPLE SPACING
After chapter titles
Before major subheadings
Before footnotes
Before and after tables

Title Page

A good title should concisely state the main topic and identify the variables or theoretical questions studied. Think of your own experiences in searching through indexes, and try to come up with a title that could be easily indexed and easily found. Do not use all-purpose words such as *method, results, study,* and *experimental,* since they add nothing to a title's meaning.

At the top margin of the title page, flush with the right margin, type a manuscript page header containing the first two or three words of the title and the page number. (With a word processor, use the automatic header function to generate numbered manuscript page headers.) At the top of the page but below the manuscript page header, type the label "Running head:" flush left, followed by a shortened (no more than fifty characters, including spaces and punctuation) version of your paper's title, in all uppercase letters. Next, type a centered, double-spaced block of text containing the paper's title, broken into more than one line if necessary; your name, in normal order, on another line, centered; and your institution on the last line, centered. Number the title page as 1 (unless your paper contains preliminary pages numbered with Roman numerals).

Manuscript Page Header

Since papers in APA format are likely to contain tables and figures that sometimes occupy the whole page, APA style allows the page number to be omitted on such pages.

On the remaining pages, set the manuscript page header, in capitals and lowercase letters, at the upper right-hand corner, flush to the top margin. Place the page number at the end of the manuscript page header, flush to the right margin.

Abstract

An Empirical Study Using 960 characters or less, including spaces and punctuation (which is about 100 to 150 words), summarize the contents of your paper. Use your outline as a guide to cover the paper's contents concisely. Refer to nothing that is not contained in the paper. Refrain from evaluating or commenting on its contents. Define all acronyms, abbreviations (except units of measurement), and special terms. If necessary, mention authors and dates, but paraphrase, do not quote. Use the past tense to describe variables or to narrate procedures;

use the present tense to describe your results. Type all numbers as digits, not as words, unless a number begins a sentence.

A Review Article or Theoretical Article   In seventy-five to one hundred words, describe the topic, preferably using a single sentence; state the thesis. Indicate the paper's scope (for example, a selective or comprehensive review); describe the sources used. Finally, state the paper's conclusions, implications, or applications.

Quotations

Setting Up Block Quotations   A quotation of more than forty words should be set off as a block. Indent the first line five spaces and type the entire block flush with this new margin. If the block is drawn from more than one paragraph, indent the first line of the additional paragraphs; use five spaces for this indentation. Block quotations should always be double spaced in articles submitted for publication, but in student papers they may be single spaced.

Altering Quotations   While the *MLA Handbook* suggests that the word *sic* may be used to call attention to errors of logic in quotations, the *Publication Manual of the American Psychological Association* confines its use to identifying errors of spelling, punctuation, and grammar. In the APA format it should be underlined, and it should be used only within brackets inside a quotation, never in parentheses *after* a quotation.

You may silently alter the case of the first letter of a quotation to make it fit your sentence.

If you emphasize a passage by underlining it, insert the words "italics added" in brackets immediately after the emphasized words.

APA FORMAT: Parenthetical Documentation

Cite sources parenthetically in the text of your paper, using the basic form explained next. However, the APA *Publication Manual* also allows the use of footnotes (really endnotes, since they appear on a separate page at the end of the paper) for two purposes: (1) to give additional information and (2) to acknowledge permission to quote copyrighted material. These notes are signaled by superscript numerals numbered consecutively throughout the paper.

Copyright permission notes are necessary only when a research paper is to be published, so the only endnotes a college researcher is likely to use are content notes. However, the APA *Publication Manual* strongly discourages their use because they are distracting. Information that develops or supplements one of your points should be included in the body of your paper, not relegated to a content note.

Basic Form

If you have used the MLA format for drafting, recasting the parenthetical documentation into APA format is simple, since the two formats are similar. The crucial difference is that the APA format adds the date of publication after the author's name. Nearly all APA citations occur in one of these simple forms:

> Example 1:   Wilson (1983) argues that. . . .
>
> Example 2:   . . . the results were inconclusive (Wilson, 1983).
>
> Example 3:   . . . the results were inconclusive (Wilson, 1983a).
>
> Example 4:   One researcher claimed to have found "absolutely no supporting evidence" (Wilson, 1985, p. 13).
>
> Example 5:   Wilson (1985) claimed to have found "absolutely no supporting evidence" (p. 13).

The form given in example 1 is appropriate if you mention Wilson in your sentence, you are citing his entire study, and your bibliography lists only one study by him published in 1983. The form given in example 2 is appropriate if your sentence does not mention Wilson by name. The form given in example 3 is appropriate if your bibliography contains two sources by Wilson published in 1983, and you need to distinguish between them. (The designations *a* and *b* will appear after the dates in the reference list, too.) The form given in example 4 is appropriate if you quote or cite a specific passage from a study by Wilson without mentioning him by name in your sentence. The form given in example 5 is appropriate if you quote or cite a specific passage after mentioning Wilson by name.

Note that the APA format, unlike the MLA format, adds the abbreviation *p.* (for "page") or *pp.* (for "pages"). You may single out a chapter instead of a page: (Wilson, 1985, chap. 2). Note, too, that whereas a researcher using the MLA format is usually citing critical and historical texts and thus tends to quote and paraphrase specific passages, a researcher using the APA format is more likely to refer to an empirical study as a whole. Therefore, the form given in example 1 is often sufficient.

Common Exceptions to the Basic Form

Citing a Web Site   To cite a Web site but not a specific Web page, simply supply the site's address in parentheses, thus: (http://www.apa.org). No bibliography entry is necessary if you are citing the entire Web site. (A specific Web page should be cited parenthetically by author and date, like any other source.)

Citing a Nonprint Source   A personal communication such as an interview should be cited in the body of your paper as follows:

> N. L. Walker (personal communication, May 16, 1994) said that early researchers encountered unexpected difficulties in replicating the study.

Personal communications should not be included in your list of references.

Citing Two or More Works by the Same Author   Place the dates of the two works in chronological order.

> (Wilson, 1984, 1985)

Citing a Multiauthor Work   Cite a work by two authors by using both names for every citation. Note that the APA format uses an ampersand (&) to replace the word *and* inside parenthetical citations.

> (Wilson & Smith, 1983)
>
> A recent study by Wilson and Smith (1983). . . .

Cite a work by three to five authors by naming all the authors in your first citation. In subsequent citations, list only the first author's surname followed by *et al.*, not underlined (note that *et* is not followed by a period). Thus, the first citation is

> (Wilson, Smith, & Jones, 1991)

A later citation is

> (Wilson et al., 1983)

If a work has six or more authors, cite the first author's surname followed by *et al.* in every citation.

> (Wilson et al., 1990)

Exception: If two works in your reference list shorten to the same *et al.* form, list the authors *with as many names as needed* to distinguish the entries.

Citing a Work Listed by Title   A work with no author should be alphabetized by title in the list of references. A parenthetical citation should contain the first two or three words of the title, plus the date. In the reference list, capitalize only the first letter of the title, but in the text of the paper, capitalize the first letter of each major word.

> ("Early Remains Discovered," 1991)

Citing a Work Listed Under Anonymous   The APA format, unlike the MLA format, uses *Anonymous* as the author for some entries, but only for works that are specifically *signed* "Anonymous."

> (Anonymous, 1993)

Citing a Work by a Corporate Author   Spell out the name of a corporate author each time it appears in a text citation. But if the name is long and the abbreviation is familiar, or if, according to the APA *Publication Manual*, it is "readily understandable" (170), introduce an abbreviation in brackets in the first text citation and use just the abbreviation thereafter. Thus, the first time, use

    (Federal Communications Commission [FCC], 1990)

Later, use

    (FCC, 1990)

Consolidating Parenthetical Citations   You may cite more than one work in a parenthetical citation. When citing works by one author, list them chronologically.

    (Smith, 1983, 1985, 1989)

When citing works by more than one author, list them alphabetically.

    (Smith & Jones, 1982; Thomason & Johnson, 1981; Withers &
    Cruikshank, 1990)

Citing a Secondary Quotation   When citing a source quoted or cited by another source, use this form.

    Smathers (1984) drew the same conclusion (as cited in Berman, 1989).

The original work by Smathers should be included in the list of references, even though it was not directly consulted.

APA FORMAT: The List of Works Cited

General Principles

List all authors' names in inverted order: last name followed by initial(s). Use an ampersand (&) before the last author's name. In listing an edited book, put the name of the editor(s) in the author position, followed by *Ed.* ("editor") or *Eds.* ("editors"), enclosed in parentheses, without underlining. Spell out a corporate author's name in full. Next, type the year of publication in parentheses, followed by a period. Capitalize only the first letter of the title and subtitle, plus the first letter of any proper names. Do not enclose an article title in quotation marks. Some of the instructions that follow reflect APA's preferences for manuscripts submitted for publication rather than for the final versions printed in its journals. For instance, unlike the *MLA Handbook*, the APA *Publication Manual* instructs manuscript typists to include a list of works cited, titled "References," but a student paper may contain a list of works consulted, titled "Bibliography."

A manuscript submitted for publication should be double spaced throughout, but a student paper may be single spaced within bibliography entries.

Listing Multiple Sources by a Single Author

List the author's name in full for each entry, and place the entries in chronological order. If the same author's name begins several entries with different coauthors, alphabetize the entries by coauthors' names.

Whitlow, B. F. (1982). The entry level. . . .
Whitlow, B. F., & Brown, L. W. (1984). The significance of. . . .
Whitlow, B. F., Chatterjee, M. N., & Brown, L. W. (1989). Factors influencing. . . .
Whitlow, B. F., Chatterjee, M. N., & Brown, L. W. (1990). Variables in conducting. . . .

Listing Books

Besides giving the information listed in the section "General Principles," immediately after a book title give in parentheses any additional information needed for accurate retrieval—for example, the number of the edition or the number of the volume used (2nd ed., Vol. 3).

A book reference concludes with the book's publication information. Since the date has already been given, list only the city of publication and the publisher; use a colon to separate the two items. Omit unnecessary words in the name of the publisher, such as *Publishers, Co.,* or *Inc.* But do not omit the words *Press, University Press,* and *Books.*

Here is a basic book entry.

Becker, E. (1969). Angel in armor: A post-Freudian perspective on the nature of man. New York: Braziller.

A Book in a Numbered Edition

Beck, R. C. (1986). Applying psychology: Understanding people (2nd ed.). Englewood Cliffs, NJ: Prentice-Hall.

An Edited Book

Brockman, J. (Ed.) (1977). About Bateson: Essays on Gregory Bateson. New York: Dutton.

A Book by a Corporate Author

National Clearinghouse for Mental Health Information, Division of Scientific and Public Information. (1981). Anorexia nervosa. Rockville, MD: U.S. Dept. of Health and Human Services, Public Health Service, Alcohol, Drug Abuse and Mental Health Administration, National Institute of Mental Health.

A Translation

> Freud, S. (1962). <u>Civilization and its discontents</u> (J. Strachey, Trans.). New York: Norton. (Original work published 1930)

Listing Articles

Articles in Periodicals First, list the author and the article's title, following the instructions given in the section "General Principles." After the journal's title, list the volume number, following a comma, and underline continuously from the first letter of the journal's title to the last digit of the volume number. If each issue of the journal is separately paginated, list the issue number in parentheses, not underlined; if the journal is continuously paginated, list only the volume number. Use *p.* ("page") or *pp.* ("pages") before the page numbers in a reference to a newspaper article.

A Journal Article In a journal separately paginated by issue, use this style.

> Remley, T. P. (1993). Rehabilitation counseling: A scholarly model for the generic profession of counseling. <u>Journal of Applied Rehabilitation Counseling, 24</u>(4), 71-73.

In a continuously paginated journal, use the following form.

> Strauss, C. C., & Last, C. G. (1993). Social and simple phobias in children. <u>Journal of Anxiety Disorders, 7</u>, 141-152.

An Article in a Magazine

> Kantrowitz, B. (1994, February 14). The metaphor is the message. <u>Newsweek, 123</u>, 49.

An Article in a Newspaper

> Denlinger, K. (1994, February 11). In search of past, Pell finds despair. <u>Washington Post</u>, p. C1.

An Article in a Collection

> Mufson, L. H., Moreau, D., Weissman, M. M., & Klerman, G. L. (1993). Interpersonal psychotherapy for adolescent depression. In G. L. Klerman & M. M. Weissman (Eds.), <u>New applications of interpersonal psychotherapy</u> (pp. 129-166). Washington, DC: American Psychiatric Press.

Note that when it is not in the author position, an editor's name should not be inverted.

Listing Other Kinds of Sources

INTERNET ### An Article from a Web Site

> Kraut, R., Lundmark, V., Patterson, M., Kiesler, S., Mukopadhyay, T., &
> Scherlis, W. (1998). Internet paradox: A social technology that
> reduces social involvement and psychological well-being?
> American Psychologist, 53, 1017–1031. Retrieved January 8, 1999
> from the World Wide Web: http://www.apa.org/journals/amp/
> amp5391017.html

(Note that the APA's guidelines [in the *Publication Manual* and at the APA Web site] are inconsistent about supplying a period at the end of references. The examples I have supplied follow their guidelines.)

A Recording

> Ellis, A. (1986). Effective self-assertion [Cassette Recording].
> Washington, DC: American Psychological Association.

If you must include a specific number to identify the recording, change the brackets to parentheses: (Cassette Recording No. 20307).

A Film

> Whitely, J. (Director). (1972). Albert Ellis: A demonstration with an
> elementary school-age child [Film]. Alexandria, VA: American
> Personnel and Guidance Association.

A Personally Conducted Interview   Cite personal communications only in the body of your paper; do not include them in the list of references.

Sample Paper: APA Format

Running head: NEGATIVE EFFECTS OF DAY CARE ON INFANT

DEVELOPMENT

The Potential Negative Effects of

Day Care on Infant Development

Lisa Hewitt

Wright State University

APA

APA

Abstract

A selective review of research on infant development in day care versus home care shows that negative effects upon infant-parent attachment have been well documented. Infants placed in day care at an early age tend to be insecure and more avoidant of their mothers. Other characteristics of children enrolled in day care at early ages include uncooperativeness, increased aggressiveness towards peers and parents, and more frequent illness. Long-term effects of infant day care have not been adequately studied, primarily because of the inherent limitations of the Strange Situation Test.

The Potential Negative Effects of

Day Care on Infant Development

Many mothers have entered the work force over the past 30 years. In fact, of the mothers with children under 6 years of age, 20% were employed outside their homes in 1960, and that number grew to 50% by 1980 and is still growing (Barglow, Vaughn, & Molitor, 1987, p. 945). This increase will have major consequences for the youth of America.

There is much controversy over the impact that day care has on the emotional and developmental well-being of children. Belsky, one of the most noted psychologists in the field of infant development, has reversed his former view that day care has no adverse effects on infants. Research involving children over the age of 2 shows no adverse effects of day care on development. But what about infants who are placed in day care within the first 2 years of life? Studies have shown that the negative emotional and intellectual effects of day care are great among these young children. For this reason, and because the early years of a child's life are crucial to later development, mothers should seriously consider staying at home for at least the first 2 years of their babies' lives.

Many researchers have pointed out that a secure infant-parent attachment is crucial to the later emotional well-being of the infant. Research has designated the first 2 years of life as the time when this important bond is developed (White, 1981). Day care within the first 2 years of life has a negative effect on infant-parent attachment.

In searching for a standard, reliable way to assess the quality of infant-parent attachment, early researchers determined that this attachment could not be assessed solely by observing episodes of

APA

crying upon separation, or even reluctance to approach a stranger. Instead, they concluded that attachment could best be measured by evaluating the behavior of the child toward the parent upon reunion following separation (Belsky, 1988, p. 243). Thus a new attachment testing procedure, known as the Strange Situation test, was developed by Ainsworth and Wittig (1969; as cited in Gamble & Zigler, 1986). The test employs a series of situations involving the infant, a parent, and a stranger. Stress on the infant is gradually increased through various separations from, and reunions with, the parent in the presence and absence of the stranger. The infant's behavior during reunion is closely monitored and scored in a standardized fashion.

Application of the Strange Situation Test led to three main characterizations of infant attachment behavior: secure, anxious avoidant, and anxious resistant. Secure infants actively sought contact with the parents during reunion. These infants also played independently while a parent was in the room. Anxious avoidant infants psychologically avoided a parent during reunion and showed signs of conflict during free play. These infants moved away from a parent during reunion, aborted attempts to approach the parent, or avoided making direct eye contact with the parent. The third class, anxious resistant infants, showed some anger and physical resistance to the parent during reunion. These infants sought some contact with the parent, but even after the contact they might cry or push away a toy offered by the parent (Ainsworth Blehar, Waters, & Wall, 1978; Belsky, 1988; Gamble & Zigler, 1986).

The Strange Situation Test has limitations. Infant behavior is highly complex, and it is difficult to develop one method that can accurately assess varying behaviors. Nevertheless, the Strange Situa-

tion Test has been used extensively in many attachment studies,
and its usefulness has not been disproved. In order for the test to be
appropriately used, however, it should be employed only on infants
below the age of 20 months. The developers of the test themselves
have suggested that the results might not be appropriate for infants
above this age (Gamble & Zigler, 1986, p. 30).

In the last few decades many studies have attempted to assess
the impact of day care on infant-parent attachment. Two highly regarded studies have been carried out in recent years (Barglow et al.,
1987; Belsky & Rovine, 1988). Both studies used the Strange Situation Test to assess infant attachment, and both studies raised some
disturbing implications about day care for infants.

In the Barglow, Vaughn, and Molitor study, 170 randomly selected pregnant women were chosen to participate. The women
were subjected to a series of psychological tests to determine their
attitudes towards motherhood and infant rearing. To eliminate biases in the sample, the experimenters excluded women from the
study if they described any risk conditions that might have contributed to adverse developmental outcomes. After testing was completed, 110 of the women were chosen to have their infants complete
the study. Data were gathered using the Strange Situation Test
when the infants reached 12 months of age. The 110 infants were
categorized into two groups: the at-home group in which the mother
was the primary caregiver and was never absent from the home for
more than 4 hours per week, and the at-work group in which infant
care was performed by a substitute in the infant's own home for at
least the 4 months prior to the testing date. In the at-work group,
46% of the infants were classified as either anxious avoidant (31.5%)

APA

or anxious resistant (14.5%), and 54% of the infants were classified as secure. In the at-home group, only 29% fell into one of the insecure classifications (9% anxious avoidant and 20% anxious resistant), while 71% of the at-home infants were classified as secure.

From these data Barglow et al. concluded that "routine, daily separations, resulting from a mother's working outside the home on a full-time basis during the last 4 months of her infant's first year of life, significantly increase the probability of an insecure-avoidant infant-mother attachment" (p. 951). Further analysis of the data brought the experimenters to the conclusion that infants interpret daily separation from their mothers as rejection, leading to avoidant behavior in the Strange Situation Test.

Belsky and Rovine's study (1988) was conducted using 149 first-born infants chosen at random prior to birth. The infants were observed using the Strange Situation Test at 12 months with their mothers and again at 13 months with their fathers, and the subjects were sorted into two categories: (a) secure and (b) insecure (composed of both anxious avoidant and anxious resistant categories).

In assessing the infant-mother attachment, Belsky and Rovine determined that infants in full-time day care were most likely to be classified as insecure (47%). High-part-time-care infants (between 20 and 35 hours per week of nonmaternal care) were next most likely (35%). Among the infants with small amounts of day care (10 hours or less per week), 21% were insecure; 25% of the infants who were cared for solely by their mothers were insecure.

Although these results show a slightly higher rate of insecurity for home-care infants versus infants in day care 10 to 20 hours per week, the statistically significant finding is the difference between

infants in day care more than 20 hours and those in day care less than
20 hours per week. From the data collected, Belsky and Rovine concluded that "infants in nonmaternal care for more than 20 hours per
week are more likely than their counterparts with less (or no) care to
be classified as insecure in their relationship with mother" (p. 164).

In assessing the infant-father attachment at 13 months, Belsky
and Rovine found that 29% of boys in care less than 35 hours per
week were insecure in their attachments to their fathers. But a total
of 50% of the boys in full-time care were classified as insecure.
These data indicate that infant boys in full-time care are much more
likely to develop insecure infant-father attachments than boys in
care less than 35 hours per week.

Because only 14% of the girls in care for more than 10 hours per
week were classified as insecure in their infant-father attachments,
the researchers concluded that infant boys are more likely than girls
to become insecure in their relationships with their parents if placed
in full-time child care. Further study is needed in the specific area of
infant attachment based on sex differences.

These studies do not emphatically prove that infant child-care
leads to insecure infant-parent attachments. However, the data
show that there is a higher risk of developing an insecure attachment if an infant is placed in day care before the age of 2. If infant
day care leads to insecure infant-parent attachments, what are the
consequences? Although there has not been enough empirical research to determine the effect of insecure attachment on later child
development, some experts have expressed hypotheses based upon
their own observations. Sroufe has stated that "ultimately . . . these
[insecurely attached] infants were quite emotionally dependent as

preschoolers, requiring a great deal of contact, guidance, and disci-pline from their teachers" (p. 289). Independence, Sroufe has pointed out, is not enhanced by early avoidance of parents but is built by ef-fectively using emotional closeness.

Belsky has echoed some of Sroufe's ideas, citing several studies that were not focused on infant day care but that "reported associa-tions between anxious avoidant attachment in infancy and subse-quent noncompliance, aggressiveness, social withdrawal, and behavior problems more generally" (p. 250). A follow-up study of 3- and 4-year-olds who as infants had been cared for in a Syracuse Uni-versity day-care center showed that the children previously classi-fied as having insecure attachments showed increases in aggressive behavior and decreases in cooperativeness (Schwarz, Strickland, & Krolick, 1974; as cited in Belsky, 1988). Another study showed that children displayed more fear and threw more frequent temper tan-trums when they had experienced day care as infants (Rubenstein & Howes, 1983; as cited in Belsky, 1988).

These studies did not determine what caused the anxious avoidant infant-parent attachment in the infants. These studies did, however, provide some independent verification that infants classi-fied as anxious avoidant are likely to experience other behavioral problems later in life.

One of the reasons why infant day care leads to insecure attach-ment might be the high turnover rate among day-care professionals. Wingert and Kantrowitz have pointed out that 41% of all child-care professionals quit each year. Marcy Whitebook has stated that "turn-over among child-care workers is second only to parking-lot and gas-station attendants" (qtd. in Wingert, 1990, p. 92). It is unlikely that infants will develop healthy bonds with adults if their caregivers are constantly changing.

Another hazard of infant day care is the increased risk of exposure to disease. Zinsmeister has indicated that day-care centers contribute to higher levels of diarrhea, dysentery, epidemic jaundice, hepatitis, and inner-ear infections (1988, p. 44). A baby's immune system, Zinsmeister pointed out, is especially prone to disease exposure since it is not fully effective until around the age of 2.

It is true that some experts still believe that infant day care need not cause serious problems, particularly if the day care is of high quality. But precisely because most of the day-care assessment research to date has been conducted in relatively high-quality centers that are not typical of those used by most families (King & MacKinnon, 1988, p. 394), the negative effects of day care in society at large may be more severe than the studies have indicated. In any case, it is unlikely that the most extraordinary child-care worker can equal the care given by enthusiastic parents during a child's crucial development years.

A few studies have compared substitute and maternal care of infants. The key findings are those of Rubenstein, Pedersen, and Yarrow (1977), who examined several caregiving behaviors and rated the caregiver's effectiveness at these behaviors. They found that "mothers expressed more positive affect, engaged in more playful interactions, and offered a greater variety of experiences to the infants" (p. 530). Generally, mothers were observed to provide more stimulating environments for infants than did substitute caregivers.

Commenting on the difficulty of finding excellent caregivers who are essentially hired to do for money what a mother would do simply out of love, Zinsmeister (1988) strongly advocated parental care:

APA

The quest for a human child-rearing system is more than an

engineering problem. It is a values problem. So long as we

continue to debase parenting, only the debased will be

willing to take it on. So long as people perversely want

what they are not willing themselves to give, there can be

no solution. The only way out of the natural shortage of

good child care is for every parent to devote more of his

own time to his children, instead of hunting frantically, and

quixotically, for more and better hired care. (p. 45)

The exact "safe" age at which mothers can feel secure in placing

their children in day care is not known. Researchers have empha-

sized the desirability of avoiding day care during the first 2 years of

life due to the development of the infant-parent bond during this pe-

riod. Does this mean day care is safe at age 2? Unfortunately, the

Strange Situation Test has not been proven effective for children

above the age of 20 months, so studies in this area are limited. Re-

search needs to be done to find a new method of measuring the ef-

fects of day care on older children.

In the end, a parental decision about day care is not easy. Par-

ents need to weigh all the evidence and options carefully to deter-

mine what is in their child's best interest. Perhaps White (1981) has

best stated the point:

It's a one-time opportunity. Babies form their first human

attachment only once. Babies begin to learn language only

once. Babies begin to get to know the world only once. The

outcomes of these processes play a major role in shaping

the future of each new child. (p. 16)

References

Ainsworth, M. D. S., Blehar, M. C., Waters, E., & Wall, S. (1978). Patterns of attachment: A psychological study of the strange situation. Hillsdale, NJ: Erlbaum.

Ainsworth, M. D. S., & Wittig, D. (1969). Attachment and exploratory behavior of one-year-olds in a strange situation. In B. Foss (Ed.), Determinants of infant behavior (Vol. 4, pp. 111–136). London: Methuen.

Barglow, P., Vaughn, B. E., & Molitor, N. (1987). Effects of maternal absence due to employment on the quality of infant-mother attachment in a low-risk sample. Child Development, 58, 945–954.

Belsky, J. (1988). The "effects" of infant day care reconsidered. Early Childhood Research Quarterly, 3, 235–272.

Belsky, J., & Rovine, M. J. (1988). Nonmaternal care in the first year of life and the security of infant-parent attachment. Child Development, 59, 157–167.

Gamble, T. J., & Zigler, E. (1986). Effects of infant day care: Another look at the evidence. American Journal of Orthopsychiatry, 56, 26–42.

King, D., & MacKinnon, C. E. (1988). Making difficult choices easier: A review of research on day care and children's development. Family Relations, 37, 392–398.

Rubenstein, J. L., Pedersen, F. A., & Yarrow, L. J. (1977). What happens when mother is away: A comparison of mothers and substitute caregivers. Developmental Psychology, 13, 529–530.

Rubenstein, J., & Howes, C. (1983). Adaptation to toddler day care. In S. Kilmer (Ed.), Advances in early education and day care (Vol. 3, pp. 39–62). Greenwich, CT: Jai Press.

APA

APA

Schwarz, J. C., Strickland, R. G., & Krolick, G. (1974). Infant day care: Behavioral effects at preschool age. <u>Developmental Psychology,</u> <u>10,</u> 502–556.

Sroufe, L. A. (1988). A developmental perspective on day care. <u>Early</u> <u>Childhood Research Quarterly, 3,</u> 283–291.

White, B. L. (1981, November). Viewpoint: Should you stay home with your baby? <u>Young Children,</u> 11–17.

Wingert, P., & Kantrowitz, B. (1990, Winter/Spring [Special Edition]). The day care generation. <u>Newsweek,</u> 86–92.

Zinsmeister, K. (1988). Brave new world: How day-care harms children. <u>Policy Review, 44,</u> 40–48.

CRITIQUE   Lisa Hewitt's paper is an example of a selective review article. It focuses on the question "What evidence is there to show that infant day care has negative effects?" Lisa concentrates on short-term behavioral effects, though she briefly considers other effects. At the beginning of the paper, she uses Belsky's change of opinion to capture the reader's attention. She defines and limits her topic well: first day care, then day care for children less than two years old, then the effects of such day care upon parent-child attachment.

Lisa does a good job of explaining a crucial item, the Strange Situation Test, though she should explain its standardized-scoring procedures. She notes limitations and shortcomings in the research she discusses. She keeps the paper well focused on its controlling idea, and she implicitly addresses her paper to parents who would like to know, judging from the literature, whether they should or should not entrust their infants to day-care workers.

The main shortcomings of Lisa's paper resulted from the need to keep the paper fairly short and manageable. Her review of the literature is very selective, and the reader gets little sense of the huge extent of the body of literature dealing with the effects of infant day care. She often cites later reviews and evaluations rather than the original sources. She should probably have presented the data from the Rovine study by using a table. Finally, I think that she should probably have ended the paper with her own writing rather than with a quotation. Some writers feel that a good quotation can provide an effective conclusion; but shouldn't the reader's final impression be of the writer rather than of one of the writer's sources?

APA

■ ■ ■ EXERCISE 15
Citing and Listing Sources

This exercise is designed to give you some practice in MLA documentation. If your paper will be converted to one of the other formats, you may adapt this exercise to fit the APA, CBE, or Chicago conventions by substituting APA, CBE, or Chicago for MLA. (CBE and Chicago conventions are discussed in the next chapter.)

Figure 7.1 (pp. 218–220) reproduces the title page, the copyright page, and page 154 from the book by Stephen Jay Gould. Its subject is the Burgess Shale, a rich source of fossils from one of the earliest periods of life on earth.

1. The sample page of text depicts a strange pre-Cambrian creature called *Hallucigenia*. It was given its name in 1977 by a scientist named Simon Conway Morris. Write a sentence in which you explain that Morris gave the creature that name because of "the bizarre and dream-like appearance of the animal." Be sure to quote Morris's exact words. Assume that this is the first time you have mentioned Morris in your paper and that you are using only one source by Gould. Include appropriate MLA parenthetical documentation.

2. Using the reproduced title page and copyright page, write an MLA bibliography entry for Gould's book.

Wonderful Life

The Burgess Shale
and the Nature of History

STEPHEN JAY GOULD

FIGURE 7.1 Title Page, Copyright Page, and a Text Page from Gould

Copyright © 1989 by Stephen Jay Gould
All rights reserved.
Printed in the United States of America.

The text of this book is composed in 10½/13 Avanta, with
display type set in Fenice Light. Composition and
manufacturing by The Haddon Craftsmen, Inc.
Book design by Antonina Krass.

"Design" copyright 1936 by Robert Frost and renewed 1964 by Lesley Frost Ballantine.
Reprinted from *The Poetry of Robert Frost*, edited by Edward Connery Lathem, by
permission of Henry Holt and Company, Inc.

Library of Congress Cataloging-in-Publication Data
Gould, Stephen Jay.
Wonderful life: the Burgess Shale and the nature of history / Stephen Jay Gould.
p. cm. Bibliography: p. Includes index.
1. Evolution—History. 2. Invertebrates, Fossil. 3. Paleontology—Cambrian.
4. Paleontology—British Columbia—Yoho National Park. 5. Burgess
Shale. 6. Paleontology—Philosophy. 7. Contingency (Philosophy)
8. Yoho National Park (B.C.) I. Title.
QE770.G67 1989
560'.9—dc19   88-37469

ISBN 0-393-02705-8

W. W. Norton & Company, Inc., 500 Fifth Avenue, New York, N. Y. 10110
W. W. Norton & Company Ltd., 37 Great Russell Street, London WC1B 3NU
4 5 6 7 8 9 0

FIGURE 7.1   Title Page, Copyright Page, and a Text Page from Gould *(continued)*

154 | WONDERFUL LIFE

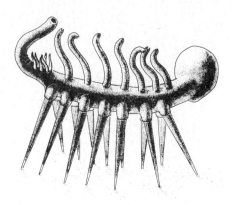

3.34. *Hallucigenia*, supported by its seven pairs of struts, stands on the sea floor. Drawn by Marianne Collins.

are talking about symbols, Simon chose a most unusual and truly lovely designation for his strangest discovery. He called this creature *Hallucigenia* to honor "the bizarre and dream-like appearance of the animal" (1977c, p. 624), and also, perhaps, as a memorial to an unlamented age of social experiment.

Walcott had assigned seven Burgess species to *Canadia*, his principal genus of polychaetes. (Polychaetes, members of the phylum Annelida, the segmented worms, are the marine equivalent of terrestrial earthworms, and are among the most varied and successful of all animal groups.) Conway Morris later showed (1979) that Walcott's single genus was hiding remarkable disparity under one vastly overextended umbrella—for he eventually recognized, among Walcott's seven "species," three separate genera of true polychaetes, a worm of an entirely different phylum (a priapulid that he renamed *Lecythioscopa*), and *Hallucigenia*. Walcott, mistaking the strangest of all Burgess creatures for an ordinary worm, referred to this oddball as *Canadia sparsa*.

How can you describe an animal when you don't even know which side is up, which end front and which back? *Hallucigenia* is bilaterally symmetrical, like most mobile animals, and carries sets of repeated structures in common with the standard design of many phyla. The largest specimens

FIGURE 7.1 Title Page, Copyright Page, and a Text Page from Gould *(continued)*

Figure 7.2 (pp. 222–223) reproduces the table of contents of an issue of the *Journal of the History of Biology* and the first page of an article by Faye Marie Getz.

3. Write a sentence in which you quote Getz's observation that "interest in various disasters ebbs and flows with the times." Include appropriate MLA documentation. Assume that this is the second time you have mentioned Getz by name and that you are using only one source by Getz.

4. Using the reproduced pages, write an MLA bibliography entry for Getz's article.

Journal of the History of Biology

SUMMER, 1991: VOLUME 24, NUMBER 2

Editors: Everett Mendelsohn, Harvard University

Shirley A. Roe, University of Connecticut

Staff Editor: Julia A. McVaugh

CONTENTS

FIGURE 7.2 Table of Contents and the First Page of an Article from the
Journal of the History of Biology

Black Death and the Silver Lining: Meaning, Continuity, and Revolutionary Change in Histories of Medieval Plague

FAYE MARIE GETZ

Department of the History of Medicine
University of Wisconsin Medical School
Madison, Wisconsin 53706

Humanity can rest assured that no disaster, however terrible, is without redeeming social content. At least this is what one supermarket tabloid would have us believe. A headline in point: "Even though 55 million died, Black Death that Wiped out Europe Had a Good Side!" The accompanying article began, "The horrifying Black Death wiped out more than 55 million people in Europe during the Middle Ages — but the catastrophe changed the world forever by giving birth to the Renaissance." According to an interview with a much-published medievalist, famous authorities agree that the Black Death not only reduced Europe's population from 75 million to 20 million, but it also put an end to those dismal Middle Ages and "nurtured geniuses like Michelangelo and Leonardo da Vinci." The piece ends with the comforting observation that this awesome slaughter indeed had "a silver lining."[1] One shudders to contemplate the death of 55 million people as a recipe for social renewal. But the thesis that the article presents, wedged though it may be between advertisements for secret good-luck charms and miracle diet pills, has an undeniable appeal. History, like a novel, ought to make sense, and how could the death of most of the population of Europe have happened for no good reason?

It is undeniable that interest in various disasters ebbs and flows with the times. We no longer share Voltaire's fixation on the meaning of the Lisbon earthquake,[2] nor does the huge mortality of the influenza epidemic of 1918 stir writers into somber contemplation of last things.[3] But interest

1. *National Enquirer*, May 6, 1986.
2. Voltaire made the Lisbon earthquake of 1755 the focus point of *Candide* (1759).
3. Major Greenwood, in his popular *Epidemics and Crowd-Diseases: An*

Journal of the History of Biology, vol. 24, no. 2 (Summer 1991), pp. 265–289.
© 1991 *Kluwer Academic Publishers. Printed in the Netherlands.*

FIGURE 7.2 Table of Contents and the First Page of an Article from the *Journal of the History of Biology (continued)*

CHAPTER 8

RESEARCH PAPER FORMATS:
CBE and Chicago

If you skipped Chapter 7 because you are using CBE or Chicago format, go back and read "Overview of Research Paper Formats" to be sure that you understand the chief points of difference between the four major formats covered in this book.

I've chosen to use CBE citation-sequence format as a model for papers in the sciences for two main reasons: First, the *CBE Manual* is the most thorough of the style manuals in the sciences, and second, the citation-sequence format, which scientists commonly use, is the only scientific format that differs drastically from the three other common forms of documentation (author-page, author-date, and Chicago footnote-style citations).

Research writers often have to convert MLA-style papers to Chicago format to meet the requirements of specific disciplines or editors. For example, research papers in the humanities are usually written in MLA format, but writers of theses and dissertations are often required to use Chicago format. If you ever need to convert a paper from MLA to Chicago format, use the following list to speed your work. It summarizes the major changes needed.

Key Changes to Make When Converting from MLA to Chicago Format

1. Add a title page.
2. Indent block quotations five spaces, not ten.
3. Add an extra line space before and after block quotations.
4. Use superscript citations and endnotes instead of parenthetical citations and list of works cited.
5. In citing articles, in addition to the volume number give either the issue number or the month/season of the issue, but not both. Use one of the forms on page 245.
6. In giving publishers' names, write out "University Press" in full, or use the abbreviation "Univ. Press." Except for the phrase

"University Press," omit such words as "Press," "Company," "Incorporated," and "Books," but leave names intact: "W. W. Norton" rather than "Norton," for example.

7. Subsequent references to a source already cited take the form "6. Higham, 16." If the source and page number are the same as in the previous note, use the form "Ibid." If the source, but not the page number, is the same as in the previous note, use the form "Ibid., 17."

8. If you are required to attach a list of works cited, use hanging indentation, but indent the second line three or four spaces instead of five.

9. In giving inclusive page numbers, express the second number by giving only the digits that differ from the first, thus: "153–5."

10. Use the word "reprint" rather than the abbreviation "rpt."

11. When citing an alphabetical reference work, use the abbreviation "s.v." (Latin, *sub verba*, literally "under the word"), thus: *The New Grove Dictionary of Music and Musicians* (1980), s.v. "Improvisation."

CBE CITATION SEQUENCE FORMAT:
General Appearance

Review the comparison of formats at the beginning of Chapter 7. The following sections present the details you will need to use the CBE format for your research paper. But to get an overview of its main features, read this checklist. It shows at a glance the basic stylings your paper should have.

CBE CITATION SEQUENCE FORMAT:
CHECKLIST OF MAIN FEATURES

1. Provide a title page and abstract; imitate the sample paper's format (see pp. 231–232).

2. Use 1- to 1½-inch margins.

3. Double-space everything, including block quotations.

4. Type a page number or manuscript page header at the top right.

5. Indent block quotations five spaces.

6. Cite sources by using superscript numbers that refer to the numbered bibliography at the end of the paper.

7. Title the bibliography "Cited References." List the sources in their order of appearance. (*Option:* List the sources alphabetically.) Capitalize only the first letter of titles, subtitles, and proper names; use no underlining or special fonts.

CBE

> 8. Use hanging indentation in the bibliography.
>
> 9. Avoid footnotes and endnotes.

The numbered system of documentation, called citation sequence format, is used most frequently by research writers in biology, chemistry, computer science, health sciences, mathematics, medicine, nursing, and physics. There are several style manuals for specific disciplines; see those listed in "A Research Writer's Bookshelf" in Chapter 1. Rather than attempt to cover briefly all the variations in the scientific style manuals, I will discuss in some detail the number system described by the *CBE* [Council of Biology Editors] *Manual*.

Student papers will generally be expected to emulate one of two major types of published research: (1) research articles (described in the APA *Publication Manual* as "reports of empirical studies") and (2) review articles (see "Types of Research Papers in Psychology and the Social Sciences" in Chapter 7).

The *CBE Manual* gives a thorough treatment of scientific style conventions, but it is designed for editors, not for students. It says nothing about many aspects of preparing a student paper. It can be frustrating to use: If you look up *margin* in its index, hoping to find out what margin width you should set, you will find nothing. On the other hand, you *will* find *buckyballs* and other unusual words in the index. Since the *CBE Manual* is difficult to consult, the following pages provide clarifications intended specifically for student use.

Headings and Subheadings

The *CBE Manual* recommends that levels of headings be designed by placement and by typeface. In descending order of importance, use headings (1) centered, (2) flush left spaced above text, and (3) flush left but running into the paragraph. Use (1) all capitals, (2) capitals and lowercase, and (3) underlining. You may use italics and small capitals in word-processed manuscripts.

Margins and Spacing

Set margins within the range of 1 to 1½ inches. Double-space throughout.

Title Page

The *CBE Manual* encourages the use of informative titles. The title should, if possible, begin with a term that indicates the paper's main topic, with subordinate terms introduced in descending order of importance: "Hypersonic Stimulation's Effects upon Sleep Cycles in Canines." On the title page, type the title and your name, using upper- and lowercase capitalization. (Articles submitted for publication normally also include the author's byline and address.)

Abstract

Starting either on the title page or on a new page, type an abstract that summarizes, preferably in a single paragraph, the methods, findings, and conclusions of the paper. The abstract of a long review article may simply indicate the

CBE

paper's topics rather than summarize its evidence and conclusions. The text of the paper itself may also begin on the title page if the layout and typography make it easy to tell where the abstract ends and the text begins.

Quotations

Setting Up Block Quotations   The *CBE Manual* says only that long quotations may be set off by "indenting the quoted text" (177) in published research. I suggest using the APA format: Indent block quotations five spaces and double-space them.

Altering Quotations   You may handle mistakes in quoted material by inserting, immediately after the mistake, the word *sic* (underlined) and followed by your correction; enclose these two items within a pair of square brackets.

If you underline part of a quotation to emphasize it, use a bracketed insertion within the quotation to indicate the alteration.

```
"You may emphasize some [emphasis mine] words."
```

CBE CITATION SEQUENCE FORMAT:
Documentation

The *CBE Manual* offers two main choices in documentation format: (1) the name-year system, which closely resembles the APA format and which is often used in biology and the earth sciences; and (2) the citation sequence system, which is used in most of the applied and medical sciences.

The citation sequence system itself offers two more choices: The references may be listed (1) in alphabetical order or (2) in the order in which they are cited in the body of the paper. What follows is a discussion only of the citation sequence format using references listed in the order in which they are cited.

Basic Form

The citation sequence system is simple and relatively inflexible. Cite a source by inserting a superscript (in a font one or two points smaller than your text font if you are using a word processor) immediately after your reference to it:

```
A later epidemiological study[7] failed to replicate these findings.
```

The number indicates that the reader should see source 7 in your list of references. The number should be repeated each time the source is cited in the body of your paper. Some instructors may prefer that citation numbers be inserted within parentheses on the line rather than as superscripts: ". . . study (7) failed. . . ."

Footnotes to Text

The *CBE Manual* says that you may use footnotes or endnotes to present important explanatory or documentary material that would be distracting if it were included in the body of your paper. Letter your footnotes with superscript lowercase letters ([a], [b], [c], and so on) throughout the paper; do not begin a new series on each page.

Consolidating Citations

Several sources may be cited at once: "The results[4–6] . . . ," or "Smith noted[4,7,11]. . . ."

CBE CITATION SEQUENCE FORMAT:
The List of Cited References

General Principles

Type the first line of each entry flush left; indent subsequent lines. List all authors' names in inverted order: last name followed by initials. When a source has more than one author, use semicolons to separate the authors' names. In listing an edited book, put the name of the editor(s) in the author position, followed by the word *editor* (or *editors*), without underlining. Place the title first when listing a work with no author, or use the word *Anonymous*, without underlining, enclosed in brackets, in the author position. Capitalize only the first letter of the title, plus the first letter of any proper names. Do not underline any titles, including titles of books, journals, and articles. Use abbreviations in the titles of journals. Place a period after each major element in a reference (author, title, publication data).

Since the CBE citation sequence system requires you to use abbreviations in journal titles in your list of references, you should be careful to record exactly the abbreviated journal titles you encounter during your source gathering. If you are unsure how to abbreviate a specific journal title, consult the *American National Standard for Bibliographic References* (New York: American National Standards Institute, 1977); it is the standard authority on title abbreviations. A useful guide is the tenth edition of *Periodical Title Abbreviations* (New York: Gale Research, 1996). Lists of recommended abbreviations are also printed in *Index Medicus* and *Chemical Abstracts*. But be forewarned: Periodical title abbreviations vary greatly and are thus a bibliographer's nightmare.

Avoiding Mistakes by Imitating Examples

The *CBE Manual*'s Chapter 30 ("Citations and References") lists a fairly broad array of special kinds of sources. When in doubt, check the examples found there.

Listing Books

An entry for a book should include the following items, in the order listed.

1. name(s) of author(s) or editor(s), last name with initials

2. title

3. place of publication

4. name of publisher

5. year of publication

6. number of pages

Two forms may be used for page numbers: 459 p (meaning that the book has a total of 459 pages, not counting Roman numeral pages) or p 459 (meaning that only page 459 has been cited in your paper).

Note that the CBE citation sequence format abbreviates publishers' names according to fairly complex guidelines (see *CBE Manual* 747). For example, University Press becomes Univ Pr; John Wiley & Sons becomes J Wiley; and Little, Brown and Company becomes Little, Brown.

Here is a basic book entry.

1. Smith GP II. Genetics, ethics and the law. Gaithersburg, MD: Associated Faculty Pr; 1981. 241 p.

An Edited Book

2. Flack HE; Pellegrino ED, editors. African-American perspectives on biomedical ethics. Washington, DC: Georgetown Univ Pr; 1992. 203 p.

A Book by a Corporate Author

3. President's Commission for the Study of Ethical Problems in Medicine and Biomedical and Behavioral Research. Screening and counseling for genetic conditions: a report on the ethical, social, and legal implications of genetic screening, counseling, and education programs. Washington, DC: GPO; 1983. 122 p.

A Translation

4. Freud S. Civilization and its discontents. Strachey J, translator. New York: Norton; 1962. 109 p. Translation of: Das Unbehagen in der Kultur. Vienna: Internationaler Psychoanalystischer Verlag; 1930.

Listing Articles

An entry for a journal article should include the following items, in the order listed.

1. name(s) of author(s), last name with initials

2. title and subtitle of article, separated by a colon

3. title of journal, abbreviated

4. year and month (for weeklies, include the specific date)

5. volume number (for journals with separately paginated issues, include the issue number)

6. inclusive page numbers, with the second number given in the shortest form possible (for example, 176–9)

Articles in Periodicals

An Article in a Journal with Separately Paginated Issues

5. Murray TH. Ethics, genetic prediction, and heart disease. Am J Cardiol 1993;72(10):80D–84D.

An Article in a Newspaper

6. Gorner P. Human gene breakthrough. The Chicago Tribune 1993 Dec 16; Sect A:1(col 2).

An Article in a Collection

7. King PA. The past as prologue: race, class, and gene discrimination. In: Annas GJ; Elias S, editors. Gene mapping: using law and ethics as guides. New York: Oxford Univ Pr; 1992. 94–111.

Listing Other Kinds of Sources

A Videotape

8. Conceiving the future [Videocassette]. Alexandria, VA: PBS Video; 1993. 1 videocassette: 57 min, sound, color, 1/2 in.

A Journal Article from a Web Site

9. Budd, JM; Sievert, ME; Schultz, TR. Phenomena of retraction: reasons for retraction and citations to the publications. JAMA 280: 296–7; 1998. Available at: <http://www.ama-assn.org/sci-pubs/journals/archive/jama/vol_280/no_3/jpv71004.htm>.

(*Note:* The fifth edition of the *CBE Style Manual* was written before the Web had emerged as a key medium of information. My sample entry is based upon the application of standard CBE principles of format to electronic citations.)

Sample Paper: CBE Citation Sequence Format

1

Ethical Dilemmas of Releasing Human Genome Information

Todd A. Rose

CBE

2

Abstract

Information obtained from the Human Genome Initiative (HGI) could lead to discrimination against individuals by insurers and employers. Genetic mapping may alter employers' practices in hiring and promoting. The release of genetic risk profiles to employers could lead to discriminatory hiring, placement, and promotion. Since insurance is based upon a concept of sharing an unidentified risk, the identification of genetic risk factors could result in inequitable insurance practices. To ensure that risks are equally uncertain for all clients, legislators should protect the privacy of individual genetic profiles. The release of individual genetic profiles should be limited to the medical profession solely for preventive medical use.

CBE

3

Todd A. Rose

Dr. Maner

English 344

11 March 1999

Ethical Dilemmas of Releasing Human Genome Information

Like archaeologists digging through Egyptian sands to discover a hidden tomb, geneticists are searching for hidden treasure in a remote location--the human cell. A 15-year project known as the Human Genome Initiative (HGI) began in 1990 and is slated to cost $200 million per year[1]. The scope of the project rivals such megaprojects as the Manhattan Project and the Apollo missions.

When completed, HGI will specify the exact location and function of each gene within the human cell. This information will have a tremendous impact upon the understanding of the role of genetics in illness. The fact that a human's entire genetic profile will be deciphered within the next decade is a biological milestone. As Annas states, "we will enter a new realm--taking not simply a quantitative step, but a qualitative one"[2]. But despite the growing excitement in the scientific community as to the benefits of this new knowledge, the Human Genome Project threatens to open a Pandora's box of ethical dilemmas. Information obtained from HGI could lead to discrimination against individuals by insurers and employers. Therefore, release of HGI findings should be limited to the medical profession solely for preventive medical use.

To explore the role of genetics in illness, one must examine the function and location of genes. Each cell has a specific role it must play depending on its location in the body. For example, a cell can exist as part of an organ, as a transporter of oxygen in blood, or as

CBE

4

an antibody in the immune system. Each cell contains genetic material, or DNA, which instructs it how to function. Human genetic material can be thought of as a tree trunk with twenty-four branches, each branch representing a chromosome, and each leaf representing a gene.

Genes are complex configurations of DNA, a substance comprising four bases: adenine, cytosine, guanine, and thymine. Each base has a single counterpart with which it bonds: adenine bonds with thymine, and cytosine bonds with guanine. These combinations are known as base pairs. The sequence of base pairs in a gene determines its function.

Phase one of HGI will fashion a physical map which identifies each gene on the DNA model, and phase two will determine each base pair sequence. Considering there are roughly 100,000 genes with 3 billion base pairs, cataloging each base pair sequence and its significance will be a formidable task[1]. The role of genes in disease formation is constantly becoming clearer, as Lammers and Peters point out:

> Some 4000 diseases are thought to be genetic in origin. Of these, sickle-cell anemia and others result from a misplaced base letter in a single gene. In other cases . . . the problem stems from a discordant ensemble of genes. The ability to locate the individual gene or gene sequence responsible for each disease could revolutionize biomedicine in the 21st century[1].

In addition to targeting which gene causes a specific illness, genetic profiles might indicate a person's risk of developing a disease. Lee points out that prejudices could evolve over one's predisposition to illness, and a tendency to categorize groups of people based on

CBE

5

their genetic profiles could materialize[3]. Also, disclosure of one's genetic profile could have a detrimental effect. As Murray points out, "experience has shown that the process of explaining genetic risks is complex; understanding often comes slowly and painfully, the psychological burdens of genetic disease can be massive, and not everyone wants to know his or her own risk"[4].

More importantly, releasing HGI findings to the private sector will leave the individual at a disadvantage due to monetary prospects for employers and insurers. Murray points out that "New uses of genetic tests are evoking controversy. In these proposed uses, the test is being done not for the good of the person being tested, but rather for some organization"[4]. Joyce says, "more real, however, is the potential of genetic mapping to change the way people are employed, promoted or insured"[5]. Yet some interesting issues arise from viewing this from the perspective of each institution.

The employer's aim is to maximize profits to keep the business successful. It is an accepted fact that the single largest business expenditure is employee-related costs. Therefore, is it not in the best interest of the business, employer, and existing employees to hire individuals who will help maximize profits while generating minimal costs?

Murray points out that as the cost of insuring employees and their families continues to grow, businesses are searching for more ways to decrease their share of the burden[4]. Options that have been implemented over the past decade include sharing of health insurance costs with the employee and decreasing the scope of insurance benefits.

CBE

6

A viable option that business is now considering is to use genetic screening to decide which prospective employees carry the least risk for illness. The Council on Ethical and Judicial Affairs says that organizations may be hesitant to employ those whose genetic profile indicates a propensity for future health problems[6]. This option may also be used against existing employees. As Lee observes, "As medical costs climb and predictive genetic medicine grows, employers will be pressed to screen their employees to pinpoint who may be too costly to be allowed free coverage"[3]. This seems like outright discrimination on the part of business. There are antidiscriminatory laws in place for such factors as age, religion, and race, but what about an employee's tendency to become ill in the future?

It is important to note here that having the propensity for a disease is not the same as having a disease. The council points out that the judicial system has "consistently rejected employers' arguments that they should be able to deny employment to applicants whose future work might be compromised by health problems"[6]. However, forms of discrimination are already built into the system, as Lee points out:

> Certainly companies now engage in routine comprehensive testing for drugs, AIDS, high blood pressure and so forth. They routinely give lie detector tests, handwriting analysis, and written psychological questionnaires that assess one's "honesty" or "maturity." It makes good economic sense for a company to require medical examinations for job applicants to look for the presence of diseases as well as to guard against future problems in order to reduce costs and increase productivity. There is no reason in principle why genetic testing would not be added to

CBE

the list. Corporations today often act as insurers and health care providers. The health of the workers ultimately affects the productivity and determines the cost of the companies' health care[3].

From this perspective, genetic screening will augment existing policies. By eliminating those who threaten to incur high costs in health care and lost time at work, companies are simply looking out for their best interests and those of their employees.

There are many instances in which screening could filter out those who pose a risk to public safety. For example, should a commercial jet pilot be allowed to fly if his genetic profile indicates a high risk of coronary heart disease? Or should a physician lose his license if he is at risk for Alzheimer's? Joyce states, "normally American companies cannot screen applicants for vulnerability to some 'future' illness. But a court has ruled that a company may reject a job applicant if it is 90% certain that he or she would have a heart attack in a particular job"[5]. Conversely, the council points out that "a more effective approach to protecting the public's safety would be routine testing of a worker's actual capacity to function in a job that is safety-sensitive"[6].

Genetic screening also benefits employers by enabling them to measure an employee's ability to tolerate stressful work environments. Examples of such stress factors include exposures to hazardous chemicals and to temperature extremes. The goal, according to the Office of Technology Assessment, is to "place those workers most susceptible to a specific risk in the least hazardous environments"[3]. This would decrease an employee's risk to illness or disability from prolonged exposure to a hazardous climate.

CBE

8

However, it is the legal responsibility of the employer to provide a safe working environment for any employee. The job of the industrial hygienist is to assess hazards, to anticipate health risks, and to implement countermeasures to insure worker safety. It is also the responsibility of O.S.H.A. to enforce occupational safety regulations in the workplace. In this context genetic screening would be discriminatory, because it would disqualify individuals from jobs that might offer promotional or economic opportunities.

Aside from the employer, the insurance industry has the most to gain from HGI. Murray points out that "insurance works on the principle of sharing risk. When the risk is equally uncertain to all, then all can be asked to contribute equally to the 'insurance pool' "[4]. However, access to genetic data from HGI would radically change this concept. Using clients' genetic profiles, insurers could redistribute benefits according to their risk factor[3]. Some argue that this would be outright unfair. Why?

> Just as non-smokers would have cause for complaint if insurance companies were required to offer the same terms to cigarette-smokers as to themselves, people free of specific genetic defects would rightly complain if those carrying defective and potentially damaging genes were knowingly offered insurance on standard terms[7].

Granted, cigarette smoking is a voluntary decision, but this scenario illustrates a valid point: releasing genetic information to insurers would cause the industry to become inequitable. Lammers and Peters observe that "the ability to map the genome may render insurance companies irrelevant and dictate a whole new system of medical security and death benefits"[1]. Murray claims that once one

CBE

9

insurance company begins using gene profiles, competing companies will follow suit. His theory states that once profile screening is available, people will want to assess their predisposition for genetic diseases. Individuals who are "high risk" will purchase more benefits. The insurers call this "adverse selection--the tendency to purchase insurance when one expects to file a claim"[4]. In addition, insurance organizations that use profiles will offer discounts to the genetically fortunate. Consequently, lower rates will incite bidding wars which will force the remaining companies to use profiles to avoid losing their market shares[4].

How, then, can insurance companies remain equitable? The key phrase is stated above by Murray: "when the risk is equally uncertain to all." Insurers' access to HGI findings would eradicate this crucial element that makes insurance work. For example, if an insurance company discovered that a client's property was sitting on a fault line, it would undoubtedly charge a higher premium or refuse coverage. Insurance companies provide a service for profit just like any other business, and when they can target a potential liability, they will try to eliminate it. The leader of a genetic testing committee for insurers says that insurance "companies traditionally identify good and poor risks and charge premiums commensurate with those risks, . . . [and] the company has the right to whatever information the applicant has bearing on himself and his present or future family"[8].

A legal consultant states that "insurance companies already ask about family history, blood pressure and smoking, [so] they already make crude assessments of people's genetic and lifetime 'risks.' Knowledge of the genome will merely make this assessment more accurate"[9].

10

Now that the motives for insurers and employers regarding HGI have been established, what are some possible countermeasures to prevent discrimination? A possible solution is to enact legislation to deny specific groups access to HGI findings:

> We must legislate to make genetic discrimination illegal. However, that argument has not worked with AIDS. Insurance companies have reacted to the spread of the virus first by demanding HIV tests from all single men, later denying mortgages and life insurance to those who tested positive[3].

Persons diagnosed as carrying the HIV virus only have the potential of developing a serious illness; their situation "differs little in effect from inheriting a gene that too will cause a disease later"[3].

Scientists agree that the technology and resources exist to complete the Human Genome Project, so the acquisition of this knowledge will supersede ethical considerations: "the desire to know will transcend the fear of knowing"[3]. Muschel makes a related argument: "One might similarly have argued against the possible value of Mendeleev's Periodic Table for chemical and physical science"[10]. However, Annas notes that despite scientists' efforts to contain HGI findings, they "certainly have little influence over its use, as they had little influence over the use of the atomic bomb"[2].

Extending access to HGI data to insurers and employers will have serious and detrimental effects upon individuals. It is impossible for discrimination not to occur because the lure of economic gain is persuasive. Consideration of the individual in the equation will inevitably be sacrificed for economic reasons.

On the basis of contemporaneous methods of screening workers and insurance clients, employers and insurance companies have

CBE

11

proven that they cannot handle sensitive information without discriminating. Therefore, release of genetic information to the private sector will only encourage discriminatory practices, and this is a direct infringement on an individual's right to privacy. Supervision of sensitive gene data must be used because unlike the supersecret Manhattan Project, HGI research is an international effort involving hundreds of scientists and technicians.

Hypothetically, if employers and insurers gain access to individual genetic profiles, there are two major obstacles confronting them. First, genetic science is not absolute like physics or math; rather, it identifies a risk factor. According to the Council on Ethical and Judicial Affairs, "genetic tests are poor predictors of disease and even poorer predictors of disabling disease . . . Many individuals who carry the gene will never show manifestations of the gene . . . [and] the extent of the gene's effects may differ widely from person to person"[6]. In addition, behavioral changes can alter or hinder a genetic abnormality. For example, persons having diabetes or coronary heart disease can suppress their illness by following special diets[6].

The second obstacle is legislation such as the Human Genome Privacy Act, proposed by Congressman John Conyers, which asserts an individual's right to privacy regarding his or her genetic profile. The act specifically targets employers, insurers, and educational institutions, denying them access to profiles[11].

Findings from the Human Genome Project will undoubtedly benefit the medical field by enhancing preventive medicine: "if you can detect a higher risk of breast cancer, a woman could have mammographies more often"[5]. In addition, doctors could counsel patients as to which diseases they are at risk for and take measures to prevent

12

their onset. Furthermore, HGI research could make reversal of genetic abnormalities possible, as Lammers and Peters point out:

> Knowing this structure may allow us to find chemical and mechanical tools to change it--fixing it where it has gone wrong in an individual and improving it where it puts whole populations at risk . . . [and] to use the new means at hand to reduce human suffering as much as we can while protecting human freedom and dignity[1].

Research in the interest of society is difficult when there exists a possibility for exploitation and economic gain. It is important to note that "ethics as such is not an objective discipline. Rather it tends to employ principles that vary with time and people"[12]. Assuming this to be true, should we expect that future generations will be required to submit genetic resumes?

CBE

13

Cited References

1. Lammers A; Peters T. Genetics: Implications of the Human Genome Project. Christ Cent 1990 Oct 3; 868+.

2. Annas GJ. Who's afraid of the human genome? Hastings Cent Rep 1989;19(4):20.

3. Lee TF. The Human Genome Project: Cracking the genetic code of life. New York: Plenum; 1991. 323 p.

4. Murray TH. Ethical issues in human genome research. FASEB J 1991 Jan;5:55–60.

5. Joyce C. Your genome in their hands. New Sci 1990 Aug 11; 52–5.

6. Council on Ethical and Judicial Affairs, American Medical Association. Use of genetic testing by employers. JAMA 1991; 266:1827–30.

7. Bad luck insurance. Editorial. Nature 1990;347:214.

8. Insurance costs and genetic testing. Lancet 1990;335:1331.

9. Brown P; Concar D. Where does the genome project go from here? New Sci 1991 Aug 17;13–4.

10. Muschel LH. Letter. Science 1990;247:270.

11. Davies K; Gershon D. Law to keep labels off genes. Nature 1990; 347:221.

12. Grisolia S. Mapping the human genome. Hastings Cent Rep 1989 July/Aug;suppl:18–9.

CRITIQUE Todd Rose's paper is a good example of how a potentially overwhelming topic can be effectively narrowed. It also shows how a scientific topic can be handled from a humanistic, ethical perspective. The ethical issue he discusses is a fascinating aspect of the Human Genome Initiative. His approach to the topic is reflective yet persuasive. Todd's thesis is clear and predictive, and he places it so that it is easy to spot as the controlling idea.

The major shortcoming of Todd's paper is the documentation. Major studies of genetics and ethics are overlooked, and several brief editorials are used rather than more substantial sources.

CHICAGO FORMAT: General Appearance

The following sections present the details you will need to use the Chicago format for your research paper. But to get an overview of its main features, read this checklist. It shows at a glance the basic stylings your paper should have.

CHICAGO FORMAT: CHECKLIST OF MAIN FEATURES

1. Provide a separate title page; imitate the sample paper's format (see p. 249).
2. Use one-inch margins.
3. Double-space everything, including block quotations.
4. Type the page number on each page at the top right.
5. Indent block quotations five spaces.
6. Cite sources by using superscripts numbered consecutively throughout the paper.
7. Do not include a separate bibliography when you provide numbered endnotes.
8. Use normal paragraph indentation in the endnotes. Use hanging indentation in the bibliography.
9. Use the basic forms for endnotes.

Remember that the *Chicago Manual of Style* offers a wide range of format choices under two main headings. In its Chapter 15 (in the 14th edition), the manual describes what is generally known as the Chicago style (sometimes also called the humanities style, or the Turabian style); this style uses notes and (sometimes) a bibliography for research documentation. The manual's Chapter 16 describes an alternative system of author-date citations and reference lists; this alternative format is very much like the APA format and is used in the natural sciences and social sciences.

The following paragraphs focus on the Chicago humanities style, highlighting the differences between it and the MLA style.

CHICAGO

Settings for most features—such as margins, spacing, and justification—are the same as in the MLA format. But block quotations should be indented five spaces in the Chicago format (as opposed to ten spaces in MLA), and an extra line space should precede and follow each block.

CHICAGO FORMAT: Documentation

Review the comparison of research paper formats at the beginning of Chapter 7. Footnotes or endnotes may be utilized in the Chicago format. Footnotes are normally used in theses and dissertations; endnotes are normally used in research papers. Use one or the other, never both. If you are in doubt, consult your instructor.

Basic Form

In the body of your paper, insert superscript numerals, ordered consecutively from the beginning of the paper to the end, in place of the parenthetical documentation used in MLA format. The superscripts may direct the reader either to a footnote at the bottom of the current page or to a page of endnotes at the end of the paper.

A Note Citing a Book

    1. Frederick Neumann, <u>Ornamentation and Improvisation in Mozart</u> (Princeton: Princeton University Press, 1986), 257.

Notice that the note has three parts separated by commas: author, title, and page number. Publication information appears inside parentheses. The publisher's name may be presented in unabbreviated or abbreviated form, but the *Chicago Manual* stipulates "Univ. Press" rather than the MLA abbreviation "UP."

A Note Citing a Journal Article

    2. Glen Jeansonne, "The Apotheosis of Huey Long," <u>Biography</u> 12 (Fall 1989): 283.

Some journals give issue numbers; others give a specific month (or season) of issue. The *Chicago Manual* allows several variations in handling journal dates and issue numbers. All of the following formats are acceptable; but notice that you should list *either* the issue number *or* the specific month (or season), not both.

    2. Glen Jeansonne, "The Apotheosis of Huey Long," <u>Biography</u> 12, no. 4 (1989): 283.
    2. Glen Jeansonne, "The Apotheosis of Huey Long," <u>Biography</u> 12: 283 (Fall 1989).
    2. Glen Jeansonne, "The Apotheosis of Huey Long," <u>Biography</u> 12 (4): 283 (1989).
    2. Glen Jeansonne, "The Apotheosis of Huey Long," <u>Biography</u> 12, 4, (1989): 283.

CHICAGO

Whichever style you adopt, stick to it consistently throughout your paper. One pleasant feature of the Chicago format is that you may, if you wish, simply use the issue number for every journal article, whether the journal is continuously or separately paginated.

A Note Citing an Article in a Popular Magazine

3. Whitney Balliett, "Jazz: Celebrating the Duke," New Yorker, 29 Nov. 1993, 136.

Notice that the issue of a popular magazine is identified simply by date. The date and page number(s) are set off by commas.

A Note Citing a Web Site

4. James Williamson, Melville Study Guide [online], February 1998 [cited 11 Jan. 1999]; available from World Wide Web: <http://www.mmd-cod.ca/iso/ud578/idiom/illus.htm> [approx. 15 screens].

(*Note:* The fourteenth edition of the *Chicago Manual of Style* was written before the Web had emerged as a key medium of information. Its editors recommended consulting the latest documentation guidelines from the International Standards Organization. My sample entry is based upon official ISO guidelines supplied at <http://www.nlc-bnc.ca/iso/tc46sc9/standard/690-2e.htm#7.12.1> [accessed January 11, 1999]. Visit this Web site for the latest ISO guidelines.)

Common Exceptions to the Basic Form

A subsequent reference to a source already cited uses the following format.

5. Balliett, 137.

If you cite more than one work by Balliett in your paper, use a short title to identify the specific work.

6. Balliett, "Jazz," 85.

You may use the abbreviation "ibid." (for the Latin *ibidem*, "in the same place") to refer to the source cited in the note immediately preceding, provided that only one source has been cited there.

7. Ibid., 87.

Standing by itself, *ibid.* indicates that you are citing precisely the same page of the same source. For example, to cite still another passage from Balliett on page 87, you would use this form.

8. Ibid.

Avoid long strings of *ibid.*s. Try to consolidate notes in the manner described in the discussion of the MLA format (see "Consolidating Citations" in Chapter 7).

CHICAGO FORMAT: The List of Works Cited

The *Chicago Manual* uses bibliographic conventions similar to those of the *MLA Handbook*, but there are some differences. For one thing, in the Chicago format the second and subsequent lines of each entry are indented three or four spaces instead of the five spaces specified by MLA.

Another difference is that the Chicago format offers two possible conventions for handling inclusive page numbers. The first makes hyphenated inclusive numbers look good on the page, but it is so complex that I will not even describe it. The second convention is elegantly simple: When you list inclusive numbers, the second number is represented only by the digits that differ from the first number: thus 4–10, 82–5, 98–121, 606–18, 1592–606.

The Chicago format also handles some abbreviations differently from the MLA format. The *MLA Handbook* tells you to use "rpt." for "reprint" or "reprinted," but the *Chicago Manual* tells you to use the full word "reprint."

Listing Books

Here is a basic book entry.

Neumann, Frederick. <u>Ornamentation and Improvisation in Mozart</u>. Princeton: Princeton University Press, 1986.

Compare this with the note format in sample note 1 shown previously.
A translation of a book has the following format.

Bach, Carl Philipp Emanuel. <u>Versuch über die wahre Art das Clavier zu spielen</u>. Berlin: 1759. Trans. and ed. William J. Mitchell as <u>Essay on the True Art of Playing Keyboard Instruments</u>. New York: W. W. Norton, 1949.

Listing Articles

Articles in Periodicals

A Journal Article

Jeansonne, Glen. "The Apotheosis of Huey Long," <u>Biography</u> 12, no. 4 (1989): 283–301.

Compare this with the note formats in sample note 2 shown previously.

An Article in a Popular Magazine

Balliett, Whitney. "Jazz: Celebrating the Duke." <u>New Yorker</u>, 29 Nov. 1993, 136–47.

Compare this with the note format in sample note 3 shown previously.

CHICAGO

Articles in Books

An Article in a Collection

> Buszin, Walter E. "Criteria of Church Music in the Seventeenth and Eighteenth Centuries." Festschrift Theodore Hoelty-Nickel: A Collection of Essays on Church Music. Ed. Newman W. Powell. Valparaiso, IN: Valparaiso University, 1967. 14–21.

Note that the copyright page of this book listed "Valparaiso University," not Valparaiso University Press."

An Article in a Reference Work

> Horsley, Imogene, Michael Collins, Eva Badura-Skoda, Dennis Libby, and Nazir A. Jairazbhoy. "Improvisation." The New Grove Dictionary of Music and Musicians. 1980.

Notice that all the authors are listed in a Chicago bibliography entry, although a Chicago *note* to a source with more than three authors may substitute *et al.* for all the names following the name of the first author.

INTERNET Listing Other Kinds of Sources

A Web Site

> Williamson, James. Melville Study Guide [online]. February 1998 [cited 11 Jan. 1999] Available from World Wide Web: <http://www.mmd-cod.ca/iso/ud578/idiom/illus.htm> [approx. 15 screens].

CHICAGO

Sample Paper: Chicago Format

The Death and Rebirth of Improvisation

Martin Maner

Wright State University

1

The Death and Rebirth of Improvisation

The cultural revolution known as romanticism has been inten-
sively analyzed by twentieth-century historians, but some aspects of
the shift from classicism to romanticism remain puzzling. Why, for
example, did musical improvisation decline? During the baroque and
classical eras, musicians were trained to improvise complex musical
embellishments and even to create entire compositions spontaneously, but by the romantic period, improvisation came to be abandoned in favor of the relatively strict performance of written scores.
From a modern perspective, this change seems paradoxical, because
modern listeners think of spontaneity as a characteristic of
romanticism.

Of course, the decline did not happen overnight, and the
greatest composers of each era--baroque, classical, and romantic--
cultivated their improvisational skills. Bach, Mozart, and Beethoven
were all famous extemporizers. Nevertheless, historians generally
agree that musical improvisation reached a high point in Bach's lifetime (1685–1750), declined during Mozart's (1756–1791), and virtually disappeared during Beethoven's (1770–1827), though the causes
of this change remain uncertain.

Bach's legendary improvisatory skills were most fully demonstrated during his visit to the court of Frederick the Great on May
12, 1747. Probably hoping to get from Frederick some financial support and perhaps a title as well, Bach arrived after a long coach journey and was immediately hurried to the king's music room without
even being given a chance to change his clothes.[1] At Frederick's
request, he improvised on each of the king's newly acquired piano-
fortes; then Frederick played a theme and asked him to improvise

CHICAGO

upon it, on the spot--a request that Bach obligingly fulfilled. Finally, Frederick asked for an extemporaneous six-part fugue upon the same theme--a task that Douglas R. Hofstadter compares to "playing sixty simultaneous games of chess--blindfolded."[2] Again Bach obliged, astonishing Frederick and his retinue. Bach later reworked these improvisations, wrote some additional canons and other pieces based on the same theme, and published the entire collection less than two months later, at his own expense,[3] as the Musical Offering, one of his greatest works.

Bach's period represents the pinnacle of the improvisatory tradition. On the violin, Tartini and Corelli, and on the keyboards, Buxtehude, Frescobaldi, Handel, and Scarlatti were famous as improvisers.[4] Bach himself marked "not only an undreamed-of peak but also a kind of conclusion."[5]

Although improvisation began to decline after the middle of the eighteenth century, Mozart, too, had phenomenal improvisatory abilities. By his own report, he once improvised a whole sonata, and he often played extemporaneous fugues or thematic variations.[6] Yet because he was conscious that musicians were losing the ability to improvise, Mozart showed his distrust of other players by writing down cadenzas and ornamentations rather than leaving them to individual discretion.

Although Beethoven was also famous for improvising, as a composer he did more than perhaps anyone else to insure improvisation's decline. As Dennis Libby puts it, Beethoven was

a figure of such forcefulness and individuality that a creative collaboration in which the performer added something of his own to

3

the composer's conception became increasingly unthinkable, and the performer was made to feel that his highest calling--going beyond the traditional good taste to an almost spiritual mission-- was to subject himself to the composer's will as the means by which his masterpieces were communicated to the world.[7]

Here Libby hints at one explanation of the decline of improvisation: The cult of individual genius in the romantic era destroyed the art of individual musical improvisation by elevating the composer and demoting the performer. The great romantic soloists still did extemporaneous cadenzas to show off their skills, but most music students were confined to studying great compositions and mastering them. As apprenticeship and imitation were replaced by reading as a standard way of learning music, music became a bookish art.

In studying the history of improvisation during this period, one immediately encounters an almost insurmountable problem. Musical notation can at best only approximate the subtleties of a live performance, as any jazz player knows after looking at a written transcription of a familiar jazz solo. How can one say anything for certain about an art that by its very nature cannot be accurately recorded in writing or in print?

The answer is that in the absence of direct evidence, historians have to some extent reconstructed the lost art of baroque and classical improvisation by using indirect evidence of several types. First, there are many handbooks or instruction manuals on improvisation. Second, although not every improvisatory nuance can be written down, nevertheless one can reconstruct the lost art by studying transcriptions of improvisations ranging from the early 1500s

CHICAGO

4

through the romantic era. A third source of evidence is the study of what might be called "written improvisations," that is, compositions in which the composer "take[s] ornaments ordinarily left to improvisation and write[s] them out in unambiguous and final form."[8] For example, Bach published "a 'self-embellished' version of his own composition."[9] Mozart left us many samples of cadenzas for his concertos. He often wrote them out for pupils, family members, and musicians who commissioned the works.[10]

Since it was through keyboard improvisation that the baroque masters "achieved a far-reaching synthesis of the horizontal principle of melodic ornamentation with the vertical one of polyphony and chordal playing,"[11] and since keyboards were the composers' most frequent instruments of choice and were most fully discussed in teaching manuals, the really crucial evidence about the decline of improvisation appears in handbooks teaching keyboard improvisation in the baroque and classical eras. An examination of these handbooks will, first, confirm that a decline did in fact occur in the time of Mozart and, second, show that the transformation of music into what I have called a "bookish" art was a primary cause of improvisation's decline.

Extemporaneous composition of autonomous, self-contained musical works occurred in several forms. One of these, the prelude, derived in part from the social requirements of specific settings. In church, the organist's chorale prelude provided transitions between parts of the service. (The continued need for transitional music in church helps to explain why improvisation remained "a required part of the church organist's training" in the nineteenth century, especially in France.)[12] The instrumental prelude served a similar

CHICAGO

5

function in the salon, and it, too, survived longer than most improvisational forms: "The improvisation of preludes, mostly by keyboard players, before the performance of a written composition, continued to flourish in the early nineteenth century. To begin with the work itself, especially in the informal atmosphere of the salon, was considered poor taste."[13]

Perhaps partly in response to these social needs, nineteenth-century keyboard handbooks continued to teach the improvising of preludes, though the instruction became increasingly rudimentary. For instance, in his Systematische Anleitung zum Fantasieren auf dem Pianoforte (Systematic introduction to improvising fantasies on the pianoforte, c. 1829), Carl Czerny taught some basic tricks of harmony, and his remarks on extemporaneous composition "reveal that technical agility [had] now taken precedence over truly creative spur-of-the-moment invention on the piano."[14]

As the nineteenth century progressed, teaching manuals increasingly presumed that the reader had little competence in improvisation. Grétry's Méthode simple pour apprendre à préluder en peu de temps avec toutes les ressources de l'harmonie (1802) discussed using chord progressions to construct preludes in three ways: playing chords or arpeggios based upon them; interjecting rapid passages between chords; and developing a fugue using a motif from the melody or the bass line. F. Kalkbrenner's Traité d'harmonie du pianiste: Principes rationnels de la modulation pour apprendre à préluder et à improviser (1849) gave instructions on how to develop stock harmonic formulas and how to splice such passages together in improvising preludes. Both these works show that improvisation

6

was on the decline, for they were "primarily introductions to keyboard harmony for the musically illiterate."[15]

Partimento techniques of improvisation upon the harpsichord and organ gave rise to other forms of extemporaneous composition including character pieces such as toccatas and fugues. Standard school exercises known as Probstücke ("test pieces") required a student to take a bass part, the basso continuo, and improvise upon it using the technique known variously as thoroughbass, figured bass, or, in German, Generalbass. The art of partimento improvisation originated in Italy but became an especially important part of musical training in Germany during the eighteenth century, as evidenced by an abundance of German training manuals and partimento collections.[16] As thoroughbass declined in the eighteenth century, so too did partimento improvisation.

The purest form of extemporaneous composition was known as the fantasia, or fantasy, which was usually written out as merely a series of bass notes, lacking even bar lines to guide the improviser. At least until the end of the baroque era, the fantasy was regarded as the supreme form of extemporaneous composition. In a treatise published in 1767, for example, J. S. Petri described the fantasy as "the highest degree of composition . . . where meditation and execution are directly bound up with one another."[17] Bach, Mozart, and Beethoven were all famous for their improvised fantasies. But by the time Czerny published his Systematische Anleitung in the early nineteenth century, "signs of an increasing shallowness of improvisation doctrine were noticeable."[18] Abandoning the idea that the fantasy should be a coherent form of extemporaneous composition, Czerny described the fantasy merely as "spinning out, while playing . . .

CHICAGO

7

any idea of one's own or someone else's into a kind of musical composition."[19]

In seeking to identify the causes of the general decline of extemporaneous composition, music historians frequently argue that extemporaneous performances by inadequately trained musicians led to improvisation's decline:

> Great composers, with specific requirements for the realization of their music, restricted the traditional freedom of performance, and promoted this by notating more than had previously been usual, or possible, in order to secure unspoilt performances. This applies equally to Haydn and Mozart and, of course, Gluck.[20]

But as a real explanation of the decline of improvisation, this argument seems circular, because it essentially says that improvisation declined because some players improvised badly. Nor is it fully satisfactory to say that "[w]ith the decline . . . of the composer-performer, in whom the art had usually reached its peaks, improvisation gradually died out,"[21] since this, too, amounts to saying that improvisation declined because there were no longer any skilled improvisers.

To escape this circularity, one must ask what changes in the training of musicians caused the art of improvisation to be lost. One possible answer has already been suggested: The essential skills in musical improvisation are best taught through apprenticeship and imitation, but in the eighteenth century the master-apprentice relationship was gradually supplanted by the treatise-reader relationship. One skill in particular, the art of thoroughbass, was so complex

CHICAGO

8

and so performance oriented that it could not be adequately passed on by means of printed treatises.

Thoroughbass was essentially a system of musical shorthand whereby a keyboard player could instantly create an appropriate accompaniment to a written bass line. After arising in the late sixteenth century, thoroughbass notation spread rapidly from Italy to other countries. So important was thoroughbass that "the period from 1600 to 1750 is sometimes simply called the 'thoroughbass period'."[22]

In its most basic form, thoroughbass required the keyboard player to play the written bass notes with the left hand while the right hand improvised a three-part (and later four-part) accompaniment to the other vocal or instrumental parts. Keyboard instruments were regarded as "foundation" instruments whose function was to hold together, through improvised accompaniment, the harmonic and melodic movement of the other voices.

The filling out of harmonies is known as the "realization" of a thoroughbass. In choral and ensemble performances, a realization normally was a relatively sparse accompaniment, but with the addition of melodic embellishments it could be so elaborate as to become an extemporaneous composition.

Because it was essentially a complex, professional art of accompaniment, thoroughbass was an essential skill for every musical apprentice, but it was peripheral for the musical amateur. Thoroughbass handbooks of the baroque and classical eras often clearly stated that they were intended for professionals or at least for those who intended thoroughly to master music (including composition).[23] Many of the most important writers of treatises

CHICAGO

9

emphasized that extemporaneous composition and embellishment simply could not be learned from a book and that treatises should therefore be treated skeptically.[24]

Music historians have tended to make it sound as if the decline of thoroughbass were merely a final symptom of the decline of improvisation: "With the gradual decline of the thoroughbass in the second half of the eighteenth century, the last traces of improvisation in Western ensemble music disappeared."[25] But perhaps the decline of thoroughbass was not just a symptom of a general deterioration but, rather, one of its prime causes.

Among twentieth-century scholars, George J. Buelow, Robert Donington, and Hermann Keller have recognized the importance of thoroughbass as a foundation for improvisation. Keller emphasizes that thoroughbass began as a technique but evolved into a unifying stylistic principle in musical composition.[26] Learning thoroughbass thus served as a gateway to learning all the other musical skills, including improvisation. It thus seems likely that the decline of thoroughbass contributed to the deterioration of improvisational skills.

For a keyboard player, figured-bass notation conveniently facilitated improvisation by providing a method of working out chord voicings by their "feel," or the physical sensation of the intervals between chord tones. However, in the eighteenth century, the new and influential system worked out by Jean Philippe Rameau "deterred rather than aided" this physical, or motoric, sense of intervals.[27] Rameau analyzed harmonies by seeing all chords as inversions, or vertical displacements, of a few fundamental chord structures. This insight laid the foundation for modern theories of

CHICAGO

harmony, but by undermining thoroughbass as a method of instant composition, Rameau's new system contributed greatly to the decline of improvisation.

The decline was further hastened by broad changes in musical training. During the period 1600–1800, particularly in Protestant countries, musical training became a common part of general education. For the aristocracy and middle class, it became a popular avocation; for professional musicians it became an object of methodical study rather than a skill achieved by imitation and "osmosis."[28] To understand what was lost, one must understand the benefits of the earlier system of education by imitation and apprenticeship. These are well illustrated in the history of the Bach family.

Johann Sebastian Bach learned music from his father, a town musician in Eisenach. Later he was apprenticed to his older brother in Ohrdruf.[29] He traveled to study under other masters; while serving as church organist at Arnstadt, he once angered his superiors by overstaying his leave after making a journey by foot to study under Dietrich Buxtehude.[30] He taught his son, C. P. E. Bach, who in turn taught his own younger brother, Johann Christian, for four years in Berlin after Johann Sebastian died. C. P. E. Bach had other successful pupils, such as Carl Fasch, later an accompanist to Frederick the Great.[31]

It is not hard to see how musical apprenticeship far surpassed book learning as a method of acquiring skill in improvisation. For one thing, the master musician could recognize and nurture the improvisatory skills of a particularly gifted apprentice. Furthermore, the instructor could immediately intervene to correct misconceptions and mistakes during performance. In writing down rules of

CHICAGO

11

thoroughbass for Anna Magdalena Bach, J. S. Bach wrote that "the remaining precautions that one must keep in mind are shown better through oral than written instructions."[32] One of Johann Sebastian Bach's pupils gives us an intimate glimpse of the master's direct intervention:

> When Sebastian Bach performed church music, one of his most capable students always had to accompany at the harpsichord [at rehearsals]. It may indeed be imagined that no one dared to come forth on such an occasion with some kind of scanty thoroughbass accompaniment. Besides, one had always to be prepared to find Bach's hands and fingers suddenly mingling among the hands and fingers of the player; without further disturbing these, they would supply the accompaniment with volumes of harmonies which impressed the students even more than did the unsuspected presence of their strict teacher.[33]

Although printed texts were good ways of conveying general rules, direct intervention was a more effective way of explaining exceptions. Writing in 1702, St. Lambert said that the good music instructor "teaches a general rule as if it had no exceptions and awaits the occasion when such an exception occurs to talk about it, because it will then be more easily understood."[34]

In teaching improvisation, the master musician could also interact with the student by closely analyzing an extemporaneous piece. In his Versuch, C. P. E. Bach describes how the close and watchful eye of the music teacher should be focused on every detail of a pupil's improvised accompaniment:

12

32. The student, in receiving instruction, must first play each example and then write it out in two staves. The ear and eye will thereby learn to distinguish clearly between the good and the bad.

33. However, nothing must be taken for granted; both written and played versions must be judged. Every note must be justified. Objections should be raised which the student must answer by giving reasons why, for example, this or that note and no other must be used.[35]

Of course, not only professional musicians but also musical amateurs often learned their craft under the guidance of teachers. But in a royal or aristocratic household, the music master was a hired servant who was unlikely to impose the same strict standards that he would set for an apprentice. While he was the music instructor of Frederick the Great, Johann Joachim Quantz could express his dissatisfaction with the king's mistakes only by coughing, so that Frederick once exclaimed, after a performance particularly fraught with royal blunders, "What are we to do about Quantz's cold?"[36]

As musical amateurism spread and musical apprenticeship declined, vicious circles of causation were set in motion. Bad improvisations by unskilled amateurs helped to fuel composers' mistrust of performers, leading them to leave less and less to the player's discretion. The lack of improvisational space, in turn, contributed to an increasing neglect of improvisational skills among professional musicians. Meanwhile, the composer's fuller transcription of middle voices rendered unnecessary the professional musician's training in

CHICAGO

13

thoroughbass technique; and as thoroughbass declined, so did the improvisational skills that it had fostered.

While it is impossible to assign an exact date to the death of improvisation, Türk's reference, in 1791, to the "pretty general neglect" of thoroughbass suggests how much had been lost by the end of the century. Perhaps the clearest early indication of a decline occurs in C. P. E. Bach's introduction to Sechs Sonaten fürs Clavier mit veränderten Reprisen (1760), where he says that in publishing musical variations so that his readers will be spared the trouble of "having either to invent them themselves or to have others write them down and then themselves learn them by heart," he believes himself to be "the first, so far as I know, to work in this manner."[37]

The key example of a transitional figure is Mozart, for "in Mozart's early church music we find spots that are not fully harmonized and obviously count on organ chords. Such spots seem to disappear in his mature sacred works."[38] Just as Mozart gradually eliminated thoroughbass passages, he increasingly tended to write out, in full, the ornamentation of passages that once would have been freely embellished by the performer. Badura-Skoda points to his Rondo in A Minor (K511) as "one of the most beautiful examples of fully written-out ornamentation of the 18th century."[39] The insistence upon fidelity to a written score reaches a new height with Beethoven, who on more than one occasion was angry to learn that performers had added notes to his compositions.[40]

Although improvisation declined because of a complex set of mutually reinforcing causes, at the highest level of explanation, the decline of improvisation was related to the impact of an increasing reliance upon printed texts--especially instructional treatises and

CHICAGO

14

printed musical scores--rather than the direct transmission of skills from masters to apprentices.

Speaking pessimistically, the rise in the number of jazz improvisation handbooks in recent years may suggest that jazz improvisation, too, has entered its phase of decline, and that the rulebook will reassert its tyranny over the musician once again. But speaking more optimistically, the mechanical reproduction of improvised music has actually restored at least one aspect of the old system of apprenticeship: Recordings now make it possible for apprentice improvisers to study and imitate the masters intuitively. Thus our mechanical devices--first our phonographs, and now our tape recorders and CD players--may paradoxically help us preserve and foster the most unmechanical of musical art forms, improvisation.

CHICAGO

15

Notes

1. Otto L. Bettmann, "Bach at Potsdam," American Scholar 52 (1982/1983): 84.

2. Ibid., 85.

3. Ibid., 86.

4. Jeff Pressing, "The History of Classical Improvisation," Part 2, Keyboard, Dec. 1984, 66.

5. Ernest T[homas] Ferand, "Historical Introduction," Improvisation in Nine Centuries of Western Music: An Anthology with a Historical Introduction (Cologne: A. Volk Verlag, 1961), 14.

6. The New Grove Dictionary of Music and Musicians (1980), s.v. "Improvisation. I. Western Art Music. 3. The Classical Period."

7. Ibid., s.v. "Improvisation. I. Western Art Music. 4. After 1800."

8. Ferand, 16.

9. Ibid.

10. Frederick Neumann, Ornamentation and Improvisation in Mozart (Princeton: Princeton University Press, 1986), 257, and Performance Practices of the Seventeenth and Eighteenth Centuries (New York: Macmillan-Schirmer, 1993), 547–8.

11. Ferand, 14.

12. The New Grove Dictionary of Music and Musicians (1980), s.v. "Improvisation. I. Western Art Music. 4. After 1800."

13. Ibid.

14. Ferand, 21.

15. The New Grove Dictionary of Music and Musicians (1980), s.v. "Improvisation. I. Western Art Music. 4. After 1800."

16. Ferand, 19.

CHICAGO

17. Ibid., 21.

18. Ibid.

19. Ibid.

20. The New Grove Dictionary of Music and Musicians (1980), s.v. "Improvisation. I. Western Art Music. 3. The Classical Period."

21. Ibid., s.v. "Improvisation. I. Western Art Music. 4. After 1800."

22. Ferand, 18.

23. F[ranck] T[homas] Arnold, The Art of Accompaniment from a Thorough-Bass as Practised in the XVIIth & XVIIIth Centuries (1931, 2 vols.; reprint, New York: Dover Publications, 1965), 1: 308–12.

24. Frederick Neumann, "The Use of Baroque Treatises on Musical Performance," Music and Letters 48 (1967): 322.

25. Ferand, 19.

26. Hermann Keller, Schule des Generalbass-spiels, mit Auszugen aus den theoretischen Werken von Praetorius, Niedt, Telemann, Mattheson, Heinichen, J. S. und Ph. E. Bach, Quantz und Padre Mattei, und zahlreichen Beispeilen aus der Literatur des 17. und 18. Jahrhunderts (Kassel: Barenreiter-Verlag, 1931); trans. and ed. Carl Parrish under the title Thoroughbass Method: With Excerpts from the Theoretical Works of Praetorius, Niedt, Telemann, Mattheson, Heinichen, J. S. & C. P. E. Bach, Quantz, and Padre Mattei, and Numerous Examples from the Literature of the 17th and 18th Centuries (New York: W. W. Norton, 1965), 91. See also George J. Buelow, Thorough-Bass Accompaniment According to Johann David Heinichen, rev. ed., Studies in Musicology, no. 84 (Ann Arbor: UMI Research, 1986), 22–4, 275; Robert Donington and George J. Buelow, "Figured Bass as Improvisation," Acta Musicologica 40 (1968): 178.

27. William J. Mitchell, Introduction, <u>Essay on the True Art of Playing Keyboard Instruments</u> (New York: W. W. Norton, 1949), 18.

28. <u>The New Grove Dictionary of Music and Musicians</u> (1980), s.v. "Education in Music. IV. 1600–1800."

29. <u>The New Grove Dictionary of Music and Musicians</u> (1980), s.v. "Education in Music. IV. 1600–1800."

30. Barry Kopetz, "Bach's Fantasia in G: An Interpretive Analysis," <u>Instrumentalist</u> 48, no. 1 (1993): 25.

31. Mitchell, 1–2.

32. Keller, 15.

33. Ibid., 96.

34. Neumann, "Use," 322.

35. <u>Versuch über die wahre Art das Clavier zu spielen</u> (1759), trans. and ed. William J. Mitchell under the title <u>Essay on the True Art of Playing Keyboard Instruments</u> (New York: W. W. Norton, 1949), 176.

36. Bettmann, 84.

37. Ferand, 20.

38. Neumann, <u>Ornamentation</u>, 254.

39. <u>The New Grove Dictionary of Music and Musicians</u> (1980), s.v. "Improvisation. I. Western Art Music. 4. The Classical Period."

40. Ibid., s.v. "Improvisation. I. Western Art Music. 3. The Classical Period and 4. After 1800."

CRITIQUE   Writing the paper succeeded in its main purpose, which was to make me write outside my field, as a student again rather than as a professor. I was able to find a bit of a fresh slant in three areas. First, the music historians have been interested in reconstructing baroque and classical performance practices, so they have focused mostly on the details of ornamentation rather than what seems to me a much more fascinating thing, true extemporaneous composition, the subject of this paper. Second, as far as I could find out, not much has been written on the shift from an apprenticeship-based to a text-based system of education, so I tried to pull together a discussion of that interesting episode in social history. Third, only a few of the authorities seemed to recognize the importance of the motoric or physical sense of interval that was lost when thoroughbass went out of fashion, so I tried to emphasize its importance.

The primary shortcoming of this paper, then, is that it makes only a very modest contribution to the field of music history by pulling together all the usual explanations for the decline of improvisation and synthesizing them from several slightly unusual angles. But as a survey of causal explanations, it serves well enough as a sample student paper. I learned a lot from writing it and had a lot of fun doing so.

The major problem I faced in writing this paper was that I was torn between two audiences. Normally such a paper would be written for music specialists, but this paper had to serve as an example comprehensible to non-musicians consulting my textbook. The result was that I put the least specialized (and therefore least original) material in this sample paper, while setting aside some more specialized material for publication in music journals. I then submitted a revised, more specialized paper to some top-line journals in musicology and music history. It was rejected three times, but not without encouraging and helpful comments from the editors and peer evaluators. (Some top music scholars commented on it, which was intimidating!) I then decided to compromise by tailoring the paper for a different audience: a conference of eighteenth-century scholars *not* specializing in music. In this form the paper was accepted for presentation at a conference on the impact of the printing press in the eighteenth century. I spruced it up by using my computer to write some examples of harpsichord improvisation, and I had a great time presenting the paper and the music at a February conference in sunny Florida. I also created a Web site (with musical examples that you can listen to) at <http://www.wright.edu/~martin.maner/improv01.html>. I still hope to publish some other offshoots of this paper in academic journals.

CHICAGO

CHAPTER 9

WRITING THE ROUGH DRAFT

■ ■ ■ QUICK VIEW

Early outlines should be informal and flexible; later, detailed and more formal outlines are useful in solving problems in revising. No matter how short your paper is to be, use the topic headings in your notes to generate an outline before you draft.

Drafting is most efficient if you write the body before the introduction and conclusion. Thus, strategies for writing introductions and conclusions come at the end of this chapter.

Many writers have difficulty blending quotations smoothly into the body of their paper. The section titled "Smoothly Incorporating Quotations and Paraphrases" discusses some specific methods for blending.

If you are concerned about the nature of your audience and the degree of formality you should strive for in your writing style, read "Style and Usage: 'To Whom Am I Speaking?' or 'Who Am I Speaking To?'"

If you tend to procrastinate or to develop writer's block, be sure to read "Developing Good Working Habits."

If you are afraid that you will later have to throw away your early drafting efforts to change your whole line of argument at the last minute, read "The Advantages of Early Drafting" and "Redrafting to Give Your Paper a New Slant."

Unless you have already worked out your own system for drafting a research paper when using a word processor, do *not* skip "Assembling the Rough Draft on a Word Processor." This section discusses some important options, and it might save you some time.

OUTLINES

Before drafting, you should create a working plan. But an effective informal plan may be simply a list of your best arguments in the order in which you plan to discuss them. Some writers produce livelier draft material if they delay creating a fully detailed, formal outline until *after* much of the drafting has been done. But writing a detailed outline before writing the rough draft has certain undeniable advantages.

ADVANTAGES OF A DETAILED PREDRAFTING OUTLINE

1. The outline provides a unified working plan.
2. The outline allows you to group and to categorize your source notes.
3. The outline inspires confidence.
4. The outline can help you subdivide your argument logically.

For many (perhaps most!) writers, however, a detailed outline's advantages are outweighed by the following disadvantages.

DISADVANTAGES OF A DETAILED PREDRAFTING OUTLINE

1. Most writers don't know what they want to say until they actually begin to say it. A detailed outline kills the process of spontaneous improvisation that underlies the writing of good prose. The outline produces stiff transitions and dull lists—the worst features of mediocre academic writing.
2. A detailed outline may prevent discovery and development by enforcing a sense of finality too early in the drafting process.
3. Many writers are not working from a tidy stack of note cards that they can sort and arrange under outline headings. Instead, they have a mixture of highlighted photocopies, note cards, open books, and drafts. This mass of material remains difficult to organize, even after a formal outline is completed.
4. A detailed outline creates a false sense of security because it looks logical and orderly even if it really is neither.
5. Writing a formal outline requires mastery of a set of conventions that some writers find perplexing. Learning the complex skills of outlining thus further inhibits the process of discovery.
6. Many writers are fully capable of organizing a fairly long paper entirely in their heads. An outline can sometimes be an unnecessary inconvenience. After all, when you build a house, you need a detailed blueprint; but when you build a napkin holder, a rough sketch will do.

Am I saying that you shouldn't outline? No, I'm not. Even skilled writers benefit from the disciplined organizational patterns created by outlines. But create your outline in gradual stages to encourage rather than stifle your exploration of your topic. Thus, your formal outline may not reach its final, fully detailed form until you have completed your rough draft and are beginning your preliminary draft.

Outlining in Stages to Save Time

If you organize your paper in stages, you will end up writing several outlines rather than just one. At first, you may think that this strategy will create more work for you and make the outlining process harder than it needs to be. But rest assured, the multiple outlines will save time, not waste it.

Your drafting and outlining should move through several phases: First, you should write informal plans, or "scratch outlines." You have already done some scratch outlines when you wrote lists of topics or questions during the prewriting and topic-formulating phases. You should redraft these lists as often as necessary while you gather information and write potential sections of your paper. When you sit down to put together your rough draft, you should complete your last scratch outline: *a list of topic headings put in the order in which you plan to discuss them, with related items placed together.* Some topic headings may refer to entire paragraphs or longer passages that you have already written; some topic headings may refer to individual note cards or highlighted passages; and some may refer to photocopies or to passages in books that you have checked out from the library and have nearby. While you have been taking notes and making drafts, you have probably followed, to some extent at least, the key principle of good organization: *Put related items together.* If you keep following this principle, your paper should automatically fall into outline form as you proceed. If working this way is uncomfortable for you and makes you feel disorganized, stop! Write a formal topic outline after reading this chapter, and use it as a guide in writing your rough draft.

The key aspect of drafting is organization: finding a way to fit all your various bits and pieces into a continuous argument. The task is daunting, even depressing. To keep your spirits up, remember that this is to be a *rough* draft. Your goal is simply to get the whole paper together in some form, accepting the fact that it will be clumsy, unedited, choppy, and even (horrors!) a bit disorganized at first. The rough draft will be followed by revisions (moving or cutting entire paragraphs or portions of the paper), which will be followed by editing. Right now what you are doing is assembling the raw material of your paper into an overall shape, just as an artist draws a rough pencil sketch before proceeding to paint. A good way to clarify your overall plan is to ask a collaborator to listen as you briefly summarize your paper. Your collaborator's questions may help you clarify your ideas—and your plan—before you draft.

During this phase of the writing process there are two crucial *don't*s to keep in mind.

1. Don't spend much time editing or polishing your writing yet. You are working on the general design of the paper; a focus on awkward sentences or phrases will only distract you from the larger organizational problems. Besides, you may later have to cut a sentence you've polished

carefully, or you may move it to another location where it will have to be revised to fit its new context.

Nevertheless, if you are drafting a few paragraphs or pages per day, use Hemingway's technique: Review and lightly edit the previous day's draft before moving on to write new material. This is a good way to maintain continuity if your drafting has to occur in bits and pieces. It also helps prevent unnecessary repetitions.

2. Don't use lists as ways of connecting subtopics, even when you arrange things in categories. If you tell yourself, "I have four points to make," and then you list them ("First, . . . Second, . . ."), you may fool yourself into thinking that you are being organized when really all you may be doing is shutting down your thought processes. A random grocery list, for example, will not guide you efficiently through the store until you have grouped related items together: fresh produce, paper goods, dairy products, and so on. Once you have grouped things together, you have categorized them in a meaningful way. Remember that a random series is a list; a categorized series is an outline!

Alternative Ways of Outlining and Drafting

The best way to enjoy the advantages of outlines while avoiding their disadvantages is to keep the early outlines simple and to elaborate them as the paper develops. The process I prefer looks like this:

1. *scratch outlines* (as many as necessary)
2. rough draft
3. *topic outline*
4. preliminary draft
5. *sentence outline*
6. final draft

For those who prefer to write a formal outline before writing the rough draft, the process might look like this:

1. *scratch outlines* (as many as necessary)
2. *topic outline*
3. rough draft
4. *revised topic outline*
5. preliminary draft
6. *sentence outline*
7. final draft

Finally, for those who prefer to have the paper's plan completely established before drafting, here is the best strategy.

1. *scratch outlines* (as many as necessary)

2. *topic outline*

3. *revised topic outline*

4. *sentence outline*

5. rough draft

6. preliminary draft

7. final draft

Since a scratch outline is just a list of topics placed in the order of their relationship to each other, it is streamlined, easy to use, and easy to revise. Thus it provides a flexible working plan that does not inhibit spontaneity.

A topic outline is a bit more complex. It uses indentations and a special system of lettering and numbering to show the logical relationship between subdivisions. However, it is essentially just a more elaborate type of list because it contains no sentences—only words and phrases that identify the paper's subtopics. Write it after completing the rough draft because it will help you identify and rectify problems with your paper's organization.

A sentence outline is still more complex. It uses complete sentences, rather than words and phrases, to summarize the paper's subdivisions. After the topic outline has been revised and has guided you through a revision of the rough draft, you have probably solved your paper's major organizational problems. At this point, the sentence outline carries you a step farther. It forces you to examine each paragraph to see whether it makes a statement and develops a point. In other words:

> A topic outline helps you organize; a sentence outline helps you argue forcefully and maintain good continuity.

What follows is a sample scratch outline of the opening paragraphs of Todd Rose's paper, "Ethical Dilemmas of Releasing Human Genome Information" (see pp. 231–242). Notice that a scratch outline does not convey much information to anyone except the writer. It is short and highly compressed, it does not show the relative importance of the ideas listed, and it does not spell out the connections between ideas. However, if you compare the scratch outline to Rose's paper, you will see that he had a clear plan in mind. The scratch outline served merely to remind him of the points he intended to make and the sources he intended to use.

Sample Scratch Outline

Introduction to the Human Genome Project

Cost

Scope

Purpose

"Qualitative step" (Annas 20)

Thesis

Purpose of identifying genes

Definition of base pairs

Phases 1 and 2 of the Human Genome Project

3 billion base pairs (Lammers 868)

Genetic diseases (Lammers 868)

Types of Outlines

During the drafting process, you may find your paper's argument going in unexpected directions, and the scratch outline will leave you free to develop some new lines of argument spontaneously. You also may find that you repeat yourself as you draft, or that you can't find a way to introduce some subtopics that you originally planned to discuss. Don't worry. False starts, digressions, repetitions, and unintentional omissions are all normal parts of the drafting process.

To fix these problems, you may need to turn your informal scratch outline into a formal outline. The following side-by-side comparison, of the two types of formal outlines—topic outlines and sentence outlines—will show you why I suggest making a topic outline first and a sentence outline later, to guide your final revision. (Sentence outlines are discussed in Chapter 10.)

Topic Outline		*Sentence Outline*	
Advantages	*Disadvantages*	*Advantages*	*Disadvantages*
Brief	Ambiguous	Unambiguous	Lengthy
Easy to evaluate at a glance	Omits details	Detailed	Hard to evaluate at a glance
Flexible list of things to be discussed	Doesn't make assertions—just lists items; allows writer to drift into exposition	Forces writer to make assertions; strengthens argumentative focus	Tends to prevent flexible reworking of argument if used during drafting
Leaves transitions to be worked out later	Doesn't help clarify connections between ideas	Clarifies connections between ideas	Tends to inhibit revision once transitions are worked out
Good for pre-planning and revising		Good for editing	

Generating a Topic Outline

Let's briefly retrace the development of a sample topic as it moved through the steps discussed in previous chapters. One of my students wanted to discuss the superconducting supercollider, an expensive government project (canceled in 1993) that was designed to use the latest technologies to produce high-energy atomic collisions. At the early stage of topic development, Wendy decided to focus on the debate about the cost-effectiveness of the supercollider. This formulation of the topic suggested that she could easily develop her argument in two major sections: costs and benefits. In filling out the topic statement exercise, Wendy wrote the following rough plan of development.

Topic: The Supercolliding Particle Accelerator

Thesis (or hypothesis): Its benefits will outweigh its costs.

As Wendy did research on her topic, she found that the costs of the project fell into two categories: start-up costs and operating costs. Therefore, she used the following topic headings in marking her photocopies and notes.

costs—start-up

costs—operation

While researching the potential benefits of the new device, Wendy found that some sources discussed the kinds of new knowledge that could be generated by means of research using the accelerator. Although this material was relevant to her topic, she decided that her real interest lay in finding out whether the device would yield only theoretical knowledge or would really have practical, dollars-and-cents benefits. Accordingly, she began marking her sources with the following topic headings.

benefits—knowledge

benefits—potential profits

In writing her rough draft, Wendy used a scratch outline with these main headings.

costs—start-up

costs—operation

benefits—pure knowledge

benefits—potential profits

After letting the rough draft sit for a couple of days, Wendy returned to it and gave it a careful, critical reading. The first half of the paper seemed relatively well organized, because it followed a straightforward, chronological plan; start-up costs naturally came first, and operational costs naturally came later. However, the sections on benefits seemed disorganized because, despite her attempts to separate "pure knowledge" from "potential profits," Wendy's draft kept jumping back and forth between the two categories. Her draft also seemed to go back and forth between civilian and military examples.

It struck her that "potential profits" didn't accurately describe the military examples, anyway, because when the government develops weapons for national defense, profit is a secondary consideration. She decided to use the following topic labels, which are more precise.

benefits—theoretical knowledge

benefits—practical applications

This change involved more than just quibbling over labels. The terms *theoretical* and *practical* are antonyms—words that have opposite meanings. The use of antonyms clarified the thought processes that underlay her pattern of organization. This change exemplifies one of the most important rules of organization.

> Whenever possible, organize your material by means of mutually exclusive (that is, nonoverlapping) categories.

The effects of a change like this carry forward into the revising process. When Wendy later revised her work for clarity and coherence, she inserted the words *theoretical* and *practical* in places where they helped to clarify the reader's perception of her pattern of organization.

Now the clarifying term *practical* enabled her to subdivide her confusing discussion of military and civilian applications by separating the two topics; both civilian and military applications of knowledge in the development of new technologies could be considered "practical" as opposed to "theoretical."

Wendy made one last change: She substituted the more formal term *development* for *start-up*. Her revised scratch outline now looked like this.

costs—development

costs—operation

benefits—theoretical knowledge

benefits—practical applications

practical applications—military

practical applications—civilian

To convert this scratch outline into a formal topic outline, all she had to do was add indentations to show which topics were main headings and which ones were subordinate. Finally, letters and numerals were added to show how the parts relate to each other. Here is the resulting *brief topic outline*.

Topic: The Supercolliding Particle Accelerator
Thesis (or hypothesis): Its benefits will outweigh its costs.
  I. Costs
      A. Development
      B. Operation
  II. Benefits
      A. Theoretical knowledge
      B. Practical applications
          1. Military
          2. Civilian

Although it is brief and may require further division into subtopics, an outline of this sort can serve as an adequate road map for revision. When Wendy revised, she marked her rough draft by labeling subsections in the margins. For example, next to one misplaced paragraph she wrote, "Move to section on civilian applications."

The Developed Thesis

Completing the topic outline at the revision stage of the drafting process has another advantage: The topic outline can help in the drafting of the final version of the thesis, the developed thesis. As originally stated, Wendy's undeveloped thesis stakes a general claim but does not specifically mention every subdivision of the argument; her developed thesis, in contrast, briefly mentions each subtopic discussed in the paper.

Undeveloped thesis: The new supercolliding particle accelerator's benefits will outweigh its costs.

Developed thesis: Although the new supercolliding particle accelerator will be expensive to develop and to operate, the theoretical knowledge gained will yield practical applications that will more than repay these costs.

Wendy could have used these statements in the paper's introduction (undeveloped thesis) and conclusion (developed thesis) to clarify the focus of her argument and to predict the paper's pattern of development.

As it turned out, however, she decided to use the more developed statement as her undeveloped thesis, because it left adequate room for surprises (What knowledge? What practical applications?) while providing a detailed, highly accurate map of the subtopics her paper would discuss. She came up with another statement, still more detailed and complex, to serve as her developed thesis.

Remember the crucial point: From the first thesis statement, the reader should get a good understanding of the direction of the argument, and the final statement should remind the reader of the specific points you covered. In this way a paper goes somewhere, develops its argument, and contains surprises. If the developed thesis is fully stated at the outset, there are no surprises and thus no sense of development. (See Chapter 3, "Generating an Argument.")

The Rules of Outlining

An outline is more than just an organized list; it is a formal way of dividing a topic. When we divide something, we must divide it into at least two parts. Therefore, the primary rule of outlining is this:

> 1. If you divide a topic or subtopic, divide it into at least two parts.

The second rule ensures that the outline will show the relationship between parts.

> 2. Related points should be expressed in related form. Use parallel (or antithetical) phrasing wherever possible.

(We just saw the advantages of setting "theoretical knowledge" in parallel with "practical applications." When two antonyms are placed in a parallel relationship, the relationship is said to be *antithetical*.)

The third rule establishes conventions for lettering and numbering the parts of an outline.

> 3. Roman numerals precede Arabic numerals, capitals precede lowercase letters, parentheses set off the lowest subdivisions, and levels of indentation match vertically.

The standard labels look like this:

I.
   A.
   B.
      1.
      2.
         a.
         b.
            (1)
            (2)
               (a)
               (b)
II.

Note that any subdivision can contain further subdivisions, but each level of subordination must have at least two parts. Thus, although it is quite unbalanced, the following skeleton outline follows correct labeling conventions because each level has at least two parts.

I.
   A.
   B.
      1.
      2.
   C.
      1.
         a.
         b.
            (1)
               (a)
               (b)
            (2)
      2.
   D.
      1.
      2.
      3.

II.

    A.

    B.

From this outline you can tell at a glance that major topic I receives much fuller development than major topic II, and that underneath major topic I subtopic C receives highly detailed development. I emphasize this point because writers so often get confused about it: *An outline can be unbalanced as long as there are two or more subdivisions at each level of subordination.*

What should you do if you find that you have only one subdivision where the rules call for two or more? There are several possibilities. If the outline helps you see that you have only one supporting example where you should have two or more, then *create more supporting examples.* But if you cannot create matching subdivisions, the rule is to *consolidate, promote, or omit.* That is, make the single heading part of the heading above it (consolidate headings). Or move the single heading up to the next level of subordination (promote a capital-letter heading to the level of a capital-Roman-numeral heading, for example). Or, finally, omit it altogether.

The fourth rule of outlining is meant to ensure the unity of the outline (and thus of the paper itself).

> 4. Try to limit the number of main headings (capital Roman numerals) to six or fewer.

This rule is not as arbitrary as it may sound. Everything you have been doing up to this point has been aimed at producing a highly unified paper supporting a single thesis statement. A proliferation of subheadings may destroy the unity you've been working so hard to achieve. Your thesis sentence can comfortably contain only a few subtopics, and these subtopics should (ideally) be the headings of the main subdivisions of your outline. If you create a host of major subheadings, your plan of organization is liable to deteriorate into a list. One main purpose of the outline is to force you to group the various parts of your paper under a tightly focused, limited group of main headings.

Outlines Generated Automatically by Word Processors

Some word-processing software has built-in outlining capability. One type of software requires you to mark phrases or sentences that will later be part of an outline; after your draft is completed, the word processor automatically assembles an outline from the marked passages. Another type of software merely supplies automatically generated letters and numbers, appropriately indented, after which you type your selection headings.

The automatic outliner I use is a handy tool for organizing and reorganizing drafts. If you move or promote a heading (by turning a third-level item 1 into a second-level item B, for example), the outliner automatically promotes and renumbers all the subheadings at the same time. This feature speeds up the process of revising an outline.

STARTING THE ROUGH DRAFT

Once you have put topic headings at the top of each note card, at the top of each drafted paragraph, or in the margins of your photocopied sources, you can complete your outline by assembling all your material and reviewing it item by item. Although I can't give you an invariable rule, an outline for a ten-page paper should probably be less than two double-spaced pages. If your outline becomes unmanageably long, perhaps you have too much material to cover in the paper's required length. If so, review Chapter 2, "Finding and Narrowing Your Topic," before you draft long sections that must later be discarded.

Step-by-step research writing texts normally advise you to write the introduction first. However, there are several disadvantages to this approach.

1. The introduction and the conclusion are the most difficult parts of the paper to write. It is less discouraging to begin with the body paragraphs.

2. The fullest and most forceful statement of your argument should come at the end of the paper. Once you have written the conclusion, you can simplify it and paraphrase it to write an effective introduction that states only the main points developed in the paper.

3. Often you will find your most effective ideas and key phrases while drafting the body and the conclusion. These ideas and phrases can then be used in the introduction to arouse the reader's interest in what follows.

For the sake of efficiency, write the body of the paper first, then the conclusion, and, finally, the introduction. If this method makes you feel lost and directionless, then write an introduction first, but keep it simple. Make it one or two paragraphs long, and put the thesis statement at the end of it. You may feel that this positioning of the thesis is trite and predictable, but remember that your paper will be read by an instructor who is probably reading dozens of papers. The thesis should be easy to spot. Occasionally, it is effective to use an *implicit thesis*, one that is not fully stated until the end of the paper. But this method is risky; it can make the paper look unplanned and unfocused. The advantage of the implicit thesis is that it avoids giving away the whole argument at once, but this advantage is also preserved in the method discussed in Chapter 3, "Generating an Argument": Start with an *undeveloped thesis statement* and end with a *developed thesis statement* (see pp. 32–34 and 276).

As you draft, try to maintain continuity. Sometimes you will find that paragraph transitions fall into natural patterns, such as chronological, spatial, cause-effect, or comparison-contrast. When considering how to order your subtopics, keep in mind the following cardinal rule of organization.

> Unless some other pattern (such as *from cause to effect*) is needed, move from the weakest points to the strongest points.

By dispensing with your weakest points first and ending with your strongest, you leave the reader with a positive impression. (See "Other Types of Transition" in Chapter 10 for a fuller discussion of patterns of organization.)

Whatever method you use to move from paragraph to paragraph, don't worry if you find that some paragraph transitions are abrupt in the rough draft. They can be smoothed out later by means of paragraph hooks. A *paragraph hook* connects paragraphs by making key phrases in a paragraph's opening sentence echo key phrases in the preceding paragraph's last sentence. This useful all-purpose technique for ensuring continuity is discussed in detail in Chapter 10, "Revising the Rough Draft."

Smoothly Incorporating Quotations and Paraphrases

Most of your source material should be presented as paraphrases. (On the relative proportions of paraphrasing and quoting, see Chapter 6, "Gathering Information.") Since you write the paraphrases yourself during note taking or drafting, they are easy to blend with the passages that surround them.

Smoothly blending quotations into your draft can be tricky, though. A long quotation (in MLA format, a quotation of more than four typed lines) should be set off in a separate block (see p. 162). Normally, a block quotation should be announced by a complete sentence ending with a colon or a period. This sentence serves as a bridge between the general point you are developing and the support offered by the quotation. Here is a good example from a student's paper.

General point. The cartoons were not vulgar or unsuitable for children--

they simply contained a few items that a child could not

Lead-in bridge. have understood. Shull and Wilt sum up the idea nicely:

Supporting   Only an adult would understand many of the verbal
quotation.
and visual references that make up so much of the

cartoons' impact. As a whole, the cartoon industry

could not afford to make "kiddie" cartoons, because

their product would then be severely restricted in its

appeal. . . . (6)

Bridge to the   Virtually all of the Warner cartoons contained some of
next point.
these "verbal and visual references" that Shull and Wilt

describe. A good example is. . . .

The important function fulfilled by the first bridge sentence is that it helps the reader understand why the writer is quoting the passage. He could have omitted the bridge sentence, inserted a colon after "understood," and inserted "Shull and Wilt" before the page number in the parenthetical documentation; this structure is technically correct. But his voice would have been lost in the process, and the quotation would have seemed like an unnecessary repetition of the general point. So remember the following general principle:

> The key to the effective use of quotations is to signal their importance with a clear lead-in bridge sentence.

When using shorter quotations, you must choose between quoting an entire clause or short phrases. The effects can be quite different, as these examples illustrate.

As Steven Schneider says, "Stories often trafficked in unavoidably 'adult' concerns and were replete with topical or real-world references" ("Alternative" 125).

Steven Schneider claims that these tales dealt with "unavoidably 'adult'" matters and were full of "topical" and "real-world" elements ("Alternative" 125).

In the first example, the introductory verb ("says") hints that Marcum agrees with Schneider; by quoting the entire sentence he expresses agreement and respect. In the second example, the introductory verb ("claims") signals potential disagreement, and the carving up of the quotation into fragments suggests a skeptical attitude toward the quoted material; one suspects that Marcum may go on to say that Schneider overstates his case.

In general, quote short passages in their entirety to avoid the awkward dismembering of quotations (see pp. 161–162). Brief quotations can be used to suggest skepticism or even disrespect for the quoted matter. Sometimes, they may be necessary for the sake of close verbal analysis: "Keats can simultaneously exploit the positive connotations of 'forever warm' and the negative connotations of 'a burning forehead'; warmth is associated both with passion and with illness." Here the fragmentary quotations are justified by the need to compare two closely related phrases.

To make a quotation fit into its surrounding context, you may tailor it by making certain kinds of alterations, such as bracketed insertions and ellipsis marks to indicate the omission of words. See the discussion of altering quotations in Chapter 7 (pp. 163 and 198). Here is the key rule to ensure the smooth incorporation of quotations.

> When you quote a phrase or clause, the resulting sentence must be smooth, grammatical, and logical in its construction.

Now examine the following example, which violates this rule.

The first victim of Pope's attack is: "Arcadia's Countess, here, in ermin'd pride, / Is there, <u>Pastora</u> by a Fountain side" (7–8).

In grading a paper, I would normally mark this sentence with the abbreviated comment "awk[ward] incorp[oration] of quotation," but the awkwardness in this example is both typical enough and complex enough to deserve some detailed comments here. The student has constructed the sentence in the belief that any string of words can be made the subject of *is*. This mistake occurs frequently in papers on literature; chunks of language are often singled out for analysis and dropped into sentences where they do not belong. In this example, the phrase "Arcadia's Countess" cannot function as the predicate of one clause and the subject of another. The incorporation is made doubly awkward by the misuse of the colon; a colon should be preceded by a complete main clause. Another typical mistake is the failure to provide any sort of bridge to a controlling point. The student has simply said, "The first victim is so-and-so." A mere listing is the weakest sort of transition. Notice how the bridge statement in the following revision solves all these problems at once.

> Pope introduces the theme of hypocrisy by attacking the pretentious, inconsistent behavior of a noblewoman who plays different roles in different settings: "Arcadia's Countess here, in ermin'd pride, / Is there, Pastora by a Fountain side" (7–8).

Verbs to Introduce Quotations

Writers may think that the reader will be bothered by too many repetitions of an all-purpose verb such as *says* or *writes*. Actually, though, readers pay little attention to the verbs that introduce quotations. However, some variations in introductory verbs are desirable, such as *Walker says* or *Ingram argues*. Variations are especially useful for showing your attitude toward a quotation: *Nelson demonstrates* shows that you regard Nelson's point as proven, whereas *Nelson claims* shows that you are skeptical. But avoid striving for variety by using coy introductory verbs that call attention to themselves, such as *Jackson avers*. Do you not deem this verb starchy and inappropriate in virtually any context? (Yes, I'm pulling your leg with the word *deem*, another stiff and inappropriate verb.)

ASSEMBLING THE ROUGH DRAFT FROM NOTES

If you have gathered most of your information in a research journal stored as a word-processing file, you should be able to assemble much of your rough draft simply by reorganizing portions of your journal. If you have collected stacks of books, notes, and photocopies, you have a more difficult task ahead. In either situation, though, here are the essential steps.

1. If you have not already done so, assign a topic heading to every quotation, paraphrase, summary, or draft portion you plan to use. (Don't vandalize library books by marking them. Use bookmarks or removable,

gummed notes to mark passages you plan to quote or paraphrase in your paper.)

2. Compile a list of these topic headings.

3. Use the topic headings to assemble a plan—either an informal plan, such as a scratch outline, or a formal plan, such as a topic or sentence outline.

4. Use the outline as a guide for your rough draft.

5. As you draft, use the outline to help you blend, topic by topic, the material you've gathered.

This is the traditional method of drafting. Figure 9.1 illustrates the essential steps.

ASSEMBLING THE ROUGH DRAFT ON A WORD PROCESSOR

Although for efficiency's sake, most writers use word processing for as much of the note-taking and drafting processes as possible, some writers are more comfortable doing their drafting in longhand. There is something about the slow, steady rhythm of writing by hand that encourages a thoughtful approach. Other writers find that the flexibility of word processing encourages them to do too much editing and fussing with details during the drafting stage; word processing actually gets in the way for them. Still other writers lack the typing skills necessary to make word processing an efficient mode of drafting. Finally, some writers have simply grown used to the typewriter and prefer to use it, even though it forces them to retype the entire paper when they revise and edit.

A shortcoming of word processing is that the video screen displays text in chunks smaller than a full page, making it hard to establish continuity during the drafting process. Many writers who use word processing find that they cannot edit on-screen text as well as they can edit printed copy.

Although you may choose to work with the rough draft on-screen, there are some advantages to printing out a hard copy of the rough draft. The great American short story writer Eudora Welty used to revise a story by laying it out across the floor so that she could walk alongside it, noticing the relative lengths of its various parts and considering alternative ways of arranging them. Before word processing, many writers used to revise by using scissors and tape to move portions around until the new arrangement satisfied them. So you should find the process that works best for you.

For several reasons, I find that I must print text to edit it. First, I inevitably spot mistakes in hard copy that I missed when I was reading text on the screen. Second, I can revise and edit hard copy by crossing out passages, by drawing circles around blocks that I intend to move, and by writing ideas, questions, and criticisms in the margin; in this way, I can see at a glance how my various changes affect each other. But if I edit on screen, each change takes effect as soon as I have made it, and I often forget what I have done and what I intended to do next.

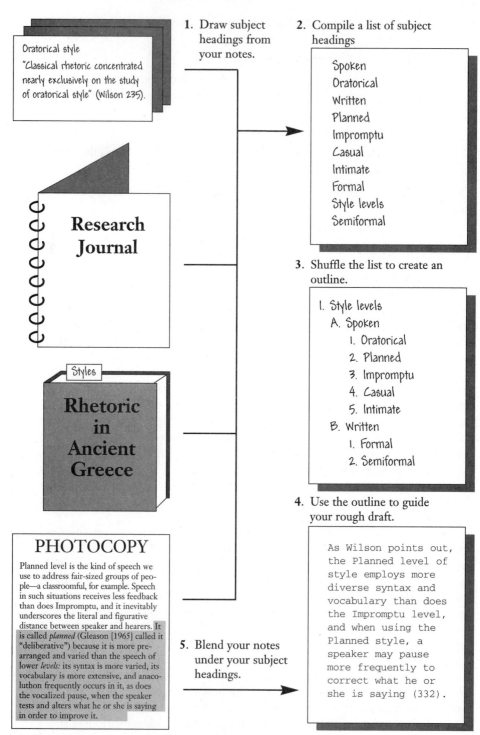

1. Draw subject headings from your notes.

Oratorical style
"Classical rhetoric concentrated nearly exclusively on the study of oratorical style" (Wilson 235).

Research Journal

Styles

Rhetoric in Ancient Greece

2. Compile a list of subject headings

Spoken
Oratorical
Written
Planned
Impromptu
Casual
Intimate
Formal
Style levels
Semiformal

3. Shuffle the list to create an outline.

I. Style levels
  A. Spoken
    1. Oratorical
    2. Planned
    3. Impromptu
    4. Casual
    5. Intimate
  B. Written
    1. Formal
    2. Semiformal

4. Use the outline to guide your rough draft.

PHOTOCOPY

Planned level is the kind of speech we use to address fair-sized groups of people—a classroomful, for example. Speech in such situations receives less feedback than does Impromptu, and it inevitably underscores the literal and figurative distance between speaker and hearers. It is called *planned* (Gleason [1965] called it "deliberative") because it is more prearranged and varied than the speech of lower *levels:* its syntax is more varied, its vocabulary is more extensive, and anacoluthon frequently occurs in it, as does the vocalized pause, when the speaker tests and alters what he or she is saying in order to improve it.

As Wilson points out, the Planned level of style employs more diverse syntax and vocabulary than does the Impromptu level, and when using the Planned style, a speaker may pause more frequently to correct what he or she is saying (332).

5. Blend your notes under your subject headings.

FIGURE 9.1 Traditional Method of Drafting

I also make mistakes when the word processor's on-screen display does not truly represent what the printer will later generate.

Some aspects of using on-screen copy and hard copy will be discussed later in Chapter 10 on revising and Chapter 11 on editing. For now, the important thing is to decide on the drafting method that is most comfortable for you and that will simplify editing and revising later. I suggest drafting on screen but editing printed copy.

Word processing allows you to assemble a rough draft quickly by means of cutting and pasting. Because there are many kinds of word-processing software on the market, I can offer only generic advice. Experiment with your word processor to find techniques that work for you.

The biggest advantage of using word processing is that there is no copying or retyping involved during drafting. It is very time-consuming to take notes on note cards, to assemble them into outline form, and to type them into the rough draft. Furthermore, each time you have to retype notes, you run the risk of introducing mistakes. In contrast, pasting draft sections together is a process that word processors can perform quickly and flawlessly.

Remember to print your draft material frequently. With a printed copy, you can look at the entire draft at once; with a word-processing file displayed on a computer screen, you can look at only one small chunk of information at a time. You may also want to share printed draft material with a collaborator to see whether your draft is clear and effective.

Here's another reminder: After each work session, make a backup copy of your draft. Store the backup on a separate disk so that you will not lose all your work in case of a disk failure. *Never* keep all your work on just one disk or on an unbacked-up hard drive.

The most effective backup technique is to copy an entire floppy disk. Here's why: In a single work session you may make changes in several different files, such as a draft, a bibliography, and a research journal. As long as you store them together on one disk, you don't have to remember which files you've altered; just back up the whole disk.

You may want to keep several numbered versions of the draft as it develops. That way you can always return to an earlier draft if you decide that today's changes were no good.

One method for drafting on the word processor is to assemble all your notes, ideas, and draft sections in a single long file, preferably in the form of a research journal. Store a backup copy of it, calling it "Journal Backup" or "Archive." Then return to the original copy of the long file and rename it "Draft 1."

If you have not already done so, type topic headings above each individual quotation or section of notes or draft material. (It helps to use capital letters in these temporary headings to distinguish them from the actual text of the paper and to make them easy to spot.) Then *copy* (without permanently removing) each topic heading, pasting the copied heading at the beginning of the file. Next, shuffle the initial list of topic headings, putting them in a logical order to assemble a scratch outline. Print out the outline, so that you have a hard copy of it; and paste it into a separate file, so that you can tinker with it later. From this point on, keep the printed copy of the outline at your side as you work. To complete the assembly of the rough draft, go through all the research material, cutting each section and pasting it under the appropriate heading in the outline without worrying about continuity and transitions. Finally, cut out all the subject headings.

This method has several advantages. For one thing, all your notes and draft materials are safely stored in an archive file (with a backup copy of the archive file on another disk). This archive file remains unchanged, so you can refer to it any time if you inadvertently cut something from your draft and forget to paste it back in.

Another advantage is that your outline takes shape gradually from the topic headings you have created. As you cluster related topic headings, you will find that the outline virtually creates itself. The key thing to remember is that you must carefully create a well-planned outline at the beginning of the file *before* you begin pasting draft materials together. It is easy to reorganize at the outlining stage, but it becomes harder as the drafting proceeds.

Another advantage of this method is that your outline is temporarily stored in the same file with your draft materials. Hence you can assemble the draft without constantly having to open another file.

One problem with this method is that some word processors paginate automatically, so that as you move material around, the page divisions constantly change. The solution is to insert "hard page breaks" (perhaps one per subtopic) to impose your own pagination. When you are done drafting, cut the hard page breaks and repaginate the draft. Remember, you can use the "search" function to jump automatically to selected subject headings.

Whatever word-processing methods you use when you cut and paste quotations and paraphrases, be sure that you include the documentation (author and page number) with each cut. Once you've cut something and pasted it into a new location, it's easy to forget where it came from. If this should happen, remember that you have your archive file to refer to.

Also, whenever you cut and paste blocks of text, keep track of the amount of remaining disk space. A long paper stored with lots of other files can result in a "disk full" message and the loss of draft material. So shift files to other disks as the need arises. Disks are cheap, but your time is expensive.

Finally, put tips and reminders at the beginning or end of the draft file. When you reach the end of the drafting process, you have a page full of reminders, and you can check to see that you have finished all your drafting chores.

STYLE AND USAGE: "To Whom Am I Speaking?" or "Who Am I Speaking To?"

As the heading suggests, speakers and writers of standard American English do not always agree about what constitutes correct usage. The relative pronoun *whom* is the object of the preposition *to* in the heading's first question—and strictly speaking, the second question should therefore read, "Whom Am I

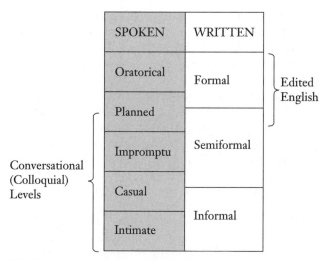

FIGURE 9.2   The Levels of Style. *(Source: Wilson xii.)*

Speaking To?" However, few speakers of standard American English use this form. (When the pronoun occurs at the beginning of a sentence, the subject form *who* is commonly substituted for the object form *whom*. For a sensible and authoritative explanation, see *who* in *The Columbia Guide to Standard American English*.) Some purists would further complicate matters by suggesting that a sentence should not end with a preposition. Thus, for purists, "To whom am I speaking?" is the "correct" usage. There's just one problem: Most speakers of standard American English feel that they are being overly formal and proper when they use this form and that they should do so only when holding a teacup, pinkie finger extended.

The problem for the research writer is to decide what level of formality is appropriate for the assigned paper. When you are in doubt, ask your instructor—without going to the extreme of asking about every point of usage that arises. In general, most research writing aims at the stylistic level commonly called *semiformal* or *moderately formal*. Figure 9.2—a chart by Kenneth G. Wilson (editor of *The Columbia Guide to Standard American English*), using concepts originally formulated by Martin Joos and H. A. Gleason—may help to clarify the levels of style.

The research writer aims for the level of style that lies precisely where semiformal and planned styles overlap, at the lower level of edited English. That is, research style is seldom oratorical or elevated. You should aim to strike a compromise between informality and formality, and you should feel comfortable when reading your work aloud.

Note that the style of this book is sometimes more casual than the style of research writing. I use first-person and second-person pronouns (*I, you*) freely, and I often use contractions rather than full verb forms (*you're* rather than *you are*). Research writing, in contrast, uses *I* very sparingly, and it never uses verb contractions.

Since a research paper is usually written within a specific academic discipline, expectations may vary from subject to subject and from instructor to instructor. For instance, a literature professor may welcome and reward subjective *I* statements, but a medical science professor may expect avoidance of the words *I* and *me*. When in doubt, ask your instructor.

In addition to choosing an appropriate stylistic level, research writers have to estimate their audience's likely level of expertise. Here I think it is useful to distinguish between an *actual* and a *hypothetical* audience. Your actual audience is most likely your course instructor. Your hypothetical audience may be an imaginary group of peers. Your goal is to satisfy the first by pretending to write for the second.

What does this guideline mean? It means, for one thing, that in writing a research paper on *The Sun Also Rises*, you should not waste time summarizing the plot. You are writing for a hypothetical audience of people who have read the novel; otherwise, they would be unlikely to want to read your paper.

For another thing, you have to make some decisions about what constitutes "common knowledge" for your hypothetical audience. For example, a study of renaissance poetry should not define the term *metaphor* (unless some very special problem of definition is being addressed), nor should a medical science paper define *respiration* (unless, again, some special problem is being discussed). As a check, have a collaborator read your paper for common knowledge, clarity, and comprehensibility.

In general, you can assume that you are writing for a well-educated group of college students majoring in the discipline of the research paper. A highly specialized term may require definition, but a term that can be found in a desk-size college dictionary should not. (Thus *arteriosclerosis* should not require a definition, but *serous retinopathy* might.) If you must use a large and highly specialized vocabulary in your paper, a separate glossary may be the best solution.

> If you are using word processing, create a *macro* for each specialized term that has to be used frequently; then you can call up each term with just a keystroke or two. Besides saving time, you can avoid the embarrassment of misspelling a term that you use throughout your paper.

DEVELOPING GOOD WORKING HABITS

Overcoming Writer's Block

Writer's block can mean many different things, but usually the phrase describes an inability to begin drafting. Often, writer's block is a direct result of perfectionism. Unrealistically high expectations about your own work can result in a sense of disappointment in advance.

Experienced writers get over writer's block by lowering their expectations. Remember that the rough draft is going to be *rough*. Remember, too, that human beings often find creative solutions by making what at first appear to be mistakes. If you feel blocked, try one or more of the following techniques for lowering your expectations.

1. Do some freewriting. Set down your thoughts about your topic in any form at all. Useful draft portions or ideas will start to surface. Turn off the self-critical part of your mind; remember that you will be revising and editing later. Accept whatever words come, no matter how foolish or awkward. You can throw away the foolishness later and keep the good ideas.

2. Shift to a different audience. Forget the teacher who will be reading your paper. Instead, start writing a letter to a friend, explaining your frustration with the paper and telling him or her what the paper is about. Before long, you will find yourself drafting. Lift the useful parts from your letter and use them as draft portions.

3. Turn down the brightness control on your word processor until you can no longer see what you are writing. You will make lots of mistakes, but you will be drafting without criticizing or editing your work.

4. Talk to a collaborator about your work before you start drafting.

Using Collaboration in Drafting

Just as writing a letter to a friend can help you overcome writer's block, talking to a friend about your paper or sharing some draft material can help you move forward when you feel stalled. Informal collaboration is helpful at virtually every stage of the writing process. The key advantage of sharing your material is that someone else's questions may help you clarify the purpose of your writing. In addition, the other person may know something useful about the topic or may be able to direct you to someone who does.

The actual drafting of a paper is unavoidably solitary and lonely, but most teachers are more than willing to look at rough drafts or to listen to your preliminary ideas. In fact, they would prefer to help you solve problems early in the writing process rather than later when you have committed time and energy to a topic or an approach that isn't working.

A useful collaborator, then, might be a teacher, a tutor, a roommate, a friend, or a family member. A collaborator need not be an expert in the subject you are dealing with. If you ask someone for help, though, you should make it clear that during the drafting stage you want the collaborator to refrain from offering detailed suggestions about such matters as style, editing, and revision; explain that these problems will be tackled later. And be careful about the ethics of collaboration. A collaborator may offer questions, suggestions, and information, but the actual writing must be your own—every word of it!

During drafting, a collaborator can be especially helpful in what most instructors call *developing the topic*. By asking for clarification, suggesting that more examples are needed, or pointing out an abrupt topic shift, a collaborator can show you how an audience is likely to respond to your work. You are too close to it to judge it accurately during drafting; a collaborator can give you a much-needed second perspective.

The Advantages of Early Drafting

Perhaps the most common mistake college research writers make is to delay writing until they have collected all their sources and notes. But if you have been following my advice and keeping a research journal, the journal has probably already proved to you that much is to be gained by beginning your drafting process *before* you have done much source gathering or note taking. Before looking at sources, you may know little about your subject, but your ideas may be fresher for that very reason. Also, by writing down what you know, you discover the gaps in your knowledge, and these gaps help you formulate the questions you want to answer. If nothing else, early brainstorming and drafting help you formulate a clear hypothesis that guides your search for information and evidence.

There is a still more important reason for early drafting. Soon after you have collected and have read a substantial body of source material, all the various writings will begin to blur together in your mind. You will begin to lose track of who said what. All the sources' voices become a babble of information that will begin to drown out *your* voice. Your mind will be rich with information about your subject, but you will begin to lose your sense of direction. I have seen many students become stymied once they have read all the relevant source material because they came to feel that everything had been said. Early drafting can prevent this sense of being overwhelmed by source material.

Now, let's assume the worst possible case: Your hypothesis has been authoritatively proved (or disproved) by one or more of your sources. Does this mean that you must now either drop your topic or write a purely informative, nonargumentative rehash of someone else's work? Of course not. It simply means that someone has answered your original research question. But what you have written during the process of research should now enable you to ask a new question and formulate a new hypothesis that may be a modification or an offshoot of the first. After all, in most subject areas the final word is never spoken. There is always more to be said; there are always new questions to be asked. Similarly, if a source you discover late in the research process forces you to rethink your entire paper, it is not a disaster. You are simply continuing to learn about your subject, right up to the last minute.

Redrafting to Give Your Paper a New Slant

Let's say you are writing a paper on Nicolo Paganini, the great violin virtuoso of the nineteenth century. Your initial hypothesis is that Paganini was primarily a master showman and a charismatic figure—not so much a great musician as a great celebrity. The topic seems to be working, because there is enough information on Paganini but no article or book that focuses exclusively on his celebrity status. Then, near the paper's due date, a requested interlibrary loan article arrives at your library. When you read it, you discover that the article is a thorough proof of your own hypothesis.

Here is a real dilemma. Through no fault of your own, you have discovered that you are duplicating someone else's published work—an unplanned and unintentional violation of one of the cardinal rules of research. You now have four options, none of them very pleasant.

1. Scrap the entire project. (This, of course, is what you feel like doing.)
2. Pretend that the interlibrary loan source never arrived, and write the paper without paying any attention to it.
3. Write the paper as planned, but incorporate references to the new source throughout the body of the paper.
4. Rewrite the paper so that it asks a new research question and states a new hypothesis.

As you have noticed, the options are arranged in order, from least desirable to most desirable. We can rule out option 1 because no one wants to throw away weeks of work, especially when tuition dollars and course credits are at stake. We must rule out option 2, because it is dishonest. You *have* seen and read this new source, and nothing can undo this fact. To pretend to ignore the source could even be dangerous: Your instructor may have read this very article and may suspect plagiarism; or while checking sources, the instructor may spot the article and consider you remiss for omitting the best available source. Option 3 is somewhat more acceptable, but your constant references to the new source will make it seem as if you had relied on this source from the very start; your paper will look like a one-source argument with sprinklings of material from other sources. The injustice here is that you have done original research, original drafting, and original organization of material—yet after the incorporation of this new material, it will seem as if you *haven't* done these things.

This scenario, by the way, is based on the experience of a student in one of my courses. He chose option 4 and was able to pull it off without much trouble. But he did one important thing: When the new source arrived, he came to me and explained the situation. He felt that his well-constructed research paper had just been shot out from under him. Because he had been drafting at every step of the research process, however, we were able to back up and refocus what he had already written. First, we talked for a while, brainstorming ideas related to his former hypothesis: Perhaps Paganini was a master self-promoter, but to what extent was this conscious and planned, and to what extent was it a lucky accident? Rumors circulated that Paganini was in league with the devil and had traded his soul for demonic powers over the violin and over his audience. How had these rumors got started? Did Paganini himself start or encourage them? Eventually, the student redirected his paper to focus on a specific issue not fully discussed by the late-arriving source, and the hypothesis got revised to look like this: "Paganini promoted his own musical career by intentionally creating a cult of followers, by encouraging rumors that he was satanically inspired, and by employing stage techniques that literally hypnotized his audience." I was impressed by this student's honesty, by his enterprising willingness to redraft, and by his skillful redirection of the paper at the last minute. If disaster strikes, follow his example.

STRATEGIES FOR INTRODUCTIONS AND CONCLUSIONS

By the time you have drafted the body of your paper, you will probably have thought of various ways of writing your introduction and conclusion. However, if you find these portions difficult to write, keep a few guidelines in mind.

An introduction usually starts with a general statement and moves toward the highly focused and particular statement that is the paper's thesis. The introduction need not be long. It is generally better to risk abruptness than to write so long an introduction that the reader's attention wanders and the thesis gets buried. But do provide at least a paragraph of lead-in to the thesis. Making the thesis sentence the very first sentence of the paper deprives your reader of the opportunity to understand the general context that supports and gives meaning to your thesis. A research paper is like a contribution to an ongoing debate. Use the introduction to help the reader understand how the debate has been going.

Whatever introductory and concluding strategies you adopt, you should echo the introduction at the end of the paper without creating a long summary or restatement. Repetition is boring, and it insults the reader's intelligence.

Introductory techniques often overlap; you needn't limit yourself to just one. In the list that follows, I mention in parentheses some element of my paper's introduction (or an early draft of the paper) that embodies each technique (my paper is reproduced in Chapter 8).

TECHNIQUES FOR INTRODUCTIONS

1. Use an anecdote or a brief narrative to catch the reader's attention. (Bach improvised on demand for Frederick the Great.)

2. Prepare the reader for a special approach, if your paper uses some special approach that requires explanation. You might define a key term, for example, but only if the definition is necessary. Starting with an unnecessary definition is a common (and ineffective) strategy in student writing. (See the definitions that I slipped into the first paragraph, pg. 255.)

3. Ask the research question. Your formulation of the topic began with a research question that you are trying to answer by means of your thesis. Share your initial research question with the reader. (Why did improvisation decline?)

4. Review a problem. Your thesis was formulated to address a doubtful question; explain the problem that underlies this doubt. (It is hard to prove anything about the history of improvisation since improvised music cannot be written down.)

5. State a paradox. A paradox is a statement that at first seems to be false, contradictory, or absurd but on closer examination turns out to be surprisingly true. (Spontaneous improvisation died during the romantic period, even though the romantics valued spontaneity more than the classicists did.)

6. Challenge a standard assumption or a specific source. (Though classical music listeners and musicians may now regard improvisation as unusual, it has been common throughout most of musical history.)

7. Survey the literature. (I avoided this strategy, and I urge you to avoid it, too. An opening survey is the weakest of all introductory strategies because it encourages mindless, unfocused summary. Use an opening survey only if you can focus tightly on a specific controlling idea, perhaps a problem or an issue common to all the sources surveyed. A survey is most appropriate for a review article in APA or scientific format; research papers in the humanities tend to be strictly argumentative, and surveys are looked upon unfavorably.)

TECHNIQUES FOR CONCLUSIONS

1. Briefly echo the opening anecdote.
2. Briefly echo the opening explanation of your special approach.
3. Answer the research question.
4. Solve the problem.
5. Resolve the paradox.
6. Complete your refutation of a standard assumption or specific source.
7. Briefly repeat your argument with a developed thesis statement.
8. Suggest broader issues and directions for further inquiry.

AVOIDING THE BAD HABITS OF ACADEMIC WRITERS: An Editor's Advice

Although the next two chapters discuss revising and editing, student research writers should think carefully about the style they use even when writing their rough draft. After reading mountains of works by academic writers, any student can end up imitating the worst features of academic writing. And the more sensitive you are to the style, tone, and mannerisms of academic writers, the more likely you are to acquire certain bad habits.

The best explanation of these habits that I have found is an article by Olive Holms that appeared in *Scholarly Publishing* (July 1974: 339–349; Oct. 1974: 40–50). Called "Thesis to Book," Holms's article analyzes the kinds of changes that professional editors usually have to make to help authors convert academic theses and dissertations into publishable books. Holms's analysis is a concise explanation of how academic writers succeed in creating boring articles and books—and how editors succeed in improving them. She neatly summarizes the most common vices of academic prose—vices that student writers often acquire by osmosis as they read mediocre sources.

Holms points out that academic writers tend to forewarn the reader too much and recapitulate too much. Therefore, clearly state your thesis near the beginning of your paper, and leave it at that. I have suggested that if a repetition is necessary (by means of a developed thesis statement) at the end of the paper, it should always express the thesis in a more complex form than the introduction did. Pay particular attention to editing the first and last paragraphs of your paper.

Academic writers tend to be self-conscious; they tend to apologize for themselves and to draw attention to themselves in defining and delimiting their subject. Thus, the early pages of a book or an article are the ones a professional editor is most likely to cut. So in your introduction, come to the point. Eliminate all unnecessary repetitions here and throughout your paper.

Academic writers tend to use far too many lists and enumerations. Break the "first-second-third" habit. If a list is necessary, edit it to make sure that its elements are grammatically parallel.

Academic writers tend to quote too much. In your paper, quote only when the material is essential or when the original author's voice adds concreteness and color to what you are saying. Holms has an interesting piece of advice about how to think of your audience; she suggests that you should never underestimate the reader's intelligence nor overestimate the reader's knowledge.

Perhaps the best way to acquire a good ear for research writing is to study works by excellent writers who cover scientific and technical subjects for general readers. My own short list of personal favorites includes anything on geology by John McPhee, anything on natural science and evolutionary theory by Stephen Jay Gould, anything on medicine and biology by Lewis Thomas, and anything on neurology by Oliver Sacks. Although their books and articles are not research writing in the narrow sense, research writers can learn much from them.

▣▣▣ JOURNAL EXCERPTS
Writing the Rough Draft

Session 9

To start my draft, I copied my research journal disk file, retitling it "Rough Draft" and putting in topic headings wherever they were needed. I'm puzzling over where to discuss the problem of using written handbooks as evidence about performance practices and teaching. At first, I placed this in the introduction to the whole paper, but now I'm thinking that it's too narrow a point to deserve such placement.

Here's the first part of my scratch outline.

INTRODUCTION: EXPLAIN LIMITATION TO KEYBOARD HANDBOOKS,

FOCUS ON CAUSAL EXPLANATION OF DECLINE OF IMPROVISATION

OVERVIEW OF THE TRANSITIONAL PERIOD, 1600–1750

BACH--PINNACLE OF IMPROVISATORY TRADITION

FREDERICK THE GREAT STORY

MUSIC AS CRAFT

MOZART--TRANSITIONAL FIGURE

BEETHOVEN--CULT OF INDIVIDUAL GENIUS

IMPROVISATION--DEFINITION

SPONTANEITY

ORNAMENTATION VERSUS MELODIC AND HARMONIC

IMPROVISATION

EXTEMPORANEOUS MELODIC IMPROVISATION

EXTEMPORANEOUS COMPOSITION

Session 12

I like the introductory section comparing improvisation then and now. I really hadn't planned or outlined this section; it just came together. [In retrospect, I think that this confirms my feeling that often the best passages arise without detailed preplanning.]

■■■ EXERCISE 16

Collaboration

Have a collaborator read and comment on your rough draft. Explain that you would like to know where he or she felt lost, confused, unconvinced, or surprised. With your collaborator, discuss ways of improving your supporting evidence and your overall organization.

■■■ EXERCISE 17

Drafting Skills

One question in this exercise entails some further practice in using MLA documentation. If you wish, adapt this question by substituting the term *APA*, *CBE*, or *Chicago* for *MLA*.

1. Pretend that you're writing a paper on the problems involved in adaptation to long-term spaceflight. You've found James R. Lackner's article "Orientation and Movement in Unusual Force Environments," which appeared in the journal *Psychological Science*. Figure 9.3 (on pp. 296–297) reproduces the table of contents of the May 1993 issue plus the first page of Lackner's article (p. 134). Because it contains a lot of technical

Psychological Science

A JOURNAL OF THE AMERICAN PSYCHOLOGICAL SOCIETY

Volume 4, Number 3, May 1993

CONTENTS

FIGURE 9.3 Contents Page of *Psychological Science* and First Page of Lackner's Article

ORIENTATION AND MOVEMENT IN UNUSUAL FORCE ENVIRONMENTS

By James R. Lackner

A manned space mission to Mars might take as long as 1 year each way. Consequently, artificial gravity is being considered as a way of preventing the debilitating effects of long-duration exposure to microgravity on the human body. The present article discusses some of the problems associated with adapting to the rotation levels that might be used to generate artificial gravity. It also describes how exposure to background-force levels greater or less than the 1-G force of Earth gravity affects orientation and movement control. The primary emphasis of the article is that human movement and orientation control are dynamically adapted to the 1-G force background of Earth and that accommodation to altered force levels or to rotating environments requires a wide range of adaptive changes.

Our bodies and our surroundings have regularities that permit adaptive interaction, a "fitness" in the sense of Henderson (1913). For example, the ground on which we walk generally has stability, continuity, and persistence; that is, it has regularities that allow locomotory adaptation to it. Similarly, our bodies have persistent characteristics and properties that allow them to be controlled in a predictable way over relatively prolonged periods. The mutual fitness of Earth's environment and our bodies allows computationally simple, dynamic adaptations of movement and orientation to develop and be maintained.

A weightless environment such as an orbiting space station with life-support facilities has regularities, albeit different ones from on Earth. Its characteristics are in part artificial, that is, manmade, and to the extent that they represent significant deviations from terrestrial regularities, they invoke the need for adaptation. One key factor on Earth which is absent in a spacecraft in orbit or moving at constant velocity in interplanetary space is physiologically and physically effective stimulation of the body by the force of gravity. Minimizing the deviations from terrestrial regularities in a spacecraft would help decrease the adaptation demands on astronauts. For instance, disorientation episodes which occur during expo-

Address correspondence to James R. Lackner, Ashton Graybiel Spatial Orientation Laboratory, Brandeis University, Waltham, MA 02254-9110.

sure to weightlessness (Lackner, 1992a, 1992b) can be minimized by having an architecturally polarized spacecraft with visual ups and downs consistently maintained for all aspects of daily activities, including placement and storage of objects. The latter feature is of importance because on earth, if we misplace or drop an object, it is relatively easy to find. It is necessary only to search part of the environment, namely, the floor and other potential support surfaces. By contrast, in a weightless environment, an object can be located anywhere within the entire free volume of the spacecraft. Consequently, it easy to misplace things, and visual search strategies have to be modified from those on Earth because the whole three-dimensional interior needs to be scanned.

At the present time, long-duration space missions are being contemplated, including a manned mission to Mars that might involve as much as 2 years of travel time for the round-trip. Investigations are under way to explore how the artificial gravity generated by rotating a spacecraft or a part of a spacecraft can be used to prevent the debilitating influence of long-term exposure to microgravity on bone mineralization, muscle and cardiovascular integrity, and sensorimotor function. It is not known for certain what level of artificial gravity is necessary to prevent degenerative changes. Consequently, the safest level to use is 1 G, the background-force level of our Earth, which is certain to be adequate.

Artificial gravity is the centripetal force produced by rotation. Accordingly, to achieve a particular level of force, there is a trade-off between the radius of rotation and the velocity of rotation; centripetal force equals the radius times the square of the angular velocity in radians. The practical implication of this relationship is that the higher the rate of rotation individuals can tolerate, the shorter the radius can be. This fact is critically important for the design of a rotating spacecraft because higher rotational speeds cost relatively little to attain, whereas increases in radius can be vastly expensive.

The rates of spacecraft rotation presently being considered to generate a 1-G centripetal force vec-

FIGURE 9.3 Contents Page of *Psychological Science* and First Page of Lackner's Article *(continued)*

language that cannot be paraphrased, you plan to quote all or most of the following sentence:

> Investigations are under way to explore how the artificial gravity generated by rotating a spacecraft or a part of a spacecraft can be used to prevent the debilitating influence of long-term exposure to microgravity on bone mineralization, muscle and cardiovascular integrity, and sensorimotor function.

Practice smoothly incorporating a long quotation by drafting a passage that includes (a) a general statement that the quotation supports, (b) a lead-in bridge statement that leads to the quotation, (c) the quotation itself, and (d) a bridge statement leading to some related point about artificial gravity. (You may draw the related point from Lackner, too, if you wish.) Use appropriate MLA documentation. Assume that this is your first mention of Lackner and that this article is your only source by him.

2. Quickly read the opening of Jorunn Sundgot-Borgen's "Eating Disorders in Female Athletes," pages 176–177, reproduced in Figure 9.4 (on pp. 299–300). Then evaluate the following sentence from a classmate's paper.

> One must look at how "psychological, biological, and social factors interrelate to produce" a valid explanation of why female athletes develop anorexia, opines one researcher (Sundgot-Borgen 177).

How would you advise your classmate to alter the use of source material in this sentence?

3. If you have not already done so, review your notes and other research materials to complete a list of topic headings covering the subtopics you plan to discuss in your paper. Shuffle the topic headings until you've placed them in the order in which you plan to discuss them. Your instructor may ask you to turn in this scratch outline along with the answers to questions 1 and 2.

REVIEW ARTICLE

Sports Med. 17 (3): 176–188, 1994
0112-1642/94/0003-0176/S06.50/0

Eating Disorders in Female Athletes

Jorunn Sundgot-Borgen

Department of Biology and Sports Medicine, The Norwegian University of Sport
and Physical Education, Oslo, Norway

Contents

Summary   Eating disorders can lead to death. The prevalence of subclinical and eating disorders is high among female athletes, and the prevalence of eating disorders is higher among female athletes than nonathletes. Athletes competing in sports where leanness or a specific bodyweight is considered important are more prone to develop eating disorders than athletes competing in sports where these factors are considered less important. It appears necessary to examine true eating disorders, the subclinical disorders and the range of behaviours and attitudes associated with eating disturbances in athletes, to learn how these clinical and subclinical disorders are related. Because of methodological weaknesses in the existing studies, including deficient description of the populations studied and the methods of data collection, the best instrument or interview method is not known. Therefore, more research on athletes and eating disorders is needed. Suggestions of the possible sport specific risk factors associated with the development of eating disorders in athletes exist, but large scale longitudinal studies are needed to learn more about risk factors and the aetiology of eating disorders in athletes at different competitive levels and within different sports.

FIGURE 9.4   Opening Pages of Sundgot-Borgen's Article

Further studies are required on the short and long term effects of eating disorders on athletes' health and athletic performance.

Weight and eating disorders are not rare, and they can have long-lasting physical and psychological effects. Symptoms of eating disorders are more prevalent among female athletes than female non-athletes. Athletes competing in sports where leanness or a specific weight are considered important for performance are at increased risk of the development of eating disorders. However, studies show that female athletes competing in sports where weight is considered to be less important, also suffer from weight or eating disorders. Psychological, biological and social factors inter-relate to produce the clinical picture of eating disorders. New data indicate that specific risk factors for the development of eating disorders occur in sport settings.

This article reviews the definition, diagnostic criteria, prevalence and risk factors for the development of eating disorders in sport and practical implications for the identification and treatment of disorders.

1. Definition and Diagnostic Criteria

According to the revised third edition of The Diagnostic and Statistical Manual of Mental Disorders (DSM-III-R; American Psychiatric Association 1987), eating disorders are characterised by gross disturbances in eating behaviour and include anorexia nervosa, bulimia nervosa, eating disorders not otherwise specified (NOS), pica (craving for unnatural types of food), and rumination disorder (regurgitation of food) in infancy. Binge eating disorder (BED) has recently been included in the latest issue of the DSM (DSM-IV; American Psychiatric Association 1994) and therefore is not examined among athletes. Pica and rumination disorders are generally not a problem in sport.

Athletes are a unique population and special diagnostic considerations should be made when working with athletes (Sundgot-Borgen 1993a; Szmuckler et al. 1985; Thompson & Sherman 1993). An attempt has been made to identify the group of athletes who show significant symptoms of eating disorders, but who do not meet the DSM-III-R criteria for anorexia nervosa, bulimia nervosa or NOS (Sundgot-Borgen 1993a). These athletes were classified as having a subclinical eating disorder named anorexia athletica.

Healthcare professionals should be aware of, and experienced with, the normal needs, expectations, and performance demands on athletes. This awareness and experience can be helpful in both diagnosis and treatment (Thompson & Sherman 1993). It is assumed that many cases of anorexia nervosa and bulimia nervosa begin as subclinical variants of these disorders. Early identification and treatment may prevent development of the full disorder (Bassoe 1990). Finally, subclinical cases probably are more prevalent than those who meet the criteria for anorexia nervosa, bulimia nervosa or BED.

1.1 Anorexia Nervosa

Anorexia nervosa is characterised in individuals by a refusal to maintain bodyweight over a minimal level considered normal for age and height, a distorted body image, and intense fear of fatness or weight gain while being underweight and amenorrhoea (the absence of at least 3 consecutive menstrual cycles). Individuals with anorexia 'feel fat' while they are underweight (American Psychiatric Association 1987).

1.2 Bulimia Nervosa

Bulimia nervosa is characterised by binge eating (rapid consumption of a large amount of food in a discrete period of time) and purging. This typically involves consumption of calorie-dense food, usually eaten conspicuously or secretly. By relieving abdominal discom-

FIGURE 9.4   Opening Pages of Sundgot-Borgen's Article *(continued)*

CHAPTER 10

REVISING THE ROUGH DRAFT

■ ■ ■ QUICK VIEW

Editors and writing teachers generally use the term *revising* for the process of making the major changes needed to turn the rough draft into a preliminary draft. These changes include cutting, shifting, and adding sections. Once you have revised the rough draft, it becomes the preliminary draft—the last stage before the final draft, which you will hand in.

The term *editing* describes the smaller changes that a writer makes, sentence by sentence, to improve clarity, emphasis, readability, and flow. Although some editing inevitably takes place at every stage of the drafting process, you should delay intensive editing as long as possible to avoid wasting time polishing passages that may later be drastically revised or even deleted.

Many writers can organize a short research paper without having to use a formal outline. If your paper is short and easy to organize, you may wish to skip the portions of this chapter that deal with outlining. Read "Guidelines for Revision," "Revising to Improve the Argumentative Focus," "The Hook Paragraph Transition," "Other Kinds of Transition," and "Adjusting the Length of Paragraphs." But whether your paper is to be long or short, be sure to do Exercise 18 at the end of the chapter.

GUIDELINES FOR REVISION

The process of revision focuses mainly on two things: organization and coherence. Revise the paper's organization to make sure that every section is in the right place, and then tighten the paper's coherence by supplying firm transitions.

To revise any paper successfully, follow these guidelines.

1. Leave the rough draft alone for at least a day or two so that you can approach it like a reader encountering it for the first time.

2. Get at least one careful evaluation by a classmate, instructor, or trusted colleague so that you have another perspective.

3. Use some sort of outline to see the whole paper's plan of organization at a glance.

4. Use the outline to guide any major organizational changes that seem necessary.

5. Strengthen transitions wherever the plan of organization is likely to be unclear to the reader.

Here are some questions for your evaluator to use.

REVISION QUESTIONS FOR PEER COLLABORATORS

1. Is the overall purpose of the paper clear to you from the thesis sentence? Does the thesis adequately predict the paper's plan of development?

2. Does every paragraph and sentence in the paper clearly support the thesis? Are there portions of the paper unrelated to the thesis? (For example, are there unnecessary summaries or sections of apparent padding?)

3. Are there sufficient examples and pieces of evidence to support the thesis persuasively?

4. Is the overall organization of the paper clear and effective? Did you feel lost at any point?

5. Does the paper convey interesting insights into its subject?

6. What are the paper's main strengths?

7. What are the paper's main weaknesses?

8. What specific recommendations can you make concerning the revision of this paper?

USING THE TOPIC OUTLINE AS A GUIDE TO REVISION

Since every writer and every paper is different, giving specific guidelines about the revision process is not possible. What often happens, though, is that as you try to construct an outline that accurately shows the paper's plan of organization in miniature, you find all kinds of problems that you hadn't noticed before. Typically, these problems fall into several categories.

1. *Items in the wrong order.* You may find that you use a term extensively before you have defined it or that you have mixed up the chronological stages of a process.

2. *Items repeated.* If you are using a flexible drafting method of the kind I have recommended, the rough draft is going to contain quite a bit of thinking aloud on paper. The mind naturally tends to circle a subject as it seeks to understand it. An outline will help you spot and eliminate unnecessary repetitions.

3. *Items separated that belong together.* Any long piece of writing has to be drafted in small chunks. You may end up writing about related topics in drafting sessions that are days apart, and the connection between items may not be clear until you analyze your rough draft.

4. *Items placed together that should be separated.* Sometimes a crucial distinction simply does not become clear until you've written a lot about the subject.

5. *Items omitted altogether.* It's amazingly easy to start a portion of a draft by mentioning, say, three key factors but discussing only two of them. Sometimes this sort of mistake is impossible to spot until you construct an outline.

6. *Items that require further development.* An outline can quickly reveal that you have too few supporting examples or that you have not subdivided one topic as thoroughly as another.

GENERATING A SENTENCE OUTLINE WHILE REVISING THE ROUGH DRAFT

The topic outline has let you see the organization of your paper at a glance and has guided you through the process of making major revisions. Now that the rough draft has gone through some major changes (shifts, deletions, additions), it has become the preliminary draft. It is time to generate a sentence outline as a guide to editing.

Remember that topic outlines use sentence fragments as headings, but sentence outlines use complete sentences. For the sake of logical consistency and usefulness, *you should not mix the two types.*

If your topic outline is now satisfactory, you can generate the sentence outline in one of two ways: (1) You can take your revised topic outline and convert all the sentence fragments to complete sentences; or (2) you can take the preliminary draft of the paper itself and extract a sentence outline from it. Generally, it is better to try to extract the sentence outline from the paper, because in doing so, you will be checking the organization and coherence of the paper itself.

Here is a way to use the word processor for outlining.

USING WORD PROCESSING TO MAKE A SENTENCE OUTLINE

1. Make a copy of the preliminary draft; call it "Sentence Outline 1."

> 2. Go through "Sentence Outline 1" and cut out everything except the topic sentence of each paragraph.
> 3. Use the topic sentences to generate a sentence outline by inserting letters, numbers, and indentations.

If you are not using a word processor, you can achieve the same effect by going through a photocopy of your paper and underlining each paragraph's topic sentence.

What if you cannot find a topic sentence in each paragraph? Don't despair. Testing for topic sentences is the whole point of this step! Does each paragraph develop a controlling idea? If you can't find a controlling idea, ask yourself what the point of the paragraph is. Then put in a sentence expressing that point. Be sure that you insert the sentence in both the sentence outline and the paper.

This test for topic sentences is where the outline becomes a powerful tool in tightening up a research paper. Research writers often get so close to their subject that they forget to state their main points. Constructing a sentence outline will automatically bring a missing point to light or will reveal that a paragraph is mere padding that should be deleted.

There is one exception to this rule. Sometimes a paragraph may contain nothing but examples that support a point made in the previous paragraph. Hence, there may be no need to generate a topic sentence for the paragraph of examples. This paragraph can simply be left out of the sentence outline.

If your topic outline has accurately guided your completion of the preliminary draft, you should be able to make the sentence outline match your topic outline, point by point. If the two don't match, don't be dismayed. Again, this is one purpose of generating a sentence outline. You're looking for places where the paper got off track. Revise the sentence outline, and use it as a guide in making a few more revisions in the preliminary draft.

Finally, the second rule of outlining requires you to revise the sentence outline so that the sentences use parallel phrasing. Parallel phrasing has two purposes: to make the outline easy to read, and to ensure logical consistency in the argument. If you are not required to hand in a sentence outline, the first reason may not concern you. But the second one concerns every writer. *By putting parallel ideas in parallel form, you force yourself to examine the connections between ideas.* Here are some examples of sentences taken from the text of a student paper. The following two sentences are topic sentences from two consecutive paragraphs.

Transient students have difficulty meeting classroom requirements.

Like the educational requirements, the social aspects of school can be difficult for displaced students.

Notice that for stylistic variety the writer has made *students* the subject of one sentence and *aspects* the subject of the other. She has used some direct repetitions of keywords (*requirements . . . requirements*) and some indirect echoes that either shift parts of speech (*difficulty . . . difficult*) or employ synonyms (*transient students . . . displaced students; classroom . . . school*). These are standard ways of achieving stylistic variety while using word echoes for coherence and continuity.

In an outline, however, these sentences should be recast so that they are precisely parallel in phrasing.

```
Transient students have difficulty adjusting to a new school's

academic requirements.

Transient students have difficulty adjusting to a new school's social

environment.
```

The parallel phrasing in the outline ensures that the reader can instantly grasp the relationships between ideas. Without parallel phrasing, the connection between "academic requirements" and "social environment" may be hard even for the writer to spot.

In the paper itself, precisely parallel phrasing would be repetitious and deadly dull. More varied sentences in the paper will not confuse the reader because the paper will contain other elements (keyword repetitions, transitional phrases, emphatic phrasing) that will make the organization clear and easy to follow.

EXAMPLES OF OUTLINES USED IN REVISION

After finishing a rough draft, I always go through it paragraph by paragraph, writing out a topic outline. In doing this for my paper on improvisation, I noticed that I had too many major subdivisions and that I had not arranged them logically. The first draft of the outline had four major divisions.

    I. Introduction, explanation of paper's focus
   II. The rise and decline of improvisation
  III. Causes of the decline of improvisation
  IV. The teaching of improvisation

Just a glance at these major headings reveals the difficulties I was having in organizing the paper. Because the word *decline* occurs in two spots (headings II and III), it is not clear which subsection is the heart of the paper.

A more serious problem with this draft outline is that the paper's subdivisions have not been logically constructed to show the subordination of topics. The topics should be nested like boxes inside boxes, showing how the topics interrelate; otherwise, the outline is just an illogical list of headings. Since the broadest topic in my paper was "decline of improvisation," "causes" should be a subtopic under "decline." "The teaching of improvisation" is a clumsy and illogical label for my actual subtopic, which is "loss of apprenticeship." So the topics should be "nested" in this fashion.

Broadest: [Decline of improvisation   ]
Narrower: [Causes of the decline   ]
Narrowest: [Loss of apprenticeship   ]

When I revised the outline, "causes of the decline" became main heading III, with "loss of apprenticeship" as subheading B. I rephrased "causes of the decline" as "analysis of the decline" to create parallelism with a new heading I, "overview of the decline." Here is the revised outline.

   I. Overview of the decline
  II. Scope and methods of study
 III. Analysis of the decline
     A. Question of the decline's beginnings
     B. Loss of apprenticeship as cause
     C. Other causes

I needed section II to handle the difficult introductory material that my topic was forcing upon me: defining improvisation, explaining its history, and analyzing the kinds of evidence used to study it.

Now, here is the topic outline in its completed form, just as I used it to guide my revision of the paper.

The Decline of Improvisation in the Time of Mozart

Thesis: As apprenticeship was replaced by reading as a standard way of learning music, improvisation became a lost art.

   I. Overview of the decline
     A. Leading figures
       1. Bach
       2. Mozart
       3. Beethoven
     B. Usual explanation: shift from craftsman to genius
     C. My explanation: shift from apprenticeship to reading
  II. Scope and methods of study
     A. Sources of evidence
       1. Keyboard handbooks
       2. Transcribed examples
       3. Written improvisations
     B. Definition of improvisation
       1. Origins
       2. Spontaneity
       3. Ornamentation versus re-composition
 III. Analysis of the decline
     A. Question of decline's beginnings—sixteenth century?
     B. Loss of apprenticeship as cause
       1. Loss of advantages of apprenticeship
       2. Loss of advantages of thoroughbass
         a. Ease of composition
         b. Reinforcement of "motoric" component
     C. Other causes of decline

Finally, after revising the paper to fit this new scheme of organization, I went through the preliminary draft and took one sentence from each paragraph (with a few exceptions) to create a sentence outline. Often I had to revise these sentences to create stronger parallelism in the outline. For instance, the paper contained these sentences introducing Bach, Mozart, and Beethoven:

1. Bach's legendary improvisatory skills were most fully demonstrated during his visit to the court of Frederick the Great on May 12, 1747.

2. Although improvisation began to decline after the middle of the eighteenth century, Mozart, too, had phenomenal improvisatory abilities.

3. Although Beethoven was also famous for improvising, as a composer he did more than perhaps anyone else to ensure improvisation's decline.

Notice how I recast these sentences in the sentence outline that follows to create tighter parallelism and a more direct statement of the paper's argument. Here, for comparison purposes, is the initial portion of the sentence outline.

The Decline of Improvisation in the Time of Mozart

Thesis: As apprenticeship was replaced by reading as a standard way of learning music, improvisation became a lost art.

I. During the baroque and classical eras, musicians were trained to improvise complex musical embellishments and even to create entire compositions spontaneously, but by the romantic period, improvisation came to be abandoned in favor of the relatively strict performance of written scores.
   A. Historians generally agree that musical improvisation reached a high point in Bach's lifetime (1685–1750), declined during Mozart's (1756–1791), and virtually disappeared during Beethoven's (1770–1827), though the causes of this change remain uncertain.
      1. Improvisation reached its peak in the career of Bach, whose improvisatory skills were legendary.
      2. Improvisation began to decline after the middle of the eighteenth century, although Mozart's improvisatory skills were also phenomenal.
      3. Improvisation went into a still more rapid decline during the career of Beethoven, who was famous for improvising but who as a composer did more than anyone to ensure improvisation's demise.
   B. The usual explanation given for the decline is that the cult of individual genius in the romantic era destroyed musical improvisation by elevating the composer and demoting the performer.
   C. A better explanation is that as apprenticeship was replaced by reading as a standard way of learning music, improvisation became a lost art.

Although it is usually impossible to scan the sentence outline at a glance, when you read it carefully, you can see the underlying structure of the argument, stripped of everything but the main assertions.

REVISING TO IMPROVE THE ARGUMENTATIVE FOCUS

While you were filling your research journal or recording notes, you may have found that you were constantly pulled away from your argumentative purpose. Lots of inviting quotations begged to be included, and lots of unnecessary information got recorded.

At the revising stage, concentrate again on your argumentative purpose. As you evaluate each paragraph of your draft, ask yourself, "What question is being resolved here? What doubtful point is being discussed?" Also ask yourself whether you can challenge your sources by questioning their evidence and assumptions. You can carry out this revision to improve the paper's argumentative focus as a separate step after you have revised the draft's organization, or you can blend the two steps. But most people find argumentation a difficult skill to learn, so I suggest giving the paper a separate reading in which you concentrate just on the argumentative purpose of each paragraph.

At the revising stage, you must be ruthless. Be impatient with yourself. Cut everything that looks like padding: unnecessary information, summaries, explanations of common knowledge, and definitions of terms that your audience can be expected to understand. It will be hard, though, to part with anything that you have put a lot of work into. Thus the most difficult part of revision (that is, the most difficult part emotionally) is cutting out unnecessary passages. But if you have planned your work carefully, your rough draft should be considerably longer (perhaps 20 to 30 percent longer) than the required minimum length, if there is one. Revision should cut about half the fat; editing should cut the other half.

Recognize that there is fat to be cut. I have never seen a rough draft that did not require at least a little trimming.

THE HOOK PARAGRAPH TRANSITION

By the time you have shifted major portions of your paper, cut other portions, revised others, and added still others, you will have created many abrupt topic shifts and awkward transitions between paragraphs. So the last thing you should do before going on to edit the preliminary draft is tighten the transitions. This is really a part of the next stage, editing, but I think it is a good idea to attend to transitions before tackling any other aspects of editing.

Now is the time to take advantage of a useful writer's trick, which is to splice jarring paragraphs together by means of a *paragraph hook*. If the first sentence of a paragraph moves to a new topic too abruptly, edit it and the last sentence of the preceding paragraph by making sure that there are several repetitions or near-repetitions of keywords linking the two sentences.

Not every teacher of writing will agree with the following guideline, but I think that it is so valuable that it deserves to be a key principle of revision. If each individual paragraph is well designed, the principle holds true.

> Readers will overlook major flaws of organization as long as their attention is led smoothly from paragraph to paragraph.

To see the good effects of using the hook paragraph transition, consider the following three paragraphs of close analysis from a research paper discussing James Joyce's short story "Araby." William, the paper's author, is analyzing the text to explain the function of personification, a figure of speech in which natural or inanimate objects are given human characteristics.

Personification is not limited to the houses in "Araby," as the following quotation shows: "The space of the sky above us was the colour of ever-changing violet and towards it the lamps of the street lifted their feeble lanterns" (30). These descriptions, however nice, are more than colorful writing; they provide insight into the boy. When individuals are wrapped up in thoughts of their own, or living a solitary life, they often invent entities or give human qualities to everyday things around them. Young children and old people demonstrate this when naming toys or talking to their plants. It is essential that these descriptions give depth to the boy's condition of grieving over his unattainable love.

There are more examples of personification in paragraph three. "The cold air stung us" (30) sounds as if the air did this in a deliberate manner. The next two instances are almost becoming psychedelic in their surreal intensity: playing "till our bodies glowed" and, better yet, "shook music from a buckled harness" (30), almost creating a confusion of the senses.

Joyce is a master of this technique, which he uses sometimes in a deliberate, obvious way, while at other times, the technique can be breathtakingly subtle: "the fine incessant needles of water playing in the sodden beds" (286). Like a painter, Joyce uses the tools of the trade, such as imagery and personification, to establish the mood and mental landscape of the boy in "Araby."

The opening sentences of paragraphs 2 and 3 create problems of coherence and continuity. In paragraph 2 the transition merely introduces a list of examples

("Here are three more examples," the writer says, in effect) and is only a minor improvement on an abrupt topic shift. Besides an accumulation of examples there should be some forward development of the argument.

In the first sentence of the third paragraph, William has tried to establish a hook by using terms ("this technique," "the technique") that refer to the preceding sentence, but the reader has to puzzle over what technique is being referred to. If we take the possibilities in reverse order, from last-mentioned to first-mentioned, is William referring to Joyce's technique of creating a "confusion of the senses"? If so, how do the examples confuse our senses? (The examples are quoted but not analyzed or highlighted.) Is William referring to Joyce's technique of using images that are "psychedelic in their surreal intensity"? And given the lack of analysis, how are we to understand the way that the quoted phrases exemplify this intensity? Finally, is William referring to Joyce's technique of personification in general? If so, how do glowing bodies and musical harnesses exemplify personification?

The break between the second and third paragraphs seems unnecessary because no new topic is introduced; instead, the third paragraph blends a general concluding statement with a single unanalyzed example. A one- or two-sentence paragraph like the third paragraph is likely to be underdeveloped. This paragraph can easily be blended with the preceding one.

There are other problems that require close stylistic editing of the sort considered in the next chapter. For example, William overuses the linking verb *to be* in its various forms. In the ten sentences quoted, eight verbs are variations of *to be*. In order of appearance, the verb forms are *is*, *was* (Joyce's word), *are*, *are*, *is*, *are*, *are*, and *is*.

Besides being wordy, the passage contains some distracting shifts that reduce its coherence. The distracting items include the faulty examples (quoted descriptions that are actually not personifications at all), the irrelevant reference to "old people," and the shift in number from "boy" to "they" and back to "boy." One of Joyce's sentences, "The cold air stung us and we played till our bodies glowed," has been unnecessarily dismembered so that the connection between "stung" and "glowed" is destroyed. Furthermore, the controlling topic, personification, shifts in a confusing way so that it becomes "descriptions" and then "personification" again. The word *personification* should be repeated more frequently to ensure coherence, and other forms of the word (*personify, personifies, personifications*) could be used to give variety. If the specific topic of personification (rather than the more general topic of description) is going to govern the paragraph, then the irrelevant portion of the first quotation should also be cut.

The last two paragraphs seem to be striving to develop a contrast between obvious personifications and subtle ones. A transitional phrase such as "in contrast" might help to point up the contrast.

Here are the same three paragraphs, which I have edited primarily to achieve coherent transitions. Strikeovers show suggested major cuts, and brackets show major additions. Further stylistic editing is called for, but at this point I am concerned with topical unity and the effective use of paragraph hooks.

[Joyce personifies] ~~Personification is not limited to~~ [not only] the houses ~~in "Araby," as the following quotation shows:~~ [but the streetlights as well]: "~~The space of the sky above us was the colour of ever changing violet and~~ [. . .] towards ~~it~~ [the sky] the lamps of the street lifted their feeble lanterns" (30). ~~These descriptions~~ [Such personifications], however ~~nice~~ [pleasing], are more than colorful writing; they provide insight into the boy. When ~~individuals~~ [people] are wrapped up in thoughts of their own, or [are] living ~~a~~ solitary ~~life~~ [lives], they often invent entities or give human qualities to everyday things around them. Young children ~~and old people~~ demonstrate this when naming toys or ~~talking to their plants~~ [imagining that a car has a human face and personality]. ~~It is essential that~~ [T]hese ~~descriptions~~ [personifications, then,] give depth to the boy's ~~condition of grieving~~ [solitary grief] over his unattainable love.

[To indirectly convey the depth of the boy's emotions,] ~~There are more examples of~~ [Joyce uses subtle] personification[s] ~~in paragraph three~~. [When he writes that] "[t]he cold air stung us [and we played till our bodies glowed,]" [he makes] it ~~sounds~~ as if the air did this ~~in a~~ deliberate[ly] ~~manner~~ (30). ~~The next two~~ [In contrast, some] instances [of personification] are almost ~~becoming~~ psychedelic in ~~their surreal intensity: playing "till our bodies glowed" and, better yet, "shook music from a buckled harness" (30), almost creating a confusion of the senses~~ [the vivid way they convey the boy's lively sense of his surroundings: He describes some bushes in the backyard as "straggling" (29), as though they shared the schoolboy's life of playful loitering, and he describes rain as "fine incessant needles of water playing in the sodden beds" (31; emphasis added). But whether subtle or vividly obvious,] ~~Joyce is a master of this technique, which he uses sometimes in a deliberate, obvious way, while at other times, the technique can be breathtakingly subtle; "the fine incessant needles of water playing in the sodden beds" (286). Like a painter~~, Joyce['s] ~~uses~~

~~the tools of the trade, such as imagery and~~ personification[s] [always

work] to establish the mood and mental landscape of the boy in

"Araby."

Now read the edited paragraphs without the distracting brackets and strike-overs. Note the improvement in coherence, particularly at the paragraph break, where the inserted hook helps the reader move forward. Note, too, that using strong verbs and eliminating wordy phrases has made the revised passage shorter than the original, even though new material has been added.

Joyce personifies not only the houses but the streetlights as well:

". . . towards [the sky] the lamps of the street lifted their feeble

lanterns" (30). Such personifications, however pleasing, are more than

colorful writing; they provide insight into the boy. When people are

wrapped up in thoughts of their own, or are living solitary lives, they

often invent entities or give human qualities to everyday things

around them. Young children demonstrate this when naming toys or

imagining that a car has a human face and personality. These

personifications, then, give depth to the boy's solitary grief over his

unattainable love.

To indirectly convey the depth of the boy's emotions, Joyce uses

subtle personifications. When he writes that "[t]he cold air stung

us and we played till our bodies glowed," he makes it sound as if

the air did this deliberately (30). In contrast, some instances of

personification are almost psychedelic in the vivid way they convey

the boy's lively sense of his surroundings: He describes some bushes

in the backyard as "straggling" (29), as though they shared the

schoolboy's life of playful loitering, and he describes rain as "fine

incessant needles of water <u>playing</u> in the sodden beds" (31;

emphasis added). But whether subtle or vividly obvious, Joyce's

personifications always work to establish the mood and mental

landscape of the boy in "Araby."

One remaining problem with this passage is the rather uncertain contrast between *subtle* and *obvious* in the last paragraph. I tried to stick to William's original design, which was to conclude the passage by saying that both the subtle and the obvious examples work to convey the boy's emotions; but I am not convinced that the distinction is well supported by the examples he gives. However, this question could lead back to redrafting rather than forward to editing—and we must move on.

OTHER TYPES OF TRANSITION

Many writing handbooks urge the liberal use of transitional words and phrases, especially the conjunctive adverbs: *consequently, finally, further, furthermore, hence, however, instead, likewise, meanwhile, nevertheless, nonetheless, similarly, therefore,* and *thus,* to name only a few. But the excessive use of transition words is one of the typical vices of poor academic writing. In this chapter, for instance, I have used the word *however* only four times (aside from the student's adverbial use of the word in the quoted passage), always to mark a major turn in the line of thought. In contrast, I have used the word *but* about twenty times to mark a minor turn of thought within a sentence. Here are the stylistic principles I try to follow: Freely use coordinating conjunctions (*and, but, or, nor, for, yet, so*) to connect simple ideas within sentences. Freely use subordinating conjunctions (*although, if, since, while, because,* and others) to connect more complex ideas within sentences. Judiciously use conjunctive adverbs (*however, also, thus*) and transitional phrases (*on the one hand, on the other hand, on the contrary, at the same time, for example, in other words, on the whole*) to mark major turns and comparisons.

In general, your paper's coherence and continuity derive from the coherence and continuity of its line of thought. If the line of thought is not coherent, you cannot improve matters much by inserting transitional phrases between sentences and paragraphs, like mortar between bricks, in hopes of ending up with a well-constructed paper. First attend to the overall unity; then see whether there are spots where unannounced turns can be brought to the reader's attention by means of a word or a phrase.

ADJUSTING THE LENGTH OF PARAGRAPHS

Learning to find the right paragraph length is like acquiring a sense of rhythm in music or sports. It requires long practice, and some people never get it. Still, the following general principles can help.

1. A paragraph should develop a single idea. You may mention multiple subtopics, but you should normally develop them in subsequent paragraphs.

2. Very short paragraphs (one or two sentences long) are seldom used in academic writing, although they are common in journalism. Generally, you should further develop a very short paragraph by adding details and examples, or you should incorporate it into the paragraph immediately

before it or after it. *Exception:* A major, dramatic turn of thought may sometimes be marked by a short, emphatic transitional paragraph.

3. Very long paragraphs (approaching or exceeding a double-spaced page) are wearying to the reader and are likely to be disunified anyway. Look for the natural breaking point and use a hook to manage the transition. Even if a very long paragraph is unified by a single idea, you may need to give the reader a resting point by breaking the paragraph at a natural dividing line.

Revision is by far the hardest part of the entire writing process. No doubt it has made you tired. Try to take a break and let the paper cool off for a day or two before you tackle editing. Print out a fresh copy of the revised preliminary draft and put it away. Rest in the knowledge that all the hardest work is behind you. Editing is going to turn your already satisfactory draft into an excellent paper.

A SAMPLE REVISION

On the following pages is a portion of a rough draft by Kristin Brucker. In it she compares Samuel Johnson's poem "The Vanity of Human Wishes" with the poem it freely translates, the tenth satire by the Roman poet Juvenal. She gave her rough draft to a peer for preliminary evaluation, and her evaluator made detailed marginal suggestions for revision.

The main problem with the rough draft is that Kristin seems at first to be saying merely that sometimes Johnson used Juvenal's original examples and sometimes he substituted eighteenth-century examples. Toward the end of the draft portion, however, she makes a more interesting claim: that Johnson actually enhanced Juvenal's poem when he did his free translation of it. This claim occurs just after Kristin has stated that both poets are moralists but that they present their moral ideologies differently.

Kristin's evaluator suggested that she develop her draft by focusing more consistently upon the idea that Johnson deepened and enhanced Juvenal's poem. The long quotations could be used to support this claim, so the evaluator suggested that they be analyzed at length. The evaluator also singled out some flaws of grammar and style, marked one point that called for further research, and pointed out that the last sentence wanders away from the subject.

Johnson frequently uses contemporary examples in his poem

"ancient"?
(Democritus
was Greek.) — instead of the (Roman) ones supplied by Juvenal, but <u>not exclusively</u> — aw

so. For example, the figure of Democritus, the laughing philosopher, is

kept intact, whereas Sejanus is replaced in favor of a more current

antecedent — character, Wolsey. (This) serves a very useful purpose for Johnson. <u>By</u>

<u>placing a contemporary personage within the bounds of Juvenal's</u>

dangling
modifier

illustration, the poem's ironies and illustrations are more easily
— *repetition* —
conveyed. The key in this example is that Johnson works within the
guidelines of Juvenal's original illustration.

*at are
these?
explain,
develop.*

Juvenal presents Sejanus in this way: *Abrupt! Use a bridge sentence.*

> [. . .] Sejanus did not know the things to be desired; for in
>
> coveting excessive honours, and seeking excessive wealth, he
>
> was but building up the many stories of a lofty tower whence
>
> the fall would be greater, and the crush of headlong ruin more
>
> terrific. (201)

*he image,
r the person?*

Johnson reworks the image, using Wolsey as his subject:

> Still to new heights his restless wishes tower,
>
> Claim leads to claim, and power advances power;
>
> Till conquest unresisted ceased to please,
>
> And rights submitted, left him none to seize. (105–08)

*iet,
developed.*

Johnson and Juvenal are fairly close in meaning and illustration.

ague

There are some references to modern people in Johnson's work that
do not correspond with any given example in Juvenal's work, but the
references are not departures in and of themselves; they are used in
conjunction with other somewhat unrelated passages. For example, in

wordy

the passage dealing with beauty, a reference is/made to Sedley,

*esearch
omit.*

apparently a mistress, which serves to illustrate immorality. In this
context Johnson has not significantly altered the examples presented,

*complete
the discussion
by comparing
Juvenal.*

but instead has merely brought them into an eighteenth-century
context.

*Self-
conscious*

In conclusion, Johnson uses Juvenal's tenth satire as a
springboard for his own ideas. And yet his philosophies were not
greatly different from those of Juvenal. Both men were essentially

*Important!
Develop,
Support.*

moralists. Their basic differences lie in the approach they take in
presenting their ideologies. In this respect, Johnson's work can be
considered a fairly accurate translation of ideas. Stylistically, the

*Develop,
Support.*

works differ radically. But this does not detract from the morality or content of the piece as a whole. In order to fit Juvenal's poem into the

Johnson's poem is not a mock epic.

accepted form of the period, <u>mock epic,</u> and to preserve his own

integrity as a writer, Johnson could not avoid some changes in the

original structure of Juvenal's poem. Johnson's poem does not falsify

Juvenal's intentions; on the contrary, it enhances the work and lends

it a continuity it might otherwise have lacked.

In revising her rough draft, Kristin followed most of these suggestions. The dramatic change she made was to develop a close analysis of the long block quotations, showing how Johnson's free translation enhances Juvenal's poem. She moved a brief example (Catherine Sedley, mistress to James II) to an earlier position, where it helps to support the idea that Johnson used contemporary figures in his poem. The following pages show all the changes she made except the crucial section of additional development immediately after the block quotations; this area is marked "INSERT 4A." To see the good effect of the additional support and development supplied by this inserted passage, look at the final draft of these pages from Kristin's paper. The final draft appears immediately after the pages that show her revisions.

Johnson frequently uses contemporary examples in his poem
                    ancient   always
instead of the ~~Roman~~ ones supplied by Juvenal, but not ʌexclusively
                    Johnson keeps
~~so.~~ For example, ʌthe figure of Democritus, the laughing philosopher,
                    he replaces   with
~~is kept intact,~~ whereas ʌSejanus ~~is replaced in favor of~~ ʌa more current

character, Wolsey. ~~This serves a very useful purpose for Johnson.~~ By
using   persons in place
ʌ~~placing a~~ contemporary ~~personage within the bounds~~ ʌof Juvenal's
                    s Johnson makes
illustration, ʌthe poem's ironies ~~and illustrations are more easily~~
                    ʌclearer to his audience.   finds
~~conveyed.~~ The key ~~in this example~~ is that Johnson ʌ~~works within~~
contemporary examples of the same moral failings Juvenal discusses.
~~the guidelines of Juvenal's original illustration.~~ ʌ

To illustrate the effects of excessive ambition, Juvenal presents

Sejanus ~~in this way~~:

[. . .] Sejanus did not know the things to be desired; for in

coveting excessive honours, and seeking excessive wealth, he

was but building up the many stories of a lofty tower whence

the fall would be greater, and the crush of headlong ruin more

terrific. (201)

alters Juvenal's ⟨of a lofty tower and uses⟩
Johnson ~~reworks the image, using Wolsey as his~~
Wolsey in place of Sejanus as his example:
~~subject:~~

> Still to new heights his restless wishes tower,
>
> Claim leads to claim, and power advances power;
>
> Till conquest unresisted ceased to please,
>
> And rights submitted, left him none to seize. (105–08)

INSERT 4A

~~Johnson and Juvenal are fairly close in meaning and illustration.~~

~~There are some references to modern people in Johnson's work that~~

~~do not correspond with any given example in Juvenal's work, but the~~

~~references are not departures in and of themselves; they are used in~~

~~conjunction with other somewhat unrelated passages.~~ For example,

in the passage dealing with beauty, a reference is made to ⟨Catherine⟩ Sedley,
~~apparently~~ a mistress ⟨of James II (Mack et al. 2305)⟩, which serves to illustrate immorality. ~~In~~
~~this context~~ Johnson ~~has~~ ⟨sometimes does⟩ not significantly altered the examples
presented⟨,⟩ but instead ~~has merely brought them into an~~ ⟨uses⟩ eighteenth-
⟨examples that his readers would recognize.⟩ century ~~context.~~

~~In conclusion,~~ Johnson uses Juvenal's tenth satire as a

springboard for his own ideas. ~~And yet his philosophies were not~~
⟨Like Juvenal,⟩
~~greatly different from those of Juvenal.~~ Both men ~~were~~ essentially
a
⟨moralists. ~~Their basic differences lie in the approach they take in~~

~~presenting their ideologies. In this respect, Johnson's work can be~~
⟨However, the styles of the two⟩
~~considered a fairly accurate translation of ideas.~~ ~~Stylistically, the~~
⟨Johnson's use of balanced lines and⟩
works differ radically. ~~But this does not detract from the morality or~~
parallel sentences leads him to emphasize the repetitiveness and
~~content of the piece as a whole.~~ ~~In order to fit Juvenal's poem into~~
inevitability of human moral failings. In using the polished heroic
~~the accepted form of the period,~~ ~~mock epic, and to preserve his own~~
couplets that audiences expected in the eighteenth century,
~~integrity as a writer,~~ Johnson could not avoid some changes in the
⟨But⟩
original structure of Juvenal's poem. Johnson ~~'s poem~~ does not falsify
⟨he⟩ ⟨Juvenal's examples⟩
Juvenal's intentions; on the contrary, ~~it~~ enhances ~~the work~~ and
them much greater moral depth than they had in the original poem.
lends ~~it~~ a ~~continuity it might otherwise have lacked.~~

Here is Kristin's final draft of this section.

Johnson frequently uses contemporary examples in his poem instead of the ancient ones supplied by Juvenal, but not always. For example, Johnson keeps the figure of Democritus, the laughing philosopher, whereas he replaces Sejanus with a more current character, Wolsey. By using contemporary persons in place of Juvenal's illustrations, Johnson makes the poem's ironies clearer to his audience. The key is that Johnson finds contemporary examples of the same moral failings Juvenal discusses. For example, in the passage dealing with beauty, a reference is made to Catherine Sedley, a mistress of James II (Mack et al. 2305), which serves to illustrate immorality. Johnson sometimes does not significantly alter the examples presented but instead uses eighteenth-century examples that his readers would recognize.

To illustrate the effects of excessive ambition, Juvenal presents Sejanus:

> [. . .] Sejanus did not know the things to be desired; for in coveting excessive honours, and seeking excessive wealth, he was but building up the many stories of a lofty tower whence the fall would be greater, and the crush of headlong ruin more terrific. (201)

Johnson alters Juvenal's image of a lofty tower and uses Wolsey in place of Sejanus as his example:

> Still to new heights his restless wishes tower,
>
> Claim leads to claim, and power advances power;
>
> Till conquest unresisted ceased to please,
>
> And rights submitted, left him none to seize. (105–08)

Johnson does more than just replace Sejanus with Wolsey; he greatly complicates and enhances the moral point of the passage. Juvenal says simply that Sejanus' quest for wealth and power made his fall that much worse. Johnson, however, stresses the idea that one ambitious wish always leads to another. The tolling repetitions ("Claim leads to claim, and power advances power") suggest a process that rolls forward inevitably until the ambitious man has nothing left to wish for, nothing left to "seize." By keeping Juvenal's image of height but delaying any reference to a fall, Johnson implies that Wolsey's ambition was a moral flaw that made him unhappy even before he fell.

Johnson uses Juvenal's tenth satire as a springboard for his own ideas. Like Juvenal, Johnson was essentially a moralist. However, the styles of the two works differ radically. Johnson's use of balanced lines and parallel sentences leads him to emphasize the repetitiveness and inevitability of human moral failings. In using the polished heroic couplets that audiences expected in the eighteenth century, Johnson could not avoid some changes in the original structure of Juvenal's poem. But Johnson does not falsify Juvenal's intentions; on the contrary, he enhances Juvenal's examples and lends them a much greater moral depth than they had in the original poem.

REVISING AS SELF-CRITICISM

I recognize that I have put a lot of emphasis on outlining—more than many students are likely to feel comfortable with. I also recognize that the students *least* likely to use these outlining techniques are the facile writers who can knock off a presentable draft from just a rough mental plan. That's unfortunate, because natural writers have much to gain by trying these techniques.

I like an emblem that used to appear in books of rhetoric during the Renaissance: a picture of the closed hand and the open hand. The closed hand stood for logic; the open hand stood for rhetoric. With the closed hand of logic we do our destructive work, smashing whatever is false and empty in our own arguments or in the arguments of our predecessors, our sources. The outline is an analytical tool, a potentially destructive tool of logic; it forces us to take a cold, hard, self-critical look at what we have done. Once we have smashed away the false, the inconsistent, the repetitive, and the hollow portions of our work, then we can use the open hand of rhetoric to complete the reconstruction and embellishment of what is left. And in the process we come to see that analyzing and condensing our work is a painful form of self-criticism but also a powerful facilitator of creativity.

▪▪▪ JOURNAL EXCERPTS
Revising
Session 14

I have just spent several difficult hours reorganizing the paper. I really did not see some organizational problems until I finished my first formal outline.

I've tried to resolve several problems. In my first outline I tried to keep the introduction short to avoid plunging the reader too directly into the technicalities of defining improvisation and of analyzing handbooks as evidence. I tried a short overview with more detailed examinations later. But this meant that the same questions, composers, and writers of manuals kept popping up. The problems of repetition were driving me crazy, so I decided that I would have to reorganize before completing the rough draft.

In reorganizing, I've tried to put my best evidence last. I like the "composition made easy" quotation, and I've tried to place that late in my brief discussion of thoroughbass.

▪▪▪ EXERCISE 18
Revision

Before revising your rough draft, read the "Revision Questions for Peer Collaborators" on page 302. Then read your paper and answer the questions. Have a trusted peer read the paper and answer the questions, too.

CHAPTER 11

EDITING

■ ■ ■ QUICK VIEW

In completing the preliminary draft, you have resolved the major problems involving organization and transitions. What remains to be done is a close, line-by-line editing of the paper to improve its readability. To succeed at editing, you need to achieve a certain distance from your work; that is why you should allow a cooling-off period of at least a day or two before you edit.

Since many college writers overestimate the benefits and underestimate the limitations of computerized spell checkers and style checkers, I suggest that you not skip the section "Proofread for Mechanical Errors." It contains a discussion of proofreading software.

COLLABORATION IN EDITING

Even a collaborator unskilled in editing can help you spot aspects of your paper that need work. One simple technique is to ask a collaborator to read the paper aloud in your presence while you follow along by reading another copy. In your copy, make marginal notes alongside all the passages in which your collaborator's reading seems to falter. Occasionally, you may hear the reader put the wrong emphasis in a passage or restart a phrase or sentence. Some of these stumbles may simply be random reader's errors. (Try to find a skilled reader.) But often a spot where a reader falters is a spot that needs correcting. Perhaps faulty punctuation misled your reader; perhaps awkward phrasing made the sentence hard to read aloud. At this stage, don't worry about revising the potentially faulty passages. Just mark them for future reference.

After your collaborator has read your paper, ask him or her to answer the following questions.

EDITING QUESTIONS FOR PEER COLLABORATORS

1. Are the transitions between sections and paragraphs effective? Did you feel lost at any point? Where?

2. Is the style sufficiently clear, varied, and graceful? Where are the unclear, monotonous, or awkward passages?

3. Is the style concise? Do you see any wordy passages? Clichés? Excessive use of *is*, *are*, and *to be* verb forms?

4. Does the language seem appropriate for its intended audience? Do you see any discriminatory language? Excessively formal or informal language?

5. Have the mechanical details (spelling, punctuation, documentation) been handled accurately and carefully? What errors did you notice?

During final editing you should aim to improve the readability of the paper by cutting unnecessary words, adding connections where they are needed, shifting some words and phrases to new positions, and converting some words, phrases, and clauses to other forms of expression. These processes will be discussed later in the chapter. For now, use the following list as a ready reference to help you focus on what needs to be done.

TYPES OF CHANGES MADE IN EDITING

1. *Cut* clichés and deadwood.

2. *Add* connecting words and transitional phrases where they are needed.

3. *Shift* items to place them closer to items to which they are logically or grammatically related.

4. *Convert*

abstract language	to	concrete language
general language	to	specific language
forceless verbs	to	forceful verbs
passive voice	to	active voice
noun phrases	to	verbs
inflated language	to	plain language
discriminatory	to	nondiscriminatory language

Final editing is less confusing when you do it on a printed copy rather than on the computer screen. To avoid making the edited hard copy difficult to read, use the following guidelines and editing marks. (Proofreaders employ other marks as well, but the ones listed here are the most useful.)

EDITING AND PROOFREADING MARKS

1. To insert something, make a caret mark (∧) below the line of text at the insertion point. Write the inserted text above the line or in the margin.

2. To cut something, mark the deleted text with a horizontal line; at some point on the line, add the proofreader's mark for deletion (ℯ).

3. To move something, draw a loop around the text to be moved; from some point on the loop, draw an arrow to the insertion point.

4. To mark a new paragraph division, use the paragraph symbol (¶). To eliminate a paragraph division, write "no ¶."

5. To close an unwanted space, mark the space with the proofreader's mark for closure (⊂its⊃).

6. To transpose letters or words, use the proofreader's mark for transposition (item).

Here is a sample sentence with standard editing marks.

The unhappy customer may (again) try that restaurant, but the
who hear his
friends, family, and co-workers told a horror story may never try it

at all.

CRITERIA FOR EDITING

Hearing your paper recited by someone else is a revealing experience. If you have chosen to skip that step, though, go on to the next one: Find a good time to read your paper all the way through at one sitting. Adopt a critical and detached perspective. Don't make detailed line-by-line revisions yet; just notice and mark the problem passages.

What criteria should you apply to your work at this stage? Most editors and teachers of writing single out the following qualities as desirable in academic prose: unity, coherence, variety, conciseness, and clarity. So analyze your work in terms of these qualities.

Unity and Coherence

Does the paper have unity? Does it stick to its thesis, its announced purpose, at every step? You probably eliminated all wandering from the topic during revising. But since you are now giving the paper its last reading, this may be your final chance to notice—and mark—all extraneous material.

Is each sentence coherent and well constructed? Is your reader's attention led smoothly from sentence to sentence and from paragraph to paragraph? Revision has probably eliminated all the abrupt shifts, but check again to be sure.

Variety

Do your sentences vary expressively in length and structure? Count the length of each sentence in some sample paragraphs. If all the sentences are roughly the same length, you need to revise to achieve variety in syntax. Particularly wearying to most readers are lengthy sequences of very short (six to twelve words) or very long (twenty-five to forty words) sentences. Consider breaking up long sentences or linking short ones at appropriate points.

Many college writers strive for long series of short, simple sentences in the mistaken belief that they are emulating the style of Ernest Hemingway or that short sentences automatically guarantee conciseness. Still others write unnecessarily long and tangled sentences in order to sound impressive. Therefore, the following axiom of good style should be posted above every writer's desk as a constant reminder.

> Complex ideas usually require complex sentence structures; simple ideas usually require simple ones.

Good prose tends to move back and forth between these two poles, because good prose usually is a blend of simple and complex ideas.

Conciseness

Many writers defend the use of monotonous, simple sentences by saying, "I don't believe in being wordy; I try to be concise." The goal of conciseness is admirable, but monotonous simplicity is not the way to achieve it. Here is another stylistic axiom.

> In concise writing, every word should count.

Notice that this principle does *not* say that every sentence should be short and simple. What it does say is that concise writing conveys meaning in the fewest possible words—that is, conciseness is determined by the *ratio* between content and number of words.

To see the effects of a style that is varied but concise, read the following passage by Jacques Barzun, a leading modern historian and a fine English prose stylist (who wrote, incidentally, a good writing handbook called *Simple and Direct*). Barzun is discussing Max Beloff, a former Oxford professor of government and public administration.

> The probable cause of his not being a familiar name among us after publishing a score of books and many essays, all with a pressure on current preoccupations, is that his interests have led him into three separate regions of the past and present: Great Britain, Russia, and the United States. Our age of specialism is intolerant of breadth, even when it is accompanied by competence all around. Fame follows concentration. ("An Historian Who Writes History," *American Scholar* 62 [1993]: 103)

Notice the way Barzun's syntax moves from the long and complex first sentence (fifty-one words), to the more condensed second sentence (seventeen words), to the dramatically compressed third sentence (3 words). Barzun's prose conveys the impression of an intelligent mind at work, refining an idea, modifying it, and emphasizing it with a short, memorable statement.

You may object, "But surely it would be more concise to come to the point immediately! Barzun could simply have written, 'Beloff is unfamiliar because fame follows concentration.'" No, this strategy wouldn't work. For one thing, the word *concentration* acquires a special meaning from the sentences that precede it. For another thing, the opening sentence's complexity is expressive; it embodies a subtle process of thought by which Barzun engages in a dialogue with his reader. If it were cast into pseudo-Hemingwayese, it might look like this.

"Beloff is unfamiliar," I said.
"Everywhere?" she asked.
"Not among us—the generally well educated."
"Hasn't written much?" she asked.
"On the contrary—lots of books and essays."
"Outdated interests?"
"No—his books are current. But they deal with Great Britain, Russia, the United States. . . ."
"Too many separate regions, then?"
"Yes."

There is no real gain in conciseness here. The Hemingwayese dialogue uses fifty-one words, although, admittedly, it is easier to read than Barzun's sentence. But the complexity of Barzun's sentence is expressive in its own way; it supplies a series of modifications of a unified central idea. If we use indentations to indicate the major ideas (left margin) and the minor qualifications (indentations), we can see that Barzun's sentence is well constructed. It moves from general to particular, setting the reader up for the more dramatic, more compressed sentences that follow it.

The probable cause
   of his not being a familiar name
      among us
         after publishing
           a score of books
           and many essays,
               all with a pressure on current preoccupations,
                  is that
                     his interests have led him
                        into three separate regions
                           of the past and present:
                              Great Britain, Russia, and the United States.

Despite its length, Barzun's sentence is clearly and logically constructed. Barzun makes demands upon the reader's ability to hold a complex series of ideas in suspension; but then, aware of these demands, he gives the reader a rest by condensing the whole idea into a simple three-word sentence. Notice, too, that Barzun achieves extra emphasis through repetition, variation, and compression.

Clarity

Clarity is the result of applying all the previous criteria. If a piece of writing is unified, coherent, varied, and concise, it will be clear. The best way of understanding how to achieve clarity, therefore, is simply to take some muddy, unclear passages and clear them up by applying the editing criteria.

EDIT FOR COHERENCE

Writing is coherent when it leads the reader's attention smoothly from point to point and directs it emphatically toward the important items. Careful outlining should produce coherent connections between the paper's major sections, but sometimes coherence breaks down within individual sentences or paragraphs. Consider this simple sentence, which shows that even short statements can be incoherent.

Respect should underlie proper motivation, not personal gain.

In a coherent sentence, you should be able to see instantly how the parts are connected. Usually, writers strive to put related items close to each other. But in the quoted example, the writer has delayed the phrase "not personal gain" so that its relationship to "respect" is obscured. Is the writer saying that personal gain should not underlie proper motivation, or that respect should not underlie personal gain? Grammatically, "personal gain" could be either the object of the verb "underlie" or part of its compound subject. The sentence becomes clear if we simply shift the "not" phrase so that it is next to its most closely related idea.

Respect, not personal gain, should underlie proper motivation.

Once the related items have been placed next to each other, another problem can be seen more clearly: "respect" is an attitude, but "personal gain" is a goal. Good editing should make sure that items placed in a parallel relationship are truly equivalent to each other. Thus, we rephrase the sentence so that it compares the two attitudes.

Respect, not a desire for personal gain, should underlie proper motivation.

In miniature, these changes exemplify several editing principles that help improve coherence:

> Put related items close to each other.
> Make sure that parallel items are logically and grammatically equivalent.
> Supply unambiguous connections between items.

Now consider a longer and more tangled sentence.

> The first part of my paper will establish that there was a change in attitude toward fairies by remarking on the fear of Elizabethans before *Midsummer Night's Dream* and their movement toward endearment of the fairies after *Midsummer Night's Dream*.

Since this sentence is part of a thesis statement, its incoherence may have the disastrous effect of misguiding the reader's perception of the paper's entire argument. A clear danger signal is the sentence's amazingly high number of prepositions (*of, in, toward, by, on, of, before, toward, of, after*). Prepositions make the sentence wordy, but they also make the reader work hard to see which items are connected.

The major problem with this sentence is the wordiness of the main clause ("The first part . . . will establish that there was . . .") followed by the vagueness of a promise to discuss something ("by remarking on . . ."). If the writer had avoided the promise to discuss and had made a clear, argumentative statement, these coherence problems might never have cropped up.

The repetition of the play's title is also wordy and distracting. Pronoun substitutions (*he, she, it, they*) should replace unnecessary repetitions as long as a substituted pronoun clearly refers to one, and only one, preceding item.

Sometimes, it is hard to disentangle wordiness from incoherence; the two flaws tend to occur together. In this sentence, the first strikingly faulty connective is the second *of*, because in English "fear of Elizabethans" can mean either fear felt by or fear directed toward Elizabethans. Admittedly, the second meaning is silly and can be eliminated once the reader has puzzled over the sentence a bit; but good editing should eliminate all distractions, *especially* the silly ones.

Another faulty connective is "endearment of," which suggests that people were trying to get fairies to like them. (Another silly distraction!) Standard English usage of the word *endear* requires a reflexive pronoun (*himself, herself, myself, ourselves, themselves*): to endear *himself* to someone. To use *endear,* the writer could make the fairies the subject of the clause; but a more drastic simplification is to use the strong verb *like:*

> The first part of my paper will show that Elizabethans were afraid of fairies before *Midsummer Night's Dream* but came to like them after the play became popular.

The unnecessary "first part of my paper" should also be cut.

> Elizabethans were afraid of fairies before *Midsummer Night's Dream* but came to like them after the play became popular.

The coherence of this sentence is secured by parallelism of the main verbs: "were afraid . . . but came to like." (*Fear* would be simpler and stronger than *were afraid,* but this substitution would produce distracting alliteration: *feared fairies.*)

The next example may look coherent at a first glance, but examine it closely.

> When these satellites are being launched, there is the possibility of an accident that will release the radioactive isotopes powering the satellites into the atmosphere.

The problem here is that "into the atmosphere" is placed near "powering," giving rise to momentary misreading. The sentence intends to focus on the danger that isotopes will be released "into the atmosphere," but the misplacement of the phrase leads the reader to concentrate on the idea that the isotopes are "*powering the satellites into the atmosphere.*" (This problem with incoherence may even strike an instructor as a factual mistake, because isotopes power the satellite's onboard systems, but combustible fuels supply the energy used to *launch* the satellite.) To correct the problem, the writer should shift "into the atmosphere" so that related words are together.

> When these satellites are being launched, there is the possibility of an accident that will release into the atmosphere the radioactive isotopes powering the satellites.

After the main source of incoherence has been eliminated, the problems of wordiness become more apparent: the repetition of "satellites" and the inert, all-purpose main clause ("there is the possibility of . . ."). Condense the opening clause ("When these satellites are being launched") into a phrase: "During launch." Condense "there is the possibility" into "may," and condense "an accident that will release" into "an accident may release." The resulting sentence gains coherence because the elimination of wordiness puts the related ideas closer together.

> An accident during launch may release into the atmosphere the radioactive isotopes powering the satellites.

Incoherence is especially likely to occur whenever a series of complex items must be packed into a sentence, as in a thesis sentence or a definition. Notice how hard it is to disentangle the series of elements in the following definition of chronic fatigue syndrome.

> By definition, the patients have been ill for at least six months, have significant functional impairments, and have no evidence of any chronic physical or psychiatric illness that could account for the chronic fatigue and prevents the patient from performing usual activities 50 percent of the time.

This sentence is hard to read because it is difficult to figure out which elements are meant to be parallel. The first three occurrences of the word *have* are clearly parallel, and the sentence runs smoothly until we reach the relative clause beginning with the word *that*. "Could account for . . . and prevents" is a particularly awkward sequence.

If we try to indent portions of the sentence to show which ideas are major and which are minor, the sentence's grammar suggests the following arrangement:

> By definition, the patients
>   have been ill for at least six months,
>   have significant functional impairments,
>   and have no evidence of any
>   chronic physical or psychiatric illness

> that could
>> account for the chronic fatigue
> and prevents the patient
>> from performing usual activities
>> 50 percent of the time.

This indentation reveals that a major element has been awkwardly relegated to a minor position in the sentence: Logic tells us that being unable to perform usual activities 50 percent of the time is one of the major characteristics of chronic fatigue syndrome, but the grammar of the sentence subordinates this idea to a minor clause. The awkward parallelism of two logically nonequivalent items ("could account for" and "prevents") causes further confusion, as does the shift in number from *patients* to *patient*. Finally, for precision's sake, the writer should say "*at least* 50 percent of the time."

The major step in solving the problem of incoherence is to make *prevents* another parallel item in the opening series of verbs. But unfortunately, *patient* is the subject of those verbs, whereas *illness* is the subject of *prevents*. Probably this shift in subject is what led the writer to construct such an awkward sentence in the first place. The solution is to find a new verb and make *patients* the subject of a coherent parallel series. A secondary result of this change is that now the singular *patient* can be eliminated, and the pronoun *their* can be inserted to further strengthen the sentence's coherence.

> By definition, the patients
> have been ill for at least six months,
> are unable to perform their usual activities
>> at least 50 percent of the time,
> have significant functional impairments,
> and have no evidence of any
>> chronic physical or psychiatric illness
>> that could
>>> account for their chronic fatigue.

A minor but persistent source of problems in putting related items together is that English employs some words that tend to wander far from the words they modify. The chief culprits are the words *only* and *even*. In informal spoken English, *only* is commonly used to modify an entire idea.

We are only at home on Wednesday nights.

The sense of this sentence is, "We are at home on Wednesday nights—and only then." In edited English, *only* should be placed next to what it really modifies, which is "on Wednesday nights."

We are at home only on Wednesday nights.

The reason for this more precise placement is that in many contexts, all-purpose adverbs such as *even* and *only* can create ambiguities. Compare the meanings of the following sentences, some of which are ambiguous.

Only Michelangelo could have achieved this beauty.

Michelangelo only could have achieved this beauty.

Michelangelo could only have achieved this beauty.

Michelangelo could have achieved only this beauty.

Michelangelo could have achieved this beauty only.

In edited English, the rule is that *only* and *even* should come just before the words they modify.

Although the main way to improve coherence is simply to put related items together, you must also find pleasingly varied ways to link these items. Nothing is more monotonous than prose in which every sentence has two halves joined by *and* or a semicolon. So here are some other strategies you can consider using.

OTHER METHODS OF IMPROVING COHERENCE

1. Use standard patterns of organization (chronological, spatial, or the like).
2. Use clear transitional sentences (paragraph hooks). (See "The Hook Paragraph Transition" in Chapter 10.)
3. Use repetitions or variations of keywords.
4. Use synonyms and related words.
5. Use clear, consistent connecting pronouns.
6. Use parallel sentence structure to link related ideas. (See "Generating a Sentence Outline While Revising the Rough Draft" in Chapter 10.)
7. Use transitional phrases. (See "Other Types of Transition" in Chapter 10.)
8. Use appropriate and consistent verb tenses.
9. Use a variety of grammatical patterns such as subordinate and coordinate clauses, participial phrases, and appositives to avoid choppy sentences.

But remember that you must use these techniques judiciously in combination with techniques for achieving variety. In the following sentences, a student writer has used keyword repetitions and pronoun links, but the effect is nevertheless incoherent because of the monotonously short, choppy sentences.

Ira Klein was main film editor for the disputed CBS documentary. He said that he had warned them all along that it was unfair. Klein was the nineteenth and final witness for Westmoreland. He said that Crile had known about the documentary's distortions.

The choppy syntax makes the writer seem to be jumping from one idea to another. The third sentence is especially distracting because of its lack of connection with the sentences before and after it.

Combining short sentences to achieve variety in length can transform a sentence built around the verb *to be* (the example's entire first sentence) into a phrase tucked neatly into one of the other sentences. Furthermore, the second and fourth sentences can be linked by a simple coordinating conjunction (*and*). Because of the resulting variety of sentence rhythm, making just these two simple changes produces a much more coherent passage.

> Ira Klein, main film editor for the disputed CBS documentary, was the nineteenth and final witness for Westmoreland. He said he had warned them all along that the documentary was unfair and that Crile had known about the documentary's distortions.

THREE COMMON MISTAKES THAT DESTROY COHERENCE

Faulty Parallelism

The following stylistic principle is involved when a writer uses parallelism to achieve coherence.

> Good prose moves forward by first arousing and then satisfying expectations.

At the level of overall structure, we have already seen the importance of giving the reader a preview of the paper's pattern of organization and then maintaining that pattern consistently. At the level of sentence construction, the same principle holds. Once a series has been initiated, the reader expects the series to be completed. Each item should, as far as possible, be expressed in parallel form. The parallelism should be grammatical (verbs parallel to other verbs, nouns parallel to other nouns, and so on) and logical (attitudes parallel to other attitudes, causes parallel to other causes).

Here is an example of faulty parallelism between grammatically nonequivalent items.

> It seems more likely that Eveline is afraid of becoming like these objects rather than of simply missing them.

The problem is that the "more . . . than" elements are misaligned.

> It seems
> *more likely that*
>   Eveline is afraid
>   of becoming like these objects
> *rather than*
>   of simply missing them.

From this indented diagram you can see that the writer intends to contrast the phrases "of becoming like these objects" and "of simply missing them." But the transitional phrases that should highlight the contrast ("more likely that . . . rather than") have been placed in front of grammatically nonequivalent items: a clause ("Eveline is afraid") and a phrase ("of simply missing them"). The faulty parallelism can be corrected by creating two parallel clauses.

> It seems
> > *more likely that*
> > > Eveline is afraid of becoming like these objects
> > *than that*
> > > she is afraid of simply missing them.

Somehow, though, this revised version seems worse than the original, even though it is grammatically correct. Do you see what's wrong?

The problem is that the "more likely that . . . than that" phrasing repeats "afraid" and uses two weak verbs: "is . . . is." Replacing "is afraid of" with "fears" and using "not that . . . but that" sets up a simpler, more emphatic contrast.

> It seems that Eveline fears
> > not that she will miss these objects
> > but that she will become like them.

These examples reveal a general (but not inflexible!) rule: Correct problems of faulty parallelism first; then if parallelism has led you to use wordy constructions, go back and edit for conciseness. In the sentence just analyzed, we might think that contrasting phrases such as "more likely . . . than" would lend emphasis to the sentence. But it turns out that the "not . . . but" phrasing, coupled with a simple verb, is actually much stronger. Simplicity can be more emphatic than complexity.

Not only . . . but also is a particularly bothersome construction that often leads to problems with parallelism. Notice the faulty parallelism in the next example.

> The automatic braking system not only aids in inclement weather but in dry weather as well.

The "not only . . . but" phrasing leads the reader to expect that two grammatically equivalent items will be paired. Instead, the writer has placed a verb after *not only* and a prepositional phrase after *but.* Furthermore, the reader expects the coupling "but also" rather than "but . . . as well." The indentation diagram illustrates the faults.

> The automatic braking system
> > not only
> > > *aids* in inclement weather
> > but
> > > *in dry weather as well.*

Granted, this is not a serious mistake. But its effect is to distract the reader momentarily, and good editing aims to remove every such distraction, no matter how minor.

To straighten out the parallelism, move "not only" so that it precedes the first prepositional phrase, and use "but also" rather than "but . . . as well."

The automatic braking system aids
> not only
> > *in inclement weather*
> but also
> > *in dry weather.*

Dangling Modifiers

One form of grammatical incoherence, the dangling modifier, is so named because a modifying phrase "dangles" without securely attaching itself to the subject of the sentence. A dangling modifier is usually the result of a writer's change of strategy in midsentence. First, the writer sets down a modifying phrase, usually a sentence opener with a present participle (an *-ing* word):

Growing larger with each eruption, ...

After this participial phrase the writer intends to say, "the river of lava engulfs the village." But after fussing with the remainder of the sentence, the writer forgets that the first phrase will end up modifying the sentence's subject.

Growing larger with each eruption, from our secure vantage point we saw the river of lava engulf the coastal village.

The thought of the observers growing larger with each eruption is grotesque, isn't it?

Remember that sentence openers are particularly liable to lead to this kind of problem. Since the participial phrase modifies the subject of the sentence, you must revise either by altering the subject or by altering the modifying phrase.

Growing larger with each eruption, the river of lava engulfed the coastal village as we watched from our secure vantage point.

Or:

We watched the river of lava grow larger with each eruption until it engulfed the coastal village.

Be sure to check all your introductory clauses for dangling modifiers and correct them as appropriate.

Tense Shifts

One distracting form of incoherence occurs when a writer inadvertently shifts verb tenses or uses an inappropriate combination of tenses. An inadvertent shift looks like this:

Darwin returned from his voyage convinced that natural selection is the key to understanding evolutionary change. He realizes that his theory would meet with resistance from religious conservatives.

Here the writer shifted quite properly to the present tense *is* to express a universal truth but forgot to return to the past tense in discussing Darwin's reaction. Revised for consistency, the passage looks like this:

Darwin returned from his voyage convinced that natural selection is the key to understanding evolutionary change. He realized that his theory would meet with resistance from religious conservatives.

Inappropriate combinations of tenses often occur when the writer misuses the three types of past tense: past (*received*), present perfect (*has received*), and past perfect (*had received*).

By the time Johnson retired, he received his pension.

In English, action prior to a past action should be conveyed by a verb in the past perfect tense.

By the time Johnson retired, he had received his pension.

Occasionally, you simply cannot avoid shifts in verb tense. In writing about the content of literary works, for example, scholars generally use the summarizing present tense: "The protagonist deals with his problem." Similarly, in MLA format the verbs introducing quotations are normally put in the present tense: "Herbert hints at his grief by using the word 'passing-bell.' " However, in talking about an author's life, a writer normally uses the historical past tense: "At this time Herbert lived in London." So within a single paragraph a writer may shift from historical past to summarizing present and back again. The rule of thumb for editing these passages is to keep the shifts few and unobtrusive. If possible, put a paragraph break between shifts in order to use a single tense within a paragraph.

EDIT FOR CONCISENESS

Cut Clichés and Deadwood Phrases

Clichés are expressions or ideas that have lost their impact through overuse. Many were once vivid metaphors—which is why they became popular in the first place—but overfamiliarity has deadened them.

dead as a doornail

happy as a lark

fresh as a daisy

pretty as a picture

free as the wind

to beat a point to death

to blow one's own horn

to feather one's nest

Enough! Do you feel the anesthetizing effect of these phrases? Taken one at a time, they cause momentary numbness; taken in gulps, they cause brain damage. Cut them from your writing.

Occasionally, you can bring a cliché back to life by giving it a witty, unexpected twist; this is a favorite device of broadcast and magazine newswriters. But how easily it can misfire! If you have ever heard your local television newscasters bantering lamely about a story covering the horse show at the county fairgrounds ("And some fairgoers were there just to horse around." "Thanks, Chet, but you'd better rein in your impulse to raise horse laughs. And speaking of rain, here's Betty with the forecast."), you have probably been cured of this habit.

Deadwood phrases are like clichés, but they are usually mere connectives without any thought content at all. They serve a useful purpose in spoken English, since they enable us to put phrases and sentences together quickly, like carpenters assembling a house from prefabricated sections. However, in edited English, you should usually replace deadwood phrases with shorter, more concise connectives.

Replace	*With*
at this point in time	now
due to the fact that	because
in the event that	if
in the not too distant future	soon
on many occasions	often
the way in which	how

Convert Abstract and General to Concrete and Specific

Good prose is usually characterized by specific, concrete language rather than abstract, general language. I've lumped these four terms together because the concrete and the specific often accompany each other. But the terms sometimes need to be distinguished carefully, since they are not synonymous. The word *food*, for example, is concrete but general.

Abstract usually refers to something that is remote from actual experience; its antonym, *concrete*, refers to something that can be seen, heard, felt, tasted, smelled, or measured. *General* refers to something that encompasses an entire class or category; its antonym, *specific*, refers to a single item.

The reason good prose tends to use specific, concrete language can be stated as a principle of style.

> A reader will tend to see the implied generalities in a sentence if it is stated in specific terms; but if it is stated in general terms, the reader will not pause to imagine the specifics.

I suspect that this principle has always been true—but never truer than in the present media-saturated age. We are used to thinking in images. Thus, when I write, "Do dishes like caviar and truffles make you hungry, or are burgers and fries more to your liking?," you immediately grasp the general point (and perhaps rush off to the restaurant of your choice). Translated into general language, the question says something like "Do *gourmet dishes* make you hungry, or are *ordinary fast foods* more to your liking?" But this version is surely less appetizing.

Granted, both sentences get the point across. Nevertheless, the first version is preferable because it supplies specific and concrete word pictures; it gives the senses, as well as the mind, something to grasp. There is no danger that the general point will be misunderstood, because the mind travels easily from specific to general.

The reverse is not true. If I write, "Should you use deadly force to protect yourself against an attack?," you are not likely to imagine specific forms of deadly force or specific forms of attack. (Of course, you *may*, but we are discussing a general tendency. Modern readers tend to be hurried and nonvisual in their response to the printed page.) But notice what happens if I write, "Should you use a gun or a knife to protect yourself against a mugger, thief, or rapist?" Now if you are a normal, twentieth-century American (or even if you are not), you have some vivid mental images, and you have still grasped the general point of the question. Much has been gained and nothing lost.

But academic prose, I hear you arguing, naturally tends to be abstract and general, if only because it usually deals with abstract and general topics. Granted. I am saying only that as far as it is possible, you should fight against the tendency. Make your case in terms as specific and concrete as your context allows.

Remember, too, that the qualities of concreteness and specificity are relative, not absolute. It is impossible to say, with finality, "This word is general (or specific)." Another term, still more general or specific, can always be found.

> food
> > sandwich
> > > meat sandwich
> > > > hamburger
> > > > > grilled hamburger
> > > > > > grilled hamburger with onions

Notice that this series goes from general to specific and from less concrete to more concrete. (*Food* is concrete because it can be tasted, but the word *food* evokes no specific tastes.)

The same principle applies to the concepts found in academic writing.

> conflict
> > regional conflict
> > > ethnic and religious regional conflict
> > > > the war in Bosnia

Use the most specific, concrete language appropriate for your context.

Some academic disciplines rely heavily upon specialized terminology that may seem unnecessarily abstract and general. The current trend, even in highly technical disciplines, is to use specific, concrete, plain language. But bear in mind that word choices depend upon context and audience. Although the word *reward* may sound refreshingly plain and direct in comparison to *positive reinforcement*, context may require a research writer to use the term most commonly employed by behavioral psychologists. Sometimes abstract technical terms have the added advantage of allowing researchers to discuss emotionally distressing topics in emotionally neutral language. If you are in doubt about specific vocabulary items, ask your instructor what usage he or she prefers. (Interestingly enough, the psychological and social sciences are starting to avoid clinical-sounding language. The third edition of the APA [American Psychological Association] *Publication Manual* used the word *subject* in describing human experiments; the fourth edition specifies that the word *participant* always be used. This is no mere quibble, since the first word connotes victimization and the second connotes informed consent!)

Convert Forceless Verbs to Forceful Verbs

Perhaps the most universally accepted principle of stylistic editing is the idea that good prose tends to be verb centered. That is, it relies heavily upon strong, active verbs rather than upon nouns, adjectives, and adverbs. A single verb can convey movement, describe action, and show relationships between ideas that would require many adverbs and adjectives. Compare the effects of the following sentences.

> Abruptly, and in an angry tone of voice, she called out: "Matthew!"
>
> "Matthew!" she exploded.

The second sentence conveys all of the nuances of the first sentence but in far fewer words. Abruptness and anger are implied in the verb *exploded*.

In the game of chess, the queen is the most powerful piece because it can move in several directions; the rook is the next most powerful, because it can sweep horizontally and vertically. The bishop and knight are next; and the pawns are the lowliest pieces because they can merely trudge forward slowly and capture pieces diagonally adjacent to them. Similarly, in the English language, verbs are the most powerful elements, analogous to queens in chess, because they can convey so many things. Nouns come next. Adverbs are less powerful because they can merely modify verbs, adjectives, and other adverbs. Adjectives are weaker still, since they can modify only nouns and pronouns. Even weaker are the connective elements—prepositions, pronouns, and conjunctions—that function only in tandem with more powerful words. Weakest of all are the articles (*a, an, the*).

Strongest among the verbs are those that convey sensory content, such as

> *explode, bloom, grasp*

or those that have precise denotative meaning, such as

> *accelerate, categorize, explain*

Verbs with less force include the all-purpose verbs that we use with great frequency and flexibility:

> *get, run, do, make*

Often these verbs acquire denotative precision and force from lesser words, such as prepositions, that modify their meaning:

make up, make over, make out, make do with

Chief among the verbs lacking force is the verb *to be* in its many forms:

is, are, was, were, has been, have been, will be

Weak, wordy prose tends to be marked by two related symptoms: (1) a predominance of verbs that lack force, and (2) a frequent use of weak connectives, especially strings of prepositions. Here is a sentence that possesses the typical symptoms of wordiness.

> One possibility as to why the severity of problems related to geriatric alcohol consumption is so great is the fact that many of the elderly alcoholics are also taking some type of medication.

Notice that the sentence contains three uses of the verb *to be* ("is . . . is . . . are") and six prepositions ("as to . . . of . . . to . . . of . . . of"). Thus, nine of the sentence's thirty-one words are forceless and inert.

We can eliminate part of the wordiness by reducing deadwood phrases to more concise equivalents or near-equivalents.

Replace	*With*
one possibility as to why	perhaps
is the fact that	because

Sometimes, phrases can simply be trimmed without any loss of meaning: "many of the elderly alcoholics" can become "many elderly alcoholics"; "severity of problems . . . is so great" can become "problems . . . are so severe"; "are also taking" can become "also take."

Perhaps

~~One possibility as to why~~ the severity of problems related to geriatric
are severe   because
alcohol consumption ~~is~~ so ~~great is the fact that~~ many of the elderly alco-
take
holics ~~are~~ also ~~taking~~ some type of medication.

Here is the edited result.

> Perhaps the problems related to geriatric alcohol consumption are so severe because many elderly alcoholics also take some type of medication.

The sentence has been reduced from thirty-one to twenty-one words; of these, only one is a form of the verb *to be*, and only two are prepositions.

Notice that editing for conciseness does more than merely change the sentence cosmetically. The first version is sloppy and unfocused; the edited version is direct and forceful. Careful editing affects the reader's impression of the writer: A clear, concise style contributes powerfully to the writer's credibility by creating a persuasive ethos. (See "The Three Bases of Persuasion" in Chapter 3.)

One word of caution: Stylistic editing requires good judgment. You cannot eliminate all forms of the verb *to be*, nor should you. Simply try to follow the general principle of verb-centering your writing, and apply the principle flexibly.

Convert Passive Voice to Active Voice

To clear up a point of confusion at the outset, not every use of the verb *to be* entails what grammarians call the passive voice. When we use the passive voice, we take the object (recipient) of some action and make it the subject of a sentence containing a participle and a form of *to be*.

Escobar's arrival *was seen* by the villagers as yet another sign of impending disaster.

Converting passive voice to active voice generally produces a more direct and forceful sentence.

The villagers saw Escobar's arrival as yet another sign of impending disaster.

There is a double gain in conciseness: Both the *to be* verb and a preposition (*by*) have been eliminated.

But sometimes the passive voice is necessary or even desirable. For example, the following sentence stresses the power of a natural disaster.

A hurricane leveled the coastal cities.

In a context stressing the helplessness of the cities rather than the force of the tornado, passive voice might be more appropriate.

The coastal cities were leveled by a hurricane.

Furthermore, some academic writing favors the passive voice precisely because it can be less forceful in one special way: It can remove the reader's sense of a human agent at work. And in some disciplines, writers use the passive voice to convey objectivity and scientific detachment. For example,

The questionnaire was distributed to a random sample of under-graduates.

may be preferable to

I distributed the questionnaire to a sample of undergraduates that I had randomly selected.

Find out your instructor's views about the specific conventions of writing in your discipline. In the humanities, writers usually avoid the use of passive voice constructions to express detachment or impartiality.

The preceding example raises a related point: Can you use *I* in a research paper? Or should you use some roundabout construction such as *in the opinion of this writer*? The general answer to this question is that in all academic disciplines research writing aims to avoid distracting, personal elements. Put yourself in the background; put your topic and your argument in the foreground. You should seldom use *I* or *me*. You certainly should never use a barbaric substitution such as *in this writer's opinion*, which calls more attention to you (and your self-consciousness) than the more direct *I think*. Should you use *I think*, then? If your intention is to identify a statement merely as your opinion, no—never. Readers understand that the statement is your own if you do not cite a source. If the statement is unsupported opinion, then you should discard it. If it is supported opinion, then it is part of your argument; and you simply make the assertion and support it with argumentation or a citation.

One exception to the general principle—an exception that not all teachers agree about—is the use of first-person statements to acknowledge uncertainty about a fact or an interpretation. Many readers will not be bothered by the following statement.

> I think that Johnson already possessed a draft of the Gulf of Tonkin Resolution, though sources disagree on this point. [Your documentation now indicates the sources.]

But notice that even here, you could avoid the use of a first-person pronoun simply by replacing "I think that" with "probably."

Convert Noun Constructions to Verbs

One of the glories of the English language is its richness of vocabulary—a diversity of word choices stemming chiefly from importing words from other languages, especially Latin, Greek, and French. (English is also rich in words of Germanic origin; but strictly speaking, they are not imported, since English is itself a Germanic tongue.)

In diversity lies peril, however. Many simple verbs, especially those derived from Latin, have corresponding nouns formed by the addition of standard suffixes such as *-ion*, *-ation*, *-ence*, and *-ment*.

revise	revision
consider	consideration
consult	consultation
fragment	fragmentation
differ	difference
refine	refinement

Dozens of examples could be listed, but these are enough to show the general principle.

These nouns have in turn become parts of standard phrases, generally in combination with standard (or, as linguists say, *idiomatic*) prepositions that precisely indicate the noun's shades of meaning.

give consideration to

in consideration of

show consideration for

This diversity may be glorious, but its perils show up in a sentence like this:

> The committee met to give consideration to revision of the company's charter.

This sentence violates two of the stylistic principles already discussed: It is not verb centered, and it contains unnecessary prepositions. Both problems can be solved at a single stroke by spotting the verbs buried in noun phrases and converting them back to verb forms.

Replace	*With*
to give consideration to	consider
the revision of	revising

Here is the edited result.

> The committee met to consider revising the company's charter.

Besides being more concise than the original, the revised sentence is considerably less stuffy. Its plainness leads to the next conversion principle.

Convert Inflated Language to Plain Language

The diversity of synonyms and near-synonyms in English gives writers an incomparable range of alternative ways of expressing an idea. Particularly abundant are near-synonyms for things that our culture considers important, such as money. Without even dipping into the huge repertoire of slang words, I can immediately list the following standard American English terms.

> money, cash, wages, salary, stipend, fee, honorarium, remuneration, currency, coins, bills, compensation

The national origins of these terms range from ancient India (*cash*, from Sanskrit by way of Tamil and finally to English by way of Portuguese traders), to ancient Rome (*salary*, from the Latin word for money given soldiers to buy *sal*, "salt"), and to medieval England (*wages*, from an Old English word for a soldier's pay).

If their origins are diverse, their shades of meaning and connotations are equally so. We tend to use the word *wages* to denote money paid to a working person on an hourly, daily, or weekly basis; whereas *salary* denotes a stated compensation for services rendered over a longer period, usually a year. A *fee* is a one-time payment for a service, but an *honorarium* is given to a professional person for services for which a fee is normally not required. Thus, etiquette suggests that one should offer a professor an *honorarium* rather than a *fee* for giving a lecture.

Using inappropriate terms can cause stylistic incongruities when the language is incorrect for the situation. For example, one of my uncles would never say "Let's go into the living room for an after-dinner drink." Rather, he would say (and it deserves to be set off for its grandness):

> Let us adjourn to the parlor for a postprandial libation.

(Please note that he was being funny!) Unless you are using ponderous language for humorous effect, use the plainest language appropriate for the context.

> In research writing, stick to the level of moderately formal English unless you are striving for some special effect, such as irony, humor, or shock. And think carefully about whether such effects are appropriate for the context you have established.

Occasionally, you may need to use a fancy or unusual word simply because no simpler synonym is available. The word *avuncular* is my favorite example because no other word even comes close to its meaning. Notice how the *New American Heritage Dictionary* is forced to define the word at length: "of, pertaining to, or resembling an uncle, especially a benevolent uncle." And how badly the definition fails to convey the flavor of the word! (The editors might have been wiser to put a picture of Walter Cronkite in the margin.)

Finally, choose one word from a group of synonyms on the basis of its emotional flavor—its connotation. People feel dignified if they are part of an *assembly;* they can still like themselves if they are part of a *group;* but no one wants to be part of a *mob.* Choosing a word for its emotional flavor is a legitimate part of what is known as semantic argument: using the connotations of words to persuade the reader. If the town meeting degenerated into violence, call the mob a mob. However, beware of pushing the semantic loading too far: If you call the U.S. Senate a mob, you risk alienating your readers.

Convert Discriminatory to Nondiscriminatory Language

The problems of racism, ageism, and sexism in our society are real and serious. For a writer, unconsciously sexist language is the most likely danger, simply because gender is a linguistic phenomenon as well as a biological one. But as the popularity of the mocking term *politically correct* shows, there is a danger that in steering away from the pomposity and male chauvinism of sexist language, we may steer directly into pomposity of an equally ridiculous sort.

For example, the term *chairman* carries an undeniably sexist implication; it suggests that the chair at the head of the corporation or committee table naturally belongs to a man. Some argue that English is full of compound words containing the word *man* and that to replace them all with *person* creates monstrosities. *Chairperson* is relatively innocuous, but what do you think about *statesperson* or *telephone lineperson?* The words *poetess* and *aviatrix* are sexist in their implication that women who are poets and aviators are so rare as to require unusual, gender-related nouns; these words, thankfully, have gone the way of the dinosaurs, while the word *comedienne* is heading that way. But what a minefield the area of gender-related words has become!

Many of these problems of diction now have solutions: *Stewardess* has become *flight attendant,* and *chairman* has become *chair.* As time passes, gender-neutral forms will gradually become normal and unconscious parts of standard usage. The clumsiest terms will be replaced by more graceful ones.

Unfortunately, the English language creates unavoidable gender problems in the handling of pronouns, though. English has three singular nominative pronouns (*he, she, it*), with matching forms in the objective and possessive cases (*him, her, it; his, hers, its*). Two kinds of problems crop up when these words are used.

The first involves the relative pronoun *who* and indefinite pronouns such as *each, everyone, everybody,* and *somebody.* Edited English has traditionally treated these terms as singular pronouns requiring matching masculine pronouns.

> Has everybody brought *his* protractor?
> Who has forgotten *his* protractor?

Although no pressing issue of gender bias is involved here, contemporary speakers and writers of American English increasingly use a plural pronoun to avoid having to make a choice of gender.

> Has everybody brought *their* protractor?
> Who has forgotten *their* protractor?

As a writer, you have the choice of violating a rule of gender neutrality, on the one hand, or a rule of pronoun agreement, on the other. You may offend some purists in either case. Since research writing is only moderately formal, the formal rule of pronoun agreement doesn't necessarily decide the issue. The best solutions are to use *he or she* and *she or he* sparingly or, most commonly, to cast the entire construction into the plural.

> Have all of you brought your protractors?
> Have all of the students forgotten their protractors?

The second kind of problem is more clearly gender related. If a writer wishes to avoid repetition by using a pronoun to refer to a singular gender-neutral noun, the singular masculine form may strike some readers as implying gender bias.

> A *doctor* should be ready to answer questions after *he* supplies a diagnosis.

Many readers will feel that the writer thinks that doctors automatically are or should be male. How should this pronoun reference problem be solved?

One school of thought argues that *he* is routinely used as a gender-neutral pronoun and that no special effort should be made to avoid its use. The crucial weakness of this argument is that while the exclusive use of male pronouns may be innocuous in some contexts, in others—such as a piece of writing that touches upon the occupational fitness of women serving as, say, medical doctors or fighter pilots—the male pronoun contributes to the perpetuation of sexist attitudes.

To write *he or she* for every occurrence of a singular pronoun, on the other hand, is cumbersome and self-conscious. This phrasing should be used sparingly; it is appropriate primarily in gender-sensitive contexts, to make the language inclusive.

Another alternative is to vary the use of gender, chapter by chapter or section by section. A drawback is that some readers may find this technique distracting.

Again, the most desirable alternative is usually to avoid the problem altogether by using plural rather than singular forms. Thus, the sample sentence about the doctor's diagnosis could be revised in this way:

Doctors should be ready to answer questions after they have supplied their diagnoses.

It will be impossible for you to eliminate all sexist language if you are unconsciously sexist. By definition, you are not aware of your own sexism, and you deny it when it is pointed out to you. Reading this section on editing to eliminate sexist language may sensitize you to certain recurrent forms of gender-biased language; but if you write "female lawyer" or "male nurse" simply because you think that these persons are so rare or so odd that their gender deserves special mention, you are unlikely to see the implicit sexism in your own writing. A collaborator who is sensitive to gender issues may be able to help you edit.

PUNCTUATE FOR CLARITY

Every conscientious writer occasionally consults a basic writing handbook for questions about punctuation. Since this chapter emphasizes editing research writing to make it clearer, we'll look at a few cases in which punctuation can affect the clarity of a piece of writing.

The comma can be a tricky punctuation mark; its improper use or omission can badly mislead the reader. Consider this example:

Bulimics need constant applause and parental approval is certainly no exception.

In this sentence, the first seven words initially seem to express a complete idea: "Bulimics need constant applause and parental approval." Then the jarring appearance of the word *is* makes you reshuffle the clause in your mind so that "parental approval" becomes its grammatical subject. A comma prevents the misreading.

Bulimics need constant applause, and parental approval is certainly no exception.

Incidentally, an even better revision is this:

Bulimics need constant approval, especially from their parents.

The unrevised sentence forces the reader to connect "constant applause" and "parental approval" in an implicitly awkward way, something like this: "Parental approval is no exception to the kind of constant applause bulimics need." But this revision takes us beyond the effects of punctuation. So let's return to the focus of this section.

Here is another example of a comma omission from the same writer.

Our culture tells us that in order to be successful, happy and fulfilled people must be slender and attractive.

The effect is similar to the first example, but this sentence is even more ambiguous. Does the writer mean that happy and fulfilled people must be slender and attractive to be successful, or that people must be slender and attractive to be successful, happy, and fulfilled? Surely the second is the intended meaning, and it could have been secured by the addition of a comma after *fulfilled*. Whether or not a comma should follow *happy* depends upon which rule you employ: "Use commas to separate every item in a series," or "Use commas to separate every item except the last in a series." The rule given in the *MLA Handbook* (and in most other handbooks) is to use a comma to separate every item, including the last.

An acid test for evaluating your sensitivity to punctuation's subtle ability to affect meaning is the use of commas to set off nonrestrictive elements in a sentence. Compare these two sentences. What difference in meaning do you perceive?

The students who complained of headaches were sent to the health center.

The students, who complained of headaches, were sent to the health center.

The first sentence indirectly asserts that only *some* of the students complained of headaches, and only these students were sent to the health center. The second sentence indirectly asserts that *all* the students complained of headaches and were sent to the health center.

In the first sentence, the relative clause ("who complained of headaches") *restricts* the assertion to a subcategory of students; therefore, it is called a *restrictive clause*. A restrictive clause should not be set off with commas. In the second sentence, the relative clause is *nonrestrictive*; it refers to all the members of the category (students), and it should be set off with a comma at each end. The presence or absence of punctuation can thus affect a sentence's meaning.

Particularly in the sciences and social sciences, many editors prefer to reserve *which* for nonrestrictive clauses and *that* for restrictive clauses. The APA *Publication Manual*, for example, offers the following example of a sentence containing a nonrestrictive clause.

The animals, which performed well in the first experiment, were used in the second experiment.

To make the clause restrictive, use *that* instead.

The animals that performed well in the first experiment were used in the second experiment.

But note that the *that/which* distinction will not help you resolve ambiguities when you must use the pronoun *who* to refer to persons.

Like clauses, phrases may function restrictively or nonrestrictively. Here's an example.

Author Anne Tyler has written many books, short stories, and articles since her first book, *If Morning Ever Comes*, was published in 1964.

In this sentence the phrase "first book" specifies which book is meant, and the title is merely additional information; the title is an *appositive phrase* and is set off with commas because it is nonrestrictive. If, however, we cut the word *first*, the appositive becomes restrictive, and we omit the two commas around the title.

Author Anne Tyler has written many books, short stories, and articles since her book *If Morning Ever Comes* was published in 1964.

Thus the distinction between a restrictive and a nonrestrictive phrase may be quite subtle and may even hinge upon a single word.

PROOFREAD FOR MECHANICAL ERRORS

Nothing can replace a careful, word-by-word scanning of the paper as the last step in editing. However, computer technology has placed some marvelous tools at the writer's disposal, and it is foolish not to use them if you have a clear sense of their capabilities and limitations. The following lists give the details about spell checkers and style checkers.

COMPUTERIZED SPELL CHECKERS

Here is what they do well.

1. They quickly scan your paper for improper spellings.
2. They allow you to add customized dictionary entries for unusual words, proper names, and specialized terminology.

Here is what they don't do.

1. They don't spot homophone errors (*their/there, vein/vain/vane*).
2. They don't spot the misuse of similar words (*lie/lay, compliment/complement, eminent/imminent/immanent, illusion/allusion*) or related word forms (*go, goes*).
3. They don't recognize most names and unusual words. A spell checker will allow you to add an unusual word to a customized dictionary, but if you misspell it when you add it, the spell checker will never again flag the misspelled form.
4. They don't recognize British or archaic spellings. You should reproduce quoted British text exactly as written, but you should not add British spellings to your customized dictionary because inadvertent uses of these spellings elsewhere in your writing will become invisible to the spell checker.

COMPUTERIZED STYLE CHECKERS

Here is what they do well.

1. They offer certain kinds of rudimentary advice on style. For example, they highlight passive verb constructions and ask whether you wish to keep them. They do automatic readability analyses by counting average sentence lengths and word lengths.
2. They highlight common wordy phrases and suggest alternatives.
3. They spot mechanical errors, such as the omission of the second quotation mark in a pair.

> Here is what they don't do.
>
> 1. They don't provide reliable, flexible advice for making subtle stylistic revisions. A skilled editor will find that many of their flags are unnecessary or false. You should never slavishly follow the stylistic advice they give, though it may often prompt a useful excursion to a handbook of style.
>
> 2. They have trouble handling writing that requires unusual punctuation or syntax. For instance, a linguistics paper that contains many words and phrases used as examples may stir up dozens of false warnings.

Although a style checker may produce some helpful advice, to use a style checker effectively, you must know grammar and usage extremely well. Unfortunately, if you know grammar and usage well, you will find about 90 percent of the checker's advice to be irritating, useless, and wrong. Thus, using a style checker can be like having a highly intrusive, semiliterate, borderline psychotic shouting instructions at you while you write.

If you do not know grammar and usage well, the style checker can lead you to produce ghastly writing. The reason is that all languages, especially word order–dependent languages like English, require the writer or speaker to make countless subtle distinctions on the basis of context. But even the best and most popular style checkers use very primitive algorithms to evaluate context. One leading style checker *always* flags the word *rather*, for example, labeling it a "vague adverb" even when it is used—appropriately and precisely—in the standard formation "[something] rather than [something else]."

To illustrate what style checkers don't do, I've used one to "correct" some excellent English prose. Here is a famous passage from a meditation by John Donne, one of our great prose masters.

> No man is an island, entire of itself; every man is a piece of the continent, a part of the main. If a clod be washed away by the sea, Europe is the less, as well as if a promontory were, as well as if a manor of thy friend's or of thine own were. Any man's death diminishes me, because I am involved in mankind; and therefore never send to know for whom the bell tolls; it tolls for thee.

In using a style checker on this passage, I decided to take, in every case, the *first* advice the style checker offered. My intention was to duplicate the choices that an unskilled user might make. Here is the result.

> No man is an island, entire of itself; every man is a piece of the continent, a part of the main. If some clods are washed away by the sea, Europe is the lessness, also if a promontory were, also if a manor of thy friend's or of thine own were. Any man's death diminishes me, because I am involved in people. Therefore never send to know for whom the bell tolls; it tolls for thee.

It was amusing to see the checker arrive at the gender-neutral phrasing "involved in people," creating a new John Donne, the warm, politically correct Anglican divine. Also, Donne is given something of a Gertrude-Stein-ish flavor in that magical phrase "Europe is the lessness." And thank heavens the style checker got rid of that dreadful subjunctive construction, "if a clod be washed."

But this is hardly fair, you say. After all, Donne used archaic, poetic language; and the style checker, in its prosaic way, was simply trying to flatten it into concise, neutral, modern prose. (I love the chipper tone of its dialogue boxes as it mangles text. "Next problem?" it asks, waiting for you to press a button and have done with some more Donne.)

All right, then, let's give it a paragraph by John McPhee, who is widely considered one of our living masters of nonfiction prose.

> In the many fractures of these big roadcuts, there is some suggestion of columns, but actually the cracks running through the cuts are too various to be explained by columnar jointing, let alone by the impudence of dynamite. The sill may have been stressed pretty severely by the tilting of the fault block, Kleinspehn says, or it may have cracked in response to the release of weight as the load above it was eroded away. Solid-earth tides could break it up, too. The sea is not all that responds to the moon. Twice a day the solid earth bobs up and down, as much as a foot. That kind of force and that kind of distance are more than enough to break hard rock. Wells will flow faster during lunar high tides. (*Basin and Range* [New York: Farrar, 1981], 6–7)

Again I followed the advice given by the style checker in every case, including some faulty capitalization. I obeyed the style checker's command to get rid of passive voice constructions, which led to phrasing that suggests that McPhee wants to blow the reader up. Of course, McPhee's two longest sentences had to be chopped up to satisfy the style checker's readability criterion, and important connections between ideas were thus destroyed.

> In the many fractures of these big rodents, there is some suggestion of columns. However, the cracks running through the cuts are too various for me to explain by columnar jointing, let alone by the impudence of dynamite. The sill may have been stressed pretty severely by the tilting of the fault block, Kleinspehn says. It may have cracked in response to the release of weight as the load above it was eroded away. Solid-earth tides could break it up, too. The sea is not all that responds to the moon. Twice a day the solid earth bobs up and down, as much as a foot, and That kinds [sic] of force and that kind of distance are more than enough to break hard rock. Wells will flow faster during lunar high tides.

Some day style checkers may be reliable tools for unskilled writers. That day has not yet arrived. Until then, ask not for whom the prompt blinks.

USE GLOBAL SEARCHES TO EDIT DETAILS

Most word processors have a search function that allows you to type a word (or any other string of characters) that the computer will then find throughout your paper. The search function can be used to check the paper rapidly, one last time, for entire categories of potential mistakes.

1. Before handing in the final draft, update the list of works cited by searching for each author's name. During revision you may have eliminated the use of some sources. Cut them from your source list to avoid having your bibliography look like it's padded.

2. Check all the parenthetical documentation by searching for the left parenthesis mark: "(". Scan each citation for accuracy of form and accuracy of page numbers.

3. If you know that you tend to make certain kinds of mistakes (such as the spelling *it's* for *its* and vice versa), use the search function to scan every occurrence of these words. To be sure that you have avoided the use of contractions, search for apostrophes. Check for proper use of the semicolon by searching for every occurrence.

4. A word of warning: Use global "search-and-replace" functions extremely carefully. (Try them first on a temporary backup copy of your paper.) You cannot simply search for "<period>-<space>-<space>" and globally replace it with "<period>-<space>," for instance, because the computer will replace every "<period>-<space>-<space>," including those that occur in charts or in other spots where you may not want changes made.

These final steps may sound time-consuming, but the computer does them quickly and easily.

Your paper is finished! Salute yourself for a job well done.

■■■ JOURNAL EXCERPTS

Editing

Session 18

In editing, I caught many tense shift problems, especially in sections dealing with historically distant treatises. I had to run through the whole paper once looking just at verb tenses.

Session 20

I found some real bloopers: I misdated a composer by a century; I inserted a quotation with no author cited and the wrong short title; there were inconsistencies in titles of primary sources cited indirectly (inevitable with foreign titles); there was a bibliography entry not cited after I finished all the cutting; I had a major source's name misspelled in all the parenthetical citations (Bettmann, spelled with one *n*)—global search was useful for this one; there was one quotation out of context, requiring revision of the surrounding passage. Also, I found that I had globally replaced *18th century* with *eighteenth century*, but this resulted in a substitution inside a quotation that contained the numerical form.

Only two major chunks needed to be shifted to new locations. I added some transitional sentences, or signposts; most important was a signpost statement saying that I would first show that the decline occurred and then explain why. I cut some repetitious restatements of the thesis.

■ ■ ■ EXERCISE 19

Editing

Identify the flaws in each of the following sentences, and name the editing principle(s) that should be applied. Then edit the sentences. Use the standard editing marks described in this chapter.

Since this exercise is a test of editing skills, edit these sentences; do not loosely paraphrase them. An editor does not rewrite extensively but, instead, strives to keep as much of the language and meaning of the original sentences as possible while eliminating wordiness, incoherence, and other flaws.

1. Not only does he attack the natives of Rome, but the foreigners as well.

2. They live in more expensive homes, drive more expensive cars, wear more expensive jewelry and clothing than do blue-collar workers.

3. When the group of pioneers arrived at Chimney Rock, after a series of battles, they decided that they must push farther westward.

4. Hitchcock's film, *North by Northwest*, is a masterpiece of action and suspense.

5. A first important step in accepting and successfully working with the adult learner in the university setting is acquiring an understanding of why adults are returning to the educational setting in such record numbers.

6. Many people are beginning to question the traditional medical treatments they customarily receive in America in an attempt to gain some level of control over their own health care in a profession dominated by males.

7. The teacher felt that his remuneration was insufficient.

8. The story's opening paragraph symbolically details how confined the narrator is by his environment simply by describing the neighborhood.

9. The stress caused by this medication was found to be very dangerous because of the fact that the woman's heart was already strained due to the changes of her body during the duration of the pregnancy.

10. Marketing analysts say that people expect quality, safety, and then price, in that order, when buying a new car.

CHAPTER 12

SPECIAL PROBLEMS IN RESEARCH WRITING

■ ■ ■ QUICK VIEW

Researchers sometimes encounter special problems in the course of their research: For example, a topic may turn out to be overwhelming, or a search for information may lead beyond what the library and the Web can supply. MLA-style papers may require more documentation than can be handled by parenthetical citations. At times the researcher must understand what constitutes "fair use" of copyrighted material. This chapter briefly addresses all these concerns.

TRYING TO DO TOO MUCH

The classic mistake that students make is choosing too ambitious a topic. Some students spend way too much time constructing imaginary plans for papers before ever looking at what the library has to offer. Soon the plans have sprouted subtopics within subtopics, like battlements and turrets attached to elaborate castles in the air. After a tremendously creative period of brainstorming and idea generating, these students trudge off to the library and find that their topics are completely unworkable, either because there is no information available or because there is too much.

The best way to avoid this pitfall is to heed the following advice: Go to the library and survey the available information while you are developing your topic. Be modest and humble in your choice of a subject. It is better to treat a small subject thoroughly than to treat a large subject superficially. Decide on the scope of your paper only after you have estimated the amount of information available. Choose a topic you can master thoroughly.

Gathering sources is another stage of research at which some students can begin to run amok. Turned loose to pursue a topic independently, they feel intoxicated by their freedom and try to include too many sources.

Be flexible rather than dogged at this stage. Perhaps your initial interest in medieval representations of unicorns (to take a really narrow example) turned out to be too limited; without scrapping what you have done so far, you could broaden the topic to medieval representations of mythological beasts in general or to medieval bestiaries.

In contrast, if you are swamped by material (as I was, to some degree, in compiling a bibliography on improvisation in the eighteenth century), then find a way of narrowing the topic by selecting one aspect, a narrower historical period, or a specific example. (I found that most sources discussed musical ornamentation as a form of improvisation; and by narrowing my definition of improvisation to exclude ornamentation, I was able to eliminate many of them.)

One thing is certain: Perfectionism will stop you cold at this point if you let it. It has been said that people who want every convenience in their dream house will never lay a foundation, much less build their house. And at this point you need to lay a foundation—a list of sources that will furnish you with knowledge on a specialized topic. You are about to become an expert. Approach the task patiently and realistically; remember to finish well ahead of deadlines. Make your perfectionism work for you, not against you.

SPECIAL PROBLEMS IN FINDING SOURCES

Finding Books Outside Your Library

Occasionally, a researcher wants to locate (or just verify the existence of) a book not owned by a local library or an article in a locally unavailable periodical. As an answer to this need, there are trade bibliographies and union catalogs, including many regional catalogs too numerous to list here. Average undergraduate researchers generally will never need to consult these books, since interlibrary loan librarians usually will carry out such searches.

Trade Bibliographies Trade bibliographies are book lists compiled primarily for booksellers and librarians. For a detailed explanation, see page 89. Here are the most important titles.

Books in Print

Cumulative Book Index

Union Catalogs A union catalog is a giant library catalog that lists the holdings of many, sometimes thousands, of cooperating libraries. Here are the most important ones.

National Union Catalog: A Cumulative Author List. A continuation (to 1983) of *National Union Catalog, Pre-1956 Imprints* (see below).

National Union Catalog: Books. A continuation (to the present) of *National Union Catalog: A Cumulative Author List.* Microfiche.

National Union Catalog, Pre-1956 Imprints (on-line).   An author catalog of
the Library of Congress and about a thousand other libraries in North
America. Comprehensive list of American books. Many mistakes; corrections listed in supplement. Complemented by the *MARC* and *REMARC*
databases, available on-line. (*REMARC* lists Library of Congress holdings
cataloged from 1897 to 1980. Besides listing recent books in foreign languages, *MARC* lists English language books cataloged by the Library of
Congress after 1968; it is updated monthly.)

Online Computer Library Center (OCLC) (on-line).   The largest union catalog; may be searched by author, title, Library of Congress call number,
ISBN number, or *OCLC* number. Much more efficient than the *National
Union Catalog*. Designed for librarians but sometimes available at public-
access terminals. Searching requires some acquired expertise; see the *OCLC
Searching Guide* generally found at public-access terminals, or ask a librarian
to search for you. *OCLC* is a standard tool for locating copies of books for
interlibrary loan. Begun in 1967, *OCLC* now has several thousand partici-
pating libraries. Its records should be regarded as comprehensive only from
the early 1970s on, though some libraries are retroactively entering books
they had already cataloged before joining the system. (See *WorldCat*, below.)

Research Libraries Information Network (RLIN) (on-line).   Less comprehensive than *OCLC*, requiring even more expertise to carry out searches. But
RLIN permits a greater variety of search techniques, such as keyword
searches. Like *OCLC*, *RLIN* is a standard tool for locating copies of books
not available locally.

Union List of Serials in Libraries of the United States and Canada.   The standard tool for locating a library that subscribes to a periodical not available
locally. Continued, for serials published after 1950, by *New Serial Titles: A
Union List of Serials Held by Libraries in the United States and Canada*.

WorldCat (on-line).   Based on the *OCLC* database, this worldwide library
catalog indexes over thirty-five million books. Covers dissertations. Particularly useful for tracking down early and rare sources, even manuscripts.

Special Ways of Finding Sources

This chapter has focused primarily upon carrying out subject searches in
catalogs and indexes. But some students may encounter special research problems that require special kinds of resources.

Conducting an Information Search by Mail and E-Mail   Sometimes, you
can gather a lot of information by correspondence. This technique will not work
for a short-term project; but if you have an entire quarter or an entire semester,
early inquiries may turn up results in time for use in the final draft.

I have had several students use imaginative and effective correspondence
methods. Word-processing programs allow the user, through what is called "mail
merge," to merge a form letter with a list of addressees so that the computer will
produce a stack of individualized letters of inquiry. One student used a form

letter of this sort to solicit research information from about three dozen area veterinarians.

One of my students wrote about the successful sales strategies of Mary Kay Cosmetics and sent a draft of her paper to the company's founder. Mary Kay wrote back within a week with detailed comments on the paper. (It's not hard to see why this energetic woman has been so successful.)

Journals often list the academic affiliations of their authors. Having noticed that the writer of a book on eighteenth-century music teaches at Indiana University, I visited the university's Web site, looked up his address, e-mailed him, and got some interesting hints for my paper on improvisation.

Information-gathering methods are limited only by your imagination. The Government Printing Office offers thousands of free publications. Private organizations, too, often provide information in pamphlets and free publications. *The Encyclopedia of Associations* (Detroit: Gale Research, updated annually) lists addresses and information about more than twelve thousand organizations devoted to special topics and interests.

Using Citation Indexes   Sometimes, a thorough search by subject and keywords fails to turn up an adequate list of sources. Let's say that you have found only one source that deals with precisely your topic. A citation index will let you find, year by year, sources that have cited that source.

A citation index is thus a strange sort of index; essentially, it is an index to footnotes. Its usefulness becomes apparent when you apply it to hard-to-research topics, because a given authority will be cited by other authorities working in the same field. If you then search the same citation index to find out who is citing those sources, you can generate a working bibliography even on the most unusual topic, though you will have to weed out quite a few unrelated sources that cited your original source only in passing.

A citation index can be surprisingly useful in the humanities, because by looking up, say, Plato, you can compile an extensive bibliography of authorities who cited Plato in any given year. And because citation indexes are interdisciplinary, they cross subject boundaries that other indexes might not cross.

Although citation indexes can sometimes produce magic solutions, they are generally used as a last resort. They are highly condensed, they use tiny print, and they require some practice. In academic subject areas, there are three citation indexes.

INTERNET

Arts and Humanities Citation Index (on-line)

Science Citation Index (on-line)

Social Sciences Citation Index (on-line)

Guides to Indexes

Another problem that sometimes crops up is that you know you wish to search for articles in a certain periodical but you don't know where to find an index to it. For example, you know that *Downbeat* is the standard periodical dealing with jazz, but you don't know if it is covered by the *Music Index*. What you need is a guide to indexing, one that lists periodicals by name and then lists indexes that cover them. One of the following guides should answer your question. (You may need to look in more than one.)

> *Chicorel's Index to Abstracting and Indexing Services*
>
> *OCLC database* (lists indexes on-line under entries for individual periodicals. See pg. 353, *WorldCat*)
>
> *Ulrich's International Periodicals Directory*
>
> *Standard Periodical Directory*

INTERNET

Using a Database Instead of a Card File for the Bibliography

If you are used to working with computers, you might consider using a database rather than note cards. Whether you choose the kind of database program found in most "office suite" software or more specialized software such as Pro-Cite or End-Note, database records can be sorted, marked, and formatted more handily than note cards.

Courtesy in Electronic Communication

Gathering information over the Internet and the Web often involves person-to-person communication through e-mail, newsgroup postings, and the like. The speed of such communication means that misunderstandings can arise like brush-fires. When you write e-mail or postings, observe good "Netiquette" through courtesy, respect, impartiality, and restraint. (See p. 41 on the ethics of the research writer.)

INTERNET

COPYRIGHT LAW AND THE ETHICS OF RESEARCH

The legal and practical problems in resolving current problems such as software copyright violations are complex, but the *ethical* aspects of respecting intellectual property rights are simple. For the student concerned about the ethics of library research, I offer these thoughts. The essential question for a library researcher is "To what extent may I mechanically duplicate the research writings of another person without violating that person's intellectual property rights?"

In the United States, intellectual property rights are governed by the Copyright Act of 1976 (Public Law 94-553), which took effect on January 1, 1978. The fundamental principle of this new law is elegantly simple: Copyright, or intellectual ownership, begins the moment a new creative work is recorded in some tangible form. Thus, copyright does not depend upon any kind of legal registration—though, of course, published materials are registered for copyright in order to protect them. The crucial thing is that *the moment you express a new thought on paper in your own words, that thought and those words become your intellectual property.* If you simply diagram a new dance step on a cocktail napkin, that dance step becomes your intellectual property the moment you create it. Any tangible form of recording a creative work, such as the tape recording of a song on a cassette, creates this intellectual property right.

However, some forms of expression may not constitute a sufficient element of creativity to justify copyright protection. For example, a song can be copyrighted, but an *arrangement* of an existing song cannot be copyrighted unless it is so strikingly original that it constitutes a new creative expression in its own right. Consequently, a judge may have to rule upon the artistic merits of a song arrangement to decide whether it can be copyrighted. The complexities of this relatively new law are still being thrashed out in the courts. For concerned college research writers, the key issues revolve around the use of photocopies and the question of what is known as "fair use" of copyrighted material.

Although the concept of fair use is in a state of flux as the lawyers battle over the fine points, the main thing you need to know is that a researcher may freely make single photocopies of copyrighted material as long as the copy is meant to be used only for research purposes. Fair use is a legal concept that becomes an issue to a research writer only when he or she submits writing for publication. If the piece is accepted for publication, the publisher must decide whether any of the quotations or other borrowed materials require permissions from the original copyright holders. Quotation without permission is legal only if the writer has made fair use of the material. Short quotations or small quantities of pictorial illustrations to support an argument or to illustrate a critical review are examples of fair use. But the concept of fair use can become complex if the borrowing could affect the market for the original work, if the amount borrowed is substantial, or if the original is misrepresented in some way.

In general, the changes in copyright law and the courts' interpretations of that law have had a greater impact upon teachers than upon students. The criterion of educational fair use suggests, for instance, that an instructor may make multiple copies of copyrighted material for class use only if the material is brief; if the material is not something like an exercise that is used and then discarded; if the instructor thinks of doing it spontaneously at a time when it is too late to secure permission from the copyright holder; if the students pay no more than the copying cost; and if the instructor distributes this material only once. (The assumption is that there will be plenty of time to get permission for subsequent copying.) A customized anthology of copyrighted material is clearly *not* fair use.

So you needn't worry about the technical concept of fair use until you have your paper accepted for publication. In your research you may make photocopies freely to help you gather your sources. If you follow the guidelines noted in this book about avoiding plagiarism and using sources well, you need not worry about the ethics of borrowing material for your paper. In summary, use your sources honestly and use them well.

DOCUMENTATION USING ENDNOTES OR FOOTNOTES

If you must use notes, the *MLA Handbook* recommends endnotes on a separate page or pages at the end of the paper. *Use footnotes (that is, notes at the bottom of each page) only if told to do so by your instructor.* The use of endnotes *throughout* the paper is treated in the *MLA Handbook* in Appendix B; the use of occasional endnotes with parenthetical documentation is very briefly discussed in the *MLA Handbook* in section 5.5. The following tips on format apply to both cases; but note that if you use endnotes for all your documentation, a separate list of works cited may not be necessary. Check with your instructor.

Superscripts in the Body of the Paper

Insert a superscript number, not preceded by a space, at the end of the sentence, phrase, or clause that contains the citation. (Normally, a citation occurs at the end of the sentence, but see Chapter 7, p. 167, for exceptions.) In typewritten text, manually roll the paper down half a line in order to raise the superscript number; in word-processed text, choose the appropriate menu item for superscripts.

Number the superscripts consecutively throughout your paper. Since inserting a new note forces you to renumber the entire sequence—a process that can lead to confusion and mistakes—avoid inserting notes until you prepare the final draft. Some word processors have automatic footnote and endnote systems that renumber superscripts each time you add a new citation. But check your citation system to make sure that it handles notes appropriately. (Some systems use tiny fonts for superscript numbers and texts, other systems allow only footnotes, and still others allow only endnotes.)

Form for Footnotes and Endnotes

Endnotes should start on a new page, numbered like the pages that precede it. Use the centered title "Notes," without underlining or quotation marks. (See the sample page of endnotes in Jill Colak's paper in Chapter 7.) Endnotes and footnotes differ from bibliography entries primarily in the way they are punctuated. A typical bibliography entry breaks a source listing into three parts separated by periods: author, title, and publication data. An endnote, in contrast, is punctuated like a sentence, with a single period at the end; publication information is tucked into parentheses.

Sample Bibliography Entry Listing a Book

Bailey, Derek. <u>Musical Improvisation: Its Nature and Practice in Music</u>. Englewood Cliffs, NJ: Prentice, 1980.

Sample Endnote Citing a Book

[1]Derek Bailey, <u>Musical Improvisation: Its Nature and Practice in Music</u> (Englewood Cliffs, NJ: Prentice, 1980) 139.

Notice several other differences in form: The bibliography entry uses hanging indentation, but the endnote indents the first line and runs the other lines flush with the margin. The bibliography entry lists the last name first, for purposes of alphabetization; the endnote lists the author's name in normal order. Finally, the bibliography entry refers to the entire source, but the endnote cites a specific page.

An endnote citing a periodical article is also punctuated like a sentence, and the page numbers refer to a specific passage rather than to the entire source. Compare the following examples.

Sample Bibliography Entry Listing a Journal Article

> Swain, Joseph. "Form and Function of the Classical Cadenza." <u>Journal of Musicology</u> 6 (1988): 27–59.

Sample Endnote Citing a Journal Article

> [2]Joseph Swain, "Form and Function of the Classical Cadenza," <u>Journal of Musicology</u> 6 (1988): 28–29.

For guidance on the format of endnotes that refer to other kinds of sources, see the *MLA Handbook* (Appendix B).

Later Endnotes to a Source Already Cited

If you are using endnotes with parenthetical documentation, there will be no later endnotes to a source already cited; all subsequent citations will appear in parentheses. If you are using the nonstandard variation of the MLA format that employs endnotes throughout the paper, the endnotes should contain the same type of short citation described in Chapter 7 (pp. 164–167).

Here are two examples.

> [3]Swain 32.

> [4]Bailey 140.

Do not use the abbreviations *ibid.*, *loc. cit.*, and *op. cit.*

Placement of Footnotes

Remember: Use *endnotes* unless your instructor specifically requires footnotes. The first footnote on a page should begin four spaces below the last line of text. Single-space within footnotes, but double-space between them. If a footnote spills over onto the next page, double-space after the last line of text on the new page, insert a solid line, double-space again, and continue the note. Footnotes for the new page should come immediately after the continuation of the note from the previous page.

If you are forced to use footnotes in preparing a typed final draft, type all the footnotes first to see how many lines each one requires. Then, before you type each page, make a faint pencil line near the foot of the page to show how much space you need to leave for footnotes. Otherwise, you will find yourself having to retype pages because you have failed to leave enough space.

Some word processors allow you to enter footnotes in the body of your paper; the word processor will automatically separate these notes and place them appropriately at the bottoms of your pages. But before you decide to use this feature, run a few sample pages to be sure that the word processor formats the notes correctly.

Using Endnotes with Parenthetical Documentation

Even in a paper using standard MLA format with parenthetical documentation, you may use endnotes for two purposes:

1. to provide bibliographical information that is too long for parentheses
2. to provide an explanation that would disrupt the continuity of your paper

The *MLA Handbook* suggests that you avoid long, essaylike notes. If an explanatory digression is necessary, you should find a way to fit it into the main body of your text. However, special problems occasionally require brief explanations that would be distracting if they were included in your text. For example, once while writing about a collection of short stories by Max Beerbohm, I had to draw the reader's attention to the complex publication history of a collection to which Beerbohm added a new story years after the book's first publication—a story that clashed with its companion stories, many critics felt. A note combining bibliographical information with a brief explanatory comment allowed me to avoid having the body of my paper go off on a tangent. The note looked like this:

[5]Seven Men and Two Others (1950; Oxford: Oxford UP, 1980) differs from the original Seven Men (1919) in that it contains the story "Felix Argallo and Walter Ledgett," originally published as "Not That I Would Boast" in the London Mercury (May 1927: 27–43). Although it was added later, this story matches its companions thematically.

■ ■ ■ EXERCISE 20
Carrying Out a Special Information Search

1. Find the e-mail address for at least one of the authors you cite in your paper (or, if that is inappropriate for some reason, have your instructor give you the name of a source to track down). Write a brief, courteous, easy-to-answer e-mail message inquiring about something specific related to the paper you are writing. Submit it to your instructor before sending it. (Hint: Journal articles often indicate a source's academic affiliation. Once you know the writer's academic institution [if there is one], it is easy to visit the college or university Web or Internet site and to

consult the faculty directory. Remember, too, that most academic organizations publish directories of their members.)

2. Create a postal mailing list (not e-mail) for three to five sources (individuals or organizations) on your topic or a topic assigned by your instructor. Write a brief, courteous, easy-to-answer letter inquiring about something specific related to the paper you are writing. Submit it to your instructor before sending it to the members of your mailing list. (Hint: Be sure to consult the guides to organizations mentioned in this chapter.)

CHAPTER 13

MECHANICS

■ ■ ■ QUICK VIEW

This chapter explains the research paper's mechanical details, such as its physical appearance; its handling of names, numbers, and dates; its punctuation; and its page layout. Differences between the major formats are highlighted to save you the trouble of searching for details in other style manuals. For example: Should you use the full name of an author whom you mention not in a parenthetical citation but in one of your sentences? (Answer: In MLA format, yes, use the full name when you first mention the author; in APA format, no, always use the surname by itself.)

The section on punctuation is specifically designed to focus on the most common mistakes made by college research writers. You should not skip it, especially since punctuation conventions in research writing differ somewhat from the conventions you may encounter in your everyday reading.

ALL FORMATS: General Appearance

Just as a job applicant should be well dressed, your paper should make a pleasing first impression. Use an old ribbon for making drafts, but run the final draft with a fresh ribbon; if possible, use a laser printer.

Use good-quality paper, thirteen-pound bond or heavier; never use light-weight onionskin paper. If you must use erasable paper, or if you have to use a lot of correction fluid to make a presentable draft, get your instructor's permission to hand in a photocopy instead of the original. (Erasable paper should not be handed in because it inevitably gets smudged.)

Perhaps these physical aspects of the paper seem trivial; you feel that your audience should evaluate your paper on the basis of its content rather than its appearance. But physical details may unconsciously affect an instructor's evaluation, even if he or she promises to grade only on the basis of content.

If you are using a word processor, always choose a nonproportional font rather than a proportional one. To tell which kind you are using, print out some sample text. If an *i* or an *l* occupies as much horizontal space as an *m* or a *w*, the font is nonproportional. If an *i* or an *l* occupies less space than an *m* or a *w*, the font is proportional, and you should choose another. The reason is that proportional fonts make it difficult to evaluate mechanical details. For instance, many proportional fonts print spaces as units smaller than normal characters.

You should always avoid special fonts such as script typefaces that resemble handwriting or sans serif fonts that resemble simple block lettering. They make the typescript hard to read and may irritate your instructor. Your goal is to eliminate all distractions and to make the paper as easy to read as possible. The ideal font should be either ten or twelve characters to the inch, nonproportional, with serifs. Courier is an example of a good, easy-to-read font.

Never use a justified (straight-edged) right margin. Word-processing software inserts spaces to achieve this effect, and it often puts spaces in awkward spots, such as inside parenthetical citations. This presentation makes it look as though you have committed mechanical errors in your handling of the paper's format.

MLA FORMAT MECHANICS

The *MLA Handbook* provides fairly detailed guidance in its section on mechanics (Chapter 2). It discusses spelling and hyphenation; punctuation; italics; names, numbers, and titles; quotations; and languages other than English. Instead of repeating the handbook's treatment of all these topics, I will give solutions to the most common mistakes writers make. For more detailed instructions, refer to the *MLA Handbook*, particularly for rules governing the handling of sources in languages other than English, a topic too complex to discuss here.

Corrections

If your paper is word processed, reprint any pages on which you made corrections. If your paper is typed, and if your instructor allows last-minute changes, a very brief handwritten correction may be made in ink above a mistake. Below the line, put a caret (^) indicating the insertion point. A page with many corrected mistakes should be retyped.

Fasteners

The finished product should be fastened with a simple paper clip—no plastic binders, folders, or staples that would make the paper inconvenient to handle. If you use a paper clip, your instructor can easily disassemble your paper to compare passages or to lay the works-cited list to one side for easy reference.

Spelling and Hyphenation

If you frequently misspell words, you should use an automatic spell checker on all your written work. But be sure to review the discussion of its limitations in Chapter 11.

Most word processors can automatically hyphenate words at the end of lines; however, you should turn off the automatic hyphenation. The only really reliable guide to hyphenating is a desk-sized dictionary; many automatic hyphenators perform the job incorrectly. Also, papers without hyphenation are easier to read.

Punctuation

Colon

Problems

1. The colon is easy to confuse with the semicolon.
2. The colon is easy to misuse when you are introducing an example, list, specification, elaboration, or quotation.

Solutions

1. Memorize the rules for correct use of the semicolon (p. 367). Use the colon only to separate volume numbers from page numbers, to separate titles from subtitles, and to serve as a sign introducing an example, list, specification, elaboration, or quotation.

2. When using a colon to introduce something, make sure that the colon follows a *complete main clause*.

Incorrect Example: The cargo bay contained: three instrument clusters, a telescope, and a portable hoist. [The colon is preceded by a sentence fragment.]

Correct Example: The cargo bay contained several items: three instrument clusters, a telescope, and a portable hoist. [The colon is preceded by a clause that could stand alone as a complete sentence.]

When it introduces a long quotation, the colon may be followed by either a capital or a lowercase letter. A single space should always follow a colon.

Comma

Problem

The mistake that students make most often is to confuse the compound sentence, which uses a comma, with the compound verb construction, which doesn't.

Solution

Check to see whether you have a compound sentence or compound verb construction.

Compound sentence: The exploration party [first subject] eventually found [first verb] the base camp, and they [second subject] rested [second verb] overnight before going on.

Compound verb construction: The exploration party [subject] eventually found [first verb] the base camp and rested [second verb] overnight before going on.

Exception: When the main clauses in a compound sentence are very short, you may omit the comma.

See a standard handbook for the fine points of comma usage.

Dash

Problems

1. The dash is often overused or used inappropriately.

2. The dash is often typed incorrectly.

Solutions

1. Use the dash only to set off emphatic parentheses (strong interruptions in the flow of thought), parenthetical lists with internal commas, or summarizing appositives.

Correct Example (emphatic parenthesis): The notion that a wealth of quoted material strengthens the arguer's case—true though that notion may be—overlooks the distracting, disunified effect of strings of quotations.

Correct Example (parenthetical list with internal commas): Many music historians—including Ferand, Thomas, and Neumann—focus primarily upon improvised ornamentation.

Correct Example (summarizing appositive): Excessive cost, inefficient procurement, and tardy deliveries—all these features of the present system contradict wise operating principles.

2. Type the dash as two adjacent hyphens running flush against the words on each side.

Ellipsis Mark

Problems

1. The ellipsis mark is often typed incorrectly.

2. The ellipsis mark is often overused.

Solutions

1. An ellipsis mark consists of *three periods* inside square brackets with a space after the first and second periods.

   Exception a: If the ellipsis occurs immediately after the end of a sentence, place the ellipsis mark after the period that ends the quoted sentence.

Exception b: When omitting a line or more of poetry in a block quotation, type a line of spaced periods where the omission occurs.

2. Use the ellipsis mark whenever you omit material *within* a quoted sentence. But avoid overusing ellipsis marks at the beginning or end of quoted passages. If a passage is clearly less than a complete sentence, use no initial or terminal ellipsis mark. If the passage *can stand alone* as a complete sentence in its quoted form but actually was a longer sentence in the original source, show the omission with an ellipsis mark.

3. Use "hard spaces" (see your word processor's documentation) to prevent an ellipsis mark from breaking awkwardly at the end of a line.

Hyphen

Problem

Writers may have difficulty distinguishing between compound adjectives, which often use the hyphen, and phrases, which don't. Check to see whether your construction is a compound adjective or a phrase.

Solutions

Compound adjective: We studied the twentieth-century novel.

Phrase: We studied the novel's development in the twentieth century.

1. When in doubt about whether to hyphenate a compound adjective, use an unabridged dictionary to see whether it is listed in hyphenated form. For more detailed guidance, see the *MLA Handbook* (secs. 2.2.6 and 2.2.10).

2. Generally, the hyphen is *not* used with compounds containing *-ly* adverbs (*highly motivated*) or *too, very,* or *much* (*very informed*).

3. The hyphen is used to form a compound adjective that precedes the noun it modifies: *role-playing exercise,* but *an exercise in role playing;* a *one-by-one analysis,* but *we analyzed them one by one.*

4. When several hyphenated compounds share a common base, the base can be omitted in every compound but the last: *1-, 2-, and 3-minute presentations.*

Italics and Bold Fonts

Problem

Student papers prepared by word processing often use italics and boldface type inappropriately.

Solutions

1. Italics and bold fonts should never be used without permission from your instructor. Use underlining or italics but never both in the same paper. The reason is that research paper conventions are based on the preparation of typed manuscripts that may be edited for publication. Every occurrence of a special font such as bold typeface and every

occurrence of italics mixed with underlining calls for special editorial handling—a time-consuming process.

2. The *MLA Handbook* recommends underlining the spaces between words in titles, though it leaves open the option of broken underlining (spaces not underlined).

Parentheses and Square Brackets

Problem

Parentheses and square brackets are often confused with each other.

Solutions

1. Use parentheses (a) for setting off parenthetical documentation and (b) for setting off sentence interrupters that are too emphatic for commas. (Dashes and parentheses are roughly equivalent in their degree of emphasis. Let other nearby punctuation govern your choice.)

2. Use brackets (a) for any interpolations (insertions) that you make in quoted material or documentation, (b) for parentheses within parentheses, and (c) for missing items of information in bibliography entries.

Correct Example (missing information in bibliography entry): Ferand, Ernest T[homas] [when the title page lists only Ernest T. Ferand]

Quotation Marks

Problems

1. Quotation marks are often incorrectly placed when used with other marks of punctuation.

2. Writers sometimes are confused about the use of American (" ") and British (' ') quotation marks.

Solutions

1. *General Rule:* At the end of a quotation, the quotation mark *follows* a period or a comma but *precedes* a colon or semicolon. The quotation mark *precedes* question marks or exclamation points unless they are part of the quoted material.

   Exception a: When the end of a quotation is followed by parenthetical documentation, the period comes after the parenthesis.

Correct Example: Herbert Gardner says that the snowfall was "the heaviest in years" (112).

   Exception b: Parenthetical documentation that follows a quoted question or exclamation requires an added period.

Correct Example: James suddenly said, "What a damned fool I've been!" (12).

2. Use American (" ") rather than British (' ') quotation marks. In quoting from British texts, convert British conventions to American ones. For example, a quotation inside a block quotation should be set off with American quotation marks, even when you are using a source punctuated in the British style.

Semicolon

Problem

The semicolon is often misused, creating sentence fragments.

Solution

Use the semicolon only where a period could otherwise serve to separate two closely related sentences.

Incorrect Example: Spending on highway construction will reach a new peak; the highest per capita expenditure in ten years.

Correct Example: The under-twenty population continued to increase into the 1990s; however, enrollment began to decline in 1987.

Exception: You may use the semicolon to separate items in a long series when the items contain commas.

Correct Example: The president's itinerary included Denver, Colorado; Des Moines, Iowa; and Springfield, Missouri.

Names, Numbers, and Dates

Names   The first time you mention a person in the text of your paper (not in the parenthetical documentation), use the person's name in full. After that, use the last name only. In your text and bibliography, omit titles (Sir, Mr., Mrs., Dr.).

Although the *MLA Handbook* gives some instructions on handling the names of titled members of the nobility (sec. 4.6.1), its advice does not resolve the question of how to document a source whose surname differs from the name given after the inheritance of a peerage. A good example is George Gordon, who became Lord Byron after he inherited a family title. Common sense suggests the following solution. Since in the body of the paper you will refer to the author simply as Byron, it would be confusing to cite his writings parenthetically by using the name Gordon. And since parenthetical citations should match the alphabetized list of works cited, you should list the poet's writings under the name Byron, with the author's full name given as it appears in standard reference works: Byron, George Gordon, sixth Baron.

But students of English literature and history should be warned that British social customs set up pitfalls for unwary Americans. For example, Lady Mary Wortley Montagu inherited her title, but she married a commoner named Montagu; thus Lady Mary is correct, but Lady Montagu is not. A useful explanation of British titles appears in Donald Greene's *Age of Exuberance* ([New York: Random, 1970], 53–55). In any case, the *MLA Handbook*'s rule of omitting titles must be tempered with sensitivity to traditional rules of etiquette.

Numbers   Use Arabic numerals, not Roman numerals, throughout your paper. (See "Guide to Converting Roman Numerals" in Chapter 7.) *Exceptions:* Roman numerals are used for outline headings and for individuals in a series (Richard III). Lowercase Roman numerals are often used for page numbers in introductions and prefaces.

In the body of your paper, spell out numbers that can be written in one or two words. You may mix numerals and words in expressing very large numbers (3.2 million). If your paper requires the frequent use of numbers, use numerals for all technical units of measurement. When using symbols ($, %), always pair them with numerals rather than words. Do not begin a sentence with a symbol or numeral; recast the sentence if necessary. To avoid distracting the reader, avoid shifting forms when comparing numbers. For example, "The study found that 5 out of 45 respondents had missed from 3 to 12 weeks of work" is correct, even though it breaks the rule of spelling out numbers that can be expressed in a word or two.

When indicating ranges of numbers (as, for example, in citing the pages of an article), always use two digits for the second number if it is greater than 9, unless three or more digits are needed to prevent ambiguity (2–6, 9–13, 68–93, 124–48; but 196–212, 1225–304).

Dates   In the bibliography, always give dates in the form 3 May 1955 rather than May 3, 1955. In the body of your paper, you may use either form, but be consistent. Centuries should be spelled out in lowercase letters; decades may be represented in words (the nineteen-fifties, the fifties) or numbers (the 1950s, the '50s [note that no apostrophe appears before the *s*]).

When indicating a range of years, write the beginning and ending dates in full unless they fall within the same century (1660–1798, but 1803–12).

Titles

The title (and subtitle, if there is one) of your paper should be neither underlined nor enclosed within quotation marks. Follow the normal conventions of capitalization: Capitalize the first letter of the first word in the title and subtitle, plus the first letter of all other words except articles (*a, an, the*), prepositions (*of, by, from,* and the like), coordinating conjunctions (*and, but, or, nor, for*), and the *to* in infinitive verbs. Capitalize words that follow hyphens. Use a colon to separate the title from the subtitle.

Capitalize the title of a work mentioned in your paper according to the same conventions, even if it is capitalized in some other way on its title page or in a list of sources in some non-MLA format. (But note the different capitalization conventions for titles in languages such as Latin and German [see *MLA Handbook* sec. 2.8].)

A title is usually set off with quotation marks if the source is short or has been published within another work. *Exception:* Underline the title of a long work, such as a novel or a play, that has been published in an anthology. A title is usually set off with underlining if the source is long or has been published separately. The following list illustrates common types of sources and how to handle them. (See also p. 167.)

Underlining	*Quotation Marks*
Book titles	Chapter titles
Periodical titles	Short story titles
Play titles	Article titles
Titles of long poems published separately	Titles of short poems published in collections
Album (CD or cassette) titles	Song titles
TV show titles	Individual TV episode titles
Pamphlet titles	

Ambiguous Cases   One of Pope's satires frequently appears in collections, yet it was initially published separately, and its middling length does not clearly indicate which category it should fall into. Separate publication suggests that the title should normally be underlined, but it frequently appears in both forms: "The Rape of the Lock" and The Rape of the Lock.

Exceptions   The following titles are neither underlined nor enclosed in quotation marks.

1. *Generic titles.* Certain titles are generic because they are all-purpose descriptive words, just as a package of generic sugar might be labeled merely "Sugar." Examples are portions of books (chapter 5, introduction, preface, act 3) and books and musical works identified by form and number (Symphony No. 5, Juvenal's fifth satire) or by general description (Clinton's inaugural address).

2. *Sacred writings.* Some examples are the Bible, Genesis, the Koran, and the Talmud. (For the special abbreviations used in documenting biblical quotations, see the *MLA Handbook* [secs. 6.7.1 and 5.4.8].)

3. *Names of series of books and names of editions.* Some examples are the Physics Monographs Series and the Twickenham Edition of the Poems of Alexander Pope.

Titles Within Titles   Sometimes the title of a long work contains the title of a short work (see example 1). Sometimes the title of a short work contains the title of another short work (see example 2). Sometimes a short work contains the title of a long work (see example 3). And sometimes the title of a long work appears within the title of another long work (see example 4).

Example 1.   "The Aleph" and Other Stories

Example 2.   "Characterization in 'The Dead' "

Example 3.   "Moby Dick as a Satire"

Example 4.   A Reader's Guide to Paradise Lost

The MLA format handles the fourth type of title within a title in a way that strikes many readers as odd: The title of *Paradise Lost* reverts to nonunderlined type. Although this looks unsightly in a typed paper, remember that the convention derives from manuscripts edited for publication. A typesetter will convert the underlining to italics if the paper is published.

Tables and Figures

Insert a table or an illustration in the text of the paper, placing it as close as possible to the passage that it illustrates. A table should be preceded by a title (such as Table 1) and a descriptive caption, typed flush left. Under the table, type "Source:" followed by the author's name (in normal order) and publication information. An illustration should be followed by a numerical title (Fig. 1), a short description, and a source citation. See the *MLA Handbook* (sec. 3.7) for examples.

APA FORMAT MECHANICS:
Differences from MLA Format

Corrections

If you are handing in a word-processing printout, correct all mistakes on disk and print out a fresh copy; make no handwritten corrections. If you are handing in a typed manuscript, you may use tape, correction fluid, or correction paper to cover and type over errors. You may type a correction directly over the line or word to be corrected. If the page requires many corrections, retype it.

Punctuation

Colon When a colon introduces a complete sentence, its first letter should be capitalized.

Hyphen In mathematical formulas, put a space before and after a hyphen to use it as a minus sign.

Italics, Bold Fonts, and Underlining Like the MLA format, APA uses underlining to represent italics. If you use a word processor, do not use the italic or bold fonts.

Writers in psychology and the social sciences frequently use underlining for some additional purposes: to indicate genus and species names; to highlight a technical term the first time it is used; to mark some mathematical symbols; to mark some test scores and scales; and to indicate the volume numbers in reference lists.

When using underlining to emphasize part of a quotation, put the words "italics added," not underlined and not in quotation marks, in square brackets after the emphasized passage.

In published papers, symbols for vectors are typeset in bold typeface. In a typed or word-processed paper, indicate bold typeface by drawing a wavy line under the letter or symbol.

Parentheses and Square Brackets   Use parentheses enclosing lowercase letters to set off items within a sentence or paragraph.

> The subject was asked to evaluate (a) the product's flavor, (b) its appearance, and (c) its texture.

In contrast, a series of paragraphs listing related items—such as a set of conclusions or the steps in a process—may be set off with Arabic numerals not enclosed in parentheses.

> 1. Faculty participants showed the greatest diversity of response to the survey's questions about. . . .
> 2. Student participants displayed a narrower range. . . .
> 3. Staff participants most consistently tended. . . .

A complete sentence enclosed in parentheses should contain a period inside the parentheses. (It should look like this.) A fragment inside parentheses should not conclude with a period; it should be tucked into the sentence (like this) and placed before the punctuation (like this).

Names and Numbers

Names   In the text of your paper, refer to an author by surname only. *Exceptions:* Use an author's initial or initials to distinguish between authors with identical surnames or to identify the source of a personal communication. (See p. 200.)

Numbers   In contrast to the choices offered in the *MLA Handbook*, the APA *Publication Manual* states a single rule: Use words to represent numbers below 10; use numerals for all numbers 10 and above.

But the APA editors note several exceptions. They suggest the use of numerals to represent numbers below 10 in the following instances:

> 1. groups of related numbers (4 of 21 cases, lines 2 and 13)
> 2. units of measurement (a 2-mg dose, 5 cm long)
> 3. mathematical functions, ratios, fractions, decimals, percentages, percentiles, and quartiles (divided by 2, in the 2nd quartile, nearly 5%)
> 4. scores and points on a scale (rated 3 on a 5-point scale)
> 5. money, time, age, population samples or numbers of participants (received $3, in 3 weeks, after 2 hours, the 3-year-olds, 5 subjects)
> 6. specific places in numbered series (Group 4, Figure 6, page 8)

Titles

The capitalization of a title depends upon its place of appearance. In the *body of your paper*, capitalize according to these rules.

> 1. Capitalize all words of four letters or more, excluding conjunctions, articles, and short prepositions.
> 2. Capitalize the second word in hyphenated compounds.

In the *list of references*, capitalize according to these rules.

1. Capitalize only the first letter of (a) the first word, (b) a word following a colon or dash, and (c) proper nouns.

2. Do not capitalize the second word in hyphenated compounds.

Mathematical Equations

Simple mathematical equations may be incorporated directly into lines of typed text as long as they do not project above or below the line. Display (set off) complex equations as independent blocks of text, with quadruple spacing above and below. Display simple equations in this fashion, too, if they must be numbered for later reference.

Some typed characters may be ambiguous: "X" may stand for a variable or for the multiplication sign, "l" may stand for the number one or "el," and so on. Therefore, identify an ambiguous character by providing a circled label, like this: χ.

Tables and Figures

Short tables may be incorporated into the body of your paper. Long tables and all figures should appear on separate pages following the page on which the table or figure is first mentioned. A caption should be typed below the figure.

Use a table only for crucial data, and design it carefully to reveal the data's significance clearly. The paper's text should discuss the table's highlights and general significance, not every item in the table. Use Arabic numerals to label all tables in order of appearance: "Tables 1, 2, 3, 4," not "Tables 1a, 1b, 2a, 2b." In your text, refer to a table by name: "Table 2," not "the table above."

Whereas a table is typeset and is therefore relatively inexpensive to produce, figures are artwork—graphs, diagrams, charts, or photographs—that must be reproduced photographically when published. Since they are expensive, figures are not often used in APA journals. In student work, where publication cost is not a factor, figures can be used more freely. An effective figure can be physically pasted onto a page and then photocopied; or a figure can be created with computer graphics programs, scanners, and clip art. Most word processors now have desktop-publishing features that allow graphics to be incorporated directly into the body of a paper. Like tables, figures are given numeric labels (Figure 1) in order of appearance; type a figure caption below the figure.

For more specific guidance on designing and incorporating tables and figures, see the APA *Publication Manual* (secs. 3.62–3.86).

CBE FORMAT MECHANICS:
Differences from MLA Format

Punctuation

Ellipsis Mark   Use an entire line of spaced periods to show that you have omitted one or more paragraphs from a block quotation.

Italics and Bold Fonts   In a word-processed paper, you may use italic type; in a typed paper, use underlining to indicate material that should be italicized if your paper were to be published. Use italics or underlining for the words *see* and *see also* in cross-referencing. Underline genus and species names, mathematical constants or unknowns, and other specialized scientific expressions described in the *CBE Manual* (169–171).

Bold type should be used for a vector in mathematical expressions. In a word-processed paper, you may use bold type; in a typed paper, indicate bold type by manually drawing wavy lines beneath the bold characters.

Period   A raised period without a space on either side may be used for some special purposes in scientific papers, especially as a multiplication symbol. In a row of three with spaces, raised periods may be used to indicate an ellipsis in mathematical formulas.

Quotation Marks   The *CBE Manual* recommends placing quotation marks before or after other punctuation at the end of a quotation, depending on whether the other punctuation was or was not present in the original passage. Here are some examples of acceptable punctuation.

No period in original: Poindexter called this "the delayed-impact effect".

Period added: He reacted by shouting "Foul!".

Period in original: He is reported to have said "The trial period is over."

▪▪▪ EXERCISE 21

Mechanical Errors

Edit the following page from a sample research paper. It contains many examples of mechanical errors, virtually all of which are covered in this chapter. (A few of the errors require familiarity with the features of MLA format covered in Chapter 7.)

Professor Maner

John Williamson

English 251

May 25, 1999

Marianne Moore's Use Of Irony

Like the plants and animals she wrote about, Marianne Moore's poems are elegantly designed. She disliked unneccessary fuss, and she found ways to communicate concisely, leaping from one point to another rather than moving in a series of tiny steps. Ironic humor was one of her favorite devices because: like a knight on a chess-board, irony jumps over obstacles, combining indirection with economy of movement. Moore deserves to be recognized as one of the great ironists of twentieth century poetry.

Although Moore is often praised for her mastery of technique; her irony is seldom discussed. Blackmur is one of the few critics who has commented on her use of quoted material to achieve just the right ironic tone. Moore, he points out, "...resorts, or rises...to the said thing, captures it, sets it apart, points and polishes it to bring out just the special quality she heard in it." [Blackmur, 77] A good example occurs in Moore's poem, "Silence". The language she quotes is incisive and true, but it is subjected to ironic undercutting in the final line. To understand Moore's irony in this poem, the reader must pay close attention to tone, and notice how the tone is reinforced by changes of rythm.

"Silence" opens with a regular iambic line, then moves into prose rythms with the quotation. It *sounds* like a quotation, and it is fairly accurate, however Moore has altered it to make it sound life-like. Her retouched version is more ambigous than the original, and is more convincingly "real" in its slightly awkward phrasing.

CREDITS

Page 44, From Margot Peters, "The Phonological Structure of James Joyce's 'Araby'" *Language and Style* 6 (1973): 135–36. Reprinted by permission of the author. Page 45, From Lewis H. Lapham, Michael Pollan and Eric Etheridge, *The Harper's Index Book*, Owl-Holt, 1987. Copyright © 1987 by Harper's Magazine. All rights reserved. Reproduced by special permission. Page 80, Fig. 4.7 Reprinted from *Humanities Index* with permission from H.W. Wilson Company. Page 105, From *Louis Armstrong: An American Genius* by James Lincoln Collier. Copyright © 1983 by James Lincoln Collier. Reprinted by permission of Oxford University Press. Pages 106, 107, From *The Complete Poems 1927–1979* by Elizabeth Bishop. Copyright © 1979, 1983 by Alice Helen Methfessel. Reprinted by permission of Farrar, Straus & Giroux, Inc. Page 109, Copyright page from *The Dubliners*. Reprinted by permission of Penguin Books. Page 128, From David Goodstein, "Pariah Science: Whatever Happened to Cold Fusion?" *American Scholar* 63 (1994). Reprinted by permission of the author. Pages 218–220, From *Wonderful Life: The Burgess Shale and the Nature of History* by Stephen Jay Gould. Copyright © 1989 by Stephen Jay Gould. Reprinted by permission of W.W. Norton & Company, Inc. Page 222, From *Journal of the History of Biology* 24 (No. 2), 1991. Reprinted with permission from Kluwer Academic Publishers. Page 287, Fig. 9.2 From *The Columbia Guide to Standard English* by Kenneth G. Wilson. Copyright © 1993 Columbia University Press. Reprinted with the permission of the publisher. Page 296, Fig. 9.3 From *Psychological Science* 4:3 (May 1993). Reprinted with permission from Blackwell Publishers. Page 297, From James R. Lackner, "Orientation and Movement in Unusual Force Environments," *Psychological Science* 4:3 (May 1993). Reprinted with permission from the author. Pages 299–300, From Jorunn Sundgot-Borgen, "Eating Disorders in Female Athletes," *Sports Medicine*, Vol. 17, No. 3, 1994. Reprinted with permission from the author.

INDEX

EXAMPLES OF FOUR DOCUMENTATION FORMATS

CBE numbered-source format, citations (see pages 227–228)

Like the patient with Tourette's syndrome who saw his ailment as somewhat comic,[1] Skloot said chronic fatigue syndrome made him feel that a whimsical comedian had rewired the circuits in his brain.[2]

CBE numbered-source format, bibliography items (see pages 228–230)

1. Sacks 0. An anthropologist on Mars: seven paradoxical tales. New York: AA Knopf; 1995. p 100.
2. Skloot F. Home remedies. Am Sch 1995 Winter; p 70.

Chicago format, citations (see pages 244–246)

Many early novels were written for literate servants, especially waiting-maids.[1] For this very reason, early male readers felt that the new literary form "could not be important."[2]

Chicago format, endnotes (see pages 245–246)

1. Ian Watt, <u>The Rise of the Novel: Studies in Defoe, Richardson, and Fielding</u> (Berkeley: University of California Press, 1957), 47.
2. Mona Scheuermann, "Woman's Place: Finding and Evaluating Women's Contributions to Literature in English," <u>The Age of Johnson</u> 5 (1992): 395.

MLA format, parenthetical citations (see pages 164–168)

Although "cunningly planted" symbols always complicate Joyce's writings (Burgess 69), Higham says that divergent readings can be reconciled if one closely analyzes Joyce's style (15).

MLA format, bibliography items (see pages 168–179)

Burgess, Anthony. <u>Re Joyce</u>. New York: Norton, 1968.
Higham, Anne S. "An Aspect of Style in 'Araby'." <u>Language and Style</u> 15 (1982): 15–21.